1, 2, 5, 6

RED *and* BLUE
NATION?

RED *and* BLUE NATION?

Consequences and Correction of America's Polarized Politics

PIETRO S. NIVOLA
DAVID W. BRADY
editors

HOOVER INSTITUTION ON
WAR, REVOLUTION AND PEACE
Stanford University

BROOKINGS INSTITUTION PRESS
Washington, D.C.

Red and Blue Nation? Consequences and Correction of America's Polarized Politics
may be ordered from:
BROOKINGS INSTITUTION PRESS
c/o HFS, P.O. Box 50370, Baltimore, MD 21211-4370
Tel: 800/537-5487; 410/516-6956; Fax: 410/516-6998

Library of Congress Cataloging-in-Publication data
Red and blue nation? : consequences and correction of America's polarized politics / Pietro S.
Nivola and David W. Brady, editors.
    p.   cm.
Summary: "Analyzes the consequences of the gulf between 'red states' and 'blue states' and its
impact on voter behavior, congressional lawmaking, judicial selection, and foreign policy.
Discusses proposals to change the electoral system and congressional rules of engagement and
presents policies and reforms for alleviating the underlying causes of political polarization"—
Provided by publisher.
  Includes bibliographical references and index.
  ISBN-13: 978-0-8157-6080-1 (cloth : alk. paper)
  ISBN-13: 978-0-8157-6079-5 (pbk. : alk. paper)
  1. Political parties—United States. 2. Party affiliation—United States. 3. Polarization
(Social sciences) 4. United States—Politics and government. I. Nivola, Pietro S. II. Brady,
David W. III. Title.
  JK2261.R28 2006
  324.273—dc22   2006034595

9 8 7 6 5 4 3 2 1

The paper used in this publication meets minimum requirements of the
American National Standard for Information Sciences—Permanence of Paper
for Printed Library Materials: ANSI Z39.48-1992.

Typeset in Adobe Garamond

Composition by Circle Graphics
Columbia, Maryland

Printed by R. R. Donnelley
Harrisonburg, Virginia

In memory of our esteemed colleague and friend

NELSON W. POLSBY

1934–2007

Contents

Foreword

Is partisanship as American as apple pie—and as the two-party system? How much partisanship is inevitable? How much is healthy? How much is destructive? And what about this habit we Americans have fallen into of color-coding our nation in a way that suggests we're really two nations?

All these questions are in order, I believe, to introduce this book, since they are ones that my colleague at Brookings, Pietro Nivola, his co-editor, David Brady of the Hoover Institution, and the authors address in this second volume of their study of partisanship. Fittingly, their title for the series—*Red and Blue Nation?*—is punctuated with a question mark. The answers offered in these pages, while diverse in perspective and prescription, are forcefully argued, clearly expressed, rooted in sound scholarship, and highly constructive.

The subject of partisanship—while perennial—is also highly topical. As this book goes to press, the 2008 presidential campaign is heating up. By definition, that quadrennial process is partisan; and by tradition, it is also highly paradoxical: on the one hand, Republicans and Democrats go at each other tooth and nail; on the other hand, every candidate promises, if elected, to bring the country together, to be the leader of all Americans, and to govern above the divisive bickering of the parties.

Of all the issues on the national agenda, none is more preoccupying—and divisive—than the war in Iraq. For that reason, too, this book could not come at a better time. In September 2007 the commander of U.S. forces in Iraq, General David H. Petraeus, appeared before congressional committees to report on how much progress, if any, had been made by the troop "surge" President Bush had ordered approximately nine months earlier. Petraeus's extensive and reasonably objective testimony was praised, albeit with some exceptions, by Republican members on the panels and met with almost uniform skepticism by the Democrats. One side saw the glass half full; the other, half empty.

This partisan divide reflected not just opposing opinions, but also differing perceptions, and was not limited to the lawmakers present. Much of the public seemed similarly split. In a survey conducted a few days after the hearings, the Pew Research Center for the People and Press found that a lopsided majority of Republican respondents (67 percent) shared General Petraeus's guarded optimism that the surge was making headway in defeating the Iraqi insurgency. Among the Democrats surveyed, all but 16 percent disagreed.

The clash over the Petraeus hearings was starkly illustrative of a larger reality: America's political parties are sharply polarized these days, not on all matters, of course, but certainly on the war in Iraq and, evidently, on the conduct of international affairs more generally. The polarization, moreover, does not stop there. It remains quite pronounced with regard to various social issues, and extends well beyond the political class to large segments of the mass electorate. To be sure, not every consequence of this phenomenon has been undesirable. With the two parties more clearly differentiated than they were a generation ago, voters now have shown greater interest in the choices placed before them, so turnouts have increased in recent national elections. At the same time, however, polarized parties in this country are unquestionably complicating the pursuit of responsible policies needed to meet several of the nation's most formidable challenges—not least, a steady and effective foreign policy in a dangerous world.

This conundrum, one of the worrisome implications of polarized politics, and other challenges, are assessed by the contributors here. Indeed, the broad aim of the volume is to improve our understanding of what intensified partisanship ultimately means for the health of American democracy and policymaking and in the end, to explore prudent ways of correcting ill effects.

A word more about the people behind the work presented here: Pietro, who is vice president and director of the Governance Studies program at Brookings, and David, who is deputy director at the Hoover Institution. David and Pietro conceived the project, then recruited nearly forty political scientists and journalists to contribute their time and expertise. The project received generous support from the John D. and Catherine T. MacArthur Foundation and the Rockefeller Brothers Fund.

The preceding volume, *Red and Blue Nation? Characteristics and Causes of America's Polarized Politics*, was published by the Brookings Institution Press in December 2006. It featured important contributions by Morris P. Fiorina and Matthew S. Levendusky on the extent of polarization in the body politic. E. J. Dionne Jr. wrote on the role of religion as a polarizing force in U.S. politics. Diana C. Mutz analyzed the impact of the mass media. Thomas E. Mann contributed a chapter on the effects of gerrymandering. Chapters by Pietro Nivola and William A. Galston, and by David Brady and Hahrie C. Han, helped place the polarization phenomenon in proper theoretical, empirical, and historical context.

This second and concluding volume focuses on what should be done to lower the partisan heat in today's politics. Marc J. Hetherington builds a persuasive case that American voters may in fact be "turned on" by polarized parties, in that voter participation in the electoral process has improved in recent elections. Other scholars, notably Barbara Sinclair and Sarah A. Binder, find that polarization has troubling consequences for the legislative process and for the selection and confirmation of federal judges.

Reviewing the parties' evolving priorities in the postwar period, Peter Beinart concludes that polarization—exacerbated by the Bush administration's Iraq policy—erodes the ability of the United States to formulate a unified and consistent foreign policy. David Brady, John Ferejohn, and Laurel Harbridge assess empirically whether polarization reduces accountability in the political process, as well as whether the public's trust in government, legislative gridlock, and partisan tactics designed to exclude the minority party from the legislative process have worsened in recent times.

The volume concludes with a look at the possible remedies. Pietro and his colleague in Governance Studies at Brookings, Bill Galston, discuss systemic adjustments aimed at bolstering "the center" in the electoral process, returning a measure of comity and bipartisanship to Congress, engaging the presidency more regularly with members of the legislative branch and the press, and rediscovering principles of federalism that could help denationalize various divisive issues and thus perhaps defuse some of them.

Pietro and Bill are mindful that reforms can often have plenty of unintended consequences. There is a possibility that some of the cures for polarization may turn out to be worse than the disease. But while it is not uncommon to observe public officials wringing their hands about political polarization, it is less common to hear them seriously take up potential correctives. We and our colleagues at Hoover and the authors represented here hope that this project will shed light on a subject that has generated so much heat—and elevate the discussion of partisanship to not just a higher and more constructive level, but to one that meets two standards that are important to both Brookings and Hoover: nonpartisanship and something that is both a necessary condition and a consequence of nonpartisanship—civility of public discourse.

STROBE TALBOTT
President

Washington, D.C.
December 2007

RED *and* BLUE
NATION?

1

Turned Off or Turned On? How Polarization Affects Political Engagement

Marc J. Hetherington

The scholarly debate about the existence of polarization in the U.S. electorate continues to rage. Using a wide array of survey data on people's self-reported issue preferences, Fiorina argues that preferences are not moving toward the ideological poles. Rather most voters remain moderate on most issues.[1] Others counter that the differences between party adherents have become significantly starker of late, which they take as evidence of polarization.[2] Fiorina characterizes such mass-level party differences as relatively small and, to the extent that they have increased, a function of more effective party sorting, not polarization. To use the nomenclature of the debate, the United States has experienced some *party* polarization but little if any *popular* polarization. In either reckoning, elites are at the core of whatever movement has occurred. Elected officials and party activists are more polarized by any definition, which has made it easier for people to sort themselves into the "correct" party.[3]

The author would like to thank Corey Bike for his research assistance, Pietro Nivola for his insights, and Suzanne Globetti, John Geer, Bruce Oppenheimer, and Christian Grose for various forms of assistance.

1. Fiorina, Abrams, and Pope (2006).
2. For example Jacobson (2006); Abramowitz and Saunders (2005).
3. Fiorina, Abrams, and Pope (2006).

Fiorina's pairing of consistently moderate mass attitudes with those of increasingly ideological elites suggests that a large chunk of the electorate might be turned off by the extreme choices they confront. Research on negative advertising, however, suggests that the intensity of campaigns waged by polarized elites has the potential to energize everybody, even those who express dismay over their choices. To this end, I assess the health of a political system during a period characterized by a normatively troubling disconnect between elite and mass ideology. Are we less participatory or more? Do we see our government as less responsive or more? Do we trust our government less or more?

The evidence I present generally suggests that Americans have responded well to a polarized environment even if they purport to dislike all the angry words and actions that accompany it. Lately, most measures of political participation and engagement have improved—often dramatically. In 2004, for example, adjusted turnout rates were higher than any presidential election since 1968.[4]

Examining highly aggregated data like these can be misleading. In 2004 it is quite possible that ideologues, whipped into a frenzy by polarized elites, increased their participation levels by so much that it offset demobilization among moderates. I segment my analyses by ideology to assess whether ideologues and moderates differ in their reactions to increasingly extreme choices. The findings suggest that, by and large, they do not. Changes in the behavior and attitudes of the nonideological have generally mirrored those of ideologues. This is not true across the board. For example, I demonstrate a polarization of opinion on measures of political efficacy and political trust. But such findings appear more the exception than the rule. The approximately 50 percent of the electorate that professes to be moderate or nonideological is not tuning out.

I also assess the effect of polarization on the 2006 midterm elections. Much of the Washington press corps has hailed the 2006 elections as a triumph for moderation over extremism. When given moderate options, like Robert Casey Jr. in Pennsylvania or James Webb in Virginia, voters chose them. Comparing the exit poll data from the 2006 U.S. Senate elections with the exit polls from the same elections in 2000, however, suggests a more subtle story. Moderates did not turn out in greater numbers relative to ideologues to seize back control of the government. In fact, in many of the key Senate races in 2006, they were less well represented than they were six years earlier. In making sense of the 2006 outcome, I argue that Fiorina's earlier work on voting remains critical.[5] Voters, particularly

4. See McDonald and Popkin (2001).
5. Fiorina (1981).

those with no ideological anchor, are more interested in ends than means. The most compelling narrative of 2006 is that they voted against Republicans because they perceived that they had failed, not because they perceived that they were too ideological. Moderates have had no problem embracing successful ideologues in the past, but they have shown a propensity for voting against them when they fail.

Competing Expectations

The potential effects of polarization on participation mirror the potential effects of negative advertising. Early work on negative advertising started from the fact that many Americans expressed dissatisfaction with its volume and tone during a campaign. As a result, Ansolabehere and Iyengar hypothesized that negativity, which had the potential to activate partisans because they would appreciate the pointed attacks, might demobilize independents because they were less invested in the political process and would grow weary of the angry sniping.[6] Using experimental and survey-based methods, they found some evidence that negative advertising diminished the political efficacy and perceptions of government responsiveness among unaligned voters, which, in turn, caused them to vote less.

Others suggested that negative advertising, at a minimum, ought to have no effect on turnout or, more likely, had the potential to stimulate turnout.[7] This line of research was tied to the fact that negative information tends to have a greater effect on people than positive information because the negative raises the specter of risk and, with it, anxiety, which can stimulate learning and interest.[8] Lau, in particular, has shown that these negativity biases, which all human beings possess to some degree, extend to political thinking.[9] In addition, negative advertisements tend to include more policy information than positive advertisements, which is important because information facilitates participation.[10] Although evidence has been found to support both the mobilization and demobilization hypotheses, much of the most persuasive research suggests that negativity, counter to the conventional wisdom, stimulates turnout no matter how much Americans complain about it.[11]

Compelling cases can be made on both sides for the effects of polarization as well. As Fiorina and his colleagues show, about half of Americans think of themselves as

6. Ansolabehere and Iyengar (1995).
7. Finkel and Geer (1998); Bartels (1996).
8. Tversky and Kahneman (1981); Marcus and MacKuen (1993).
9. Lau (1985).
10. Brians and Wattenberg (1996); Geer (2006).
11. Lau and others (1999); Wattenberg and Brians (1999); Geer (2006); Brooks and Geer (2007).

either moderate or are unable to place themselves on an ideological scale.[12] If both parties and their candidates move toward the ideological poles, as has been the case in American politics lately, moderate and nonideological voters may feel alienated, seeing little that they have in common with either side. Of course, ideologues would be likely to participate in greater numbers because one of the parties would be appealing more closely to them while the other party would appear to be a greater risk.

But it is also possible that polarization could have the reverse effect on moderates, especially given how even the partisan divide is today. Polarized elites will produce more heat during the campaign, providing choices rather than echoes. Both sides will attack the other as extreme, which empirically speaking is true. As evidence, Geer shows a massive increase in negative advertising through this period of elite polarization.[13] Significantly, raising the specter of risk in this manner could encourage the public to notice what is happening politically. Moreover, in comparison with ideologues, moderates know precious little about politics. It is possible that they might not even realize that the political system is not really representing their so-called preferences. While moderates might say they hate polarization, they might still respond to it positively.

Voter Turnout in a Polarized Age

As elections approach, commentators begin to wring their hands about voter apathy. Such concerns are more urgent with the nation so evenly divided between Democrats and Republicans. When a presidential election can be decided by 537 votes, as it was in 2000, more people ought to feel that their votes make a difference. But what if persistently low turnout rates are a function of the ideological disconnect that Fiorina uncovers between a centrist public and an ideological elite? A moderate public faced with immoderate choices might decide to exit the process altogether. And given that moderates make up such a large chunk of the electorate, this would have a large effect on turnout overall.

Yet despite all the worry about turnout, voters have actually begun to participate more, not less, as political elites have polarized. Figure 1-1 tells this story graphically, comparing the traditional measure of turnout (the percentage of the voting-age population [VAP]) and an adjusted measure of turnout (the percentage of the voting-eligible population [VEP]). The VAP decreased in nearly every election between 1960, when turnout reached 63 percent, and 1996, when it dropped below 50 percent. The only exceptions were a slight increase in 1984 and

12. Fiorina, Abrams, and Pope (2006).
13. Geer (2006).

Figure 1-1. *Measures of Voter Turnout in Presidential Elections, 1952–2004*

Percent

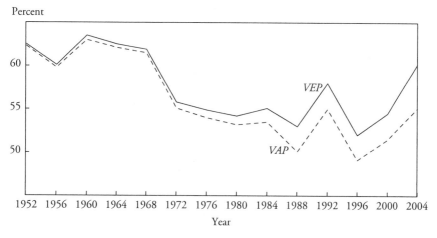

1952 1956 1960 1964 1968 1972 1976 1980 1984 1988 1992 1996 2000 2004

Year

Source: Data supplied by Michael P. McDonald of George Mason University.
a. VAP, voting-age population; VEP, voting-eligible population.

a bigger one in 1992. The general pattern of turnout decay coincided with a time when the parties at the elite level were uncommonly close ideologically. In 1976 presidential candidates Gerald Ford and Jimmy Carter were very difficult to differentiate, and measures of congressional polarization (such as Keith Poole and Howard Rosenthal's DW-nominate scores) show that the parties' ideological differences in the early 1970s represented the minimum in the twentieth century.[14]

Since 1996, as the parties have become increasingly polarized, VAP-based turnout has increased, though not enough to celebrate. Political scientists Michael McDonald and Samuel Popkin, however, demonstrate that this measure does not allow for meaningful comparisons over time.[15] Today far more people of voting age are ineligible to vote because they have been disenfranchised by past criminal acts or by virtue of their citizenship status. Therefore, the voting-*eligible* population is a more appropriate denominator in calculating voter turnout. When this statistic is used, it shows that voter turnout has surged over the last three presidential elections, from about 52 percent in 1996 to over 60 percent in 2004. VEP-based turnout was almost exactly the same in 2004 as it was in 1956, and only about 3.5 percentage points lower than in 1960. This may be something to celebrate after all: it does not appear that eligible voters are turned off by the polarized environment.

14. Poole and Rosenthal's DW-nominate data sets are available at voteview.com.
15. McDonald and Popkin (2001).

Figure 1-2. *Self-Reported Voting in Presidential Elections, 1980–2004*

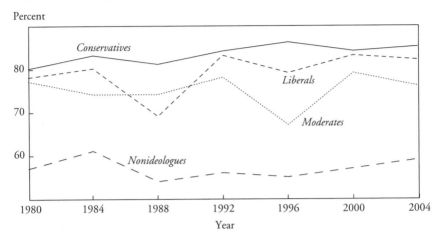

Source: National Election Studies Cumulative Data File, 1948–2004.

But perhaps the recent surge in turnout is asymmetric. Ideologues may be happier with more ideological candidates to choose from, but moderates might be more inclined to drop out. Figure 1-2 does not suggest such a pattern, however. Using data from the National Election Studies, figure 1-2 tracks self-reported turnout among four different, ideological groups: self-identified liberals, conservatives, and moderates, and people who say that they have not thought enough about their ideology to place themselves ("nonideologues"). People are notorious for reporting that they vote even when they do not, which accounts for the fact that self-reported turnout has increased from 71 percent in 1980 to 78 percent in 2004, even though actual turnout in both these elections was far less. But the important point is that self-identified moderates and nonideologues have not been turned off by increasingly polarized elites. Although moderates were much less likely to vote in 1996, their voting participation surged in 2000, such that it was nearly on par with liberals and conservatives. Moderates experienced a slight drop in 2004, as did liberals, but neither change was statistically significant. Far from tuning out, nonideologues actually show a slight upward trend in turnout since 1996.[16]

16. Although the problems with self-reported measures of turnout are legion, these results square nicely with data gathered from recent exit polls. The percentage of people who do not identify as either liberals or conservatives when polled on election day has remained constant. In 1996, 47 percent of voters called themselves moderate in exit polls, exactly the same as in 2006.

Figure 1-3. *Americans Reporting They "Care a Good Deal" Who Wins the Presidential Election, 1980–2004*

Percent

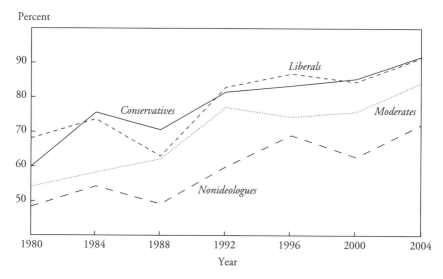

Source: National Election Studies Cumulative Data File, 1948–2004.

Determinants of Turnout

One reason turnout has increased in this polarized period may be that the factors influencing whether people vote or not have changed. In their 1993 book *Mobilization, Participation, and Democracy in America,* Steven J. Rosenstone and John Mark Hansen catalogued a range of relevant factors, including caring about who wins the presidential election and having interest in the campaign.[17] These psychological determinants of voting can be tracked over time to assess whether they have encouraged turnout, especially among moderates.

Figure 1-3 shows the percentage of Americans of different ideological stripes who "care a good deal" about who wins the presidential election. The trend since 1980 is upward among all groups, including ideological moderates and nonideologues. In fact, in 2004 more than 70 percent of respondents who failed to place themselves on the ideology scale cared a good deal whether George W. Bush or John Kerry won, a higher response than liberals and conservatives provided in 1980 in regard to their choices. This is a particularly noteworthy finding because the choice between Carter and Reagan in 1980 was not exactly a choice between

17. Rosenstone and Hansen (1993).

Tweedledum and Tweedledee. The steepest increase for moderates occurred in 1992, a possible reflection of moderates' preference for Ross Perot's pragmatic—if sometimes offbeat—candidacy. (The fact that the percentage of moderates remained relatively constant in the next two elections suggests a Perot effect.) But in 2004, with sharp ideological differences between the candidates and no centrist alternative, the percentage of moderates who said they cared about the outcome surged dramatically, approaching 85 percent.

The percentage of Americans who expressed significant interest in the presidential campaign follows a somewhat different pattern, but with the same end point. Between 1980 and 2000, the percentage remained fairly constant, with the exception of a Perot-induced spike in 1992. In 2004, however, an even larger surge occurred. In fact, a higher percentage of Americans reported that they were "very much interested" in the campaign than at any other time in the National Election Studies (NES) time series, which dates to 1952. Figure 1-4 shows that the surge in 2004 was driven disproportionately by liberals and conservatives, but it was not as though moderates and nonideologues were indifferent to the campaign. Interest levels among both groups increased. In fact, both expressed more interest in the 2004 campaign than in any other except the 1992 campaign.

Measures of Nonvoting Campaign Participation

Along with recent increases in turnout, many other measures of electoral participation have also increased, some quite dramatically. Table 1-1 shows the trends since 1980 for five measures of nonvoting participation tracked by the NES. For instance, Americans today are much more likely to have tried to influence the votes of others. In 2004, 48 percent of the public reported that they engaged in this form of persuasion, the highest level since the NES introduced this item in 1952. The median over the prior thirteen election studies was only 32 percent. And while the percentage of Americans who reported attending a political meeting or working for a party or candidate has remained fairly constant over time, the 2004 election cycle saw marked increases in the percentage of people who reported having worn a button or displayed a bumper sticker and who said they gave money to a campaign. In fact, the measures for these forms of participation tied their previous highs going back to 1952. In that sense the present polarized period has seen a remarkable increase in a range of different forms of political involvement.

Although Table 1-1 does not present figures broken down by ideology for these forms of participation, the National Elections Studies data show that moderates and nonideologues have recently become more participatory, just as liberals and

Figure 1-4. *Americans Reporting They Are "Very Much Interested in the Election,"
1980–2004*

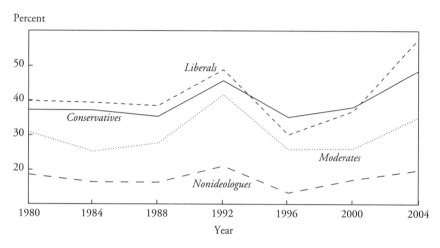

Percent

Source: National Election Studies Cumulative Data File, 1948–2004.

conservatives have. For example, the percentage of conservatives who reported trying to influence the votes of others increased by 16 percentage points between 2000 and 2004. The change in the behavior of moderates was similarly dramatic, increasing over the same period from 30 percent to 44 percent. To be sure, moderates are significantly less participatory overall than are liberals and conservatives. But it is equally important that party polarization has not demobilized moderates and nonideologues. In fact, by many measures, it has stimulated them as well.

Explaining the Pattern of Results

In terms of participation, those who do not organize their political thinking in an ideological manner appear to be turned on, not off, by today's ideologically charged environment. Why, then, do they seem more invested in politics now that it provides choices that clearly do not match their nonideological sensibilities? It is possible that those who think of themselves as moderate or without an ideology might simply miss the fact that they are choosing between more and more ideologically distinct candidates. Perhaps they are unable to discern that the choices offered them by the political system have changed. (This may not be all that surprising considering that a broad swath of Americans are so poorly informed about politics that they know little if anything about the office-seekers on the ballot.)

Table 1-1. *Nonvoting Measures of Political Participation, 1980–2004*
Percent

Year	Tried to influence others' votes	Attended political meeting	Worked for a party or candidate	Wore button or displayed bumper sticker	Gave money to a campaign
1980	36	8	4	7	8
1984	32	8	4	9	8
1988	29	7	3	9	9
1992	37	8	3	11	7
1996	28	5	2	10	8
2000	34	5	3	10	9
2004	48	7	3	21	13

Source: National Election Studies Cumulative Data File, 1948–2004.

The results in figure 1-5 provide the somewhat shocking news: moderates and nonideologues actually saw *less* distance between George W. Bush and John Kerry in 2004 than they saw between any pair of major-party presidential candidates between 1988 and 2000.[18] Liberals and conservatives, not surprisingly, never saw bigger differences between candidates, but moderates and nonideologues saw their choices as basically the same (perhaps even less distinct) in 2004 as in the preceding elections. And while the results are not presented here, the same pattern holds for a host of traditional domestic policy items tracked by the NES, including questions about government services and spending, government-guaranteed jobs and standard of living, government-run health care, government aid to blacks, and a woman's proper role in society. On all these items, moderates and nonideologues failed to see increasingly large differences between the presidential candidates.

Perhaps the answer lies in attitudes about foreign policy, which ought to be much more influential now than in the 1990s after the end of the cold war. Many political leaders are fond of saying that the terrorist attacks of September 11 changed everything. And, as it relates to people's investment in political outcomes, that may well be the case. Since terrorism in the United States is a relatively new phenomenon, it is not possible to track perceptions about candidates on this issue over time. The NES has, however, regularly asked people to place the parties and their standard-bearers on a defense spending question on a seven-point scale

18. To test the hypothesis that moderates and nonideologues have failed to perceive greater polarization on the elite level, I focus on presidential candidates because most of the evidence I have presented thus far deals with assessments of presidential elections.

Figure 1-5. *Perceived Ideological Difference between the Major-Party Presidential Candidates, 1984–2004* [a]

Mean distance

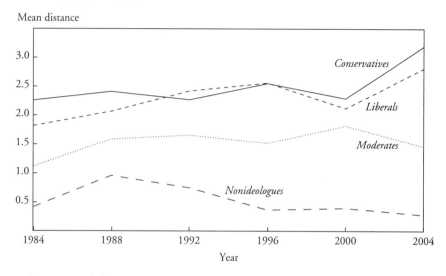

Year

Source: National Election Studies Cumulative Data File, 1948–2004.

a. To test people's ability to perceive the ideological divergence of their choices, I take the difference between respondents' placements of the major-party presidential candidates on the NES seven-point ideology scale and track it over time.

(ranging from "greatly decrease defense spending" at 1 to "greatly increase defense spending" at 7). Figure 1-6 shows the difference between people's perceptions of the Republican and Democratic presidential candidates, segmented by the four ideological groupings. The results of this analysis provide some indication that perceptions of polarization on issues matter in understanding the increase in voter engagement and participation.

Given the centrality of the cold war and Ronald Reagan's image as a strong anticommunist, it is not surprising that the public perceived the largest differences between presidential candidates in 1984. Although the perception of differences remained high on this issue in 1988, it decreased markedly after that (through 1996 for conservatives, moderates, and nonideologues and through 2000 for liberals). By 2004, however, the perceived difference between candidates had returned to levels reminiscent of 1988 for all ideological groups.

Regarding moderates, it is noteworthy that they saw greater differences between the candidates in 2004 than liberals did, which is quite rare. (It is typical for ideologues to see greater differences than moderates and nonideologues.) The raw magnitude of the recent increase is also striking. For moderates the mean

Figure 1-6. *Perceived Difference between Major-Party Candidates on Defense Spending, 1984–2004*[a]

Mean distance

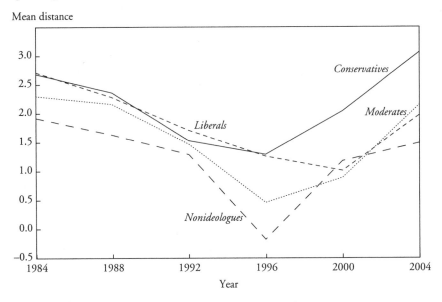

Source: National Election Studies Cumulative Data File, 1948–2004.
a. To test people's ability to perceive the ideological divergence of their choices, I take the difference between respondents' placements of the major-party presidential candidates on the NES seven-point defense-spending scale and track it over time.

perceived ideological distance between George W. Bush and Al Gore in 2000 was less than one point, but in 2004 the perceived distance between Bush and Kerry was greater than two points, more than double the difference in just one election. Conservatives saw a gaping three-point difference between the candidates, a spread 50 percent greater than that perceived by liberals, at just under two points. Although the defense spending item is not about terrorism specifically, these results probably reflect an orientation toward the use of force in the face of external threats that would be important to people assessing political candidates.

Supporting evidence for the importance of terrorism in shaping the attitudes of moderates and nonideologues comes from the 2004 National Election Study. That year's survey debuted a question that asked respondents to place themselves and the presidential candidates on a seven-point scale bounded at one pole by the statement, "Some people believe the United States should solve international problems by using diplomacy and other forms of international pressure and use military force only if absolutely necessary," and at the other pole by, "Others

Table 1-2. *Perceptions of Bush and Kerry on the Diplomacy-versus-Military-Intervention Scale, by Ideological Self-Identification, 2004*[a]
Points

Group	Mean perception of Bush	Mean perception of Kerry	Difference
Liberals	6.36	2.99	3.37
Moderates	5.94	3.13	2.81
Nonideologues	5.84	3.35	2.49
Conservatives	5.77	2.52	3.25

Source: 2004 National Election Study.
a. Higher numbers correspond to the more hawkish position.

believe diplomacy and pressure often fail and the U.S. must be ready to use military force."[19] The responses to this question cannot be compared across time, but they can be compared to the perceived difference between the candidates produced by other issues in 2004.

The results appear in table 1-2. All four ideological groups saw differences between Bush and John Kerry on the use of diplomacy versus force that were significantly greater than the increasingly larger perceived differences they saw over time regarding defense spending. In fact, the differences on the diplomacy-versus-intervention scale in 2004 were larger for all groups than they were in 1984 on defense spending, when those differences were at their maximum. On average, those who called themselves liberals placed Bush at 6.36 on the seven-point scale, suggesting that a high percentage placed Bush at the scale's maximum—a rarity in survey research. Liberals saw Kerry as 3.37 points to the left of Bush. The average difference perceived by conservatives was similarly large at 3.25 points.

More important for understanding the effect on turnout, moderates and nonideologues saw a wide gulf, too. Moderates saw Bush as 2.81 points to the right of Kerry and nonideologues perceived the gap to be about 2.5 points. These differences are very large relative to the differences these groups perceive on other issues. On defense spending, moderates never perceived a difference greater than 2.3 points and nonideologues never perceived a difference greater than two points over the nearly thirty years that the defense spending questions have been asked.

A second complementary explanation for surging interest and participation among moderates and nonideologues involves mobilization by the political parties

19. The diplomacy option is at the low end of the scale, and the military force option is at the high end; thus higher numbers correspond to the more hawkish position.

Table 1-3. *Mobilization Efforts by Political Parties or Other Organizations, 1980–2004*
Percent reporting yes

Year	Contacted by a party?	Contacted by something other than a party?
1980	24	10
1984	24	8
1988	24	8
1992	20	10
1996	26	10
2000	35	11
2004	43	18

Source: National Election Studies Cumulative Data File, 1948–2004.

and so-called 527 groups. In their classic treatment of declining participation rates between 1960 and 1988, Rosenstone and Hansen cited diminishing mobilization by parties and other social movements as the root cause.[20] The data in table 1-3, however, suggest a tremendous recent surge in these activities. As recently as 1992, only 20 percent of respondents reported being contacted by one of the parties about the campaign. By 2000 this had increased to 35 percent, and in 2004 it reached 43 percent. The percentage of people who reported being contacted about the campaign by a nonparty organization nearly doubled between 2000 and 2004, from 11 percent to 18 percent.

Figure 1-7 shows that much of the recent surge in party mobilization activities has been directed toward ideologues, as Rosenstone and Hansen would have predicted. People with resources, a group that tends to be disproportionately ideological, are thus much more likely to be contacted.[21] But parties have been more active in targeting self-identified moderates and nonideologues as well. In 1996, for example, only about 25 percent of moderates and 19 percent of nonideologues reported being contacted by a political party. In 2004 the level of contact had climbed to 41 percent and 28 percent, respectively. Taken together, it seems reasonable to conclude that people across the ideological spectrum express more interest and participate more in politics because political organizations have encouraged them to do so. In fact, a multivariate test, which appears in appendix A, confirms that both mobilization and perceived candidate polarization on defense contributed to the turnout increase among moderates.

20. Rosenstone and Hansen (1993).
21. Luskin (1987).

Figure 1-7. *Voters Reporting Contact from a Political Party, 1980–2004*

Percent

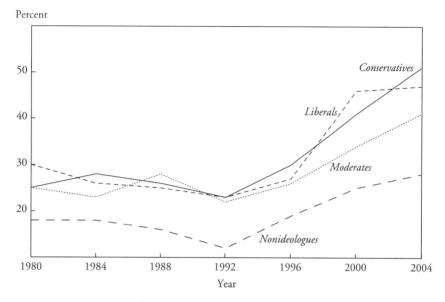

Source: National Election Studies Cumulative Data File, 1948–2004.

In sum, the increased interest and participation among all ideological groups appears to be driven by the public's polarization of perceptions about the candidates' approaches to defense and terrorism and by the enormous increase in the mobilization of voters by parties and interested groups.

Political Efficacy and Attitudes about Government Responsiveness

Political participation is not the only measure of the electorate's orientation toward politics. Elections today are generally fought between ideologues on both sides, which means that an ideologue will tend to win most contests.[22] This certainly has the potential to cause people, especially moderates and nonideologues, to believe they have less influence over the political process (their political efficacy) and to feel more concern about the kinds of policies the government might produce (their perceptions of government responsiveness).

In the National Election Studies series, external political efficacy is measured by asking people whether or not they agree with the following statements: "People like

22. See Ansolabehere, Snyder, and Stewart (2001).

Table 1-4. *External Political Efficacy and Perceptions of Government Responsiveness*
Mean scores

Year	External efficacy	Government responsiveness
1980	0.534	0.513
1984	0.627	0.518
1988	0.487	0.510
1992	0.515	0.553
1996	0.375	0.551
2000	0.463	0.566
2004	0.465	0.609

Source: National Election Studies Cumulative Data File, 1948–2004.

me don't have a say in what government does," and "Public officials don't care much what people like me think." For government responsiveness, respondents are queried about the system more generally, not their personal experience with it. Specifically, they are asked: "Over the years, how much attention do you feel the government pays to what the people think when it decides what to do?" and "How much do you feel that having elections makes the government pay attention to what the people think?"

Table 1-4 tracks the mean scores for these two indexes over time.[23] The results in these two areas are mixed. For external efficacy, the period from 1980 to 2004 produced a great deal of fluctuation. The maximum was achieved in 1984 and the minimum in 1996. As the parties have polarized at the elite level, we see a marked increase in efficacy at the mass level, but the mean in 2004 was still considerably lower than it was in any of the three election years in the 1980s.

Government responsiveness, on the other hand, is a different story. These more sociotropic evaluations of government remained relatively constant throughout the 1980s, with a mean around 0.5. The mean then increased in 1992 to 0.553 and remained relatively constant through 2000. In 2004, with the political environment particularly polarized at the elite level, people's feelings about government responsiveness shot up to 0.609, the highest mean score recorded since 1968.

23. I calculate an average political efficacy score by arraying both statements onto 0-to-1 intervals, with efficacious responses coded 1 and nonefficacious responses coded 0, and taking the mean. The average government responsiveness score was calculated in a similar manner. Unfortunately, the NES did not ask its internal efficacy question in 2004. Hence I do not track responses to this item over time.

Figure 1-8. *External Political Efficacy, 1980–2004*

Mean, bounded between 0 and 1

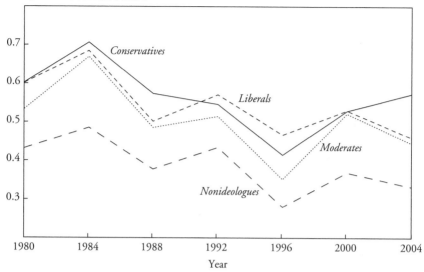

Source: National Election Studies Cumulative Data File, 1948–2004.

Given that the government is now run by ideologues, it would be reasonable to hypothesize that, at least recently, liberals would feel more efficacious (and conservatives less so) when Democrats win elections, with moderates and nonideologues probably somewhere in between. Thus one would expect to see a polarization of these opinions by ideology. In the 1980s, this was not the case. The trends, which appear in figure 1-8, run in tandem for all ideological groups, although efficacy among conservatives dropped less steeply in 1988 than it did for the other groups. In 1992 efficacy among conservatives continued to drop a bit while it increased substantially among liberals, as expected. In 1996 the trends again move in tandem, and in the aftermath of the unsettled 2000 election, liberals, moderates, and conservatives all converge on the same point. Polarization between liberals and conservatives shows up most clearly in 2004. The slight overall increase in political efficacy for the entire sample is wholly a function of conservative responses; all other ideological groups felt less efficacious.

Figure 1-9 reveals that over the time period in question, perceptions of government responsiveness generally trend upward among all ideological groups. But the responses become much more volatile in 2000 and 2004. In 2004 the same polarization of opinion that is evident for external efficacy appears for government

Figure 1-9. *Perceptions of Government Responsiveness, 1980–2004*

Mean, bounded between 0 and 1

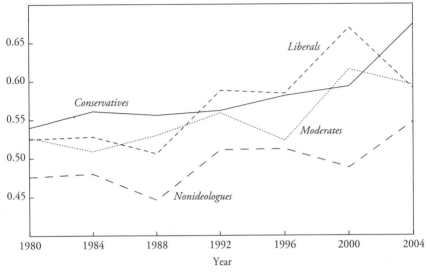

Source: National Election Studies Cumulative Data File, 1948–2004.

responsiveness as well. Between 2000 and 2004, conservatives' perceptions of government responsiveness increased by nearly 10 percentage points while liberals' perceptions of responsiveness decreased to a similar extent.

At this point, it does not appear that the polarized political system has soured moderates and nonideologues on the representativeness of the system. Efficacy in 2004 among moderates and nonideologues was low, but it was lower still in 1996. However, it is worth noting that moderates' and liberals' sense of efficacy dropped at about the same rate between 2000 and 2004. It is obvious why this would have happened among liberals, but a similar drop among moderates might suggest that they did not believe that the very conservative Bush administration and its conservative allies in Congress were responsive to people like them either.

Those less efficacious feelings among moderates in 2004 do not extend to their evaluation of the political system's responsiveness more generally, however. Moderates scored higher on the government responsiveness index in 2004 than in any other year except 2000, and the difference between 2000 and 2004 was not statistically significant. In addition, nonideologues' perceptions of government responsiveness was at its maximum in 2004. In other words, the less and nonideological appear to express more satisfaction with government responsiveness when it is run by polarized elites than when it is run by more centrist leaders.

Political Trust

Political trust is a measure of people's satisfaction with government compared with their normative expectations of it.[24] Understanding variation in political trust is important because it has a wide range of meaningful consequences. It is the key to understanding why government pursued a Great Society in the mid-1960s (when trust was very high) but a "Reagan revolution" in the early 1980s (when trust was very low).[25] Indeed, both individual- and aggregate-level studies suggest that trust is the foundation of public support for liberal domestic policies.[26] In addition, political trust increases citizen compliance with government demands such as taxpaying, engages collective restraint in the face of social dilemmas, and shapes the likelihood of voting for incumbents and third-party candidates.[27] Finally, by affording representatives greater leeway to depart from constituency ideal points, trust may enable them to place collective interests ahead of parochial concerns when allocating scarce resources.[28] In short, it is an important measure of political health and vitality.

Variation in political trust over time is shown in figure 1-10.[29] Trust was high in the 1960s before beginning a slide that lasted the duration of the 1970s. The nation has subsequently experienced some surges in political trust, notably during Reagan's first term, Clinton's second term, and, although not clear from this figure, after the terrorist attacks of September 11, 2001. Perception of government's performance seems to be central to understanding this variation over time: when people think the government is doing well, they trust government more,

24. Miller (1974).
25. Hetherington (2005).
26. Chanley, Rudolph, and Rahn (2000); Hetherington (2005).
27. Scholz and Lubell (1998); Tyler and Degoey (1995); Hetherington (1999).
28. Bianco (1994).
29. Political trust is measured as the mean of four items: "How much of the time do you think you can trust the government in Washington to do what is right?" "Would you say the government is pretty much run by a few big interests looking out for themselves or that it is run for the benefit of all the people?" "Do you think that people in government waste a lot of the money we pay in taxes, waste some of it, or don't waste very much of it?" And, "Do you think that quite a few of the people running the government are crooked, not very many are, or do you think hardly any of them are crooked?" I map this score onto a 0-to-1 interval, so that differences over time can be interpreted as percentage differences.

Figure 1-10. *Political Trust in Presidential Election Years, 1964–2004*

Mean, bounded between 0 and 1

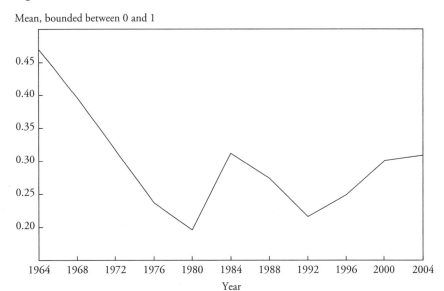

Source: National Election Studies Cumulative Data File, 1948–2004.

and vice versa.[30] In addition, it seems that the issues that people have in mind when they are asked to evaluate government are also important. Americans like the government better when it is dealing with a foreign crisis than when it is attending to economic problems, for instance.[31]

Figure 1-11 reveals that from 1980 to 2004, political trust among all ideological groups has generally waxed and waned in tandem. When liberals are dissatisfied, so are conservatives and moderates. Moreover, the groups' averages are very close together, suggesting a very low correlation between ideological self-placement and trust. This is reassuring in terms of measurement because it suggests that trust is not a short-term reflection of who is running the government. Conservatives trust government a little more than liberals when Republicans occupy the White House (and vice versa in times of a Democratic presidency), but generally not by much. In 2004, however, this relationship changed fundamentally. Although it is unclear whether this pattern will hold into the future, the period between 2000 and 2004 saw political trust among conservatives surge and

30. Citrin (1974); Citrin and Green (1986); Hetherington (1998).
31. Hetherington and Rudolph (2006).

Figure 1-11. *Political Trust in Presidential Election Years, by Ideological Self-Identification, 1980–2004*

Mean, bounded between 0 and 1

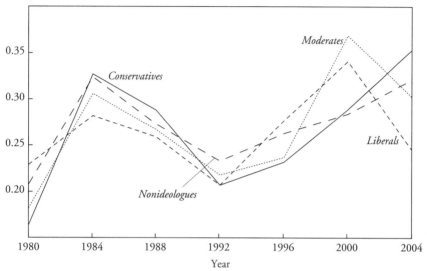

Source: National Election Studies Cumulative Data File, 1948–2004.

that of nonideologues increase a little, while political trust among liberals and moderates plummeted.

Using the entire range of the trust and ideological self-placement variables, these correlations can be tracked over time. The results of this analysis appear in the first column of table 1-5. Between 1980 and 2000, the correlation was never stronger than 0.10 in either direction and was often statistically insignificant. In 2000 the correlation for ideology was −0.09, which indicates that conservatives were slightly less trustful of the government than liberals. In 2004, however, the relationship doubled in strength to a correlation of 0.18, with conservatives (not surprisingly) more trustful of a government with Republicans controlling both the White House and Congress.

Tracking the correlations between partisanship and political trust over time reveals a similarly dramatic change (second column of table 1-5). As with correlation between trust and ideology, the correlation between trust and partisanship has generally been very modest. In the 1980s it was slightly stronger, but in the 1990s it ranged from 0.04 in 1992 to −0.11 in 1996 and to −0.07 in 2000. In 2004, however, the correlation jumps to 0.27—roughly double the previous maximum

Table 1-5. *Correlation between Political Trust and Ideology and Partisanship, 1980–2004*[a]

Year	Ideological self-identification	Partisanship
1980	−0.10	−0.12
1984	0.06	0.14
1988	0.03	0.14
1992	0	0.04
1996	−0.07	−0.11
2000	−0.09	−0.07
2004	0.18	0.27

Source: National Election Studies Cumulative Data File, 1948-2004.
a. Calculated using Pearson's *r* correlation.

correlation between the two variables. Without question the Bush presidency and the lockstep support the president received from the Republican majority in Congress has politicized what it means for ordinary citizens to trust the government in Washington.

The scholarly implications of this are rather interesting. It has been shown elsewhere that political trust is central to understanding variation in the public's policy preferences when supporting government action that requires sacrifice.[32] For example, whites need to trust the government in Washington in order to support programs such as affirmative action or aid that benefits nonwhite minority groups. Among the beneficiaries, political trust has no effect; but among those who are asked to make perceived sacrifices, political trust has a large effect. And this has been revealed to be the case over a variety of years, regardless of which party occupies the White House and holds the majority in Congress.

In 2004 the relationships between political trust and various measures of support for government action requiring sacrifice disappear. For example, among nonblacks the partial correlations between political trust and support for affirmative action and aid to blacks, respectively, are statistically insignificant in the presence of controls for partisanship and ideology.[33] In a politicized political system, then, political trust seems to mean something much different than in a less polarized one. The normative implications of this are much more serious than the scholarly ones. At no time in the four decades that the NES has been asking its current

32. Hetherington (2005); Hetherington and Globetti (2002).
33. More fully specified models like those I have estimated elsewhere produce wholly insignificant results for political trust as well. See Hetherington (2005); Hetherington and Globetti (2002).

trust-in-government questions has the difference between Republicans and Democrats been as large as it was in 2004. The only presidential year that Republican respondents showed more trust in government was 1964, the year the present trust question debuted and the year that trust was at its apex in the population as a whole. Democratic respondents in 2004, conversely, have rarely seen the government in a poorer light.

If political trust provides the reservoir of good will for governments even when times are bad, then government in the early twenty-first century is only getting it from one side of the political aisle.[34] This can have tremendous implications for certain kinds of government actions, as when the United States commits military troops abroad, for instance. Support for military action is, in part, a function of political trust.[35] Yet given the relationship between trust and partisanship that has emerged in recent years, it is little wonder that the largest partisan gulf in attitudes ever recorded about a war in the era of modern public opinion surveys is about the conflict presently occurring in Iraq. For example, partisan differences on Vietnam averaged about 5 percentage points, and for Korea, Kosovo, and Afghanistan, they ran about 12 points. But by the last months of 2004, with the Iraq war about a year and a half old, Republicans and Democrats differed on the war by an average of 63 percentage points—more than twice the maximum partisan difference achieved during the first Gulf War.[36] As the Bush administration is presently learning, it is hard to continue a war with the support of less than half the country.

Perhaps, too, we ought to be troubled by the uncommonly high levels of trust that Republicans express.[37] A compelling case for the pernicious effects of high trust could be made today. Specifically, many believe that the Bush administration will not be remembered kindly by history because of its willingness to pursue extra-Constitutional means to battle terrorism, such as the use of wiretaps without first obtaining warrants; its reluctance to ban torture; and its desire to jail suspected nonmilitary enemy combatants without habeas corpus rights. Republicans' high levels of trust may be at the heart of their support of these initiatives and, consequently, the Bush administration's willingness to pursue them.

The evidence I present below is necessarily indirect because no polls about trust in government also asked about public support for wiretapping without a warrant, torture, or limiting habeas corpus. But the preceding analysis demonstrates that

34. See the earlier studies of Easton (1965) and Gamson (1968).
35. Hetherington (2005, chapter 8).
36. Jacobson (2006).
37. The most common criticism that I have received about my work on political trust is that I have often expressed more concern about *low* levels of trust than *high* levels.

as of 2004, Republicans had much higher levels of trust in government than did Democrats and independents. Hence the vast array of public opinion polls suggesting that Republicans are much more willing than Democrats and independents to back the president on these initiatives indirectly points to the fundamental importance of trust.

In February 2006, Gallup asked Americans, "Do you think the Bush administration was right or wrong in wiretapping conversations without obtaining a court order?" In the sample as a whole, opinion was split evenly, with 48 percent expressing support and 49 percent expressing opposition. But the interesting finding is the partisan split: Republicans (83 percent supportive) were a whopping 57 percentage points more in favor of warrantless wiretapping than were Democrats (26 percent).[38]

The differences in support for the use of torture in the fight against terrorism are also striking. In December 2005, an ABC News/*Washington Post* poll asked respondents, "Would you regard the use of torture against people suspected of involvement in terrorism as an acceptable or unacceptable part of the U.S. campaign against terrorism?" Only about 30 percent of Americans said yes, with Republicans (39 percent) roughly twice as supportive as Democrats (21 percent).[39]

Finally, party differences—probably with trust differences at their core—were also evident from people's beliefs about whether or not it was acceptable for the U.S. government to "hold suspected terrorists without access to lawyers and a trial." According to an August 2006 *Time* magazine poll, 51 percent of Americans sampled supported the idea. Even without explicit mention of the Bush administration in the question, 70 percent of Republicans expressed support for neglecting habeas corpus rights while only 32 percent of Democrats did.[40] Thus the very high levels of trust in the government among Republicans in the post–September 11 world may have a darker side as well.

The 2006 Elections and the Consequences of Polarization

The sweeping Democratic victories in the 2006 midterm elections seem like a triumph for moderation over the forces of polarization. In that sense, the new Democratic majority in both houses of Congress could be the consequence of the

38. CNN/*USA Today*/Gallup Poll data (survey conducted February 9–12, 2006).

39. ABC News/*Washington Post* Poll, "Iraqi Elections, Economic Gains Lift Bush from His Career Lows," December 15–18, 2005 (abcnews.go.com/images/Politics/1001a1Bush-IraqYear-ender.pdf).

40. Data from the *Time*/SRBI Poll, "Slight Bush Gains on Heels of Foiled Terrorist Attack and Post 9/11," August 22–24, 2006 (www.srbi.com/time_poll_arc31.html).

Republicans' polarizing governing strategy. In 2006 even primary electorates—which tend to be the most extreme in American politics and are often fingered for producing the polarization evident at the elite level—seemed to produce moderation. Alabama Republicans, surely among the nation's most conservative, overwhelmingly chose incumbent Governor Bob Riley, a pro-business conservative, over the socially conservative firebrand Roy Moore, who had achieved notoriety three years earlier when he was removed as chief justice of the Alabama Supreme Court for refusing to take down a monument of the Ten Commandments installed on state property. Despite struggles during his first term, Riley had no trouble defeating Moore, winning the primary by a vote of 65 percent to 35 percent.

Alabama was not alone. The national Democratic Party provided millions of dollars in financial support to the Senate campaign of Robert P. Casey Jr. in Pennsylvania, despite his pro-life stand on abortion. Implicit in the decision of party elites to support Casey, who is the son of the former Pennsylvania governor, was the belief that voters would prefer a more moderate candidate. The socially moderate Casey trounced the ideologically extreme incumbent, Republican Rick Santorum—who had, among other things, expressed concerns about man-on-dog sex—by a breathtaking 18 percentage points. In Connecticut an activist-dominated primary gave liberal Ned Lamont the Democratic nomination over incumbent Senator Joe Lieberman, but the general electorate handed Lieberman, who ran as an independent, a 10 percentage point victory over Lamont. Similar stories can be spun about Senate races in Virginia, Montana, and Missouri. In all these states, the Democratic candidates who defeated Republican incumbents will almost certainly prove to be more moderate than the Republicans they are replacing.[41]

Moderation, however, is not the only explanation for these outcomes. Jim Webb almost certainly would not have won the Senate race in Virginia had not the Republican incumbent, George Allen, called a Webb campaign worker "macaca," an impromptu remark that was likely a racial slur despite Allen's protestations to the contrary. Jon Tester might have lost Montana by a few thousand votes rather than winning by that margin had Senator Conrad Burns, the Republican incumbent, not been so closely identified with the Jack Abramoff corruption scandal. And Republican senator Jim Talent might have survived in Missouri had Rush Limbaugh not lampooned Michael J. Fox's symptoms of Parkinson's syndrome after Fox appeared in an advertisement backing Democrat Claire McCaskill. Indeed, all these races were so close that the winning margins could

41. These outcomes also square with Morris Fiorina's view that voters would elect more moderate candidates if only they had them to choose from.

Table 1-6. *Ideological Self-Identification of Senate Electorates, 2000 and 2006*
Percent

State	Liberal	Moderate	Conservative
Montana			
2000	20	45	35
2006	19	47	34
Difference	−1	2	−1
Missouri			
2000	20	48	33
2006	20	43	37
Difference	0	−5	4
Virginia			
2000	21	49	30
2006	21	44	35
Difference	0	−5	5
Pennsylvania			
2000	21	49	31
2006	25	46	29
Difference	4	−3	−2

Source: Voter News Service, "General Election Exit Poll," November 7, 2000; Edison/Mitofsky, "Exit Polls," November 7, 2006.

easily be explained by the anti-Republican wave caused by an unpopular president's position on an unpopular war.[42]

Exit poll data on participation do not paint a picture of moderates forcefully reclaiming their government from the forces of polarization. Table 1-6 compares the percentage of self-identified liberals, moderates, and conservatives in 2000 and 2006 in the four states that elected Democrats who are expected to be more moderate than the Republican incumbents they defeated in 2006. In three of the four states, the percentage of self-identified moderates actually dropped between 2000 and 2006. In Missouri and Virginia, the decrease was 5 percentage points, and in Pennsylvania it was 3.

It is possible that moderates were more inclined to choose the Democratic candidates in 2006 than in 2000, but comparisons over time about vote choice are more difficult to make than comparisons about turnout. For example, the 2000 Senate race in Pennsylvania was nothing like the one in 2006 because the 2000

42. It is also worth noting that in two of the six Democratic Senate seats picked up—Sherrod Brown in Ohio and Sheldon Whitehouse in Rhode Island—the Democratic challengers are likely to produce voting records that are ideologically more extreme than the two Republican incumbents they are replacing.

Table 1-7. *Vote for the Republican Senatorial Candidate, by Ideological Self-Identification, 2000 and 2006*
Percent

State	Liberal	Moderate	Conservative
Montana			
2000	17	45	80
2006	9	38	83
Difference	−8	−7	3
Virginia			
2000	22	46	84
2006	12	40	88
Difference	−10	−6	4

Source: See table 1-6.

Democratic challenger, Ron Klink, ran an underfunded and uninspired campaign. Klink raised less than $4 million despite the fact that he faced a crowded Democratic primary and a well-financed incumbent in Santorum, who raised more than $10 million. And, in Missouri the Democrat on the ballot in 2000, Mel Carnahan, died in a plane crash three weeks before the election, which makes it impossible to compare the dynamics of that race with the one in 2006.

Fortunately, the dynamics of the Senate races in Virginia and Montana were relatively similar, although not identical. In 2000 Chuck Robb, the Democratic incumbent in Virginia, was an attractive moderate candidate, as was Democratic challenger Brian Schweitzer in Montana.[43] Robb lost to Allen 52 percent to 48 percent, and Schweitzer lost to Burns 51 percent to 48 percent—both close races, though not as close as either contest in 2006. Table 1-7 shows how the voting behavior of different ideological groups changed between the 2000 and 2006 elections in these two states. In both Virginia and Montana, the Republican candidate lost support among moderates—by 7 percentage points in Virginia and 6 in Montana. In both cases that was enough to cost him the election.

But it was not just moderates who jumped ship. Both of the Republican losers in 2006 lost even more ground among self-reported liberals than they did among moderates—a clear sign of polarization. Allen went from garnering the support of 22 percent of liberals in 2000 to only 12 percent after his "macaca" moment. Burns's support among liberals dropped from 17 percent to 9 percent. If either candidate had run as well among liberals as before, they would have narrowly

43. Schweitzer went on to win the governorship in Montana in 2004.

prevailed. In both states, conservatives, who were very loyal to the Republican candidates in 2000, became even more so in 2006.

We cannot know how moderates in 2006 saw the candidates relative to each other ideologically, nor can we know whether moderates saw the Republican Party as significantly closer to the ideological extreme than before. But if the results presented earlier regarding the presidential contest in 2004 are any indication, they probably did not see the Republicans as *ideologically* less attractive in 2006. Rather than voting against polarization, it seems that the best explanation for changing moderate behavior was dissatisfaction with incumbent performance. In political science, a venerable line of thinking about voting behavior suggests that most voters make decisions about ends rather than means.[44] If they think the "ins" have done well, then they return them to office. But if their retrospective evaluations of the "ins" are poor, they vote them out. Since moderate voters do not have strong ideological commitments, they are more likely than liberals or conservatives to engage in retrospective voting.

The 2006 elections were clearly nationalized, with the results a function of people's perceptions of the Bush presidency and the performance of the Republican majority in Congress.[45] According to 2006 exit polls, voters' views of the economy had improved markedly by late 2006, but they were not giving President Bush or Republicans in Congress much credit for it—which suggests that their evaluations of the political system were not as tightly tied to the economy as they usually are. Rather, Iraq and other noneconomic concerns (such as corruption) topped voters' lists of concerns. These concerns seemed to be embodied in the president's weak approval numbers.

Moderates in both Virginia and Montana had overwhelmingly negative views of President Bush. He enjoyed only 35 percent approval among moderates in Virginia and 39 percent in Montana.[46] Little wonder that they were more likely to turn to Democratic alternatives in 2006. By contrast, when Chuck Robb came up 4 percentage points short in the Virginia Senate race in 2000, Bill Clinton's approval rating in the state was 62 percent among moderates. Robb, the incumbent from the president's party, got 54 percent of moderates' votes that year. In

---

44. Key (1966); Fiorina (1981).

45. One indication that national conditions were particularly important in understanding Senate outcomes was that Republican incumbent Lincoln Chafee of Rhode Island lost despite having a personal approval rating of better than 60 percent. Rhode Islanders clearly thought a Democratic majority in the Senate would be more effective in confronting their major concerns than even the most moderate Republican the Senate had to offer.

46. I thank Dana Blanton of Fox News for providing these cross-tabulations of the 2006 exit poll data. They are not yet publicly available. When they are, I will be able to do more detailed analysis.

contrast, Allen, the incumbent in 2006, got only 40 percent of moderates' votes with the president of his party at 35 percent approval among moderates.

Although the case that the 2006 elections represented a vote against Republicans' performance rather than an outright rejection of their ideology is far from perfect, the data are suggestive.[47] Moderates over time seem to like ideologically extreme political leaders when times are good and like them much less when times are poor. According to the National Election Studies, Ronald Reagan's approval rating was 14 percentage points higher among moderates in 1984 than it was in 1982; George W. Bush's approval rating was 22 points higher among moderates in 2002 than it was in 2004; and Bill Clinton's approval rating was 21 points higher in 1996 than it was in 1994. Other than Clinton on welfare reform, none of these leaders changed all that much ideologically over time. Rather, moderates approved of them when they thought they were doing well and disapproved of them when they thought they were not. It is likely that the Republicans would have held the Congress had Bush's polarizing approach to solving problems borne more fruit. Moderates certainly did not seem to have a problem with it in 2002.

Conclusion

The results presented here generally suggest that elite polarization has stimulated participation at the mass level even though the masses remain relatively moderate. Not surprisingly, ideologues are now more engaged, but that is also true of the moderates and nonideologues among us. In the aggregate, we are seeing higher levels of voting and nonvoting participation, greater interest and investment in campaigns and elections, and improved perceptions of government responsiveness.

One major reason for the increase in participation among moderates and non-ideologues is blissful ignorance. They simply do not realize that their choices have become polarized and that, as a result, the political system today represents their interests to a lesser degree than before. Such ignorance should not come as a shock. Generations of public opinion research have demonstrated that people who favor independent and moderate identifications are not exactly modern-day Athenians, carefully weighing all available policy alternatives and, after much deliberation, charting a middle course. Rather, they simply do not pay much attention and hence do not know very much about politics. As evidence, the 2004 National Election Study included a six-item political knowledge test, asking whether people could

47. John Aldrich and David Rohde's theory of conditional party government rests on the same idea: a centrist public will support an extremist agenda in Congress provided it is effective in addressing their concerns. See Aldrich and Rohde (2001).

identify various national and world leaders, knew which party had the majority in the House, and so forth. Those who self-identified as either liberal or conservative answered an average of about 3.5 questions correctly. Moderates only answered an average of 2.8 correctly, and those who failed to place themselves on the ideology scale got a dismal 1.94 correct. "Moderation" can be a troubling thing.

It is not that this group is completely incapable, either. As a group, they did realize that the presidential candidates in 2004 presented markedly different ideas about the nation's defense and the best way to combat terrorism. Moreover, this finding is generally important to the study of polarization, suggesting that scholars should avoid aggregating a large number of issues into scales of perceived polarization or of individuals' polarization. One issue might be enough, if it is the only issue that matters at a given time.

There is also a potentially troubling polarization of ideologues' attitudes toward government. In 2004 the difference between conservatives and liberals in their trust in government was never greater.[48] This polarization may help explain party differences in support for the war in Iraq. And it may also help us understand the widespread support for more normatively troubling government programs that challenge existing notions of the importance of civil liberties.

Finally, the 2006 elections provided the nation with divided government, which the public seemed to want after five years of the Republicans' polarizing style. Although moderates were not any more likely to vote in 2006 than in 2000, they were more likely to *vote for Democrats* in several key Senate races. Whether this represented a conscious rejection of polarization is unclear, however. As recently as two years before, moderates seemed to endorse the politics of polarization by reelecting the president and Republican majorities in Congress. The 2004 vote, however, was probably no more of a vote for polarization than the vote in 2006 was a vote against it. Rather, moderate voters were simply satisfied enough with the present course in 2004 but dissatisfied when 2006 rolled around. In that sense, moderates in this polarized era are a bit like children with two bad parents: not knowing enough to understand that their interests are not being well represented by either source of power, they support one or the other as long as nothing terrible happens. But at some point the situation eventually sours, leaving them angry and looking for alternatives, which might not be any better. Thus, in politics today, even a supposed vote for moderation gave the majority to a party led by Nancy Pelosi, who is anything but a moderate.

---

48. The difference was probably even greater in 2006, although the data are not yet available to substantiate this.

Appendix A. Multivariate Analysis of Turnout Change among Moderates

Although the descriptive results of voter engagement presented in the first part of this chapter are interesting in their own right, I can also use them to explain why turnout among moderates has increased somewhat dramatically since 1996 even as candidates have become increasingly immoderate. To that end, I estimate a relatively simple voter turnout model using logistic regression analysis. Regression allows me to estimate the effect of each of the potential variables of interest while holding other potential explanations constant. I use logistic regression, specifically, because the dependent variable, whether someone reported having voted or not, is dichotomous. The independent variables of greatest interest are the amount of polarization between the presidential candidates that people perceive on defense spending, whether people reported being contacted by one of the major parties, external efficacy, and perceptions of government responsiveness. I have shown that each has changed quite a bit over time for moderates, so, provided they are predictive of turnout among moderates, all are candidates to explain change in voter turnout over time. I also control for strength of partisanship and a range of demographic factors, including race (being African American), gender (being female), age, income, education, and being from the south, to make the estimates of interest more secure.

The results of this analysis appear in table A-1. Somewhat surprisingly, neither external efficacy nor perceptions of government responsiveness had a statistically significant effect on voter turnout in 2004, so neither variable can explain why turnout among moderates was higher in 2004 than before. However, reporting contact from a party and perceived polarization of the presidential candidates on defense spending are statistically significant. Provided their values increased over time, they each contributed to the increase in reported turnout among moderates.

Recall that figure 1-2 revealed that self-reported turnout among moderates had increased markedly between 1996 and 2004. Therefore, 1996 is used as the baseline year of comparison. Specifically, I use the regression estimates in table A-1 to estimate the relative contribution to increased voter turnout that party mobilization and perceptions of polarization on defense made between the two years. To do so, I first calculate the predicted probability that someone reported having voted, holding all the variables in the model constant at their 2004 sample means. Next, I calculate the predicted probability that someone voted, substituting the 1996 value only for the independent variables of interest. I then record the difference in the predicted probabilities of voting.

Table A-1. *Self-Reported Voter Turnout as a Function of Perceived Candidate Polarization, Party Mobilization, Feelings about the Political System, and Social Characteristics, Self-Identified Moderates Only, 2004*[a]

Variable	Parameter estimate
Constant	−7.659***
	(1.659)
Perceived polarization of candidates on defense spending	0.279*
	(0.149)
Contacted by a party	1.442**
	(0.481)
External efficacy	0.372
	(0.586)
Perceptions of government responsiveness	−0.296
	(0.918)
Strength of partisanship	1.143***
	(0.275)
Race (African American)	1.532**
	(0.654)
Gender (female)	−0.607
	(0.437)
Education	0.853**
	(0.292)
Income	−0.207
	(0.199)
Age	0.040***
	(0.013)
Non-South	0.984*
	(0.449)
Cox and Snell R^2	0.28
N	279

Source: Author's calculations based on data from 2004 National Election Study.
*** $p < 0.001$, ** $p < 0.01$, * $p < 0.05$, one-tailed test.
a. Logistic regression estimates; standard errors shown in parentheses.

As the analyses above foreshadowed, the increase in perceived candidate polarization on defense and the increase in party contacts were statistically significant. In 1996 the mean absolute difference between the presidential candidates on defense was 1.76 points. In 2004 it had increased to 2.34 points. My model estimates that this increase led to a 2.1 percentage point increase in voter turnout among moderates, other things being equal. Similarly 26 percent of moderates said they had been contacted by one of the parties in 1996, while 41 percent reported this in 2004. My model estimates that this increase led to a 2.7 percentage point increase in voter turnout. In short, both variables, perceptions of increasing polarization between the presidential candidates on defense and party mobilization activities, contributed to the turnout increase.

Before one concludes that the effect of mobilization is larger, recall that the defense spending item is probably best considered a proxy for terrorism, an issue area in which the perceived difference between candidates was even larger than for defense. Unfortunately, time comparisons for perceptions of the candidates on terrorism are not possible because the National Elections Study did not ask these questions before 2004. Even so, we should not lose sight of the fact that, other things being equal, the increase in voter turnout between 1996 and 2004 among moderates would have been far less impressive had it not been for the efforts of parties to mobilize voters, even moderate ones.[1]

1. Although explaining the increase in voter turnout between 1996 and 2004 yields predictable results, it is less clear why turnout did not increase between 2000 and 2004 among moderates. Although perceptions of polarization on defense and party contact were both up between 2000 and 2004, increased turnout did not result. Of course, external efficacy and perceptions of government responsiveness dropped during the period, but neither had a significant effect on turnout. This suggests that something not included in the model offset the increases that the variables in the model would have predicted. Unfortunately the literature on voter turnout does not provide many clues. The most plausible explanation to me is the unreliability of self-reported voter turnout. Replicating this analysis with a voter validation follow-up might sharpen the results considerably.

Comments on Chapter One

COMMENT

Deborah Jordan Brooks and John G. Geer

The polarization of American politics has been a much discussed topic in recent years. Not everyone agrees about exactly what is happening, but it seems clear that—at the very least—the parties have become more polarized. This volume and its predecessor attest to the fact that there is an important debate occurring about polarization and its possible influences on American politics. And while it seems obvious to many analysts that polarizing political parties have an adverse influence on the polity, Marc J. Hetherington offers a refreshingly unorthodox perspective—one that challenges this prevailing view. Not only does he make a strong case that citizens do not become disengaged by party polarization, he shows that polarization, in fact, has some notable beneficial effects on the public.

We find much to like in Hetherington's overall position. In our comment, therefore, we will attempt to build upon his helpful analysis by delineating the theoretical links between his argument and the "party responsibility" literature that was prominent in the 1950s, mentioning a few additional empirical patterns about polarization and its most visible symptom (negativity), and discussing some of the general implications that intensified party polarization has for American politics.

Recalling the "Party Leadership" Literature

Hetherington undertakes an impressive array of analyses that exploit a range of dependent variables. His data show that polarization does not appear to be decreasing turnout, nonvoting campaign participation, interest in campaigns, political trust, and other measures of citizen political engagement. There is some uncertainty about how much elite polarization is really trickling down to the public, but even on that point, Hetherington demonstrates that people are clearly able to distinguish between the parties on two of the biggest issues of the day: defense spending and terrorism. There do appear to be differences in patterns of political trust among liberals and conservatives, with it being on the rise among the latter and on the decline among the former—a trend that is potentially troubling. But even so, most of Hetherington's indicators suggest that polarization is not harmful to the electorate and, in fact, appears to be beneficial.

Hetherington's position stands in stark contrast to the conventional wisdom that polarization has detrimental effects on the political engagement of voters. Concerns abound that polarization will result in lower turnout, less interest in elections, and a general disenchantment with politics. But like Hetherington, we agree that polarization seems likely, on average, to yield more benefit than harm with respect to the public's engagement with the political system. The most obvious benefit of polarization is to offer a sharper distinction between the two political parties. For partisans the benefit of this sharper distinction is clear: elite polarization gives partisans further reinforcement for their preexisting ideological and policy preferences. For moderates, the choices are made clear enough that one option is more likely to be preferred, at least marginally, over the alternative. For those who have lower levels of overall political knowledge, it should make the lines of differentiation on at least the most salient issues clearer than they would be otherwise. We would expect that more distinct parties, along with coverage of their differences by the media, would make most people more vested in political outcomes—and more interested and engaged in politics as a result.

While different from the views of many in the field, this position that polarization, on the whole, will benefit voters is not new. In fact, it is quite a long-standing intellectual tradition in American political science (albeit one that employed different terminology). Rather than speaking of the benefits of "polarization" per se, scholars such as E. E. Schattschneider advocated more than half a century ago for "party responsibility"—a concept which, by its nature, requires polarization between the parties. With a unified voice probably not heard before or since within the profession, the American Political Science Association called on Schattschneider to lead a task force to devise suggestions for promoting structural changes to enhance the strength and responsibility of America's political parties. The task force issued its set of proposals in a report, entitled "Toward a More Responsible Two-Party System," in a special edition of the *American Political Science Review* in 1950. The product of input from both academic and political practitioners, the report called for several improvements, including:

—more clearly differentiated and articulated party positions,
—a stronger opposition party,
—more internal party cohesion,
—more effective enforcement of party unity,
—greater party resistance to outside pressure (in order to, among other things, minimize deviance from consistent party platforms), and

—parties responsible to the public such that the public can identify party actions and agendas, and reward and punish for these accordingly in the voting booth.[1]

Ultimately, polarized parties were seen as an optimal state of affairs in that each organization could be held clearly responsible for its actions. At the time, intensified polarization was seen as a solution to a failing party system. While certainly not without rebuttal, the report has been characterized as representing a viewpoint held by much of the profession at the time.[2]

We are certainly not arguing here that we now have a perfectly "responsible" party system, even by the classic definition.[3] But when scholars express concern about party polarization in the current era, they seem to be indirectly concerned that the parties may have achieved many of the goals of the 1950 report *too* well. Those concerned with current polarization levels typically view present-day parties as being too cohesive. Enforcement of party unity is seen as too strong, with the frequent and effective deployment of powerful carrots and pointed sticks to guarantee party discipline. The opposition party is seen as too antagonistic and adversarial. And overall, parties are deemed to present unduly stark choices on issues to a mostly moderate American public.

In other words, many concerns about political polarization come down to the idea that parties have too successfully achieved many of the recommendations contained within the American Political Science Association report. According to that classic definition of the term, parties appear to be "responsible" now—or at least *more* responsible. They have become so "responsible" that they are now "polarized," in today's terms. Relatively few scholars and pundits seem to be worrying these days about weak parties with little responsibility to the public, as they did in the 1940s and 50s, and more recently during the 1970s and late 1980s, when divided government seemed like it was becoming the dominant state of affairs.

Additional Empirical Patterns

It is important to remember that the tables have turned quite quickly away from weak parties and toward stronger and more polarized ones. We think that a

1. See Committee on Political Parties (1950).
2. See Turner (1951).
3. Among other things, one might reasonably argue that the Democrats could have been more unified and platform oriented in recent years, especially during the immediate aftermath of September 11 and early in the Iraq conflict. Or one might argue that our current era of candidate-centered campaigns conflicts with the degree to which parties can be fully held responsible by the public at election time. (The 2006 midterm elections, however, seem to be a fairly convincing repudiation of that concern.)

reminder about the connection between responsible parties and polarization is warranted. In fact, the sometimes forgotten "party responsibility" debate offers a useful framework for understanding and appreciating Hetherington's many findings. Put in this larger theoretical context, it becomes easier to see why Hetherington has uncovered the benefits of polarized political debate for the public. Schattschneider would have predicted such developments—and his faith in them was among the reasons he pushed for major reforms.

When we use the old responsible party model to inform our understanding of polarization, additional empirical patterns come into sharper focus. For example, we know that negativity is on the rise in political campaigns. Scholars ranging from Darrell West, director of Brown University's Taubman Center for Public Policy, to Kathleen Jamieson, director of the Annenberg Public Policy Center at the University of Pennsylvania, have shown this trend.[4] The usual assumption of those concerned about polarization is that attacks have become increasingly personal and that such criticism undermines the political system. But the party responsibility perspective would contend that *issues* should be the source of the increase. That is, with parties polarized on issues, attacks should focus on policy differences, not personal ones. This party responsibility hypothesis appears to be correct. Geer demonstrates that issue-based negativity in presidential campaigns has increased since the 1960s, but trait-based attacks *have not*.[5] The incidence of trait-based negativity has been basically unchanged over the last forty years.[6]

This finding is critical as we consider the debate over polarization. Candidates are more likely to criticize their opponents on their issue positions or records in times of ideological polarization. But the occurrence of trait-based negativity in presidential campaigns, at least, is largely unaffected by polarization—and trait-based attack ads are the kind of campaigning that most upset the public and political observers. Voters want politicians to "focus on the issues." Polarization provides the fuel for more negativity, but in so doing, it also increases the amount of time candidates spend talking about important issues.[7] This strikes us as a good thing.

While there are silver linings to polarization and greater differences between the parties, there are concerns that lurk on the horizon. Most work by scholars has looked at the electorate as whole, with some attention to ideological moderates

4. West (2005) traces the evolution of televised political campaign ads from the 1950s to the present. For an account of negativity in the 2000 presidential campaign, see Johnston, Hagen, and Jamieson (2004).
5. Geer (2006).
6. Geer (2006, p. 86).
7. See Geer (2006).

and self-identified independents as key subgroups.[8] But we need to dig deeper on this front, examining differential patterns among important segments of the electorate. Aggregation could be masking important differences. There is no reason to think that all segments of the electorate will react in the same way to these changing dynamics.

One distinction ripe for analysis involves gender. Do men and women differ in their reactions to different types of political messages? New research shows that the answer to that question is that men and women do react differently to negative messages, with men being far more likely than women to intend to vote in response to seeing uncivil negative campaign messages.[9] Negative messages delivered in a more "civil" manner were actually quite energizing to women; it is only harsh attacks that keep them from going to the polls relative to men. Such findings would be mostly of normative importance if it were not for the fact that the partisan gender gap (men are far more likely to vote for Republicans than are women), in conjunction with turnout rates differing in response to incivility, could potentially skew the voting electorate toward the right during times of political polarization.

Looking Forward

In general, however, the benefits of polarization seem clear: a polarized system provides a chance for those competing for power to make a clearer case for why they should be given power. Of course, the other side can point to the risks associated with that position as well. As a result, this struggle can get nasty—and at times the rhetoric will cross the line of civility and even be insulting to our collective intelligence. Regardless, we need to make room for it in our politics, and moreover, we need to appreciate its contributions to the political process. Assuming that party polarization is here to stay (for a while, at least), we can expect that issue-based negativity will be a part of political campaigns as well. And we can take comfort in the fact that there is little evidence to suggest that polarization and its byproduct, negativity, are disengaging people overall from the political process.

8. For example, see Ansolabehere and Iyengar (1995); Clinton and Lapinski (2004); Finkel and Geer (1998); Goldstein and Freedman (2002); Lau and Pomper (2001, 2004).

9. Why might this be the case? Brooks (2006) shows that there are a large variety of findings from fields outside of political science—child development, linguistics, media studies, biology, evolutionary psychology, and the like—that show that men are far more comfortable with conflict than women are. They engage in it more frequently, and it energizes them when they see it. To the extent that elite polarization breeds elite conflict, then an energized response on the part of men and an enervated response on the part of women would not be surprising.

Whether parties are undifferentiated or highly differentiated, there will be complaints. One may recall George Wallace's famous comment that "there is not a dime's worth of difference" between the parties. Perhaps the broader lesson is that whatever the condition of our political system, there will be critics of it. That, of course, is part of the democratic enterprise—the opportunity to question the status quo. It is important to remember that democracy is about disagreement—about that famous battle for who gets what, when, where, and how. Political scientists John R. Hibbing and Elizabeth Theiss-Morse are convincing about the fact that people say they do not like the "battle" aspect of politics.[10] But what people say they like and dislike about democratic rhetoric does not necessarily translate into their behavior. People may not like polarization—or more likely, the negativity that accompanies it—but it seems to produce a more engaged electorate.

However, our general optimism about polarization is tempered somewhat by Hetherington's observations that liberals and conservatives are differing increasingly on matters of trust in government and, especially, that partisans may be increasingly willing to uncritically embrace the positions of their own party. That being said, we would not be surprised if major differences were reasonably confined to specific years. Of late there are certainly far more Republicans questioning the Bush presidency than had been the case during the first few years he was in office.

Since continued polarization may result in continued incivility, we are also potentially worried by the finding that incivility in campaigns appears to affect men and women differently. If elites keep their negative messages reasonably civil, women are likely to stay engaged in politics. But to the extent that it gets nasty, substantial differences are likely to emerge between the political engagement of men and women. That all suggests that polarization tempered by civility will not be harmful to the relative participation of women, but bitter and nasty politics might be.

Beyond its specific implications, the finding of gender differences in response to incivility is a reminder that Hetherington's piece on the relationship between polarization and political engagement is just a first step at examining the issue. For the most part, he is focusing on the U.S. electorate overall. In some analyses, he breaks voters out by ideology or attention to politics. But beyond those broad-brushed distinctions, big questions remain to be answered about how different types of voters are affected by polarization. Race, age, and education seem to be areas ripe for more analyses. To the extent that we are conscious about keeping all groups engaged in the political system—and especially to the extent that such differences

10. See Hibbing and Theiss-Morse (2002).

may be associated with persistent partisan voting patterns—we still need to know much more about how different types of citizens are affected by political polarization before we can be less cautious in our optimism about it.

Conclusion

It is all too obvious to call for more work in the general area. We always can profit from more research. Our main point is to generally support Hetherington's position and to do so in a way that provides a greater coherence to his findings. The rise of polarization is not necessarily a bad thing for the polity overall. More "responsible"—or at least more differentiated—parties seem to yield substantial benefits to voters, and Hetherington's paper documents many of those advantages very effectively. But we need to cast a broader theoretical and normative net in considering the question. By so doing, we will be in a better position to understand and assess the shifts in our political system. It would be very interesting to know what E. E. Schattschneider would think of the political system right now. We suspect he would find much to like—and we are very sure he would like the evidence put forth by Marc Hetherington.

COMMENT
Martin P. Wattenberg

Marc Hetherington's chapter nicely outlines evidence demonstrating that political participation in the United States has increased during this recent age of partisan polarization. Such findings are hardly surprising in light of factors that have long been known to stimulate public participation in politics. The more interested people are in politics, for instance, the more likely they are to take an active role in the political process. A highly polarized partisan environment is usually a more interesting one, and this should fire up more citizens to become politically engaged. Furthermore, as polarization between Democrats and Republicans increases, the stakes at the polls are clearly raised—and citizens become more inclined to participate in politics when they believe their involvement will truly make a difference.

Hetherington's findings that political participation, efficacy, and feelings of governmental responsiveness have been increasing in recent years are noteworthy in and of themselves. Yet it is hard to judge whether these numbers are excellent, good, fair, or poor without some perspective. The turnout rate of 60 percent of U.S. citizens of voting age in the 2004 presidential election was substantially higher than for the previous two presidential contests, but compared to typical turnout rates in other established democracies, it is nothing to brag about. In short, one of the reasons why so many observers of the American political scene continue to be concerned about U.S. turnout rates is that they are relatively low compared to other countries. Thus the most valuable commentary I can make on Hetherington's analysis is to offer a comparative perspective.

Two recent cross-national surveys—the Comparative Study of Electoral Systems and the International Social Survey Program—provide excellent sources of comparative data on the measures employed by Hetherington. Although these surveys were undertaken in established as well as new democracies, my analysis will be limited to advanced industrialized societies that have continually held elections since at least the 1970s. This confines the analysis to about twenty nations whose economic status and historical experience with democracy is relatively comparable to that of the United States. The results clearly show that the United States measures up favorably to these nations in terms of political participation, efficacy, and perceptions of governmental responsiveness. And such findings can certainly be interpreted as a very positive indicator of the health of American democracy in a polarized partisan environment.

Comparative Measures of Participation

My analysis is designed to parallel Hetherington's as much as possible. Therefore, I will first compare nonvoting measures of political participation in the United States to those of other established democracies.[11] Table 1-8 demonstrates that the United States ranks at or near the top of the list in terms of talking to other people to persuade them how to vote, showing support for a party or candidate, and donating money for political purposes. In the typical established democracy, 23 percent of citizens sampled say they have tried to persuade others how to vote during the most recent national election. In 2004 the figure in the United States was 44 percent—a level of political activity exceeded only by Canadians and equaled by the British. Similarly, only Canadians are more likely than U.S. citizens

---

11. In this and the following comparisons, the questions in the surveys I used are not exactly the same as the questions in surveys used by Hetherington. However, they clearly tap the same concepts. What is most important for my analysis is that the wording of questions in the surveys I used was the same for all of the countries.

Table 1-8. *Nonvoting Political Participation in Established Democracies*
Percentage of voting-age population surveyed

Country	Talked to other people to persuade them to vote for a party or candidate[a]	Showed support for a party or candidate[a]	Donated money to a political organization or group in the past year[b]
Australia	32	16	n.a.
Austria	n.a.	n.a.	12
Belgium	12	7	10
Canada	65	35	n.a.
Denmark	22	8	9
Finland	13	11	7
France	29	7	3
Germany	28	7	9
Iceland	22	16	n.a.
Ireland	13	8	11
Israel	32	11	13
Italy	n.a.	n.a.	3
Japan	12	4	n.a.
Netherlands	12	7	8
New Zealand	8	6	n.a.
Norway	18	7	12
Portugal	11	7	4
Spain	8	6	5
Sweden	13	3	7
Switzerland	15	6	19
United Kingdom	44	25	8
United States	44	30	21
Average	23	11	9
U.S. rank	Second of 20	Second of 20	First of 17
Nations ranking higher than U.S.	Canada	Canada	...

Sources: Responses in columns 1 and 2 are from the Comparative Study of Electoral Systems, "Module 2," 2001–05; responses in column 3 are from the European Social Survey, "Round 1," 2002–03, and from Center for Democracy and Civil Society, "U.S. Citizenship, Involvement, Democracy Survey," 2005.

a. Survey question for data in columns 1 and 2: Here is a list of things some people do during elections. Which if any did you do during the most recent election: 1) talked to other people to persuade them to vote for a particular party or candidate; 2) showed your support for a particular party or candidate by, for example, attending a meeting, putting up a poster, or in some other way?

b. Survey question for data in column 3: During the last twelve months, have you donated money to a political organization or group?

n.a. = Not available

to have actively engaged in a recent campaign by attending a meeting, putting up a poster, wearing a button, or other such activities. On this measure of participation, 30 percent of Americans said they had taken part, compared to just 11 percent in the average established democracy.

The third column of table 1-8 shows that Americans are more likely to donate money to political organizations or groups than the citizens of any of the sixteen Western European democracies surveyed. While many observers of American politics feel that the political process has been tarnished by the seemingly endless pursuit of more and more money to finance campaigns, these data reveal a positive side to American political fundraising—namely, that a comparatively high percentage of citizens (roughly one in five) donates money for political purposes. Political donors will necessarily be unrepresentative of the electorate as a whole (the poor, for instance, are naturally less likely to give money), but surely the more people who give, the more broadly representative such donors to parties and candidates will be. It may well be that the American political process is currently awash with money, but at least it is coming from a comparatively large swath of the electorate.

A second dimension of U.S. political participation that Hetherington focuses on involves mobilization efforts by political parties and other organizations. Given the extraordinary amount of money that such organizations now have to spend, it is hardly surprising that Hetherington finds they have been able to reach more people in recent years. Table 1-9 examines how this performance compares with other established democracies. The results show that only a few countries other than the United States have recently seen such a large percentage of their population being contacted by a campaign or political party. Forty-seven percent of those interviewed after the 2004 U.S. election said they had been contacted to ask for their vote, compared to an average of 24 percent in the established democracies where this question was asked.

Given that American political parties have become quite active in terms of mobilizing participation, it bears asking how responsive they are to the voters they are trying so hard to engage. Those who bemoan the growth of ideological polarization between Democrats and Republicans often criticize the parties for being dominated by supposedly unrepresentative activists who shape the parties' policymaking. Compared to parties in other countries, then, are American political parties small and elite-driven?

The answer, in fact, is no. The survey data displayed in table 1-10 indicate that no other country comes close to the United States in terms of the percentage of citizens who say they "belong" to a political party. This difference probably stems,

Table 1-9. *Contact by Political Parties in Established Democracies*
Percentage of voting-age population surveyed

Country (year)	Reported that a campaign or a party contacted them to ask for their vote[a]
Australia (2004)	29
Belgium (2003)	29
Canada (2004)	55
Denmark (2001)	23
Finland (2003)	21
France (2002)	7
Germany (2002)	13
Iceland (2003)	28
Ireland (2002)	53
Israel (2003)	18
Netherlands (2002)	14
New Zealand (2002)	21
Norway (2001)	15
Portugal (2002)	22
Spain (2004)	6
Sweden (2002)	7
Switzerland (2003)	18
United Kingdom (2005)	26
United States (2004)	47
Average	24
U.S. rank	Third of 19
Nations ranking higher than U.S.	Canada and Ireland

Sources: Comparative Study of Electoral Systems, "Module 2," 2001–05.
a. Survey question: During the last campaign did a candidate or anyone from a political party contact you to persuade you to vote for them?

in part, from the fact that belonging to a party in the United States often just means that someone is registered as a Democrat or a Republican, whereas in other countries it typically means they pay membership dues. Yet this difference is indicative of the greater openness of American parties, as evidenced by the extraordinarily high percentage of Americans who say they not only belong to a party but also *participate* in one. Whereas this figure ranges from 1 to 5 percent in other democracies, in the United States it is 14 percent. This aspect of American exceptionalism is no doubt due to the openness of American primary elections, which have yet to catch on in other established democracies. Thus, while it is no doubt true that primaries skew partisan choices toward the ideological poles, it should also be noted that widespread participation in party primaries means that Amer-

Table 1-10. *Participation in Political Parties in Established Democracies*
Percentage of voting-age population surveyed

Country	Belong to a party[a]	Belong and actively participate in a party[a]	Agree that parties encourage people to become active in politics[b]
Australia	5	1	21
Austria	22	5	27
Canada	13	5	32
Denmark	7	3	39
Finland	9	2	34
France	5	2	20
Germany	4	2	20
Ireland	9	3	42
Israel	18	5	41
Japan	5	1	15
Netherlands	10	2	21
New Zealand	11	2	28
Norway	17	3	35
Portugal	6	2	41
Spain	6	3	38
Sweden	10	3	29
Switzerland	9	4	53
United Kingdom	10	2	28
United States	42	14	64
Average	11	3	33
U.S. rank	First of 19	First of 19	First of 19
Nations ranking higher than U.S.	. . .	. . .	. . .

Source: International Social Survey Program, 2004.

a. Survey question for data in columns 1 and 2: People sometimes belong to different kinds of groups or associations. For each type of group, please indicate whether you: belong and actively participate; belong but don't actively participate; used to belong but do not any more; or have never belonged to it—a political party.

b. Survey question for data in column 3: Thinking now about politics in [country], to what extent do you agree or disagree with the following statement: Political parties encourage people to become active in politics.

icans are more involved in the internal decisionmaking (that is, selection of candidates) of parties than partisans are in other countries. Consequently, Americans are more likely than the citizens of other countries to agree that "political parties encourage people to become active in politics." Nearly two out of three Americans believe parties perform this positive function, compared to just one out of three in the typical established democracy.

Comparative Measures of Efficacy, Responsiveness, and Trust

Hetherington's trend analysis of public perceptions of political efficacy and governmental responsiveness reveals mixed findings. A comparative perspective, however, makes it clear that just holding steady on such measures is quite impressive, as the United States ranks very high on both fronts relative to other democracies. The first two columns of table 1-11 display the cross-national findings for the same two efficacy items that Hetherington examined. When asked to agree or disagree with the statement that "politicians don't care what people like me think," Americans were more likely to disagree (the "efficacious" response) than the citizens of any other established democracy except Denmark. On the question of whether people feel they have any say about what government does, Americans finished ahead of the Danes and behind only three other countries (France, Japan, and Switzerland). Thus it is clear that the United States ranks extremely high overall in terms of political efficacy.

People who believe they have a say in government and that politicians care about them are naturally inclined to feel positively about governmental responsiveness. Hence, the rank ordering of countries on these two dimensions is likely to be relatively similar. Indeed, only the Danes are more likely than Americans to say that elections ensure that voters' views are very well or quite well represented in government (see the third column of table 1-11). Such a finding is particularly impressive given that many of the countries that scored below the United States on this measure have proportional representation systems that guarantee that even small parties are fairly represented in parliament.

In the absence of proportional representation (and with only two major parties in the United States), we might expect Americans to be less likely than the citizens of other countries to say that a political party represents their views. But as the data in table 1-12 indicate, the U.S. response to this question was actually somewhat higher than the average for established democracies. Where representation in the United States really shines, though, is in terms of leaders. Table 1-12 also shows that Americans are more likely to say there is a political leader who represents their views than the citizens of all other established democracies, except for Australia. Our candidate-centered system thus helps facilitate representation by giving Americans a plethora of choices within parties, as well as between them. All told, 84 percent of Americans say that either a party or a leader stands for their political views—a figure exceeded only by Denmark, Australia, and Norway.

While Americans may feel that someone represents them, a potential problem of a polarized political environment is if one side does not trust the other side

Table 1-11. *Political Efficacy and Perceptions of the Representativeness of Elections in Established Democracies*
Percentage of voting-age population surveyed

Country	Disagree that politicians don't care what people like me think[a]	Disagree that people like me don't have any say about what the government does[a]	Feel that elections ensure that the views of the voters are well represented[b]
Australia	24	29	56
Austria	17	25	n.a.
Belgium	n.a.	n.a.	63
Canada	26	28	40
Denmark	47	41	79
Finland	30	26	48
France	26	83	61
Germany	16	24	38
Iceland	n.a.	n.a.	55
Ireland	22	25	63
Israel	21	28	47
Japan	11	77	24
Netherlands	33	39	59
New Zealand	27	33	56
Norway	31	47	n.a.
Portugal	14	21	38
Spain	25	26	64
Sweden	24	25	59
Switzerland	36	50	58
United Kingdom	23	27	40
United States	39	48	72
Average	26	37	54
U.S. rank	Second of 19	Fourth of 19	Second of 19
Nations ranking higher than U.S.	Denmark	France, Japan, and Switzerland	Denmark

Sources: Responses in columns 1 and 2 are from the International Social Survey Program, 2004; responses in column 3 are from the Comparative Study of Electoral Systems, "Module 2," 2001–05.

a. Survey question for data in columns 1 and 2: To what extent do you agree or disagree with the following statements: 1) I don't think the government cares much what people like me think; 2) People like me don't have any say about what the government does.

b. Survey question for data in column 3: Thinking about how elections in [country] work in practice, how well do elections ensure that the views of voters are represented by majority parties: very well, quite well, not very well, or not well at all?

n.a. = Not available

Table 1-12. *Comparative Sense of Representation by Parties and Leaders*[a]
Percentage of voting-age population surveyed

Country (year)	Said a leader represents their views	Said a party represents their views	Said a party or a leader represents their views
Australia (2004)	79	83	87
Canada (2004)	68	69	75
Denmark (2001)	70	80	87
Finland (2003)	47	61	70
France (2002)	59	56	71
Germany (2002)	59	57	72
Iceland (2003)	52	61	72
Ireland (2002)	64	67	74
Israel (2003)	54	66	76
Japan (2004)	51	54	52
New Zealand (2002)	68	65	76
Norway (2001)	69	80	85
Portugal (2002)	48	44	59
Spain (2004)	73	74	73
Sweden (2002)	58	75	80
Switzerland (2003)	56	76	80
United Kingdom (2005)	48	55	63
United States (2004)	77	72	84
Average	61	66	74
U.S. rank	Second of 18	Seventh of 18	Fourth of 18
Nations ranking higher than U.S.	Australia	Australia, Denmark, Norway, Spain, Sweden, and Switzerland	Australia, Denmark, and Norway

Sources: Comparative Study of Electoral Systems, "Module 2," 2001–05.
a. Survey question: Would you say that any of the parties in [country] represents your views reasonably well [column 2]? Regardless of how you feel about the parties, would you say that any of the individual party leaders/presidential candidates at the last election represents your views reasonably well [column 1]?

when the other side is in power. Marc Hetherington's analysis finds that trust in government was more related to party identification during the 2004 election campaign than ever before. He expresses concern over this development, writing that "if political trust provides the reservoir of good will for governments even when times are bad, then government in the early twenty-first century is only getting it from one side of the political aisle." On this point, I think Hetherington has exaggerated the evidence. A simple cross-tabulation from the 2004 National

Table 1-13. *Polarization between Major Left-Wing and Right-Wing Party Members on Trust in Government, 2004*[a]
Mean trust level

Country and parties	Supporters of major left-wing party	Supporters of major right-wing party	Difference
France: Socialist versus UMP/RPR[b]	39.4	52.7	13.3
Austria: SPÖ versus ÖVP	34.1	44.8	10.7
Australia: Labor versus Liberal/National	48.0	58.3	10.3
United States: Democratic versus Republican	42.4	52.5	10.1
United Kingdom: Labour versus Conservative	52.5	42.6	9.9
New Zealand: Labor versus National	54.8	48.7	6.1
Germany: SPD versus CDU/CSU	37.3	32.4	4.9

Sources: International Social Survey Program, 2004.

a. Survey question: To what extent do you agree or disagree with the following statement: Most of the time we can trust people in government to do what is right—strongly agree (100), agree (75), neither agree nor disagree (50), disagree (25), or strongly disagree (0).

Note: Party support was measured by a party identification question in Australia, France, the United Kingdom, and the United States; by intended vote in Germany; and by recent past vote in New Zealand and Austria.

b. Party abbreviations: France—UMP, Union for a Popular Movement; RPR, Rally for the Republic. Austria—SPÖ, Social Democrats; ÖVP, Austrian People's Party. Germany—SPD, Social Democratic Party; CDU, Christian Democratic Union; CSU, Christian Social Union.

Election Study reveals that 36 percent of Democrats said they trusted the government in Washington to do the right thing always or most of the time, compared to 62 percent among Republicans. This difference of 26 percentage points hardly strikes me as reason for concern. If this is the extent of the difference during the heat of a contentious election campaign, it seems likely that there would be an ample supply of goodwill when it is really needed for governing, as evidenced in the immediate aftermath of the September 11 terrorist attacks.

Furthermore, the difference between Democrats and Republicans on trust in government in 2004 was perfectly normal compared to other countries whose political systems are dominated by two large parties. Table 1-13 displays data from the International Social Survey Program, which asked an almost identical trust question on a five-point scale (as opposed to a three-point scale in the data Hetherington employed). In the United States, the difference between Democrats and Republicans on trust in government was 10.1 percentage points, compared to an average of 9.2 points between the supporters of the major left-wing and right-wing parties in the other six stable democracies. By this measure, the degree of partisan polarization regarding trust in government in the United States is hardly remarkable when placed in comparative perspective.

The Turnout Problem

This examination of how U.S. political participation, perceptions of representation, and trust in government compare to that in other established democracies has revealed many strengths of the American electoral process. From a comparative perspective, the only clear weakness is the abnormally low rate of turnout of the U.S. electorate at the polls. Fortunately, should there ever be the political will to do something about this, the experience of other countries can lead us to a clear solution. As President Clinton is said to have occasionally remarked, the solutions to most public policy problems have already been found somewhere—we just have to scan the horizons for them.[12]

If in an ideal democracy everyone votes, a simple way to realize this goal is to require people to participate. This is how Australians reasoned when they instituted compulsory voting after their turnout rate fell to 58 percent in 1922. Since then, the country's turnout has never fallen below 90 percent—even though the maximum fine for not voting is only fifty Australian dollars and judges readily accept any reasonable excuse.

In my view, political scientists have been far too cautious in recommending compulsory voting in the United States in light of what we know about the seriousness of the turnout problem and how well this solution works to correct it. It is certainly true that many Americans would object to being told that they have to show up on election day (even though they do not actually have to vote—as long as the secrecy of the ballot is sacrosanct, no law can prevent someone from casting a blank ballot). Yet engineering safety experts have not backed off their calls for mandatory seat belt laws just because some people think it is a matter of personal choice whether to buckle up or not. Nor have researchers on secondhand

---

12. This section harkens back to an article I published in the *Atlantic Monthly* nearly a decade ago—proof enough that the wheels of U.S. electoral reform move very slowly. See Martin P. Wattenberg, "Should Election Day Be a Holiday?" *Atlantic,* October 1998.

smoke backed off on recommendations to ban smoking in public places just because many people think that such restrictions violate their individual rights. Rather, these researchers have continued to try to educate people and shift public policy, achieving a fair degree of success as a result. Political scientists who are concerned about turnout should follow this model, bringing attention to the fact that compulsory voting laws are a proven solution to the problem of low turnout.

Elsewhere in this volume, Pietro Nivola and William Galston suggest that a few states experiment with compulsory voting. This strikes me as an excellent idea. Once the Australian state of Queensland demonstrated that requiring election participation worked extremely well for its state elections, the federal parliament soon adopted the requirement with little controversy at all. In the United States, the best candidate to play this role is probably Massachusetts, whose state constitution explicitly gives the legislature the right to make election attendance compulsory.[13] Once one American state tries out this reform and sees its turnout rate rise over 90 percent, chances should increase that other states—as well as the federal government—will follow and that America's turnout problem will be solved.

13. Article 61 of the constitution of the Commonwealth of Massachusetts states, in its entirety, "The general court shall have authority to provide for compulsory voting at elections, but the right of secret voting shall be preserved."

References

Abramowitz, Alan I., and Kyle Saunders. 2005. "Why Can't We All Just Get Along? The Reality of a Polarized America." *Forum* 3 (2): article 1.

Aldrich, John H., and David W. Rohde. 2001. "The Logic of Conditional Party Government: Revisiting the Electoral Connection." In *Congress Reconsidered*, 7th ed., edited by Lawrence C. Dodd and Bruce I. Oppenheimer, pp. 269–92. Washington: CQ Press.

Ansolabehere, Stephen, and Shanto Iyengar. 1995. *Going Negative: How Political Advertisements Shrink and Polarize the Electorate*. New York: Free Press.

Ansolabehere, Stephen, James M. Snyder Jr., and Charles Stewart III. 2001. "Candidate Positioning in U.S. House Elections." *American Journal of Political Science* 45 (1): 136–59.

Bartels, Larry M. 1996. "Review of *Going Negative: How Political Advertisements Shrink and Polarize the Electorate*." *Public Opinion Quarterly* 60 (3): 456–61.

Bianco, William T. 1994. *Trust: Representatives and Constituents*. University of Michigan Press.

Brians, Craig Leonard, and Martin P. Wattenberg. 1996. "Campaign Issue Knowledge and Salience: Comparing Reception from TV Commercials, TV News, and Newspapers." *American Journal of Political Science* 40 (1): 172–93.

Brooks, Deborah Jordan. 2006. "A Negativity Gap? Gender and Attack Politics in American Elections." Paper prepared for the annual meeting of the American Political Science Association, Philadelphia, August 31–September 3.

Brooks, Deborah Jordan, and John G. Geer. 2007. "Beyond Negativity: The Effects of Incivility on the Electorate." *American Journal of Political Science* 51 (1): 1–16.

Chanley, Virginia A., Thomas J. Rudolph, and Wendy M. Rahn. 2000. "The Origins and Consequences of Public Trust in Government: A Time Series Analysis." *Public Opinion Quarterly* 64 (3): 239–56.

Citrin, Jack. 1974. "Comment: The Political Relevance of Trust in Government." *American Political Science Review* 68 (3): 973–88.

Citrin, Jack, and Donald Philip Green. 1986. "Presidential Leadership and the Resurgence of Trust in Government." *British Journal of Political Science* 16 (4): 431–53.

Clinton, Joshua D., and John S. Lapinski. 2004. " 'Targeted' Advertising and Voter Turnout: An Experimental Study of the 2000 Presidential Election." *Journal of Politics* 66 (1): 69–96.

Committee on Political Parties, American Political Science Association. 1950. "Toward a More Responsible Two-Party System." *American Political Science Review* 44 (Supplement).

Easton, David. 1965. *A Systems Analysis of Political Life*. University of Chicago Press.

Finkel, Steven E., and John G. Geer. 1998. "A Spot Check: Casting Doubt on the Demobilizing Effect of Attack Advertising." *American Journal of Political Science* 42 (2): 573–95.

Fiorina, Morris P. 1981. *Retrospective Voting in American National Elections*. Yale University Press.

Fiorina, Morris P., Samuel J. Abrams, and Jeremy C. Pope. 2006. *Culture War? The Myth of a Polarized America*. New York: Longman.

Gamson, William A. 1968. *Power and Discontent*. Homewood, Ill.: Dorsey Press.

Geer, John G. 2006. *In Defense of Negativity: Attack Ads in Presidential Campaigns*. University of Chicago Press.

Goldstein, Ken, and Paul Freedman. 2002. "Campaign Advertising and Voter Turnout: New Evidence for a Stimulation Effect." *Journal of Politics* 64 (3): 721–40.

Hetherington, Marc J. 1998. "The Political Relevance of Political Trust." *American Political Science Review* 92 (4): 791–808.

———. 1999. "The Effect of Political Trust on the Presidential Vote, 1968–96." *American Political Science Review* 93 (2): 311–26.

———. 2005. *Why Trust Matters: Declining Political Trust and the Demise of American Liberalism*. Princeton University Press.

Hetherington, Marc J., and Suzanne Globetti. 2002. "Political Trust and Racial Policy Preferences." *American Journal of Political Science* 46 (2): 253–75.

Hetherington, Marc J., and Thomas J. Rudolph. 2006. "Priming, Performance, and the Dynamics of Political Trust." Paper prepared for the annual meeting of the Midwest Political Science Association, Chicago, April 20–23.

Hibbing, John R., and Elizabeth Theiss-Morse. 2002. *Stealth Democracy: Americans' Beliefs about How Government Should Work.* Cambridge University Press.

Jacobson, Gary C. 2006. *A Divider, Not a Uniter: George W. Bush and the American People.* New York: Longman.

Johnston, Richard, Michael G. Hagen, and Kathleen Hall Jamieson. 2004. *The 2000 Presidential Election and the Foundations of Party Politics.* Cambridge University Press.

Key, Valdimer O., Jr. 1966. *The Responsible Electorate: Rationality in Presidential Voting, 1936–1960.* Cambridge, Mass.: Belknap Press.

Lau, Richard R. 1985. "Two Explanations for Negativity Effects in Political Behavior." *American Journal of Political Science* 29 (1): 119–38.

Lau, Richard R., and Gerald M. Pomper. 2001. "Effects of Negative Campaigning on Turnout in U.S. Senate Elections, 1988–1998." *Journal of Politics* 63 (3): 804–19.

———. 2004. *Negative Campaigning: An Analysis of U.S. Senate Elections.* Lanham, Md.: Rowman & Littlefield.

Lau, Richard R., and others. 1999. "The Effects of Negative Political Advertisements: A Meta-Analytic Review." *American Political Science Review* 93 (4): 851–75.

Luskin, Robert C. 1987. "Measuring Political Sophistication." *American Journal of Political Science* 31 (4): 856–99.

Marcus, George E., and Michael B. MacKuen. 1993. "Anxiety, Enthusiasm, and the Vote: The Emotional Underpinnings of Learning and Involvement during Presidential Campaigns." *American Political Science Review* 87 (3): 672–85.

McDonald, Michael P., and Samuel L. Popkin. 2001. "The Myth of the Vanishing Voter." *American Political Science Review* 95 (4): 963–74.

Miller, Arthur H. 1974. "Political Issues and Trust in Government: 1964–1970." *American Political Science Review* 68 (3): 951–72.

Rosenstone, Steven J., and John Mark Hansen. 1993. *Mobilization, Participation, and Democracy in America.* New York: Macmillan.

Scholz, John T., and Mark Lubell. 1998. "Trust and Taxpaying: Testing the Heuristic Approach to Collective Action." *American Journal of Political Science* 42 (2): 398–417.

Turner, Julius. 1951. "Responsible Parties: A Dissent from the Floor." *American Political Science Review* 45 (1): 143–52.

Tversky, Amos, and Daniel Kahneman. 1981. "The Framing of Decisions and the Psychology of Choice." *Science* 211 (January): 453–58.

Tyler, Tom R., and Peter Degoey. 1995. "Collective Restraint in Social Dilemmas: Procedural Justice and Social Identification Effects on Support for Authorities." *Journal of Personality and Social Psychology* 69 (3): 482–97.

Wattenberg, Martin P., and Craig Leonard Brians. 1999. "Negative Campaign Advertising: Demobilizer or Mobilizer?" *American Political Science Review.* 93 (4): 891–99.

West, Darrell. M. 2005. *Air Wars: Television Advertising in Election Campaigns 1952–2004.* Washington: CQ Press.

2

Spoiling the Sausages? How a Polarized Congress Deliberates and Legislates

Barbara Sinclair

A majority-party member of the august Ways and Means Committee tells a senior colleague of the minority party to "shut up," and the colleague responds by saying, "You think you are big enough to make me, you little wimp? Come on, come over here and make me, I dare you, you little fruitcake."[1] The chair of the Judiciary Committee pulls the plug figuratively—by abruptly gaveling to a close—and literally—by turning off the microphones—on a hearing when his Democratic colleagues use it as a forum to criticize the president.[2] The majority staff of the same committee rewrites the summaries of Democratic amendments, claiming they "exempt sexual predators."[3] A Republican on the floor flatly states, "Like a moth to a flame, Democrats can't help themselves when it comes to denigrating and demonizing Christians."[4] A committee chair calls the police

---

1. Alan K. Ota, Liriel Higa, and Siobhan Hughes, "Fracas in Ways and Means Overshadows Approval of Pension Overhaul Measure," *CQ Weekly*, July 19, 2003.

2. Michael Sandler, "Nerves Are Raw on House Judiciary," *CQ Weekly*, July 11, 2005.

3. Therawstory.com, "Democrats Furious over GOP Efforts to Rewrite Amendments, "April 17, 2005 (www.rawstory.com/exclusives/byrne/gop_rewrites_dem_amendments_427.htm).

4. Mike Allen, "GOP Congressman Calls Democrats Anti-Christian," *Washington Post,* June 21, 2005.

Figure 2-1. *Ideological Distance between the Parties, 1947–2004*

Difference in medians (DW-nominate)

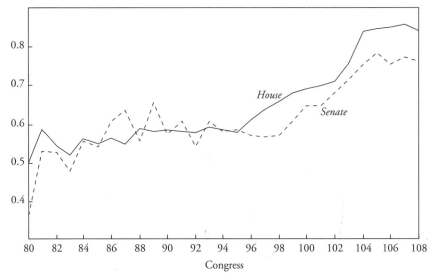

Source: Calculations by the author based on DW-nominate data from www.voteview.com.

to clear the minority-party members out of the committee library where they are caucusing.[5]

If this is the face of the contemporary Congress, no wonder public approval is so low. Although unedifying, such instances are not everyday occurrences, but are they symptoms of more serious and chronic problems with the legislative process that partisan polarization has produced? And, if so, is it true that "bad process leads to bad policy," as Thomas Mann and Norman Ornstein argue in their recent book, *The Broken Branch?*[6] Is the "meat grinder" that is the legislative process now so badly defective that it produces "spoiled sausages?"

By the 1990s, floor voting in both houses of Congress had become much more polarized along coinciding partisan and ideological lines than at any time in the previous half-century. Figure 2-1 shows the increasing ideological distance between Democrats and Republicans over time, as measured by the difference between the parties' median DW-nominate scores, which can be interpreted as locating mem-

5. Ota, Higa, and Hughes, "Fracas in Ways and Means."
6. Mann and Ornstein (2006, p. 13).

bers of Congress on a left-right dimension.[7] This polarization has constituency roots, as the chapters in the first volume of *Red and Blue Nation?* demonstrate. The voters who elect Democrats to Congress and those who elect Republicans have quite different notions of what constitutes good public policy; activists, who vote in primaries, donate money, and engage in other political acts, are even more polarized.

Because the two chambers differ in their rules and internal organization, the impact of polarization on the legislative process differs in the House and the Senate. Polarization has, however, significantly shaped the legislative process in both. Polarization has also affected the legislative product in a number of ways, but whether it has led to "bad policy" is, as discussed at the conclusion of this chapter, a difficult question to answer.

Polarization and the Legislative Process in the House

House rules allow an organized and reasonably cohesive majority to work its will. Consequently, when majority-party members are reasonably like-minded in their legislative preferences, they have strong incentives to organize enough to take advantage of the rules to pass preferred legislation, and given the size of the House, that means providing their leaders with the resources necessary to induce the needed collective action.

As the political parties in the House became more like-minded internally and as the ideological distance between them grew in the 1980s, members did, in fact, enhance their party leaders' powers and resources and allow them to use them more aggressively. For example, both parties gave their leaders more influence over their members' committee assignments, and majority Democrats urged their leaders to use their influence over the Rules Committee to control floor proceedings more tightly in order to protect legislation from hostile amendments and shield members from having to take politically difficult votes. A skillful and conservative Republican president and a political climate inimical to their policy preferences made the 1980s tough for House Democrats. The election of a Democratic president in 1992 brought hope for the achievement of legislative goals long stymied but also generated enormous pressure to produce. Furthermore, the House majority party confronted an increasingly aggressive and conservative minority intent on

7. DW-nominate scores are a commonly used measure of legislators' ideological positions. Based on legislators' roll-call votes, the scores are scaled from 1, indicating an extremely conservative member, to −1, indicating an extremely liberal member. DW-nominate scores for the 1st to the 109th Congress, compiled by Keith Poole and Howard Rosenthal, can be found online at voteview.com.

blocking majority-party initiatives whenever it could and embarrassing the majority and the chamber even when no impact on policy was possible. This context intensified Democrats' willingness to strengthen their party leadership. Without considerable leadership involvement, Democrats were unlikely to be able to achieve their legislative goals—goals now broadly shared within the party.

Thus, well before Republicans won control of the House in the 1994 midterm elections, partisan polarization had shaped the legislative process. Party leaders were more centrally involved in the prefloor legislative process, persuading and sometimes pressuring committee leaders, occasionally bypassing committees altogether, and sometimes working out substantive postcommittee adjustments to bills. Their aim was always to ensure that the legislation taken to the floor was broadly acceptable to the party's membership, passable by the chamber, and preferably enhanced (and certainly did not damage) the party's image. Democratic party leaders often brought legislation to the floor under rules that restricted amendments, thereby protecting both the legislation and their members.[8]

When Republicans became the majority party in the House in 1995, the normal legislative process was thus no longer the decentralized, committee-dominated process of the early 1970s and before. Furthermore, the factors that had led majority Democrats to alter the legislative process were still present, often in an amplified form. The House Republican membership was more like-minded in its legislative preferences than the Democrats they replaced. The party had become more uniformly conservative over the previous decade and a half, and most members, especially the large freshman class, read a mandate into the surprising 1994 election results. In the mid-1990s (and again when George W. Bush became president), Republicans saw their electoral fate tied to their legislative success. Yet the Republicans' narrow margins of control made legislative success uncertain and the prospect of losing control all too conceivable.

The combination of partisan polarization and narrow margins of control produced the legislative process in the Republican-controlled House of 1995 through 2006 described in this chapter.[9] Unified Republican control of the House and the presidency after the 2000 elections—for the first time in a half-century—further amplified the trend toward a House legislative process that favored centralization and expeditiousness and moved away from broad participation and deliberation. Unified control ratcheted up the pressure to produce and weakened incentives to include the minority in the legislative process.

8. This argument is elaborated in Sinclair (1995).
9. See also Mann and Ornstein (2006); Sinclair (2006).

Committee Decisionmaking and the Prefloor Legislative Process

House committee decisionmaking in the 1995–2006 period was far more likely to be driven by partisanship than it was during the pre-1990s period. Since the early 1990s, the committee process on just over half of major measures was partisan in the House—about double the proportion in selected earlier Congresses.[10] Committee partisanship was already high in the 103rd Congress, before Republicans won the majority. To be sure, not all bills were the product of partisan committee processes during the period of Republican control. Still, on the biggest and most consequential bills, committees tended to split along partisan lines.

Partisan polarization affected far more than the final vote in committee. The majority often excluded the minority from the decisionmaking process altogether. On many issues, Democrats and Republicans differ starkly on what constitutes good public policy, and majority Republicans knew that if they stuck together, they did not need to compromise with the minority to pass their legislation in the House. Thus committee markups often were not true decisionmaking sessions; the real decisions had been made in informal behind-the-scenes bargaining among majority-party members of the committee, often with party leadership involvement. The public markup with minority-party members present was simply a formality. The rules allow the minority to offer amendments, but consideration was perfunctory and all were voted down, with the majority voting in lockstep. Such minority exclusion seemed to be considerably more prevalent after the Republicans won control and especially after Bush became president.[11]

Majority-party leadership involvement in the prefloor legislative process, already considerable on major legislation in the late 1980s and early 1990s, also seemed even greater in the Republican era. Given the Republicans' narrow margins and the extent of partisan and ideological polarization, putting together legislation that was acceptable to the party's members, was passable, and enhanced the party's image was often difficult, requiring intensive leadership intervention at the committee stage or after the bill was reported and before it was scheduled for floor consideration. The center of gravity of the Republican Party in the House

10. Major measures are defined by the list of major legislation in the *CQ Weekly* (before 1998, *Congressional Quarterly Weekly Report*), augmented by those measures on which key votes occurred (again according to the *CQ Weekly*). This definition yields about forty to fifty bills (and some other measures such as budget resolutions and constitutional amendments) for each Congress that close contemporary observers considered major. The figure for the early 1990s onward is based on the 103rd to 105th, 107th, and 108th Congresses and is the mean percentage across these Congresses.

11. Data are not yet available, however, to substantiate this claim quantitatively.

was decidedly conservative, and the legislation that emerged from committee usually reflected that. Consequently, to pass legislation, the leadership often needed to pick up the votes of the small but crucial moderate bloc, which sometimes led to postcommittee adjustments on issues, such as social spending, to satisfy moderates.

Occasionally conservatives lost in committee, and in at least one famous case, the leadership intervened to largely reverse the outcome. The Federal Housing Finance Reform Act of 2005 was reported out of the Financial Services Committee on May 25 by a vote of 65-5. Democrats backed the bill and made the strong bipartisan vote possible because the act created a new fund for affordable housing. Many conservative Republicans opposed the fund—one called it an "experiment in socialism"—but failed in their attempt to remove it in committee.[12] To overcome the objections of conservative Republicans, the leadership negotiated and the Rules Committee made in order a manager's amendment making major changes in the bill and then prohibited Democrats from amending the amendment. Among the provisions included to placate conservative Republicans—and to which Democrats objected—was one that essentially barred nonprofit groups from using their own funds to engage in nonpartisan voter registration or get-out-the-vote activities if they had applied for or received federal housing grants.

When George W. Bush became president, the party leaders of the Republican majority in the House viewed the passage of his program as critical to the success of the party as a whole and usually worked closely with him. This also motivated postcommittee adjustments and the bypassing of committees. In the wake of the terrorist attacks of September 11, 2001, the House Judiciary Committee reported a bipartisan version of what became the USA PATRIOT Act. The Bush administration believed that bill too weak, so the Republican leadership substituted a tougher, administration-backed version for the committee-reported bill and took that to the floor.

Floor Scheduling and the "Majority of the Majority" Rule

In a now famous speech, then Speaker of the House Dennis Hastert (R-Ill.), explained that his job was to "please the majority of the majority."[13] In other

---

12. Michael R. Crittenden, "House Panel OKs Fannie-Freddie Shift," CQ Weekly, May 30, 2005.

13. Speaker of the House Dennis Hastert, in remarks entitled "Reflections on the Role of the Speaker in the Modern Day House of Representatives," Cannon Centenary Conference, Washington, November 12, 2003.

words, the Speaker would not willingly bring legislation to the floor unless a majority of Republican House members supported it. Although some commentators have interpreted Hastert's maxim as a departure from past practices, as stated it is not. Numerous studies show that House leaders have long operated under such a rule.[14] So is there anything different about how the Republican leadership applied the precept?

During three Democrat-controlled Congresses in the late 1980s and early 1990s (the 100th, 101st, and 103rd), only 8 of the 136 major measures considered on the House floor were supported by less than a majority of Democrats. And during four Republican-controlled Congresses in the 1990s and 2000s (the 104th, 105th, 107th, and 108th), 172 major measures were considered on the House floor, of which only 5 did not gain a majority of Republican votes. Although the rate at which the majority of the majority rule was violated was a bit lower during the period of Republican control, it was basically low overall.

Presidential pressure forced Democratic leaders to bring to the floor some bills that lacked the support of a majority of the majority—for example, Reagan's Contra aid package and, to a certain extent, the North American Free Trade Agreement (NAFTA).[15] Most of the other bills lacking majority Democratic support were forced onto the floor by opposition partisans, sometimes through discharge petitions but always primarily through public pressure; this was true of Dick Armey's (R-Tex.) military base closure legislation and flag-burning and balanced budget constitutional amendments.[16]

Of the legislation considered on the floor despite opposition from a majority of Republican House members, all fall into the latter category, though sometimes with a twist. Campaign finance reform legislation in the 105th and 107th Congress and the minimum wage increase in the 104th were straightforward cases where opposition partisans forced a bill onto the floor. The drug importation bill in the 108th Congress and the stem-cell research bill in the 109th were brought to the floor because Democrats and allied interest groups made them highly salient issues. Hastert agreed to schedule them in return for crucial votes from moderate Republicans on party agenda legislation. Thus the House leadership can be forced to give floor time to legislation that a majority of the majority opposes—but it does not happen often.

14. Cox and McCubbins (2005); Sinclair (1995).

15. NAFTA was governed by fast-track provisions, but presumably the Democratic leadership would have scheduled it in any case at President Clinton's urging.

16. One of the eight instances during the Democrat-controlled Congresses fits neither category; it was a vote on overturning the base-closing commission's recommendations.

Yet surely neither Hastert nor his Democratic predecessors interpreted the majority of the majority rule as really meaning a bare majority. A House leader who regularly brought to the floor major legislation that, say, 40 percent of his membership opposed would not last long. The question, then, is whether the Republican standard for the size of the necessary majority is higher than that of their Democratic predecessors. According to three different measures—the mean percentage of the majority party voting "yea" on passage votes, the percentage of passage votes on which at least 80 percent of the majority party voted "yea," and the percentage of passage votes on which at least 90 percent of the majority party voted "yea"—Republicans in the majority surpassed Democrats in the majority, and Republicans in the 107th Congress, the first Congress of George W. Bush's presidency, surpassed the Republican majority under conditions of divided control. On average, 87 percent of majority Democrats supported major legislation on passage votes in the 100th, 101st, and 103rd Congress; 91 percent of majority Republicans did in the 104th and 105th, and 93 percent in the 107th. The percentage of passage votes on which at least 90 percent of the majority party voted "yea" was 59 percent for Democrats, 68 percent for Republicans during the 104th and 105th Congress, and an astonishing 86 percent for Republicans in the 107th.

Clearly, very large proportions of Republicans voted for most of the major legislation their leadership brought to the floor. Given their narrow margins of control and a high degree of partisan polarization, however, Republicans needed higher proportions of majority-party members in order to pass legislation than their Democratic predecessors did. We cannot conclude that Republican leaders have set a higher standard of majority-party support for bringing legislation to the floor than did their Democratic predecessors without considering these conditions. Hastert spoke of being uncomfortable with bringing legislation to the floor if he did not have the votes on his side first. Yet Republicans managed to get 218 votes or more from their own ranks on only 34 percent of the votes in the 104th, 105th, and 107th Congress, while Democrats, with bigger margins, managed that on 65 percent of passage votes in the 100th, 101st, and 103rd.

Special Rules

As developed by Democratic leaders in the 1980s and early 1990s, special rules had become powerful and flexible tools for the leadership. Although Republicans had bitterly criticized Democrats' use of restrictive rules, they soon found them too useful to eschew and, in fact, greatly accelerated their use on major legislation. The Republican leadership frequently used highly restrictive rules to protect legislation and to shield its members from having to cast tough votes. In 2001–02,

44 percent of all rules allowed only one Democratic substitute.[17] Amendme. that the leadership opposed but that might pass were often disallowed. In 2003, for example, the Workforce Investment Act, the country's main job training legislation, included a provision that would allow religious groups that run federally funded job training and literacy programs to hire and fire employees based on their religious beliefs. Republicans had failed to enact Bush's faith-based initiative as a separate bill and were attempting, in this way, to enact it piecemeal. This provision—which in effect permitted discrimination—was politically tricky for some Republicans, so the rule simply barred the Democratic amendment that would have knocked the provision out. The rule for the Broadcast Decency Enforcement Act of 2004 barred an amendment supported by a considerable number of Republicans and all Democrats to roll back the Federal Communication Commission's loosening of media ownership rules. And the resolution to establish a congressional committee to investigate the governmental response to Hurricane Katrina was brought up under a closed rule to prevent Democrats from offering an amendment that would have made the investigative body an independent commission rather than a congressional committee with a Republican majority.

Majority-party members vote for such rules because the amendments at issue are often ones members believe to be bad public policy but politically difficult to vote against. In other words, the leadership is providing "cover" for members to vote their policy preferences—which are also the party position—without paying an electoral price. In addition, however, the expectation that members support their party on procedural votes has become very strong. New members are advised of that expectation during freshman orientation and are reminded during the whipping process on tough votes; Republicans who have voted against rules have been booted off the whip team.

Votes on rules fall strongly along party lines, especially when the rule is restrictive. In 2003–04 every recorded rule vote for a major measure was a party vote, pitting a majority of Republicans against a majority of Democrats. Every Republican opposed every Democrat on 41 percent of these votes, and no more than two members defected from the party position on another 27 percent. The largest number of Republican defections on any one vote was six.

Rules in Republican-controlled Congresses differed from those in the preceding Democrat-controlled Congresses in several important respects. Republicans

---

17. Data on all rules for initial consideration of legislation (except rules on appropriations bills that only waive points of order) were compiled by Donald Wolfensberger, director of the Congress Project at the Wilson Center, from Rules Committee calendars and surveys of activities.

more frequently used closed rules. During the last two Democrat-controlled
Congresses of the 1990s (the 102nd and 103rd), a mean of 12 percent of all rules
for initial consideration of legislation were closed; during the succeeding five
Republican-controlled Congresses, the mean was 21 percent, and the trend was
monotonically upward from 14 percent in the 104th Congress to 28 percent in
the 108th. On major legislation, Republicans were also more likely to use closed
rules than Democrats, but the big jump came with the 107th Congress, the first
of the Bush presidency. The percentage of closed rules on major measures from
the last three Democrat-controlled Congresses for which I have data (the 100th,
101st, and 103rd) averaged 12 percent, and no trend is evident. The mean for the
104th and 105th Congresses, which were controlled by the Republicans but with
Clinton still president, was 13 percent. The mean then jumped to 22 percent for
the first two Congresses of the George W. Bush presidency.

Republicans also made more use of self-executing rules than their Democratic
predecessors, though the frequency of such rules was on the rise before the Republicans won control. A self-executing rule provides that when the rule is adopted
by the House, the accompanying bill is automatically amended to incorporate the
text of an amendment either set forth or referenced in the rule. The new language
is "considered as adopted," and no separate vote on it is held. In the last three
Democratic Congresses (1989–94), 19 percent of rules had self-executing provisions; in the five Republican Congresses from 1995 through 2004, 28 percent of
rules had self-executing provisions. Some self-executing rules simply substitute the
committee's bill for the original bill, avoiding a redundant vote. However, self-
executing amendments are used increasingly for substantive and strategic reasons
to build support for the measure in question. Postcommittee compromises of considerable substantive significance and even completely new provisions are inserted
into a bill without a floor vote through a self-executing provision. For example,
in 1999, after the Republicans' tax bill was reported from committee, the leadership, in order to amass the votes needed to pass the bill, worked out a compromise
with moderate Republicans, and the new language was incorporated into the legislation by a self-executing provision in the rule. A postcommittee adjustment
required to pass the Gasoline for America's Security Act of 2005 was contained in
a manager's amendment that the rule specified "shall be considered as adopted."
In 2004 new tax breaks worth $12.8 billion for business were quietly incorporated
into the transportation bill through a self-executing rule.[18]

18. Dan Morgan, "Transportation Bill Hid Millions in Tax Breaks," *Washington Post*, April 7, 2004.

The rule for the lobbying and ethics reform bill the House considered in spring 2006 was, in the words of Don Wolfensberger, former Rules Committee chief of staff, "the mother of all self-executing rules," with three separate self-executing provisions.[19] A Rules Committee version was substituted for the bills reported by the committees of jurisdiction; this version deleted several major provisions in the Judiciary Committee bill that the leadership had been unable to sell to its members. The Rules Committee version was further altered by deletion of another Judiciary Committee provision. Finally, a House-passed bill regulating "527" political committees was added to the bill that would go to the Senate. This was a highly controversial measure that Republicans believed would give them an electoral advantage and that Democrats consequently strongly opposed. All of this was done automatically without votes.

Floor Consideration

House floor consideration changed significantly after Republicans took control. Suspensions, which are mostly minor matters and cannot be amended, came to take up considerably more of the time that the House was in session. In 2003 Republicans altered House rules to extend the days on which suspensions are in order from Monday and Tuesdays to Wednesdays as well. Votes on suspensions are regularly postponed so that members need not be in Washington during much of the actual consideration of the legislation. During a typical week, the House considered only suspensions early in the week: either the House was not in session on Monday or only suspensions were on the schedule. On Tuesdays only suspensions were considered, and all recorded votes from both days were postponed until 6:30 in the evening. At that time, the votes were stacked (that is, the votes were taken in succession with no legislative business in between). The first was a fifteen-minute vote; succeeding ones were shortened to five minutes. Usually the Republican leadership made sure that several recorded votes were taken because the whip counts were carried out on the floor during these Tuesday evening votes.

Since most rules for major legislation were restrictive, the amending process was seldom prolonged. Even when the Rules Committee allowed a number of amendments to be offered, the debate time it allotted was usually short—most often ten minutes for amendments other than a minority-party substitute, which might be given an hour. The fiscal year 2007 Department of Defense authorization bill, for example, was considered under two rules that allowed a total of thirty-one

19. Don Wolfensberger, "House Executes Deliberation with Special Rules," *Roll Call,* June 19, 2006.

amendments: the first rule specified one hour of general debate and made in order eight amendments; the second rule made in order twenty-three more amendments. All but one of these amendments were allotted only ten minutes of debate time (the exception was allotted twenty minutes). Such rules ensured the expeditious processing of most legislation on the floor. Thus the sort of free-wheeling, unscripted amending process that was still common in the late 1980s largely has become a thing of the past.

House majority-party leaders' control of the chair gives them valuable tools. Thus, if an important bill runs into unexpected trouble on the floor, the leadership can pull it off the floor and regroup. Democratic leaders in the 1970s and early 1980s confronted such problems more frequently than the succeeding Republican leadership because they led a less ideologically homogeneous party. However, in April 2006, after consideration had begun, Republican leaders found themselves clearly short of the votes needed to pass the rule for their lobbying reform bill. They pulled the rule off the floor, and Speaker Hastert made a deal with the Republican members of the Appropriations Committee who objected to a provision in the bill. Five hours later, the leaders took the rule to the floor again and passed it narrowly.

Even though the majority-party leadership seldom brings a bill to the floor if it does not have the votes to pass it, Republican leaders in the early 2000s found themselves in a situation that induced them to ignore that maxim on a number of occasions. They were charged with passing President Bush's often ambitious and contentious program with a narrow congressional majority. In most cases, neither they nor the president considered compromising enough to pick up a significant number of Democratic votes in order to make passage easier. The Republican leadership brought to the floor several key elements of Bush's agenda and then held open the recorded vote until they could pressure or persuade enough of their members to support the bill and pass it. They figured correctly that the imminent prospect of a very public defeat for their president and their party would soften up enough Republican members to allow them to squeak out a victory.

Control of the chair of the Committee of the Whole allowed Republican party leaders to hold recorded votes open until they could change enough votes to prevail. A normal recorded vote lasts fifteen minutes (though it is often extended to seventeen minutes to give stragglers time to get to the floor to vote). The House rule simply stipulates that a recorded vote must be held open for fifteen minutes and does not specify a maximum time. The Republican leadership took advantage of that lacuna. The best known example is the 2003 vote on the conference report for the Medicare prescription drug bill, which lasted about three hours. The vote on passage of that bill had also been extended, to about an hour. Other bills got similar treatment—legislation giving the president trade promotion authority in 2001, approval of the Central American Free Trade Agreement in 2005, and the Gasoline for America's Security Act in 2005. The only known instance in which Democrats used this tactic occurred when Speaker Jim Wright (D-Tex.) extended the vote on the 1987 reconciliation bill by about twenty minutes. Wright's action provoked a vituperative attack by Republicans, including then House member Dick Cheney (R-Wyo.) who called the Speaker "a son of a bitch."[20]

The way in which the Republican leadership ran the House floor led to members spending little time in Washington. With major legislation being considered under such highly restrictive rules, the floor time consumed was considerably less than in the past. Most members arrived just in time for the week's first recorded votes, which usually occurred at 6:30 p.m. on Tuesday, and they left after the last vote on Thursday. The House seldom had real legislative sessions on Friday. In the 1980s and 1990s, Congress was in session an average 140 days a year; in 2006 the House schedule called for votes during the day on only 71 days, with votes scheduled no earlier than 6:30 p.m. on an additional 26 days.[21]

This drastically truncated Washington workweek made it hard for committees and subcommittees to get much serious work done, particularly as work groups or collective entities. For individual members, meetings conflicted, and committees and subcommittees had difficulty getting quorums. Norman Ornstein of the American Enterprise Institute has reported a steep drop in the number of committee and subcommittee meetings: "The average Congress in the 1960s and '70s had 5,372 committee and subcommittee meetings; in the 1980s and 1990s, the average was 4,793. In the last Congress, the 108th, the number was 2,135."[22]

From the leadership's point of view, the abbreviated workweek offered several advantages. Their members had more time to spend in their districts shoring up support from their constituents, which would presumably increase the likelihood that Republicans would hold their narrow majority. Furthermore, when members are not in Washington, the leadership's control is enhanced. The opposition party—and disgruntled members of their own party—have less opportunity to plan mischief.

Why Leadership Centralization?

The Republican leadership's aggressive role in the prefloor legislative process and their tight control of the floor contributed greatly to the minority party's severe

20. Mann and Ornstein (2006, p. 75).
21. Norman Ornstein, "Part-Time Congress," *Roll Call,* March 7, 2006.
22. Ornstein, "Part-Time Congress."

discontent with the legislative process and to the hostility between the parties. House Democrats contended that Republicans had perverted the process by centralizing control in the party leadership, emasculating the committees, and excluding the minority from playing any meaningful legislative role.[23] Republicans' tactics, however, also contributed enormously to the party's legislative success—and that was key to their own members' willingness to allow the leadership to pay such a central role. Members expect their party leaders to aggressively use the resources they have given them to further the membership's common goals, including encouraging members to act as team players.

Advancement within the chamber (good committee assignments, chairmanships, and party positions) depends on the member's reputation with his or her party peers and the party leadership, providing strong incentives for members to be team players. In the wake of the 1994 elections, Republicans adopted a three-term limit for committee chairs, as they had promised. Although this had little immediate effect, its long-range impact proved to be enormous. The first chairs were termed out in 2000. With thirteen chairmanships vacant, mostly because of term limits, the Republicans' party leadership instituted a new procedure for the selection of committee chairs: aspirants were required to appear before the Steering Committee, which nominates chairs to the House Republican Conference, and were put through rigorous interviews about their legislative and communication strategies and their proposed agendas.[24]

Twenty-nine members interviewed for the vacant chairmanships. The Steering Committee did not follow seniority in choosing the new chair for six of the thirteen vacant positions. Most of the aspirants, like most House Republicans, were conservatives. However, on two important committees, a fairly moderate member—Marge Roukema (R-N.J.) from the Banking and Financial Services Committee and Tom Petri (R-Wisc.) from the Education and the Workforce Committee—was passed over for a less senior but more conservative member.[25] In filling four vacant chairmanships at the beginning of the 108th Congress, Republicans passed over Chris Shays (R-Conn.), a moderate and the chief sponsor of the detested campaign finance reform bill. For the Resources Committee, they passed over Jim Saxton (R-N.J.), a moderate on environmental issues, and

23. Jennifer Yachnin, "Quartet Offers New House Rules," *Roll Call,* December 6, 2005.
24. Brewer and Deering (2005).
25. In two other cases, the senior moderate received the chairmanship but on lesser committees. Karen Foerstel, "Choosing Chairmen: Tradition's Role Fades," *CQ Weekly,* December 9, 2000; Karen Foerstel and Alan K. Ota, "Early Grief for GOP Leaders in New Committee Rules," *CQ Weekly,* January 6, 2001.

reached down four more seniority slots to pick Richard Pombo (R-Calif.), a hard-line ally of Majority Leader Tom DeLay (R-Tex.).[26]

Interviews for sitting chairs were usually a formality. But Chris Smith (R-N.J.), who had first been chosen to head the Veterans Affairs Committee in 2000, was warned during his interview that he needed to be more of a team player. Smith had fought for greater funding for veterans' programs, against the wishes of the leadership. Smith seems not to have heeded the warning to the satisfaction of the leadership or the membership: at the beginning of the 109th Congress, the Steering Committee took away his chairmanship and even removed him from the committee altogether. "There will definitely be a perception out there that you need to be a team player if you want to succeed," said a leadership aide. "You don't need to be beholden to the leadership so much as to the Conference at large."[27]

The contest for the highly coveted chairmanship of the Appropriations Committee in 2005 illustrates the extent to which that has become the case. Three senior members actively vied for the post by raising campaign money for their colleagues; pledging to dedicate themselves to the task of deficit reduction, as the leadership and the Conference membership demanded; and committing themselves to reforming the committee internally, as DeLay had proposed. As Harold Rogers (R-Ky.) wrote in a December 10, 2004, letter to the Speaker asking for his support,

> *Our Republican Majority is on the line in the 2006 elections* and who you select to lead the Appropriations Committee will be crucial to neutralizing our biggest vulnerability—*the soaring, historically high deficit. . . . We need a disciplined, take charge leader* who won't hesitate to say "no" over and over again, and who can and will boldly retool, reorganize and re-energize the Committee. We need someone who can work *with* the Budget Committee, Leadership and our Members—not *against* them.[28]

Steering chose Jerry Lewis (R-Calif.), the second-ranking Republican on the Appropriations Committee, over senior member Ralph Regula (R-Ohio), who was considered the least conservative of the candidates. As soon as he was confirmed by the Conference, Lewis announced he was replacing Appropriations

26. Derek Willis, "Republicans Mix It Up When Assigning House Chairmen for the 108th," *CQ Weekly,* January 11, 2003.
27. Ben Pershing, " 'Team Players' Boosted in GOP," *Roll Call,* January 10, 2005.
28. Emphasis in original.

staff director Jim Dyer. Many Republicans distrusted Dyer, a long-time Appropriations aide, believing him not sufficiently dedicated to budget cutting.

In late 2002, the Republican Conference altered its rules in order to give the leadership-dominated Steering Committee the right to vote on the "cardinals," the chairs of the Appropriations subcommittees. Previously, under the Republicans, the full committee chair picked the subcommittee chairs, largely on the basis of seniority. "The goal," said a GOP aide of the change, "is to make these folks accountable."[29]

Getting ahead in the contemporary House now largely depends on a member's standing in the party and with the party leadership. Members' House lives now take place mostly within their party. All this amplifies both intraparty cohesion and interparty polarization even beyond what constituency-based ideological homogeneity would dictate.

Polarization and the Legislative Process in the Senate

The external, constituency-related forces driving polarization are similar for members in the two chambers, and floor voting is about as partisan in the Senate as it is in the House. But because of the Senate's nonmajoritarian rules, partisanship plays out differently. The Senate has the most permissive rules of any legislature in the world.[30] Extended debate allows any senator to hold the floor as long as he or she wishes unless cloture is invoked, which requires a supermajority of sixty votes. The Senate's amending rules enable any senator to offer any—and as many— amendments as he or she pleases to almost any bill, and those amendments need not even be germane. Because the majority party is seldom big enough to prevail on its own, these rules exert pressure on senators to compromise across party lines. The Senate is less partisan than the House at the committee level. Floor scheduling is the responsibility of the majority leader, who usually brings business (legislation or nominations) to the floor by unanimous consent; that, of course, requires the assent of the minority.

Nevertheless, Republicans and Democrats in the Senate diverge sharply in their policy preferences, and margins of control have been narrow since the mid-1990s. Thus, while some bipartisan cooperation is necessary just to keep the body functioning, the parties have strong incentives to aggressively exploit Senate rules for partisan advantage. At the same time, the powers that Senate rules give to the indi-

29. Susan Crabtree, "House to Maintain Ratios at Status Quo," *Roll Call,* January 6, 2003.
30. Sinclair (2000); Binder and Smith (1997).

vidual senator fuel the persistence of the individualism that developed in the 1960s and 1970s.

The Senate majority party exploits its greater influence over the floor schedule to showcase legislation it believes will aid its electoral prospects and hinder those of the minority. While hardly new, this strategy in recent years has taken the form of leaders bringing to the floor measures that appeal to the party base but have little to no chance of enactment. Thus the Senate has spent considerable time debating gay marriage, flag burning, and other such "niche" issues.

The minority party uses nongermane amendments—often in combination with extended debate—to force its issues to the floor. Recently, for example, Democrats used nongermane amendments to force consideration—often repeatedly— of an increase in the minimum wage, the extension of unemployment benefits, and the blocking of Bush administration regulations changing workers' eligibility for overtime. The Republican leadership finally scheduled a stem-cell research bill in the summer of 2006, at least in part because Democrats threatened to add it as an amendment to every bill that was brought to the floor.[31]

The minority party in the Senate uses extended debate to kill legislation outright or to extract concessions on legislation. Some sort of extended-debate-related problem is now a routine part of the legislative process on major legislation, affecting on average about half of major bills in Congress since the early 1990s.[32] Democrats sometimes objected to the consideration—not just the passage—of legislation they strongly opposed. The majority leader sometimes brought such legislation to the floor without an agreement and so, instead of asking unanimous consent that the bill be considered, moved to proceed to consider the bill. Usually he knew that he would not be able to break a filibuster against the motion to proceed but wanted to make a political point by at least having a debate on the issue. During the 108th Congress, several versions of medical malpractice legislation, the asbestos claims compensation bill, and class action lawsuit overhaul legislation

31. Molly Hennessy-Fiske, "Senate Republicans Block Boost in Minimum Wage," *Los Angeles Times,* June 22, 2006; Bill Swindell, "Partisan Flames Still Flicker with Both Sides Entrenched on Rules for Overtime Pay," *CQ Weekly,* April 24, 2004; "2004 Legislative Summary: Overtime Compensation," *CQ Weekly,* December 4, 2004; John Stanton and Erin P. Billings, "Stem-Cell Plan Eases Worries," *Roll Call,* July 12, 2006.

32. Holds and threats to filibuster, as well as actual extended-debate-related delay on the floor, were coded as filibuster problems. The definition of major legislation used here—those measures in lists of major legislation published in the *CQ Almanac* and the *CQ Weekly* plus those measures on which key votes occurred, again according to Congressional Quarterly—yields forty to sixty measures per Congress. Thus, although truly minor legislation is excluded, the listing is not restricted to only the most contentious and highly salient issues.

were stopped when the motion to proceed to consider the legislation was filibustered and the majority could not invoke cloture.[33] In the 109th Congress, a bill on class action lawsuits finally passed, but by then the majority had compromised considerably.[34]

The majority's attempt to pass the Estate Tax and Extension of Tax Relief Act of 2006—the so-called trifecta bill—right before the August 2006 recess and the minority's blocking of the attempt illustrate how both parties use Senate prerogatives for partisan purposes. Most Republicans in both chambers favored permanently abolishing (or at least severely reducing) the estate tax. The House had passed bills to that effect several times, but Democrats in the Senate had blocked them by filibustering the motion to proceed to consider. At the same time, Democrats very much wanted to raise the minimum wage, and some moderate Republicans were under electoral pressure to do so as well. Republicans put together a bill that included the estate tax cut, an increase in the minimum wage, and a number of tax cut extensions that had broad bipartisan support. It also included sweeteners targeted at specific Senate Democrats. For example, there were tax breaks for the timber industry aimed at Maria Cantwell (D-Wash.) and funding for the cleanup of abandoned mines targeted at Robert Byrd (D-W.Va.), both of whom were up for reelection. The House passed the bill narrowly with the Republican leadership using the tools at its command. Senate Majority Leader Bill Frist (R-Tenn.) scheduled a vote right before the recess and insisted that, if the bill were defeated, he would block votes for the rest of the year on its component parts, including the popular tax cut extenders. When the vote came on invoking cloture on the motion to proceed to consider the bill, it was defeated 56 to 42.[35]

Not surprisingly, the use of Senate prerogatives for partisan advantage fosters hostility between the parties and strains the relationship between their leaders. An indicative instance occurred in November 2005. Minority Leader Harry Reid (D-Nev.) employed a seldom used rule to force the Senate into a closed session to discuss the use of pre-Iraq war intelligence and why the Intelligence Committee had not investigated the Bush administration's possible manipulations, despite the chairman's promise to do so a year earlier. Majority Leader Frist took the surprise tactic as "a slap in the face" and "an affront" to himself and to Senate norms.

33. "2004 Legislative Highlights: 108th Congress, Second Session," *CQ Weekly*, December 4, 2004.

34. Seth Stern, "Republicans Win on Class Action," *CQ Weekly*, February 21, 2005.

35. David Nather and Rachel Van Dongen, "Frist Loses Estate Tax Showdown," *CQ Weekly*, August 7, 2006.

He would no longer be able to trust Reid, he said.[36] In fact, the relationship between the Senate leaders had been strained well before this incident and continued to be so. Senate rules force the leaders of the two parties to communicate and cooperate on an almost continuous basis simply to keep the body functioning at all, but their members' expectation that they also aggressively pursue partisan advantage makes the relationship difficult.

The nonmajoritarian cast of the Senate has engendered intense frustration in majorities and their leaders. Probably the most drastic sign of that frustration was Majority Leader Frist's willingness to use the "nuclear option" on presidential nominations. During the 108th Congress, Democrats blocked ten Bush nominees to appellate judgeships through filibusters. The nuclear option would have entailed a ruling by the Senate's presiding officer that cutting off debate on nominations only requires a simple majority. Democrats would, of course, have appealed the ruling, but only a simple majority is required to uphold a ruling of the chair. This strategy was dubbed "nuclear" because minority Democrats could be expected to "go nuclear" and block Senate business indefinitely if Republicans resorted to it; perhaps the term was also used because the strategy's effect on the Senate over the longer run would likely be enormous. The "Gang of 14," a bipartisan group of mostly moderate senators, forestalled the gambit just as Frist was preparing to "pull the trigger" in May 2005. The seven Democrats promised not to support filibusters on judicial nominations, barring "extraordinary" circumstances, and the seven Republicans pledged not to support the nuclear option. The agreement held throughout the 109th Congress.[37]

Unified Control, the President, and the Reconciliation Stage of the Legislative Process

Unified Republican control of the Congress and the presidency also affected the legislative process. When George W. Bush became president in 2001, it was the first time in almost a half-century that Republicans controlled both the presidency and Congress. Bush's agenda was ambitious and largely distinctly Republican (that is, it was conservative and was shared by most Republican members of Congress).

36. Emily Pierce and Paul Kane, "Gambit Raises Tensions Again," *Roll Call,* November 2, 2005.
37. Sheryl Gay Stolberg and David D. Kirkpatrick, "Heated Efforts in Senate to Avoid Filibuster Clash," *New York Times,* May 18, 2005; Sheryl Gay Stolberg, "Behind the Scenes, an Army of Senate Aides Takes on Filibuster Fight," *New York Times,* May 20, 2005; Carl Huse, "Bipartisan Agreement in Senate Averts a Showdown on Judges," *New York Times,* May 24, 3005.

The partisan polarization of policy preferences meant that getting bipartisan support for Bush's initiatives would require considerable substantive compromise, a price that most congressional Republicans and Bush himself were loath to pay. After all, Republicans finally had the opportunity to achieve policy goals they had so long sought. Yet their margins of control in both chambers were excruciatingly narrow.

Bush and the congressional leadership largely pursued a partisan strategy, one that depended on the House of Representatives—where a bare majority, if cohesive, can prevail—taking the lead and passing a bill far to the right on the policy spectrum. This would allow Republicans to go into negotiations with the Senate (where, because there is less party control, bipartisan cooperation is often necessary) in the strongest possible position. Enabling the House to play its role in this strategy required the sort of leadership control of the legislative process described earlier.

Another part of the strategy entailed recouping, in the process of reconciling the differences between the House and Senate bills, what Republicans had lost in the Senate. Implementing that strategy affected the process at the reconciliation stage. House rules give the Speaker sole power to appoint House conferees. The norms and expectations that bound the Speaker in the prereform period had loosened well before the Republicans won control of the House. The Republican leadership's greater clout vis-à-vis committee leaders, however, translated into even more significant influence over the appointment of conferees and on conference decisionmaking. For the most important and controversial legislation—especially bills that were items of top priority on the party's and the president's agenda—Hastert regularly appointed a member of the House party leadership to the conference and made him a general conferee with authority over the entire bill. First as whip and later as majority leader, Tom DeLay served on conferences on energy bills, the Medicare prescription drug bill, transportation bills, and tax bills. This kind of involvement is not completely unprecedented, yet a *routine* leadership presence in conference delegations on party agenda legislation *is* new.

In the late 1980s and early 1990s, as the Democratic Party became more ideologically homogeneous and the Republican Party moved to the right, final deals on party agenda legislation were often made within the party. Republicans took that practice a large step further and often excluded most Democrats from conference negotiations altogether. In 2003 no Democrats were allowed to participate in the energy bill conference and only two Senate Democrats (who were considered accommodating) were admitted to the negotiations on the Medicare prescription drug bill. House Democrats were routinely excluded from negotiations on tax bills.[38]

From 2001 through 2006, the House Republican leadership often intervened at the resolution stage in support of President Bush's policy preferences and specifically to avoid embarrassing the party by a Republican president's veto of legislation passed by a Republican Congress. "[Hastert] made it clear that they would not allow bills that would be vetoed to reach the president's desk," according to Nick Calio, the former Bush White House liaison to Congress.[39] Attempts to overturn new FCC media ownership rules, lift the ban on travel to and trade with Cuba, prevent the administration from revising overtime rules in such a way as to deprive some of those currently eligible of overtime pay, delay military base closings, allow concurrent receipts for veterans, and block the administration's efforts to outsource federal jobs to private companies were all the target of Bush veto threats—sometimes repeatedly. In some cases, Bush was forced to compromise but in every instance, the veto threat moved the bill toward his position. Party leaders repeatedly removed offending provisions in conference—in a number of cases, ones that both chambers had approved. Hastert made sure a transportation bill that Bush would feel compelled to veto did not emerge from conference in 2004. In June 2006, a bar on the funding of permanent U.S. military bases in Iraq, a version of which was included in both chambers' bills, was deleted from the Iraq war emergency supplemental appropriations bill before conference. The Bush administration had opposed any such language.[40]

Although conferences are supposed to restrict themselves to matters in disagreement between the chambers, going beyond that charge is far from new. However, especially in the last few years, the Republican Congress does seem to have pushed the envelope in this respect as well, sometimes but not always at the behest of the leadership. The conference report for the agricultural appropriations bill passed in late 2005 contained totally new language rewriting and weakening the

38. Amy Goldstein, "Medicare Proposal Outlined," *Washington Post,* October 23, 2003; Robert Pear and Carl Huse, "Rewriting Top Legislation Is an Invitation-Only Party," *New York Times,* October 26, 2003.

39. Ethan Wallison, "Bush and Hastert; Respect Fuels Relationship," *Roll Call,* September 22, 2003.

40. Bill Swindell, "Labor-HHS-Education: Bush Scores on Overtime Pay," *CQ Weekly,* December 6, 2003; Swindell, "Partisan Flames Still Flicker"; Andrew Taylor, "GOP Hands Appropriations Success to Bush," *CQ Weekly,* November 20, 2004; Seth Stern, "Provisions Tossed, Added in C-J-S Bill," November 14, 2005; Robert Pear, "House Approves $94.5 Billion for Military Operations and Hurricane Recovery," *New York Times,* June 14, 2006; "Rep. Tom Allen: By Removing No Permanent Bases Language, Leadership Subverts Will of Congress," *States News Service,* June 12, 2006.

legal definition of "organic food"; the bills that went to conference did not deal with the issue even peripherally.[41] Earmarks seem to have been regularly added at the conference stage.[42] Sometimes even most majority-party conferees were unaware of what was being inserted into the conference report. In fact, often no formal meeting of the conference to approve the report was held. Rather, the necessary signatures were gathered by staff, and members signed without actually seeing the final language. Although not a new practice by any means, the regular waiving of layover requirements before conference reports are voted on becomes increasingly problematic as the number of members with knowledge of what is in those reports shrinks.

Differences on most legislation are reconciled through nonconference procedures such as amendments between the chambers, but conference committees have long been the primary means of resolving differences on major legislation.[43] In recent years, however, the number of conferences has dropped significantly—from an average of eighty-one conferences per Congress in the 1980s and early 1990s to an average of just thirty-seven for the 107th and 108th Congress. In part, the drop reflects conflicts between the House and the Senate that led to bills never being sent to conference; in the 104th, for example, much major legislation that passed the House got nowhere in the Senate. The Senate's inability to pass a number of the regular appropriations bills as freestanding measures in 2002 through 2004 also reduced the number of conferences. In addition, the decrease in conferences reflects an increase in the use of informal procedures to work out interchamber differences, often under leadership aegis. On several recent important bills, the process consisted of informal negotiations followed by a "clean" bill being introduced and passed. After the Senate and House had passed their versions of the USA PATRIOT Act, no formal conference was held. Rather, key lawmakers met with administration officials to resolve the differences and then introduced a clean bill that incorporated their agreements. Such informal procedures make it even easier to exclude the minority from negotiations when desired.

41. Scott Lilly, "Skullduggery: What We Used to Call the Legislative Process," *Roll Call,* November 16, 2005.
42. U.S. Senate, Committee on Homeland Security and Governmental Affairs, "Draft Statement of Scott Lilly, Senior Fellow, Center for American Progress before the Subcommittee on Federal Financial Management, Government Information, and International Security," March 16, 2006 (hsgac.senate.gov/_files/031606Lilly.pdf).
43. Rybicki (2003). Data compiled by Elizabeth Rybicki show there was an average of eighty-one conferences per Congress for the 97th through 103rd Congress. The number drops to sixty-three in the 104th and to fifty-one for the 105th and 106th. See Elizabeth Rybicki, n.d., "The History of Bicameral Resolution Practices in the U.S. Congress," Ph.D. dissertation, University of Minnesota.

A Coequal Branch?

To enact significant legislation, Congress needs to work with the president. When an ideologically homogeneous Republican Party gained unified control of government for the first time in almost fifty years, a close, cooperative relationship was to be expected. But Congress is also supposed to be a coequal branch, to check and balance executive power. Partisan polarization combined with unified control limited the extent to which Congress adequately preformed its expected role.

Overseeing the executive and examining how the administration executes the law are fundamental aspects of Congress's charge. Such oversight is institutionalized in committee hearings and investigations, but there are other ways in which these functions can be performed. During the first six years of the George W. Bush administration, Congress largely abdicated its oversight responsibilities. When members of the congressional majority party and the president see themselves as members of the same "team" in a high-stakes battle against the opposition, ferreting out corruption or incompetence in the administration of your team's leader is unlikely to strike majority-party members as a winning strategy.

There is, however, a considerable price to be paid for abdicating oversight. A salutary wariness about possible congressional oversight keeps executive agencies, appointees, and the president himself on their toes. Some of the crony appointments and misguided decisions that later embarrassed the president and other Republicans might never have been made had there been at least a fear of oversight. Furthermore, when Congress authorizes big changes in government organization and functioning, as it did with the establishment of the Department of Homeland Security and the reorganization of the intelligence agencies, careful examination of how well they subsequently work is essential to good government. The Federal Emergency Management Agency's abysmal failure in its response to Hurricane Katrina might even have been avoided had Congress examined the agency's incorporation into the Homeland Security Department.[44]

Moreover, oversight need not be of the "gotcha" variety. During the Clinton administration, Republicans obsessively investigated old business deals and minor matters, such as the travel office firings, in hopes of finding a scandal that would irretrievably damage the president. But responsible oversight that focuses on whether the laws are being faithfully executed and whether they were effectively designed in the first place need not seriously embarrass the president; it can, in fact, help him or her get better performance out of the executive branch. Such

44. See Mann and Ornstein (2006, p. 152).

oversight often will not command headlines, however, so the incentives for members to devote the necessary time are lacking.

A related problem is the extent to which Congress has allowed the president to withhold information, both from itself and the public. The Bush presidency has been the most secretive in our history.[45] In contradiction to what most lawyers consider clear legal language, the administration blocked the scheduled release of documents from the Reagan presidency and, by executive order, gave presidents and former presidents the power to block the release of presidential documents in the future. It classified much more material than previous administrations and even reclassified documents that were already in the public domain. It refused to release information on Vice President Dick Cheney's task force that drafted the administration's energy bill, and it often stonewalled other congressional requests for information. The administration withheld information on the costs of the prescription drug benefit, even threatening an employee who proposed releasing the information before the congressional vote.[46] Yet the congressional leadership did nothing. Republican leaders saw themselves as good soldiers in the president's army, not guardians of the powers of a coequal branch.

Uninformed deference to the president's policy judgments and his claims of inherent powers was certainly driven by the events of September 11; in a time of crisis, members of Congress are loath to do anything that could be interpreted as undermining the commander in chief. It was not just Republicans who failed to ask probing questions about a possible war in Iraq and the curtailment of civil liberties at home. Eventually some members of Congress did begin to push back a bit. In late 2005, Congress overwhelmingly passed a provision sponsored by Senator John McCain (R-Ariz.) to bar the torture of detainees. And as the Iraq war worsened, many Democrats and some Republicans began to question the president's policy.

The Policy Impact of Partisan Polarization

What is the impact of partisan polarization on policy—on the legislation Congress passes or fails to pass? Sarah Binder finds that Congress is more prone to deadlock when ideological polarization is high and when different parties control Congress and the presidency.[47] I have found that the proportion of major legisla-

45. For an overview of the Bush administration's secrecy, see Rudalevige (2006).
46. Mann and Ornstein (2006).
47. Binder (2003).

tion enacted during a president's first two years in office, often the most productive period, has been somewhat lower since the late 1970s than it was in the 1960s,
but the decline came before the major increase in polarization.[48] In any case, it is
hard to argue that the George W. Bush presidency has been characterized by gridlock. To be sure, a number of major domestic policy measures favored by Bush
and most congressional Republicans—such as the curtailment of medical malpractice awards and opening the Alaska National Wildlife Refuge to gas and oil
drilling—have failed enactment. Yet much legislation that constitutes sweeping
policy change was enacted—huge tax cuts, a Medicare bill that added a component of private sector competition and prescription drug coverage, and a national
education standards bill.[49]

The question, then, is what has been the impact of partisan polarization on the
quality of legislation, on whether the policies passed are "reasonable, workable,
[and] sustainable?"[50] As Christopher Foreman notes in his comment on this chapter, characteristics of the political environment other than polarization may lead to
"bad" legislation. Haste, as a result of pressure to act quickly in response to an emergency such as the September 11 attacks, and "ordinary capitulation to the clout of
powerful economic interests" are among the likely culprits. So even if one finds
considerable "bad" legislation, care is called for in attributing it to polarization.

Anecdotes concerning the significant but secondary dimension of drafting
quality abound. Republican staffers privately admitted that much of the "Contract with America" legislation of 1995 was poorly drafted. However, very little of
that was enacted; the Senate or the president blocked it. Mann and Ornstein
report that bankruptcy lawyers contend that the bankruptcy overhaul legislation
enacted in 2005 is sloppy and unclear.[51] Some knowledgeable Republicans complained that the House leadership staffers who often got involved in legislative
substance, even drafting language, did not know enough about the matters at
issue, and so not enough expertise was brought to bear. Some House Democrats
argued that Republican Party leadership involvement in substance reduced the
value of even top committee assignments to the point that there was little incentive for members to develop expertise. And there has been some concern that top

48. Sinclair (2006, p. 356).
49. Although less sweeping, Congress also passed a production-oriented energy bill, a bankruptcy
law overhaul, and a revision in the law governing class action lawsuits.
50. These criteria for good policy are from the remarks of Thomas E. Mann of the Brookings
Institution, at the conference "The Polarization of American Politics: Myth or Reality?" Princeton
University, December 3, 2004.
51. Mann and Ornstein (2006, p. 145).

staff aides moved to K Street and lucrative lobbying careers so quickly that expertise was lost. However, systematic data that would allow a definitive assessment of quality, even in the narrow sense of drafting quality, are lacking.

Earmarking, the direction of funds to specific projects as a provision in legislation, has received a great deal of attention and criticism during the recent debate over lobbying and ethics reform. Perhaps the least anticipated difference between how Democratic- and Republican-controlled Congresses legislated was the much greater tendency of the recent Republican majority to earmark. According to a Congressional Research Service count, there were 3,023 earmarks worth $19.5 billion in 1996 appropriations bills. By 2006 the number had climbed to 12,852, valued at $64 billion.[52] Before 1995, when Congress was under Democratic control, a number of appropriations bills—for example, the huge bill funding the Departments of Labor, Education, and Health and Human Services—were largely or completely free of earmarks; in subsequent years, they became replete with them. In other appropriations bills, the sums earmarked grew enormously. The last Democratic Labor, Health and Human Services, and Education appropriations bill of the 1990s (fiscal year 1995) contained no earmarks; by fiscal year 2002, over $1 billion in the bill was earmarked.[53] The periodic transportation authorization bill has traditionally included numerous earmarked projects, but in both numbers and value, there were large increases under Republican-controlled Congresses. The number of earmarked projects averaged 325 among the three bills passed in 1987, 1991, and 1995. That increased to 1,850 earmarks (worth $9.5 billion) in 1998 and to 6,371 earmarks (worth $23 billion) in 2005.[54]

Republicans' narrow margins and their determination to maintain their control were major contributors to the explosive growth in earmarks. Political scientist James D. Savage reports that a few months before the 1996 elections, Speaker Newt Gingrich sent a memo to Appropriations subcommittee leaders urging them to support projects in the districts of politically vulnerable Republicans. Republican House leaders routinely sent the Appropriations Committee a list of lawmakers whom they thought needed shoring up.[55] Republican leaders also used

52. Jonathan Weisman, "Proposals Call for Disclosure of Ties to Lobbyists," *Washington Post,* March 27, 2006.

53. Minority Staff of the House Appropriations Committee, "Grand Old Porkers," November 2005 (www.majorityleader.gov/docuploads/pork.pdf).

54. Scott Lilly, "How Congress Is Spending the 18 Cents a Gallon You Pay in Gasoline Tax," October 2005 (www.americanprogress.org/kf/highway_earmark.pdf).

55. Janet Hook and Richard Simon, "Earmarking—A Win-Win for Lobbyists and Politicians," *Los Angeles Times,* January 29, 2006.

earmarks to build winning floor coalitions, what Democrats have labeled "internal blackmail."[56] The vote on the big transportation bill in 2005 was delayed a day so that the leadership could use the time to amass the votes need to pass the Central American Free Trade Agreement. Republicans disinclined to vote for the bill, a major Bush priority, were reportedly threatened with having their earmarks removed, and promises of new projects were used as enticements.[57] "Chairman [Bill] Thomas [of the Ways and Means Committee] joked openly about the delay in consideration of the Highway bill last summer so that the leadership could gain more support for the Central America Free Trade Agreement," Scott Lilly, a former long-time senior Appropriations staffer, reported in congressional testimony.[58]

Earmarking is not responsible for the big budget deficits; the amounts involved are a tiny percent of the entire federal budget and, furthermore, most of the money is not additional but comes out of the total amount authorized or appropriated. Some of the projects earmarked are wasteful, but many are worthy. In some smaller programs, however, the extent of earmarking has left almost no funds for nonearmarked projects; in other cases, such as the NASA budget, earmarks direct scarce funds to projects that have little to do with the agency's core mission.[59] According to Lilly, the most deleterious effect of the huge increase in earmarking is that it seriously skews how both members and staff use their time. Pursuing earmarks is a highly time-consuming process for the member, his or her staff, and committee staffs, especially the Appropriations Committee staff. Yet constituent groups increasingly expect earmarks, and an entire lobbying establishment has grown up around the pursuit of them. The result is that members and staff are left with less time to devote to legislation of broader import.[60]

Has partisan polarization prevented Congress and the president from making hard but necessary decisions on budgets and entitlements, as has sometimes been claimed? Leaders dependent on the electorate are always going to have difficulty making such decisions because tough decisions are by definition unpopular. If

56. Representative David Obey (D-Wisc.) used the phrase in a panel discussion, "A Proposal to Make Congress Work Again," Center for American Progress, Washington, December 5, 2005.

57. See the remarks of Norman Ornstein in the transcript of "A Proposal to Make Congress Work Again," Center for American Progress, Washington, December 5, 2005.

58. U.S. Senate, Committee on Homeland Security and Governmental Affairs, "Draft Statement of Scott Lilly."

59. "Special Report: A Gold Rush," *Chronicle of Philanthropy,* July 21, 2005 (philanthropy.com/free/articles/v17/i19/19000101.htm); Minority Staff, "Grand Old Porkers."

60. Scott Lilly, quoted in the transcript of "A Proposal to Make Congress Work Again," Center for American Progress, Washington, December 5, 2005.

budgetary decisions that restrain structural deficit spending are considered responsible, then the past quarter-century offers as examples the 1990 budget deal,
passed under conditions of divided control; the 1993 budget bill, passed during a
period of unified government and through highly partisan decisionmaking; and
the 1997 agreement, passed during a period of divided control and high partisanship but by bipartisan agreement. Conversely, because they increased the structural deficit, the 1981 Reagan economic program and the 2001 and 2003 Bush
tax cuts would be classified as irresponsible, as would the "smoke and mirrors"
budgets of the mid- and late 1980s. The Bush tax cuts were passed in a period of
high partisan polarization through highly partisan decisionmaking processes.
Reagan, however, had to get some opposition party votes because his party did
not then control the House. Clearly, no particular configuration of divided-
versus-unified control or level of polarization ensures responsible decisions will be
made. Furthermore, even a seemingly consensual standard, such as restraining
structural deficits, is far from consensual when actually applied to a specific case.
Supporters of the Bush tax cuts argued that they would improve economic performance and that without them the deficits would have been worse. And almost
everyone would agree that restraining deficits is far from the only standard that
should be applied to legislation.

Without some sort of broadly agreed upon standard, assessing whether the
policies enacted in recent years are "reasonable, workable, and sustainable" and
meet the needs of the American people is a fool's errand. One's own values will
inevitably color the assessment, and during a period of high polarization, any particular person's assessment is unlikely to carry much credibility with those who
have different values.

Have partisan polarization and the kind of legislative process it fostered hin-
dered Congress's ability to create policies that are congruent with public preferences? Given the vast amount of polling data available, it is perhaps surprising that
determining whether policies are congruent with public preferences is no easy
task. Public preferences about policy are seldom highly specific and are influenced
by how political leaders frame choices. What pollsters find is influenced by how
the questions are framed. Thus eminent scholars disagree on whether the public
supported Bush's tax cuts.[61] The polling data show that tax cuts were not the public's top policy priority and that self-identified Republicans were considerably
more enthusiastic about tax cuts than Democrats or independents. A more definitive answer depends on assumptions that have value implications.

61. Bartels (2005); Lupia and others (2005); Hacker and Pierson (2005).

When public opinion is both clear and intense, however, the polarized Congress does listen. President Bush's Social Security proposals went nowhere because of public opposition. Congressional Republicans, a large majority of whom probably personally supported the Bush approach, were not about to enact legislation in the face of a storm of opposition.[62] Usually, however, public opinion is less clear and less intense. What can be said is that a number of President Bush's signature legislative achievements, which were enacted through highly partisan processes, remain contested. The Medicare prescription drug bill, many of the tax cuts, termination of the estate tax particularly, and even the No Child Left Behind Act continue to excite great controversy. As a result, these major policy departures have not become broadly accepted.

Because definitive assessments of whether contemporary legislation represents "good"—and even responsive—public policy are so problematic, we are forced back to basing our assessment of the contemporary Congress on the character of the legislative process. Most participants and outside experts agree that a "good" process will, on average and over the long run, produce better policy. They also agree that, to function well, a legislative process needs to strike a balance between deliberation and inclusiveness, on the one hand, and expeditiousness and decisiveness, on the other, even if there is no consensus about what the optimal balance is.

There seems to be considerable agreement that the Republican style of lawmaking in the House tilted the balance too far in the direction of expeditiousness at the expense of deliberation and inclusiveness. Deliberation requires time, information, and at least enough inclusiveness that a range of views is heard and considered. Inclusiveness is valuable in its own right because members who are included in the decisionmaking process, even if their views do not prevail, are more likely to consider the policy results legitimate. When the minority party is routinely excluded from meaningful participation at every stage of the process, the range of views that is heard and considered is artificially narrowed, partisan hostility and bitterness are exacerbated, and—especially in a period of partisan polarization— minority partisans in the electorate are likely to feel unrepresented and consider the policy produced less legitimate.

Deliberation has too often been given short shrift in the contemporary House. The House's severely truncated workweek in Washington has been one problem. Committees and subcommittees, traditionally the most important venues for deliberation in the House, lacked the time to legislate seriously. Committees used to be forums in which members of opposing parties got to know each other, but

62. Edwards (2007, chapters 6 and 7); Jacobson (2007, pp. 206–18).

they have become much less so in recent years. Tightly controlled House floor consideration and conference decisionmaking have also provided little opportunity for deliberation. In addition, such processes often created real information problems. When, in the middle of the night, the Rules Committee allows post-committee adjustments to be inserted in legislation to be considered the next morning, or when leaders work out a conference deal and get conference committee members to sign off without seeing the language and then bring it to the floor without giving anyone the opportunity to read the bill, even the most minimal criteria for good decisionmaking are not met. Such procedures lend themselves to stealth lawmaking—sometimes provisions that neither house has approved are included, and sometimes provisions that both chambers approved are excluded. Under such circumstances, accountability is lacking.

Expeditiousness and decisiveness are important values, and in the House, a legislative process that puts no time limits on deliberation and no constraints on participation will fail. The House is simply too big. Yet one need not embrace a completely open-ended deliberative process or require every decision to be made by consensus to conclude that the balance had swung too far. Exclusionary processes in the House and in conference actually impeded expeditiousness on occasion by giving the minority party in the Senate greater incentives and justifications for obstruction.

The response of an ideologically homogeneous Republican Party to gaining unified control of the national government for the first time in almost a half-century is understandable. With their narrow margins and ambitious agenda, Republican leaders bent the legislative process toward an expeditious production of party agenda legislation, especially in the House. But in doing so, they sacrificed deliberation and inclusiveness and exacerbated partisan hostility. Congress can withstand such perturbations—but only as long as they are short lived.

Will the New Majorities Revitalize the Congressional Process?

The 2006 elections brought in new majorities in both chambers. The new Democratic leaders promised to operate in a fairer and more bipartisan manner. In the Senate, majority leaders have little choice but to deal with the minority. The large Republican minority in the 110th Congress quickly began using its prerogatives under Senate rules to extract concessions from the majority. It also sought to block measures, such as the resolution opposing President Bush's troop surge in Iraq. As in the past, the majority leadership's options were to compromise or accept a stalemate. And, as in the recent past, the only real check on the Senate minority's use of obstructionist tactics is their fear that public opinion may turn against them and threaten their electoral goals.

In the House, where the problems of minority exclusion and lack of information have been much greater, Democrats pledged themselves to some fairly specific changes. Their campaign manifesto, "A New Direction for Democrats," committed them to give members at least twenty-four hours to examine a bill before it is considered in committee, initially on the House floor, or as a conference report; to "generally" consider bills on the floor under "a procedure that allows open, full and fair debate"; to restrict recorded votes to the customary seventeen minutes; and to require regular and open conference committee meetings in which all conferees are given an opportunity to vote on all amendments. The rules package put together by the new majority and adopted by the House in January 2007, at the beginning of the 110th Congress, prohibits the Speaker from holding open votes for "the sole purpose of changing the outcome," "requires House conferees to insist that conference committees operate in an open and fair manner and that House conferees sign the final conference papers at one time and in one place," and "prohibits the consideration of a conference report that has been altered after the time it was signed by conferees." The package also contains strong language on making earmarks transparent and reinstitutes pay-as-you-go budget rules.[63]

However, as Christopher Foreman points out in his comment to this chapter, whether Democrats deliver on their promises over the course of the Congress depends on the incentives created by the institutional and political context. The new Democratic majority has ample incentives to engage in oversight of an opposition-party administration, and committees began hearings on a variety of programs and policies immediately. Considering the high degree of scrutiny to which these investigations are subject, there would seem to be as many incentives for responsible—as opposed to "gotcha"—oversight. During the campaign, Democrats promised to expand the workweek and spend more time in Washington attending to congressional duties. They delivered on that promise during their first weeks in control, and because Democrats have much they wish to accomplish, Congress seems likely to continue adhering to a longer Washington workweek. Although members complain about the increased hours and the leaders have not be able to stick to five-day weeks, the 110th Congress will almost certainly spend much more time in session than its immediate predecessors.

63. U.S. House of Representatives, Committee on Rules, *Report of Oversight Plans,* 110 Cong. 1 sess., February 7, 2007 (rules.house.gov/archives/110th_oversight.pdf).

Democratic committee leaders and members are insisting on returning to a legislative process that gives committees a greater role. To be sure, in January 2007 the new Democratic majority leadership did bring a number of bills to the floor without committee consideration first. During the campaign, Democrats had promised to pass a specific list of bills during the first 100 (legislative) hours that they controlled the House, and delivering on that promise required bypassing committees. Even so, the new Democratic committee leaders complained. Party leaders remain influential and involved in legislative substance, but strong and, in many cases, experienced committee chairs and committee members intent on legislating are tilting the balance toward more real committee deliberation.

The Democrats' pledge to include the minority in a more open legislative process is proving harder to honor. Most chairs have attempted to deliver on their vow to include the minority in committee decisionmaking, with mixed but some promising results. The issue under consideration and the role the minority decides to play, as well as committee Democrats' willingness to compromise, affect the chances of successful bipartisanship. Despite their complaints about the Republican majority's use of closed rules, Democrats brought all of their "hundred hours" agenda legislation to the floor under highly restrictive rules. The imperative of keeping their legislative promises trumped their promises about an open process. Since then, restrictive rules have been the norm rather than the exception; from January through the August recess of 2007, 78 percent of special rules restricted the amendments that could be offered.[64] On the resolution disapproving President Bush's troop surge in Iraq, rank-and-file Democrats reportedly pressed their leaders to employ a rule barring any sort of Republican alternative; those members did not want to confront the potentially tough vote that could be generated by an artfully drafted Republican substitute. To deliver on their promise of a more open floor process, the Democratic leaders will have to risk losing floor votes and occasionally require their electorally vulnerable members to cast difficult votes.

Both polarization and narrow margins persist, creating a strong temptation for the House majority-party leadership to use the tools it possesses in a heavy-handed fashion. However, House Democrats tend to be less ideologically homogeneous than the Republican majority they replaced, and that puts some constraints on such leadership. To establish a record of legislative productivity, Democrats will need to work with Republicans at least periodically, though to date active bipartisan collaboration has been rare at the House Chamber—as opposed to committee—

64. Author's calculations based on information available at the Rules Committee website (www.house.rules.gov).

level. By and large, House Republicans do not see such cooperation as in their electoral interest.

We should not expect a return to an era of ineffectual parties, party leaders with few resources, and ephemeral winning coalitions. Nor should we want that. A majority party that is vigorous and reasonably ideologically like-minded provides some coherence to lawmaking and at least the possibility of accountability. We *are* likely to see a somewhat better balance in the House between expeditiousness and decisiveness on the one hand and deliberation and inclusion on the other. If that proves to be true, it will be the result not of Democrats' greater virtue but because of a different balance of incentives, including the incentive to avoid the mistakes that cost their predecessors the majority.

Comments on Chapter Two

COMMENT

Christopher H. Foreman Jr.

What difference does partisan polarization—by which we mean the increased ideological space separating two reasonably cohesive congressional parties—make for Congress and the country? At least three underlying questions, none easily answered, invite attention. Does polarization improve or worsen the quality (or, for that matter, the quantity) of legislation? Does it bolster or undermine relations between the legislative and executive branches of government? And does it affect citizens' regard for, or influence over, government?

Problems of value judgment (how does one tell "good" from "bad" legislation?) and measurement (how much "bad" legislating or inadequate oversight do we see?) are impediments on all fronts. Barbara Sinclair's analysis necessarily leaves fundamental matters unresolved, partly because of data limitations and partly because separating polarization from other forces is difficult. Indeed, Sinclair's chapter would ideally carry a revised subtitle inviting readers to consider the combined consequences of partisan polarization, near-parity of legislative membership, a substantial recent history of Republican powerlessness in the House of Representatives, and the complicating role of the Senate's peculiar attributes. All of these factors have clearly mattered.

Sinclair's concluding emphasis on incentives is indeed appropriate. Polarization, in concert with other forces, has influenced Congress by creating incentives that predispose members and leaders to certain kinds of behavior—in some cases, arguably, extreme and unwise behavior. (On the other hand, even a moderate stance can seem unwise in the near term if it irritates or demobilizes one's supporters, perhaps spawning challenges to one's leadership.) As Sinclair and others have observed, an ideologically cohesive legislative majority sets the stage for strong leadership; members who broadly agree tend to defer to strong leaders who advance their collective interests. But the trouble comes when those leaders use their power in ways that undermine deliberation (with a correspondingly high probability of unleashing poor judgment), which they will do when they have sufficient incentives.

And we would anticipate that majority party leaders are more likely to have such incentives when their hold on power appears tenuous, which is, in turn, more likely if that power is recently acquired after a long wait in the minority. When wielding power is a relatively novel experience that could evaporate altogether with the shifting of a few seats (the parity challenge), leaders may be especially inclined to play hardball with allies and opponents alike. Sarah Binder has proposed that "when a party has been in the minority for a long time, it most likely has greater incentive to legislate when it regains control of Congress."[1] Not surprisingly, then, the 104th Congress began, as Thomas Mann and Norman Ornstein observed in their book *The Broken Branch,* "with an assertiveness unparalleled in modern American history."[2]

A key danger, however, is that leaders conditioned by such forces will overreach, and against this tendency—not polarization—citizens will likely react. One example of such a reaction is the way in which the public blamed Speaker Newt Gingrich and the Republicans for shutting down the government in late 1995 in their showdown with President Clinton over the budget.[3] Political scientist Richard Fenno argues that the Republican newcomers, who had just been elevated to the majority by the previous year's midterm elections, badly interpreted their victory, reading into it a mandate for radical change that was not politically viable.[4] The party also came across as heavy-handed in its use of the K Street Project, the intent of which was to pressure Washington's lobbying firms to hire Republican loyalists and shun Democrats. House Majority Leader Tom DeLay (R-Tex.)—ever attuned to the thinness of his party's majority—grabbed for and won additional seats in his home state with a contentious and much criticized redistricting, while overseeing fundraising practices that would provoke a career-ending criminal indictment. DeLay's determination to impeach President Clinton reflected polarization by playing to Republican base sentiment as distinct from broader public opinion, which opposed impeachment. DeLay and his colleagues in the Republican leadership clearly saw their core mission as twofold: elect (and reelect) Republican members, and enact (and promote aggressive implementation of) Republican policies. DeLay proved famously single-minded in this regard, but he would doubtless defend himself by claiming only to have played, albeit without mercy, the cards he was dealt.

Institutional Disregard

By predisposing Republicans to a sharply partisan team identity, polarization may be implicated in the notably low concern among House Republicans for the

1. Binder (2003, p. 26).
2. Mann and Ornstein (2006, p. 108).
3. Mann and Ornstein (2006, pp. 108–10).
4. Fenno (1997).

institutional health of their chamber. That is certainly one way of interpreting the anecdotes of incivility with which Sinclair introduces her chapter. Indeed, given everything that has been researched about and reported on the House Republicans over the last several years, it is reasonable to speculate that their four decades in the minority prior to 1994 may have been crucial in diminishing Republicans' concern for the House as an institution. They were not invested in such concern— and from their collective standpoint at the time, why should they have been? Who among them could recall a time when institutional stewardship offered significant benefits? (Fenno points out that notably few of the newcomers of 1994 had even served as legislative leaders in their home states.)[5] On the other hand, they could well recall how they had come to power—through unity and aggressive challenging of a "corrupt" status quo by Gingrich. And with achievement of the first all-Republican government since the early 1950s (briefly in 2001 and more durably after the 2002 elections), it could reasonably have appeared necessary to "go for broke" on remaking the political and policy landscape and not to spend much time worrying about a bit of broken furniture. Moreover, spending fewer days at work in an institution (and perhaps fewer years in it, for Republican true believers in term limits) would plausibly tend to suppress awareness of its needs.

If there is anything to this line of reasoning, it implies a long-range palliative: avoiding the near-dynastic, decades-long control of the chamber by a single party. For quite apart from polarization, such a condition may incline the majority toward irresponsible arrogance and the minority toward irresponsible desperation. It is not clear how such an outcome can be avoided, though the small majority margins of recent years suggest that there may not be much to worry about. If the House remains as evenly divided as it is currently (compared with the very large Democratic margins witnessed often in the twentieth century), the system may prove effectively self-regulating. Republican expectations of a "permanent" majority were obviously premature, but a few more turns of the wheel may quite plausibly return them to power.

The Rewards of Party Unity

Sinclair observes both that polarization had been in evidence for a long time before the Republican takeover after the 1994 midterm elections and that the House's rules amply reward majority unity. Henry Waxman (D-Calif.), now chairman of the recently renamed Committee on Oversight and Government Reform, made

5. Fenno (1997).

the latter point twenty years ago: "If we have a united Democratic position," he told a reporter, "Republicans are irrelevant."[6]

But how far are Waxman and his fellow Democrats inclined to press their new advantage? There was feverish speculation about how Democrats would behave following the 2006 midterms, which returned them to the majority in the 110th Congress, with a margin about as narrow as the Republicans had held in the 109th. We cannot foresee the future, but we can, once again, ponder the incentives facing the new majority. Perhaps the safest general prediction is that Democratic leaders will press their advantage as hard as they can, consistent with preventing defections while trying to appear fair enough to blunt the most damaging criticisms. During the 2006 campaign, future Speaker Nancy Pelosi (D-Calif.) sent strong signals that the new majority would demonstrate more transparency and inclusiveness than had prevailed before. Her acceptance speech contained predictable rhetoric of governing "in the spirit of partnership, not partisanship" and reaching "beyond partisanship to work for all America."[7] But just as predictably, the leadership moved quickly to insulate its opening "first 100 hours" of prime legislation against Republican tweaking. On the other hand, Pelosi knew that her party was both less unified than Republicans were and opposed by a president with a new incentive to veto bills he disliked. She would also likely wish to impress knowledgeable observers (the participants in this Brookings-Hoover project, for example) as being something more than a slightly kinder, gentler version of her predecessors.

Missing Sausages?

Neither polarization nor divided government means that the "meat grinder" grinds to a halt.[8] Individual issue areas regularly display bipartisan cooperation (at least of the logrolling variety) even in this more polarized legislative era. Agriculture subsidies, for example, are hardly a one-party policy. Any casual Congress-watcher can cite many instances—including landmark legislation such as the Americans with Disabilities Act, the North American Free Trade Agreement, and the 1996 welfare reform law—when recent presidents have found common ground with a significant number of opposition legislators. (At the start of the 110th Congress, immigration reform struck many observers as probably the likeliest candidate for

---

6. Quoted in Mann and Ornstein (2006, p. 73).

7. Martin Kady II, "New Majority, New Rules," *CQ Weekly,* January 8, 2007.

8. The best known statement on the effects of divided government is Mayhew (1991).

the list.) After considering the matter intensively, Yale University political scientist David Mayhew opined that "it seems unlikely that divided party control lowers the quality of statutes."[9]

But can "unspoiled sausages"—statutes that pass the quality test—emerge from a polarized legislative process? The judgment of recent critics highlights a significant deterioration of quality as a consequence of a recent decline in deliberative norms. Mann and Ornstein opine at length on the deficiencies of the 2005 bankruptcy reform law, and many would doubtless cast the 2003 prescription drug legislation in a similar light.[10] But if polarization is one villain here, it clearly has companions. They include the incentives to simple haste—evident, arguably, in the legislative response to the terror attacks of September 11, 2001—and ordinary capitulation to the clout of powerful economic interests. Again, polarization would have operated as a predisposing factor for, but not the main driver of, questionable judgment.

Polarization-tainted incentives, too, probably help us understand what Sinclair might well dub the "missing sausages," legislation that ought to have been enacted but was not. I am not speaking here of Social Security reform or a disaster policy that might have prevented or mitigated the well-known woes associated with Hurricane Katrina. Rather, I refer to the more routine failure to enact ordinary appropriations, culminating in a postelection decision by the GOP in 2006 to give up on all but two spending bills and leave the new congressional leadership to cope with the consequences.[11]

Well before the 2006 election, everyone could easily predict that the surest transformation to be wrought by the Democratic capture of at least one chamber lay in the realm of administrative oversight.[12] In particular, the Republican-led Congress had been notably reluctant to challenge the Bush administration's national security and antiterrorism decisionmaking through critical investigative hearings. Congressional Republicans had little incentive to challenge, and potentially embarrass, their team leader in the policy area most crucial to his public support and in which he had most aggressively asserted executive prerogatives.

Actually, Sinclair's somewhat broader claim that "Congress largely abdicated its oversight responsibilities" during the first six years of the Bush administration implies—correctly, I think—that congressional inquiry and supervision across the

9. Mayhew (1991, p. 183).

10. Mann and Ornstein (2006, pp. 141–46).

11. Steven T. Dennis and Liriel Higa, "GOP Punts on Spending Bills," CQ Weekly, November 27, 2006.

12. Robert Kuttner, "A Slight Oversight," American Prospect, October 3, 2006.

board were more muted than they could, or should, have been. As a long-time observer of Congress's oversight activities, I concluded that the default stance of the typical congressional Republican was roughly this: the president is our leader and he appoints reliable people to run the agencies, so we should mainly get out of the way and let them do their jobs. The point invites careful empirical verification, however, and the discussion (at least among academic political scientists) could grow a bit complicated. That is partly because congressional *oversight* involves far more than hearings and investigations, and partly because the subject overlaps with a much more nuanced ongoing discussion of congressional *influence.* One can easily imagine research claiming to show administrative "agent" behavior in the Bush era as quite compliant with the preferences of various congressional "principals," perhaps suggesting that concerns about legislative timidity have been misplaced.

In any case, time and a crucial election have rebalanced the system but without, as far as one can tell, reducing the polarization between the parties. To the extent that polarization matters—and, as both Sinclair and I emphasize, it is not even close to the whole story—we may have to content ourselves with managing its worst institutional effects. Perhaps something approaching "regular order" (if not a full-fledged return to the textbook Congress of "How a Bill Becomes a Law") and a bit more comradely, cross-party comity can be nurtured in the House of Representatives. Now that we are beyond the first wave of legislative promise-keeping by House Democrats, we shall see whether Speaker Pelosi is tempted, over time, to hold open floor votes, shut out Republican participation, and resort to the blame-avoiding chicanery of self-executing rules. It is a story turning less on intentions than on incentives.

COMMENT
Keith Krehbiel

The topic of party polarization and its consequences still elicits enough head scratching that it may be wise to reconsider the usual answer to a well-studied question: does party polarization lead to bad legislation? A reconsideration of this question gives rise to a paradoxical second question: if so, why not? The resolution of the paradox, as we will see, supports a more sanguine view of partisanship and its legislative consequences than many political observers are willing to admit.

The author appreciates helpful communications with Larry Evans, Morris Fiorina, Mattias Polborn, Eric Schickler, Alan Wiseman, and Jack Wright.

So, does party polarization lead to bad legislation? In a word, yes—or at least that is what most people believe. Therefore I will begin by summarizing this supposition and then look at it more closely.

Grounded in mainstream beliefs about how the contemporary Congress works—or, in this instance, doesn't—the consensus view of political scientists and pundits is that bad legislation is common and that party polarization is to blame.[13] According to Barbara Sinclair, for example, party polarization in Congress is a condition ripe for procedural empowerment of the majority party in either the House or the Senate. The majority party's size and its organizational and procedural advantages give rise to bold partisan initiatives (which the minority prefers to call radical proposals). The ability of the majority party to craft extreme proposals, exercise procedural control, enforce discipline, and squelch dissent within its ranks is, in various combinations, sufficient for legislative success, where success is measured by the degree to which legislation comports with what is wanted by the median member of the majority party. With less evidence but more zeal, other observers suggest that the partisan bias in legislation is the political equivalent of Isaac Newton's apple *not* falling to the ground but rather rising to the tree. "Today's governing Republican majority," wrote Jacob Hacker and Paul Pierson in their 2005 book, *Off Center,* "can justly claim that it has defied normal laws of political gravity."[14]

These observation-based beliefs can also be fruitfully grounded in an explicit theory. Consider the scenario of extreme party polarization in figure 2-2, in which an ideological space is normalized so that -1 denotes the most liberal policies possible, $+1$ denotes the most conservative policies possible, and the midpoint is a normative benchmark for good (moderate) policies.[15] Assume that the seat advantage of the majority party (on the right) is as small as possible.[16] The *extremity* of

---

13. By *bad legislation* I mean (loosely) legislation that is more extreme than what most people want, or (precisely) legislation that comports with preferences of an extreme and homogeneous majority party. *Party polarization* has two components: a large distance between Democrats' and Republicans' policy stances, and large agreement within each party about its stances. These conditions are often called (interparty) *distance* and (intraparty) *homogeneity.*

14. Hacker and Pierson (2005, p. 2)

15. The zero point may be operationalized as any of several defensible moderate policies, such as the median voter in the electorate, or the median voter within the median district (or state in the case of the Senate), or the median legislator. By default, I will define it as the first of these.

16. Sinclair identifies smallness of the majority as a key feature of polarization because, under such conditions, the majority party has an especially keen incentive to control procedures and the agenda. This assumption is not critical for the argument that follows. See also Aldrich and Rohde (2000, p. 43).

Figure 2-2. *Party Polarization and Bad Legislation*[a]

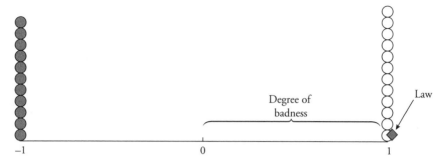

a. −1 denotes the most liberal policies possible; +1 denotes the most conservative policies; 0 (midpoint) is a normative benchmark for good (moderate) policies.

the party ensures that its most preferred policy proposals will lie at +1, and the *homogeneity* of the party ensures that, even though extreme, its proposals will receive unanimous support within the majority party and thus majority support within the legislature as a whole. Relative to the moderate benchmark of zero, this is obviously a bad outcome. Combining this simple theoretical illustration with the empirical summary reinforces the now seemingly robust *party polarization proposition:* party polarization within Congress leads to bad (unrepresentative) legislative outcomes.

But the polarization proposition prompts a second question: if party polarization *seems* to lead to bad legislation, why are things not quite like they seem? The answer, in a word, is fragility. That is, although the proposition is strictly true, for four reasons it is sensitive to small perturbations in theoretical and empirical conditions.

1. Theoretically, a small number of moderates nullifies the premise of the proposition. Empirically, congressional moderates are not extinct and seem regularly to be pivotal in lawmaking.

It is well known that throughout the latter half of the twentieth century, many Republicans in the South replaced conservative Democrats while many Democrats in the North replaced liberal Republicans. In effect (and roughly compatible with figure 2-2), the parties have become good preference sorters. "Conservative and liberal have become almost perfect synonyms for Republican and Democrat," as political scientists Nolan McCarty, Keith Poole, and Howard Rosenthal have stated.[17]

17. McCarty, Poole, and Rosenthal (2006, p. 3).

It is important to remember, however, that figure 2-2 takes this change to the limit, which is farther than data suggest is realistic. Sarah Binder, for example, has pointed out that

> the political center in Congress has shrunk markedly over the past 15 years. Hovering around 30 percent of House and Senate members in the 1960s and 1970s, the percentage of centrists in each chamber began slipping in the 1980s, and it has fallen to about 10 percent today. Centrists now can claim 11.3 percent of the House, down from 20 percent or more during the 1980s. And after peaking at 32.3 percent of the Senate during 1969–70, the first term of the Nixon administration, centrists make up less than 10 percent of today's Senate.[18]

So, should we think of the glass of moderates as two-thirds empty or as one-third full? From a theoretical perspective, the glass is full enough when, under simple majority rule, the median legislator is a moderate. Then, according to the median voter theorem, policy, too, will be moderate.[19]

Although this may seem like a sterile theoretical point, it has a noteworthy substantive basis. Even after an additional decade of alleged continued polarization since Binder observed the "shrinking middle," moderates do still exist. According to the *National Journal*'s Congressional vote ratings, for example, twenty-five representatives in the 109th Congress (2005–07) were in an interval of moderates bounded on the left by the most liberal Republican and bounded on the right by the most conservative Democrat.[20] The nonextinct status of congressional moderates is further corroborated by an informally compiled list of Senators who were regularly in the news when major legislative initiatives in the 109th Congress received traction. These include Democrats Joseph Lieberman (Conn.), Ben Nelson (Neb.), Mary Landrieu (La.), and Mark Pryor (Ark.); Republicans John McCain (Ariz.), Olympia Snowe (Maine), and Susan Collins (Maine); and independent Jim Jeffords (Vt.).[21]

18. Binder (1996, p. 37).
19. The logic extends straightforwardly to situations of greater-than-minimum majority parties, although the number of moderates needed increases with majority-party size, of course.
20. This number is almost surely biased downward, for reasons that will become clear in the discussion below of bias problems in measuring party polarization. For the 2006 evaluation, see "2006 Congressional Vote Ratings," *National Journal* (nationaljournal.com/voteratings).
21. A comparable list of less well known members of the House can also be constructed.

Why were these senators in the news so often? Probably because as moderates on many or most salient issues, they were at or near pivotal ideological positions and therefore credibly demanded compromises in order to give their support to proposed legislation—compromises often tantamount to moving policy to the center of the policy spectrum. Indeed, two of the chapters in this volume summarize approximately a dozen high-profile instances in recent Congresses in which party leaders' seemingly bold initiatives either failed because of their inability to attract moderates' votes or passed only because significantly moderating concessions were made to attract moderates' votes.[22] Either way, all it takes to counter the threat of polarization-induced bad legislation is a few moderates—and the Congress still seems to have an ample supply of them.

2. *Measures of party polarization are likely to overstate actual party polarization, especially in recent decades.*

Specifically, measures of *homogeneity within parties* are biased upward by the kind of agenda setting that empirical research has shown to be increasingly common, and measures of *differences between parties* are biased by agenda setting and compounded by researchers' censoring of data. The empirical seed of this second source of fragility is the concept of *message politics,* which political scientist C. Lawrence Evans of William & Mary has defined as "the interrelated set of electoral, communications, and legislative strategies that congressional parties employ to advance their respective messages." Evans presents a compelling argument that "over the past fifteen years the formal message operations of the House and Senate have grown more extensive and institutionalized."[23] Message politics involves coordinated inside and outside partisan games. Leaders target their outside electoral audiences with strategically filtered references to elements of the inside game of lawmaking. Increasingly, they are willing and able to appear before TV cameras as programmatic partisan entities rather than free-agent, nonpartisan position takers or credit claimers.

Moreover, when partisan leaders choose to go public, they do so on issues that have familiar characteristics. Evans explains:

In choosing their message, agenda leaders look for issues on which there is a high degree of *preference homogeneity within their party caucus* because serious divisions will make it difficult for rank-and-file members to coalesce

---

22. Sinclair in this chapter, and Brady, Ferejohn, and Harbridge in chapter 5.
23. Evans (2001, p. 219).

behind a single coherent message. . . . Among the issues that the party rank and file can unite behind, leaders search in particular for issues that can be used to distinguish their party from the opposition, that is, issues for which there is a significant *divergence of preferences between the two parties.*[24]

In other words, message politics emphasizes *exactly* the same characteristics that define party polarization. It is therefore a short step from the dynamics of message politics to bias in measures of party polarization. The point of intersection is the roll call agenda: which issues and proposals get onto it, and which are kept off it?

Consider three types of issues: *bipartisan consensus* issues, which attract large-to-unanimous coalitions; *cross-cutting* issues, which have narrower margins of approval than consensus issues but that likewise attract bipartisan support; and *partisan* issues, which unify the majority party but pit it against most of the minority party.[25] In an era of message politics, as Evans notes, party leaders act upon incentives to downplay issues of bipartisan consensus and issues that cut across parties. This includes keeping undesired legislation from reaching the floor and using rules to shield desired legislation from amendments that would elicit bipartisan support or cross-partisan opposition.[26] Such strategies clearly reduce the number of bipartisan consensus votes and cross-cutting votes and increase the proportion of partisan votes in the data sets researchers rely upon to estimate preferences. It is therefore quite possible that underlying preferences are stable over contiguous periods during which parties have comparable overlapping clusters of moderates, but an increase in message politics and the associated screening of roll calls generate an illusion (or at least overstatement) of increasing polarization. That is, differences in party means will be artificially large, and variances within parties will be artificially small, thereby making Congress appear more like the depiction in figure 2-2 than it really is.[27]

A more subtle feature of measurement techniques only makes matters worse. The most common measures of party polarization are roll call voting scales, such

24. Evans (2001, pp. 221–22). Italics added.

25. For examples of the first type, see Mayhew (1974, figure 1, p. 113) or Krehbiel (1998, figure 4.4, p. 85).

26. The resurgence of party literature is infused with this argument as it pertains to the majority party. See Roberts and Smith (2003); Rohde (1991); Smith (1989); and Sinclair (1983, 1995), as well as Sinclair's chapter in this volume. On rules, see Bach and Smith (1988); Dion and Huber (1996); and Brady, Ferejohn, and Harbridge in chapter 5 of this volume.

27. A minor exception is that *minority*-party preferences may appear artificially *heterogeneous* to the extent that majority leaders succeed at opposition-splitting message politics. See Evans (2001).

as DW-nominate scores or "inflation-adjusted" (time-comparable) ADA rankings.[28] All such measures are sensitive both to the issues on which legislators choose to vote and to researchers' selection of votes from which to calculate the indexes. Measurement of the distance between parties is confounded by two features. First, such measures are typically bounded. For example, DW-nominate scores range from −1 to +1, while percent-correct indexes such as ADA ratings are minimized at 0 and maximized at 100. In any given year, at least a handful of senators and representatives have perfect or abysmal voting records and are therefore pushed to the extremes of 0 or 100. But who is to say that the ideological score of 100 in 2007 represents the same degree of policy disagreement as a score of 100 in 1997, 1987, or 1977? Even if one puts faith in more sophisticated "inflation-adjusted" or "common-space" techniques, measures of party differences are sensitive to the share of the agenda that is composed of bipartisan consensus votes.[29] Such votes are clearly indicative of cross-party agreement, which runs counter to polarization punditry. To the extent that bipartisan consensus votes are tallied into the calculation of measures, the groups at each pole in figure 2-2 will converge and facilitate the production of moderate laws.

Do the measures, in fact, give sufficient weight to these bipartisan tendencies? Additional evidence suggests they do not. Because unanimous roll calls exhibit no variation, such votes are of no use in scaling and are consequently discarded. Also discarded in most applications are near-unanimous roll calls. Theoretically, this censoring should overstate the differences between the parties.[30] Suggestive evidence is shown in figure 2-3. Additional analysis reveals that the supposedly innocuous omission of consensus votes accounts for almost 42 percent of the variation in the DW-nominate polarization measure (difference in party means).

It seems quite likely, therefore, that the interparty distance component of polarization is inflated not only by party leaders' agenda setting but also by researchers' data censoring, both of which took a sharp upturn beginning around 1994.

---

28. See Poole and Rosenthal (1985); Heckman and Snyder (1997); Groseclose, Levitt and Snyder (1999).

29. Such procedures necessarily rely on ad hoc assumptions. The critical assumption of Groseclose, Levitt, and Snyder (1999) is that when House members move to the Senate (or, conversely, Claude Pepper goes to the House), their expected ideal points induced by their state are equal to those induced by their former district. The key assumption of Poole and Rosenthal (1985) is that ideal points may change but only monotonically and linearly.

30. Although James Snyder's original notion of "artificial extremism" lacked a party component, this is clearly an instance of his argument. See Snyder (1992).

Figure 2-3. *Party Polarization and Discarded Bipartisan Consensus Votes*[a]

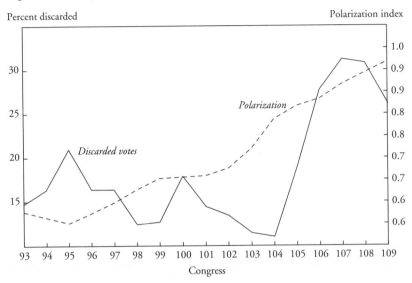

Source: Author's calculations using vote count data provided by Nolan McCarty, Princeton University. Polarization measure available online at voteview.com.

a. The replacement of teller votes with electronic voting changed floor politics significantly, so the time series begins with the initiation of electronic voting. See Smith (1989). An ordinary least squares regression of polarization on the percentage of omitted roll calls yields $b = 0.012$ ($p = 0.005$) and $R^2 = 0.418$. The correlation between the two variables is 0.647.

3. In the presence of a few moderates, supermajority procedures provide an additional guarantee that new policies will be moderate and old policies will stay moderate. The preceding median-based arguments rely on a simple-majority voting rule in which a single median voter is always pivotal. In legislative settings where a credible threat of a presidential veto or a filibuster exists, supermajoritarian logic applies. The Senate allows filibusters and has Rule XXII to institutionalize the corresponding three-fifths voting requirement. The U.S. Constitution gives the president a veto, subject to a two-thirds override in both houses of Congress. Assuming (for reasons that seem clear in light of the empirical parts of the discussion thus far) that a few moderates exist in an otherwise polarized legislature (as shown in figure 2-4), spatial characterization of legislation that can and cannot be passed is simple, intuitive, but mostly inconsistent with the proposition that party polarization in Congress leads to bad legislative outcomes.[31]

31. The algorithm is an application of the pivotal politics model. See Krehbiel (1996, 1998); Brady and Volden (2006); Messner and Polborn (2004).

Figure 2-4. *Supermajoritarianism and Good Policy with Minimal Number of Moderates*[a]

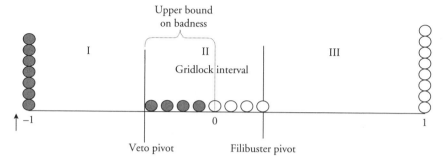

a. See figure 2.2 and text for explanation.

Supermajoritarianism reveals yet another facet of the fragility of the polarization proposition. For each of the three intervals in figure 2-4, hypothesize that existing policy (the status quo) lies in that interval and ask whether a supermajority can be formed whose members are willing to vote to move policy into an adjacent interval. If so, then such status quo policies should be dismissed as infeasible because they are not steady states given preferences and rules. If not, then such a policy is an equilibrium, and the corresponding law can then be assessed as a function of its distance from zero.

Clearly, any policy in interval I can be defeated by points in interval II because at least some of the latter are preferred by more than two-thirds of the voters (the veto pivot and everyone to his right). The same argument applies to all policies in interval III, except that they need only three-fifths of the voters to break a filibuster. This leaves only moderate policies in interval II as feasible. For any and all of these, any attempt to move left is opposed by at least a two-fifths-plus-one blocking minority on the right, and any attempt to move right is opposed by a one-third-plus-one blocking minority on the left.

Are feasible laws under supermajority procedures bad? This is not a strict yes-or-no question, but the answer is closer to no than to yes. Inasmuch as laws passed under supermajority procedures can unequivocally be good (for example, at 0), they unequivocally cannot be bad (for example, at −1 or 1). Moreover, the model clearly identifies an upper bound on badness (the distance between either of the two pivot points and zero). Furthermore, moderate policies are locked in by supermajority voting rules, and therefore, such rules are effective containment barriers against the passage of bad legislation implied by the partisan polarization proposition.

4. *Even under the conditions that most closely reflect the proposition (maximum polarization, as represented in figure 2-2), the electoral connection facilitates good outcomes on average. Under more realistic conditions (the presence of at least a few moderate legislators, as in figure 2-4), elections provide additional insurance against anomalous bad legislation.*

To appreciate the first part of reason four, suppose the original party polarization proposition were restored. That is, disregard all earlier demonstrations of fragility, and assume that party polarization exists in its extreme form and that, by implication, bad legislation regularly passes. Would such a system "defy political gravity" with an electoral accountability mechanism in place? Under a wide range of assumptions about electoral institutions and behavior, such legislative outcomes cannot be sustained. A rigorous and exhaustive demonstration is beyond the scope of this comment, but a simple example conveys the essential intuition.[32]

Assume that figure 2-2 accurately reflects the polarized state of the legislature *and* that the electoral basis for that extreme polarization is *almost* identically extremely polarized. That is, just under half of legislative districts are at −1, just under half of the districts are at +1, but one district is at 0.[33] Suppose that parties in the electorate have a firm grip on candidates they nominate and are highly ideological and non-Downsian. So, in the pivotal moderate district, the pivotal voters are indifferent toward the −1 and +1 candidates up for election, and they flip a coin to determine their votes. The obvious electoral outcome is that the elected representative of the pivotal district will flip randomly from Democrat to Republican, as will party control of the otherwise balanced legislature. Then, even in the worst case when the polarization proposition is true, bad policies will alternate randomly between −1 and +1 and will be good (moderate) on average.

More realistic scenarios can also be considered and should be given more weight. For one thing, there are many moderate legislative districts—not just a few.[34] Furthermore, postulating slightly strategic behavior leads to much more satisfactory outcomes than those caused by random, leapfrogging, extreme-policy regimes. Within any given moderate district, moderate voters have a strong incentive to elect a moderate legislator because they know that he or she would be a pivotal power broker in the legislature. Similarly, both parties in the electorate have a strong incentive to put up such a candidate because his or her victory clinches

32. See, however, Krehbiel, Meirowitz, and Romer (2005).
33. A concrete example is Colorado's seventh district. See William Schneider, "Spotlight on Center Stage," *National Journal,* September 30, 2006.
34. See Fiorina, Abrams, and Pope (2006).

majority-party status in the legislature.[35] In sum, the greater the number of moderate districts, the greater are the centripetal forces on parties in the electorate, the lower is the empirical plausibility and theoretical relevance of figure 2-2, and the more apt is the minimal-moderates scenario of figure 2-4. Once again, a bit of theory and a dose of realism illustrate the fragility of the party polarization proposition.

Finally, electoral accountability of this type is not just a normative hope. The outcomes of the 1994 and 2006 elections testify to the genuineness of election-induced constraints on overreaching parties' attempts to enact extreme legislation. Recent history reassures us that political apples, too, fall toward the center of political gravity—not away from it.

Resolution

As a strictly logical matter, the proposition of party polarization still holds because, as its two concepts are defined, party polarization is a sufficient condition for bad legislation. Why, then, the paradox? That is, if party polarization contributes to bad legislation, why suggest that bad legislation is not much of a problem?

Resolution of the "if so, why not" paradox requires clarification of the treacherous step taken from theory to data. Specifically, for the logic to work as needed in trying to rationalize prevailing empirical beliefs, the two critical concepts in the proposition must be defined so stringently that they lose their empirical plausibility. The resulting slippage can be summarized as follows. In theory, party polarization *does* result in bad legislation. In practice, however, party polarization only *may* result in bad legislation because for legislation to be significantly bad (extreme and durable), party polarization has to be exceptionally severe (essentially, there must be no moderates).

Ultimately, then, the substantive relevance of the proposition of party polarization is undercut by empirical realities. Real-world polarization does not seem severe enough to produce alarmingly bad legislation on a regular basis. Measures of polarization probably overstate the phenomenon. Supermajority procedures not only put limits on noncentrist policies but also stabilize moderate policies. And if all else fails, electoral mechanisms empower voters to repair perceived breakdowns in representative governance.

---

35. If the majority party allows one of its candidates to occupy the center, it protects its majority status. If the minority party positions a challenger at the center in a district held by an opposite party extremist, the challenger wins and the old minority becomes the new majority.

References

Aldrich, John, and David Rohde. 2000. "The Consequences of Party Organization in the House: The Role of the Majority and Minority Parties in Conditional Party Government." In *Polarized Politics: Congress and the President in a Partisan Era,* edited by Jon R. Bond and Richard Fleisher, pp. 31–72. Washington: CQ Press.

Bach, Stanley, and Steven S. Smith. 1988. *Managing Uncertainty in the House of Representatives: Adaptation and Innovation in Special Rules.* Brookings.

Bartels, Larry M. 2005. "Homer Gets a Tax Cut: Inequality and Public Policy in the American Mind." *Perspectives on Politics* 3 (1): 15–31.

Binder, Sarah. 1996. "The Disappearing Political Center: Congress and the Incredible Shrinking Middle." *Brookings Review* 14 (4): 36–39.

———. 2003. *Stalemate: Causes and Consequences of Legislative Gridlock.* Brookings.

Binder, Sarah, and Steven S. Smith. 1997. *Politics or Principle? Filibustering in the United States Senate.* Brookings.

Brady, David W., and Craig Volden. 2006. *Revolving Gridlock: Politics and Policy from Jimmy Carter to George W. Bush.* Boulder, Colo.: Westview Press.

Brewer, Paul R., and Christopher J. Deering. 2005. "Musical Chairs: Interest Groups, Campaign Fundraising, and Selection of House Committee Chairs." In *The Interest Group Connection: Electioneering, Lobbying, and Policymaking in Washington,* edited by Paul S. Herrnson, Ronald G. Shaiko, and Clyde Wilcox, pp. 141–63. Washington: CQ Press.

Cox, Gary W., and Mathew D. McCubbins. 2005. *Setting the Agenda: Responsible Party Government in the U.S. House of Representatives.* Cambridge University Press.

Dion, Douglas, and John D. Huber. 1996. "Procedural Choice and the House Committee on Rules." *Journal of Politics* 58 (1): 25–53.

Edwards, George C., III. 2007. *Governing by Campaigning: The Politics of the Bush Presidency.* New York: Longman.

Evans, C. Lawrence. 2001. "Committees, Leaders, and Message Politics." In *Congress Reconsidered,* 5th ed., edited by Lawrence C. Dodd and Bruce I. Oppenheimer, pp. 217–43. Washington: CQ Press.

Fenno, Richard F., Jr. 1997. *Learning to Govern: An Institutional View of the 104th Congress.* Brookings.

Fiorina, Morris P., Samuel J. Abrams, and Jeremy C. Pope. 2006. *Culture War? The Myth of a Polarized America.* New York: Longman.

Groseclose, Tim, Steven D. Levitt, and James M. Snyder Jr. 1999. "Comparing Interest Group Scores across Time and Chambers: Adjusted ADA Scores for the U.S. Congress." *American Political Science Review* 93 (1): 33–50.

Hacker, Jacob S., and Paul Pierson. 2005. *Off Center: The Republican Revolution and the Erosion of Democracy.* Yale University Press.

Heckman, James J., and James M. Snyder Jr. 1997. "Linear Probability Models of the Demand for Attributes with an Empirical Application to Estimating the Preferences of Legislators." *Rand Journal of Economics* 28: S142–89.

Jacobson, Gary C. 2007. *A Divider, Not a Uniter: George W. Bush and the American People.* New York: Longman.

Krehbiel, Keith. 1996. "Institutional and Partisan Sources of Gridlock: A Theory of Divided and Unified Government." *Journal of Theoretical Politics* 8 (1): 7–40.

———. 1998. *Pivotal Politics: A Theory of U.S. Lawmaking.* University of Chicago Press.

Krehbiel, Keith, Adam Meirowitz, and Thomas Romer. 2005. "Parties in the Electorate, Parties in Government, and Partisan Bias." *Political Analysis* 13 (2): 113–38.

Lupia, Arthur, and others. 2005. "Were Bush Tax Cut Supporters 'Simply Ignorant?' A Second Look at Conservatives and Liberals in 'Homer Gets a Tax Cut.' " University of Michigan, Department of Political Science.

Mann, Thomas E., and Norman Ornstein. 2006. *The Broken Branch: How Congress Is Failing America and How to Get It Back on Track.* Oxford University Press.

Mayhew, David R. 1974. *Congress: The Electoral Connection.* Yale University Press.

————. 1991. *Divided We Govern: Party Control, Lawmaking, and Investigations, 1946–1990.* Yale University Press.

McCarty, Nolan, Keith T. Poole, and Howard Rosenthal. 2006. *Polarized America: The Dance of Ideology and Unequal Riches.* MIT Press.

Messner, Matthias, and Mattias K. Polborn. 2004. "Voting on Majority Rules." *Review of Economic Studies* 71: 115–32.

Poole, Keith T., and Howard Rosenthal. 1985. "A Spatial Model for Legislative Roll Call Analysis." *American Journal of Political Science* 29 (2): 357–84.

Roberts, Jason M., and Steven S. Smith. 2003. "Procedural Contexts, Party Strategy, and Conditional Party Voting in the U.S. House of Representatives, 1971–2000." *American Journal of Political Science* 47 (2): 305–17.

Rohde, David W. 1991. *Parties and Leaders in the Postreform House.* University of Chicago Press.

Rudalevige, Andrew. 2006. *The New Imperial Presidency: Renewing Presidential Power after Watergate.* University of Michigan Press.

Rybicki, Elizabeth. 2003. "Unresolved Differences: Bicameral Negotiations in Congress, 1877–2002." Paper prepared for the History of Congress Conference, University of California-San Diego, December 5–6.

Sinclair, Barbara. 1983. *Majority Leadership in the U.S. House.* Johns Hopkins University Press.

————. 1995. *Legislators, Leaders and Lawmaking: The U.S. House of Representatives in the Post-Reform Era.* Johns Hopkins University Press.

————. 2000. *Unorthodox Lawmaking: New Legislative Processes in the U.S. Congress,* 2nd ed. Washington: CQ Press.

————. 2006. *Party Wars: Polarization and the Politics of National Policy Making.* University of Oklahoma Press.

Smith, Steven S. 1989. *Call to Order: Floor Politics in the House and Senate.* Brookings.

Snyder, James M., Jr. 1992. "Artificial Extremism in Interest Group Ratings." *Legislative Studies Quarterly* 17 (3): 319–45.

3

Consequences for the Courts: Polarized Politics and the Judicial Branch

Sarah A. Binder

The portrait of polarized parties is a familiar one to scholars and observers of the U.S. Congress. Over the past thirty years, the parties' centers of gravity have moved toward their wings, leaving few centrist legislators to hold the political center. Although we know much about the contours and causes of polarization, we know far less about its consequences. Given concerns about the breakdown in the confirmation process as the two parties quarrel over the ideological tenor of recent judicial nominees, this chapter focuses on patterns in judicial selection in the years since World War II to show that polarization has markedly affected confirmation politics and given more partisan presidents a freer hand to place immoderate judges on the federal bench.[1] Coupled with recent congressional challenges of judges' decisions and court jurisdictions, polarization has clearly left its mark on the bench—raising the prospect that the legitimacy of the unelected branch may be at risk.

I appreciate the comments and questions of my discussants, Ben Wittes and Martin Shapiro; the advice of Eric Lawrence, Forrest Maltzman, and Russell Wheeler; and the research assistance of Alan Murphy, Molly Reynolds, and Emily Zametkin.

1. On the breakdown in advice and consent for Supreme Court nominations, see Wittes (2006). On the wars of advice and consent over lower federal court judges, see Binder and Maltzman (2005).

The Dilemma of Political Courts

When we discuss the impact of polarization on the judiciary, we are directly concerned with the impact of ideologically polarized political parties on the structure,
makeup, and independence of the federal courts. It would be naive, of course, to
believe that the federal judiciary can be immune from politics. Our courts today
are almost by definition deeply "political" courts, in the sense sketched by John
Ferejohn of Stanford University in recent work in which he notes that judges
engage in policymaking, determine constitutional limits for legislatures, and
increasingly regulate the conduct of political life.[2] Not surprisingly, then, court
appointments are themselves political—something Ferejohn identifies as "inevitable
and legitimate in our governmental structure." If courts in effect legislate, the
public has an interest in who serves on the bench.

But political courts, as Ferejohn observes, need not always be partisan courts—
by which we typically mean that a party's handprint can be seen directly on the
makeup of the bench. If a governing majority party can confirm a nominee in
the face of opposition from the minority party, then one might reasonably label
the selection process—and potentially the bench on which such judges sit—as
partisan: the outcome reflects the agenda of the majority party. To the extent that
an opposition party might oppose the governing majority's nominee on ideological grounds, then a partisan process may produce immoderate judges. European
constitutional courts, for a number of reasons, tend to be less partisan and more
ideologically centrist. Because appointments to European courts typically require
supermajorities for confirmation, judges with more extreme ideological views are
unlikely to be appointed or confirmed.[3] Modes of judicial selection that require
simple majorities for confirmation, as in the United States, are far more likely to
produce immoderate judges—a tendency that has led observers to paint federal
courts as both partisan and political.

Given the political nature of the appointments process in the United States,
there is a greater risk of creating partisan courts. Unlike the process in many European nations—where judicial candidates are often drawn from government
bureaucracies—the American system gives presidents a free hand in selecting
nominees. Moreover, because the federal courts address issues central to the iden-
tities of the political parties (such as abortion, gay rights, civil liberties, and environmental protection), both parties are loath to allow their opponents easy entrée

2. Ferejohn (2002).
3. Ferejohn (2002, p. 66).

to the courts. Even judicial resignations display a partisan cast: judges are far more likely to resign from the bench when the president hails from their own party.[4]

A shift from political courts to partisan ones, then, may be a cause for concern. A key question is whether shifts in partisan control and in the ideological makeup of the two political parties produce shifts in the ideological tenor of judges.[5] If so, both the stability of the law and a prevailing norm of judicial independence may be at stake. Once judges are confirmed for a lifetime appointment, it has been generally understood that their judicial acts may not serve as a basis for their impeachment—a norm, so to say, of "hands off the courts!" As Chief Justice William Rehnquist wrote in his 2004 year-end report, "Any other rule would destroy judicial independence."[6] If the advice and consent process enables the appointment of immoderate judges, then politicians may be reluctant to respect the norm of judicial independence, which extends beyond judicious use of the impeachment power to restraint in curtailing court jurisdiction or altering the size of the Supreme Court. Moreover, if the process of advice and consent becomes more visibly partisan, the public's confidence in judges, their decisions, and the bench may decline. How judges secure appointment to the federal bench—and how polarization may affect that process—thus has important normative consequences for the law and the legitimacy of the bench.[7]

The following analysis begins by focusing on the politics of judicial selection and assessing the impact of polarization on the ideological tenor of nominees and on the likelihood of their confirmation. It then considers briefly how judicial decisions, salaries, and jurisdictions have come under fire by ideologically charged congressional majorities, and concludes with an exploration of the consequences of confirmation conflict for the public's views of the federal bench.

4. See Spriggs and Wahlbeck (1995).
5. In his comment to this chapter, Wittes argues that the use of ideological terms to describe judges' behavior is "inherently impressionistic and, as such, of limited analytical value." Still, the analytical value of considering the ideological orientation of lower court judges is well established. See, most recently, Sunstein and others (2006). For a discussion of approaches to measuring judicial ideology, see Bailey (2007). Ideology, to be sure, does not explain all variation in appellate judges' decisionmaking.
6. Rehnquist (2005).
7. I recognize that my focus on judicial selection and judicial independence excludes other arenas where polarization may be consequential. For example, the movement of legislative parties to the extremes of the ideological spectrum may affect congressional responses to court decisions and could have an impact on interpretation of the broader separation of powers model, which guides the interaction of Congress, the president, and the courts. I leave these and other aspects of judicial-congressional interaction for the future.

Why Polarization Matters

The rise of polarized parties in Congress has encouraged several scholars to consider the consequences of this development. Some studies—most notably recent
works by Barbara Sinclair and by Thomas E. Mann and Norman J. Ornstein—
identify quite clearly the procedural consequences of polarization: partisan majorities, particularly in the House, tend to exploit the rules of the game to limit participation by the minority party.[8] Even in the Senate, where supermajority rules
may constrain the majority party to consider minority views, exclusion of the
minority party has occurred, for example, by denying minority-party members a
role in conference committees on measures important to the majority party's
agenda.

What is less clear from these studies, however, is whether the warping of process
has direct policy consequences. Mann and Ornstein give several important examples, arguing that "bad process leads to bad policy."[9] Sinclair offers caution in her
conclusions about policy consequences, noting the difficulty of making objective
judgments about what counts as "reasonable" legislation.[10] Other recent work on
polarization identifies clear consequences for economic policy, concluding that
"polarization accentuates gridlock."[11] Elsewhere, evaluating gridlock at the aggregate level, I have shown that the demise of the political center has increased the
level of policy stalemate over the past half-century.[12]

Perhaps the most explicit effort to test for the policy consequences of polarization is offered by David W. Brady, John Ferejohn, and Laurel Harbridge in this
volume.[13] Assessing several claims about the shape of policy outcomes when congressional political parties diverge ideologically and become more internally cohesive, their survey of recent, major legislation leads them to deduce that immoderate
policies are, in fact, quite often moderated to an outcome that can be supported
by the median legislator. The authors conclude that the rules of the game—
including supermajority requirements in the Senate—help stabilize policy outcomes at the center.

Could congressional rules also effectively prevent the confirmation of
immoderate nominees? If that is so, then polarization should not have discernible

8. See Mann and Ornstein (2006); Sinclair (2006). Also see Sinclair, chapter 2, in this volume.
9. Mann and Ornstein (2006, p. 13).
10. See Sinclair, chapter 2, in this volume.
11. McCarty, Poole, and Rosenthal (2006, p. 165).
12. See Binder (2003).
13. See chapter 5.

Figure 3-1. *Nominee Ideology in an Unpolarized Senate*

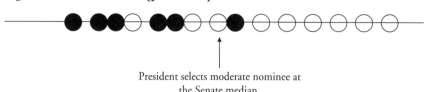

President selects moderate nominee at
the Senate median

consequences for the makeup of the federal bench. The potential for a filibuster and the need to attract the confirmation vote of the median senator might be sufficient to steer presidents to nominate centrist judges, even in periods of polarization. But if the dynamics of advice and consent actually make it quite difficult to prevent the confirmation of immoderate nominees, then polarization may have an impact on the makeup of the bench.

There is one striking difference in the process for appointees versus legislation: although bill proposals are subject to amendment, nominations confront senators with a single, dichotomous up-or-down vote to confirm. While legislative proposals offer opportunities for bargaining, negotiation, and compromise, nominations are not divisible. Although there is conceptually the potential for logrolling to secure senators' votes, on balance most nominations offer a take-it-or-leave-it proposition to senators who are sitting on the fence about whether to confirm. As discussed below, off-center majority parties can take advantage of the dichotomous nature of this kind of vote to secure confirmation of immoderate judges.

To understand how polarization theoretically affects the ideological tenor of judicial appointees, consider first a nonpolarized Senate: a chamber with two ideologically heterogeneous parties with little separation between the party medians (see figure 3-1). With a large bipartisan middle, even conservative or liberal presidents should appoint nominees who hail from the center of the political spectrum. Given that nominations are not divisible, it would be too costly for a president or his party to buy sufficient support for extreme nominees. Rather than propose an extreme nominee with little chance of securing his or her confirmation, a strategic president should appoint a nominee at the political center. As a result, in periods of low ideological polarization, we should see evidence that nominees are quite moderate. If so, nominees should attract support from across the ideological spectrum of the Senate, centered on the median senator.

By comparison, in periods of polarization, few legislators reside at the political center (see figure 3-2). In this context, presidents who are themselves distant from the center are much more likely to propose nominees who are out of the

Figure 3-2. *Nominee Ideology in a Polarized Senate*

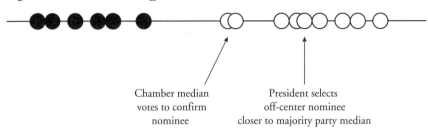

Chamber median   President selects
votes to confirm   off-center nominee
nominee   closer to majority party median

mainstream. With just a few moderate votes to secure, presidents can secure at rel-atively low cost the support of the median senator—even for a nominee who might be deemed by the median as ideologically off-center. The central reason is the dichotomous character of the confirmation vote. Unlike policy proposals that can be modified upon demand of a senator poised to filibuster, nominations are single events that pose a stark choice to moderates, particularly to those from the presi-dent's party: support a nominee, no matter how far from one's own ideological viewpoints, or accept the status quo of a vacant judgeship. Given partisan pressure to support the president and given the consequences of leaving federal judgeships vacant, moderate senators of the president's party should opt to vote for the nom-inee rather than accept the status quo.[14] That choice is all the more compelling when the existing bench is quite immoderate in the opposite direction, leading moderate senators to prefer the president's nominee to leaving the judgeship open.

If the dichotomous character of confirmation choices encourages moderates in a period of polarized parties to support off-center nominees, then the ideological makeup of confirmation coalitions in periods of polarized parties should look quite different than that of coalitions formed during periods of low polarization. In periods of low polarization, nominees should have broad support across the ide-ological spectrum. In periods of high polarization, support for the nominee should come predominantly from the president's side of the ideological median, with few senators on the opposite side voting to confirm. Polarization of Senate parties cre-ates the conditions under which off-center presidents are able to pull the courts to the right or left. In principle, these are testable conjectures, and empirical evi-dence is brought to bear on them below.

---

14. Senators from the opposition party, of course, often see the benefit of keeping judgeships vacant, particularly in the run-up to a presidential election when their party has a chance of regain-ing the White House (Binder and Maltzman 2002).

Although the discussion so far has focused almost exclusively on the interests of the median senator, other institutional forces may come to bear on the choice and fate of judicial nominations. In particular, two additional forces with potential veto powers over the selection of judicial nominees need to be considered: the senator able to sustain a filibuster (typically referred to as the "filibuster pivot") and the majority-party median. Each of these players is considered in turn.

A confirmation vote is technically a motion for the Senate to "advise and consent" to a particular nominee. Because the Senate's formal rules governing executive session dictate that this motion is debatable, the motion may be subject to a filibuster. In the face of concerted opposition, judicial nominees in theory require the support of sixty senators—the number necessary to invoke cloture on the motion and thus bring the Senate to an up-or-down vote on confirmation. Pivotal politics models of Congress (which are typically applied to the selection of policy choices rather than appointments) would imply that the nominee must be acceptable to the sixtieth senator, or else the nominee is likely to be filibustered. Extended debate by Democrats over President George W. Bush's judicial nominations in the 108th and 109th Congress (2003–06) did occur, bringing the Senate to a boiling point over the majority leader's threat in 2005 to "go nuclear" by creating a new precedent against judicial filibusters.

One might conclude that presidents are usually careful to select nominees who will pass muster with the filibuster pivot. However, it has not been unusual in recent contests over Supreme Court nominations for confirmation to occur with less than sixty votes (for example, the confirmation votes on Clarence Thomas in 1991 and Samuel Alito in 2006). Moreover, over the past decade, lower federal court nominees also have been confirmed with less than sixty votes.

Given that nominations do not lend themselves to compromise, a senator considering a filibuster faces a choice between confirming the nominee or maintaining the status quo (that is, the existing court lineup before the appointment is filled). Opposing a nominee and sustaining a filibuster in that context might be too costly for senators, leading them to vote for nominees they might oppose on policy grounds. The low salience of many nominations—even to the courts of appeals—also limits senators' appetite for sustaining a coalition to block cloture. In other words, although it is possible that Senate Rule XXII raises the bar for confirmation, it is not clear whether senators will always pursue that strategy. The question explored below is whether policy differences between the two parties—coupled with the increasing role of the federal courts in resolving controversial issues of salience to the parties—fuel senators' interest in blocking nominees appointed by the other party's president. If so, polarization should lower the likelihood of confirmation, even for appellate court nominees.

The fate of nominees is also potentially shaped by partisan control of the White House and Senate since the majority party controls access to the Senate's Executive Session—the procedural domain in which nominations and other executive business are considered by the full Senate. Because the motion to go into executive session is not debatable, the majority party leader (who enjoys the right of first recognition) wields control over the executive session agenda. In periods of unified party control, this simply means that nominees approved by the Senate Judiciary Committee should be swiftly called up by the president's party and brought to a vote in executive session. In periods of divided control, in contrast, the opposition party controls the agenda of the judiciary panel, as well as access to executive session. If off-center presidents are more likely to nominate out-of-the-mainstream nominees in periods of polarized parties, then we should expect to see the majority party in a period of both divided government and polarization proceed more cautiously in considering the president's nominees. Faced with the option of supporting the president's extreme nominees or dragging its feet on confirmation, majority-party senators might reasonably conclude that the costs of confirming an off-center judge are too great to bear. Thus, in periods of divided government with polarized parties, majorities might exercise their control over the executive session agenda to block nominees deemed too conservative or too liberal. Off-center presidents in polarized times may have a strong incentive to nominate immoderate judges, but in periods of divided government, the prospect of confirmation would decline for such nominees.

If polarization affects the dynamics of advice and consent, a number of patterns should be visible over the course of the past several decades as the parties' ideological centers have diverged in the Senate. First, at the individual level of the nominee, we should find a stark ideological difference in the confirmation coalitions supporting nominees in periods of low polarization versus periods of high polarization. Using the voting coalition as a proxy for the nominee's ideological predilection, we should see nominees broadly reflective of the median voter in less polarized Congresses and nominees more reflective of the right or left in periods of high polarization—subject to the caveat that we may be less likely to observe confirmation votes on extreme nominees during periods of divided government.

Second, if such differences are visible at the individual level, then several patterns in the ideological bent of nominees should be detectable at the aggregate level. In particular, we should find a relationship between the degree of polarization in the Senate and the average ideological position of all nominees in a given

Congress. We might also find that ideologically extreme nominees are less common in periods of divided government, since the party in opposition to the president, if it controls the Senate, should be reluctant to bring off-center nominees to the Senate floor.

Third, confirmation rates for federal judges should vary with changes in ideological polarization. As ideological differences between the Senate majority party and the president grow, confirmation rates should decline. Confirmation rates should also decline in periods of divided government, as the majority party (regardless of its preferences) should more cautiously grant access to the executive session when their party does not control the White House. Finally, we should find an interactive effect between polarization and divided government, with more aggressive gatekeeping by the opposition party when the ideological stakes of confirming presidential appointees are greater. Overall, then, we should expect to find that polarization has discernible effects on the appointment and ideological tenor of new federal judges.

The Impact of Polarization on Advice and Consent

The impact of polarization on judicial selection can be explored by bringing evidence to bear from the roll call record of the Senate in executive session from 1947 through 2006. In the discussion that follows, I present results from two different data sets on advice and consent. First, I compile confirmation statistics for all nominations to the federal courts of appeal over the postwar period, using data culled from the final editions of the Senate Judiciary Committee's *Legislative and Executive Calendar* for each Congress.[15] Second, I compile senators' roll call votes on all judicial nominations to the U.S. Courts of Appeals over the postwar period. Because roll call votes to confirm federal judges did not become the norm until Republicans made such votes de rigueur in 1997, I add observations for unanimous voice votes to confirm nominees over the entire period.

Polarization and Likelihood of Confirmation

Figure 3-3 shows the pattern of confirmation success over the past fifty years. As observers of the process have speculated, the practice of advice and consent has fallen on hard times over the past decades: there has been a steady decline in confirmation rates since the 1970s. Roughly 90 percent of appellate court nominees

15. For details on the data collection, see Binder and Maltzman (2002).

Figure 3-3. *Confirmation Rates for Nominees to the U.S. Court of Appeals,*
1947–2006

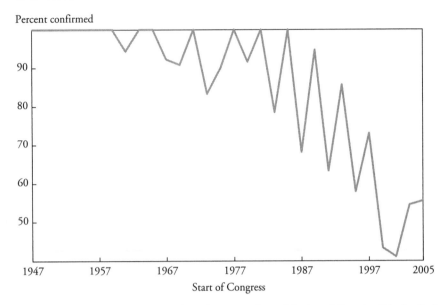

Percent confirmed

Start of Congress

Sources: U.S. Senate, Committee on the Judiciary, *Legislative Calendar* and *Executive Calendar,* final editions (80th–108th Congresses); U.S. Department of Justice, Office of Legal Policy, "109th Congress–Judicial Nominations" (www.usdoj.gov/olp/nominations109.htm).

were confirmed in the 1970s, but roughly half have been confirmed during the George W. Bush administration. Still low confirmation rates are not unique to the modern Senate. Confirmation rates dipped to 60 percent in the 62nd Congress (1911–12) and 58 percent in the 72nd Congress (1931–32)—both instances in which Democrats favored keeping judgeships vacant to save the appointments for a Democratic president.[16]

Does partisan polarization drive down confirmation rates? If the two political parties differ strongly on the fit of nominees for the federal bench—and if the courts are active players on issues that divide the parties—then we would expect stiffer opposition to presidential appointees when the differences between the parties are greater. As shown in the first column of Table 3-1, confirmation rates for appellate court nominees in the postwar period drop as the degree of polarization

16. Confirmation rates for appellate court nominees before 1947 are determined from annual volumes of the *Senate Executive Session Journal.*

Table 3-1. *Polarization and Confirmation Failure, 1947–2006*[a]
Units as indicated

Variable	Coefficient (1)	Coefficient (2)	Change in simulated failure rate (percent)[b]
Polarization	1.142***	1.075***	+30
	(.122)	(.099)	
Divided government	.081**		+15
	(.030)		
Divided government * polarization		.151**	
		(.044)	
Constant	−.592***	−.557***	
	(.079)	(.065)	
N	30	30	
F test	43.91***	59.36***	

Source: Author's calculations.
***$p < 0.001$, **$p < 0.01$ (both one-tailed tests).
a. Ordinary least squares regression coefficients; Newey-West standard errors are shown in parentheses. Simulated failure rate change calculated as polarization rises from one standard deviation below to one standard deviation above mean polarization (assuming divided government) and as party control changes from unified to divided (assuming mean polarization).
b. For the model estimated in column 1.

rises.[17] The relationship holds even after controlling for party control: as expected, divided party control of the Senate and the White House drives down the likelihood of confirmation as the opposition party takes advantage of its control of the Judiciary Committee and the executive session agenda to block nominees they oppose. Moreover, as shown in the second column of table 3-1, polarization especially matters in periods of divided government. Given that most disputes over nominees have tended to center on their policy views, opposition parties appear to exploit their control of Senate rules and practices to limit the president's ability to place nominees on the federal bench in times of deep polarization.

The substantive impact of polarization is shown in the third column of table 3-1 for the model estimated in the first column. If one assumes a period of divided government and varies the level of polarization by one standard deviation above and below the mean polarization level, the predicted rejection rate for appellate

17. The results are robust to a number of different specifications, including grouped logit and Poisson estimation. For presentational ease, table 3-1 displays the results of an ordinary least squares regression, using Newey-West standard errors to control for the possibility of serial autocorrelation over the course of the time series (at a one-Congress lag). All models estimated using Stata Version 9.2, StataCorp, College Station, Tex.

nominees in a period of low polarization is just 10 percent. In contrast, the predicted rejection rate rises to 40 percent in a period of high polarization. Change in party control also has a substantive effect on the likely rejection rate, albeit with much diminished force. Assuming a mean level of polarization, the predicted rejection rate for appellate nominees is 10 percent in a period of unified control, rising to 25 percent when control is divided between the parties. The makeup of the political parties, as well as their leverage over the agenda of the Senate, clearly alters the dynamics of advice and consent.

These results are, of course, subject to a caution against over-attributing causal effects to polarization, given that other changes in the political environment were also occurring in the postwar period. The most important of these changes was the advent of a more activist bench, as contentious social and regulatory issues (for example, abortion and race relations) became litigated in the courts. Ideological polarization of the political parties should only affect advice and consent politics if the parties have sufficient incentive to care about who sits on the bench.

That said, it is important to keep in mind that the Supreme Court's entry into controversial policy areas is often dated to the 1950s, with the Warren Court's *Brown* v. *Board of Education* decision.[18] Yet the steep decline in confirmation rates does not begin until the 1980s, a period well after the court's initial involvement in controversial issues. Polarization of the parties—which emerges in earnest in the 1980s—seems to be a critical factor in explaining confirmation conflict. Moreover, presidents' executive branch nominees also begin to encounter tough confirmations at roughly the same time, as numerous scholars have shown.[19] This also suggests that differences between the parties over the ideological tenor of policy and its implementation by the executive branch, as well as its interpretation by the courts, were critical in reshaping advice and consent politics in the Senate over this period.

Polarization and the Ideology of Nominees

Does polarization also affect the types of nominees selected by the president? The conjectures above suggest that presidents are more likely to nominate moderate judges when a large political center thrives in the Senate, even when the president himself might prefer an off-center nominee. To deviate too far from the views of the median senator would be too costly for a president seeking to secure confirmation of favored nominees. In contrast, periods of polarization—leaving few moderate senators in the center—are likely to encourage off-center presidents to

18. Wittes (2006).
19. See McCarty and Razaghian (1999); MacKenzie (2001).

select more immoderate judges, since the remaining moderates would face a stark choice between voting for the president's nominee (however extreme) or keeping the seat vacant.

To test these conjectures about polarization and nominee ideology, consider a simple comparison of the coalitions supporting confirmation in two different contexts—a period of low polarization in 1980 and a period of high polarization in 2005. If polarization is measured as the ideological distance in each Congress between the mean Democratic senator and the mean Republican senator (along a range of −1 for the most liberal senator to +1 for most conservative), polarization averages about 0.61 over the postwar period from 1947 to 2006.[20] In the 96th Congress (1979–80), polarization stood at 0.55, roughly one standard deviation below the mean polarization for the postwar period. In the 109th Congress (2005–06), polarization measured 0.982, more than one standard deviation above the mean level of polarization. Unified party control reigned in both Congresses, meaning that we cannot attribute differences in the confirmation coalitions to the opposing parties' differences of opinion about suitable nominees.

Consider first the coalition of senators in 1980 that voted in favor of confirming Stephen Breyer as President Jimmy Carter's nominee to the First Circuit Court of Appeals. Breyer was confirmed by a Democratic Congress, 80-10. As shown in Figure 3-4, Breyer secured the support of senators from across the ideological spectrum, including both liberal Democrats and conservative Republicans. The ideological character of the confirmation coalition—and thus, arguably, the anticipated ideological stance of the new judge—can be captured more precisely by calculating for all of the senators voting to confirm the ideological distance of each senator from the chamber median for that Congress. The better a nominee reflects the center of the Senate's ideological spectrum, the closer that nominee's score will be to zero. We can infer that positive or negative scores reflect nominees who are, respectively, more conservative or more liberal than the political center.

Breyer's confirmation coalition score was 0.036, indicating that the senators who supported his confirmation were almost neatly arrayed on both sides of the chamber median. Given the low polarization that characterized this Congress, we should not be surprised to find that nine of the ten Democratic senators to the right of the chamber median supported confirmation, and thirty out of the thirty-nine Republican senators to the right of the median also voted to confirm a Democratic president's nominee.

20. Ideological scores are based on McCarty, Poole and Rosenthal's DW-nominate scores (first dimension). Senators' scores and party means can be found online at www.voteview.com.

Figure 3-4. *Senators Voting to Confirm Stephen Breyer to the First Circuit Court of Appeals, 1980*[a]

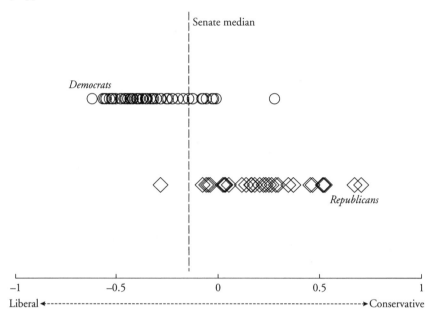

Source: DW-nominate scores from voteview.com.
a. The confirmation vote on Breyer's nomination was held during the 96th Congress on December 9, 1980.

In contrast, consider the coalition of senators that supported the confirmation of Janice Rogers Brown to the D.C. Circuit Court of Appeals in 2005 during a period of unified Republican control. As can be seen in figure 3-5, Brown's confirmation coalition is decidedly off-center to the right, scoring a 0.276. What is striking, however, are the votes of the three moderate Republicans who voted to confirm Brown, even though their ideological views place them on the opposite side of the chamber median from their Republican colleagues.

Why would these Republican moderates support a nominee who appears to be so out of step ideologically? Given the dichotomous choice of voting to invoke cloture or maintaining the status quo of a vacant judgeship, the lone moderates voted to confirm an extreme nominee appointed by their own party's president. Because nominations offer limited opportunity for bargaining, centrist legislators lack the ability to moderate a president's choices, in this case eventually allowing President Bush to put an off-center nominee on the bench. In Breyer's case, there were so many centrist senators that President Carter and the governing Demo-

Figure 3-5. *Senators Voting to Confirm Janice Rogers Brown to the D.C. Circuit Court of Appeals, 2005*

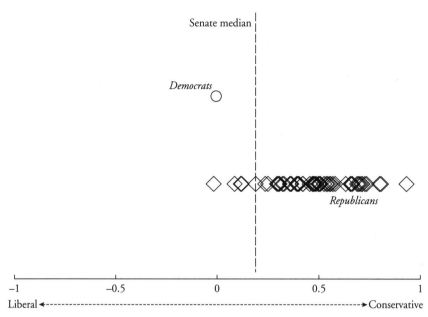

Source: DW-nominate scores from voteview.com.
a. The vote to confirm Brown's nomination was held during the 109th Congress on June 5, 2005.

crats were unlikely to have been able to buy sufficient support from those centrist legislators to secure confirmation of a more liberal nominee—even in a period of unified party control. The dichotomous character of the vote, combined with the difference in polarization across the two periods, helps to account for the confirmation of extreme nominees in the absence of a strong political center.

One might object to the comparison of Breyer's and Brown's confirmation coalitions on the grounds that twenty-five years passed between the two votes, coinciding with the period in which polarization has altered the dynamics of the confirmation process. As Benjamin Wittes of the Brookings Institution argues, "We have no way of knowing whether a Breyer confirmation in 2005 would have looked a lot more like Brown's."[21] Fortunately, we can test this counterfactual scenario by calculating the confirmation coalition score for the Senate vote on Breyer's appointment to the Supreme Court in 1994. The average distance from the Senate median of Breyer's supporters was 0.055, allowing us to

21. See his comment to this chapter.

infer Breyer's moderate character from his confirmation vote, even in a period of polarized parties.[22]

Breyer and Brown were just two of more than 500 appellate court nominees considered by the Senate from 1947 to 2006.[23] If polarization systematically encourages more partisan presidents to consider off-center nominees, then over the course of this period, a broader pattern in the ideological character of judicial nominees should be detectable. For each president's nominees, I calculate an average confirmation coalition score across all votes on that president's nominees (coding voice votes as unanimous votes). Because I am interested in whether presidents are able to secure off-center nominees as polarization increases (as opposed to knowing whether nominees are, on average, to the left or to the right of the center), I take the absolute value of the average confirmation coalition score for each president. Finally, because majority parties in periods of divided government may exercise their gatekeeping over executive session to keep consideration of extreme nominees off the floor, I calculate separate average confirmation coalition scores for each party regime for each president. For example, I calculate separate confirmation coalition scores for Bush nominees considered in periods of divided control (2001–02) and unified control (2003–06).

Figure 3-6 shows the average extremity of the confirmation coalitions during each presidential administration and associated party regime from 1947 through 2006. Given that more extreme coalitions suggest that nominees are perceived to be more off-center, a striking trend emerges: the average nomination to the federal courts is increasingly likely to be off-center over the course of the postwar period. The largest increase in coalition extremity occurred during the Clinton administration when Republicans held the Senate between 1995 and 2000, and during the Bush administration when Republicans again controlled the Senate from 2003 to 2006.[24] Overall, the correlation between polarization and coalition

22. Wittes is certainly correct that we do not know what would have happened to Breyer had he been nominated for an appellate court judgeship in 2005. Nevertheless, given that Supreme Court nominations typically receive more scrutiny than appellate court nominations, a reasonable inference is that Breyer would again attract support from across the ideological spectrum, even in a period of polarized parties and contentious confirmation contests.

23. Roll call votes on confirmations are available at voteview.com.

24. In his comment to this chapter, Wittes asks why President Ronald Reagan's appointees seem so moderate given his campaign to appoint more conservative judges. Because recorded votes were not routinely called for on confirmation votes until 1997, most confirmation votes in the Reagan era were by voice vote. The average confirmation coalition score across all recorded (nonvoice) votes on Reagan appointees was 0.11, on par with the average coalition scores for both subsequent Republican presidents and suggesting the right-of-center character of judges appointed by Republican presidents in the contemporary era.

Figure 3-6. *Average Ideological Extremity of Senators Voting to Confirm, 1947–2006*[a]

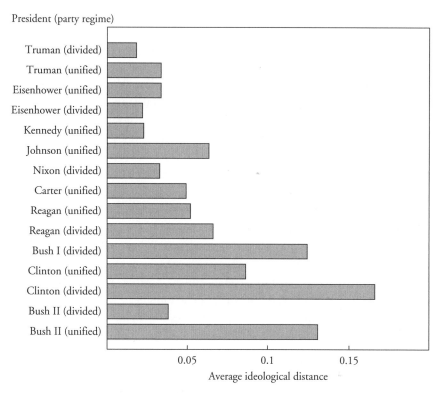

President (party regime)

Average ideological distance

Sources: Roll call votes were obtained from www.voteview.com. Voice votes on nominations determined from U.S. Senate, Committee on the Judiciary, *Legislative Calendar* and *Executive Calendar,* final editions (80th–109th Congresses).

a. The bars show the average ideological distance from the Senate median of those senators voting in favor of confirmation, averaged over all confirmation votes for each president-party regime. Voice votes treated as unanimous votes for confirmation.

extremity is positive and significant, suggesting that as the political center disappears, confirmation coalitions move off-center—at least in part reflecting the perceived ideological character of the presidents' nominees.

The pattern of coalition scores in the second Bush administration merits some more attention. In the 107th Congress (2001–02), a period of divided government with Democrats taking over control of the chamber and its committees in June 2001, it appears that nominees well reflected median Senate interests. In fact, the president nominated quite a few noncentrist candidates, whom Democrats proceeded to block in the Judiciary Committee. By and large, only those nominees deemed by Democrats to be within the mainstream were allowed to secure a confirmation vote on the floor. The result is an average confirmation coalition score for the Congress more reminiscent of the 1950s and 1960s than the 1990s. In contrast, unified Republican control in the 108th and 109th Congress (2003–06) facilitated Senate confirmation votes on more extreme nominees. Although some failed to secure cloture, the few remaining moderate Republican senators typically provided the votes for off-center nominees preferred by President Bush. As a result, the average confirmation coalition score grew markedly to 0.13, significantly higher than the mean extremity of the voting coalitions over the postwar period (0.016). Although centrists may moderate policy outcomes in periods of polarization, the vote choice confronting centrists in confirming federal judges makes feasible the appointment of immoderate judges in a polarized era.

A note of caution is in order in making sense of these confirmation coalition scores. Having a direct measure of nominee ideology would be ideal, but there is no reliable and valid way to systematically capture and compare the policy views of potential judges over time on a fixed spatial map. What can be done instead is to capture the ideological balance of senators voting to confirm a nominee. It is possible, of course, that senators' tolerance for opposition party nominees has declined over time. If so, even centrist nominees might be confirmed with off-center support in a period of polarized parties—leading to the same rising extremity of confirmation coalitions shown in figure 3-6. Of course, that does still beg the question of why tolerance of the other party's nominees would have declined, and one might reasonably conclude that senatorial intolerance for the opposing party's nominees is itself a function of polarization. Moreover, one is left with the puzzle of why candidates nominated in the same Congress for the same circuit might attract vastly different ideological support across the Senate.[25] Surely these voting coalitions must to some degree tap variation in how senators perceive the nominees' ideological orientations. This is an imperfect measure of nominee ideology for sure, but we can still confidently infer that polarization has left its mark on the politics of advice and consent.

25. Compare for example the confirmation coalition score for Consuelo Maria Callahan (–0.07) to that of Carolyn Kuhl (0.282), both women nominated by President George W. Bush to the Ninth Circuit Court of Appeals in the winter of 2003. Callahan was confirmed; Kuhl's nomination failed to secure cloture.

Second-Order Effects of Polarization

Notwithstanding the direct effects of polarization on confirmation rates and nominee ideology over the course of the postwar period, is polarization truly *consequential* for the federal courts? Are there additional effects of polarization that may raise the stakes for the judiciary? This section considers the consequences of a more contentious practice of advice and consent and explores the plausible effects of intense ideological conflict over who sits on the bench. Moreover, criticism of nominees and judges, I argue, exposes the courts to conflict and risks undermining the norm of independent courts.

Scholars have carefully delineated the impact of criticism on the president and his approval ratings. As political scientist Richard Brody has shown, the "rally-around-the-flag" phenomenon in times of crisis is less a matter of intense American patriotism than a consequence of diminished criticism of the president in such times.[26] When criticism is diminished, Americans rally around the flag, which in turn yields strong approval ratings for the president. Once the crisis recedes, other players begin to criticize the president and approval recedes. It seems quite conceivable that the nearly uniform high approval registered by the public for the federal judiciary is, in large part, a consequence of the traditional norm of judicial independence. Elites are quite typically reluctant to criticize the courts—most notably the judges of the lower federal bench—helping to sustain high approval rates of the judiciary.

But what happens when nominees and judges become the target of a party's criticism for their policy views or for their decisions on the bench? It seems quite plausible that the public's views of the bench are affected by elite debate about the courts. The heated public discourse about the Supreme Court's *Bush* v. *Gore* decision in 2000, for example, negatively affected views about the court as an institution among supporters of Al Gore.[27] However, when the media portray the Supreme Court as following legal principles, rather than engaging in the more political process of bargaining, that helps to sustain public confidence in the high court.[28]

Given the increased conflict over lower court nominees and judges over the past decade, might polarized debate over the makeup of the lower federal bench affect

26. Brody (1991).
27. See Price and Romantan (2004).
28. Baird and Gangl (2006).

the public's views of judges and the courts? Initial findings from a survey experiment incorporated into the Collaborative Congressional Election Study in the fall of 2006 strongly suggest that the public's trust in judges and the courts is far more conditional than is commonly believed.[29] In the online survey, a thousand respondents were divided into six groups. Four of the groups varied in terms of what they were told about which president (George W. Bush or Bill Clinton) appointed a fictitious federal judge (Judge Jones) and the circumstances under which he was confirmed (unanimous versus closely contested). The remaining two groups were not told which president nominated Judge Jones, but each was given different version of his confirmation circumstances.

All six groups were presented with the following scenario. Federal Judge Ralph Jones recently struck down a law that prohibited the sale of guns within one mile of any school. In the ruling, Jones argued that "although protecting children from firearms may be a justified policy, under the Constitution, Congress does not have the right to mandate local zoning codes." Respondents were then asked three questions: did they agree with Judge Jones' opinion in the case; to what degree did they trust Judge Jones to make decisions that are right for the country as a whole; and to what degree did they trust and have confidence in the federal judiciary?[30]

The results presented in table 3-2 are quite striking: they show that for two of the three groups of respondents, confirmation conflict had a strong negative impact on their appraisal of the judge and his decisions. Because the decision might be viewed as anti–gun control, it may not be surprising that Republicans' views of Jones's opinion do not seem to be affected by exposure to information about confirmation conflict. Individuals who might oppose gun control are arguably more likely to identify with the Republican Party. Thus, the Republicans' views on the subject might have been strong enough to resist any impact of confirmation conflict. In fact, confirmation conflict—perhaps a signal to anti–gun control Republicans that this judge was worth fighting for—boosts Republicans' trust in Jones's decisionmaking. Democrats, on the other hand, show lower levels of enthusiasm for Judge Jones's decision, and those exposed to confirmation conflict harbor even dimmer views of the judge's decision and significantly lower trust in him.

29. For a detailed description of the survey, see web.mit.edu/polisci/portl/cces. The experiment was designed with Forrest Maltzman of George Washington University.

30. In the cross-tabulations shown in table 3-2, trust in Judge Jones is recoded into a dichotomous variable: 1 represents individuals who "strongly agree" or "agree" that Judge Jones can be trusted to make decisions that are right for the country as a whole; 0 represents those who "disagree" or "disagree strongly" that Judge Jones can be trusted.

Table 3-2. *Respondents' Views of Judge Jones*[a]
Percent

Party affiliation	Agree with Jones's decision[b]		Trust Jones[c]	
	Unanimous vote	Contested vote[d]	Unanimous vote	Contested vote
Democrat	58	53	40	29
Republican	75	76	56	69
Independent	70	60	63	40

Source: Collaborative Congressional Election Study, George Washington University Module, 2006. See web.mit.edu/polisci/portl/cces.

a. The sample size for each question is less than 1,000 either because respondents did not answer the question or because they expressed a neutral opinion on the judge.

b. $N = 670$.

c. $N = 303$.

d. Contested vote, 53-47.

Most striking are the reactions of self-professed independents. Although their support for the judge is generally high, independents exposed to confirmation conflict drop 10 percentage points in their tendency to agree with Judge Jones's decision and over 20 points in their trust in Jones. This suggests that contested confirmation votes send a signal to independents, a signal that is interpreted as a warning about the judge's decisions—whether the signal is interpreted as a sign of partisanship, immoderation, or just plain old unsound decisionmaking. In contrast, independents exposed to a signal of unanimous support for the judge likely infer moderation from the bipartisan character of the Senate vote. Collectively, these experimental results suggest that citizens' views of judges and their decisions are shaped by what they know about a judge's pathway to and decisions from the bench. Confirmation conflict, which appears to stem directly from polarized parties' disagreements over the policy issues before the courts, also appears to shape the public's trust in the bench. Support of those inclined against the judge on policy grounds appears to drop significantly in the face of advice and consent heat.

Congressional Attacks on the Judiciary

Beyond debates over judicial selection, how has partisan debate about the courts unfolded? There is ample evidence that the conservative majorities in Congress over the past decade have stepped up their attacks on federal judges. The Terri Schiavo case is certainly the best known example, as conservative Republicans led by then majority leader Tom DeLay criticized the federal judges who opposed intervening in the state battle over removing Schiavo's feeding tube. As DeLay

stated on the day Schiavo passed away, "The time will come for the men responsible for this to answer for their behavior," suggesting that impeachment proceedings against the judges might be warranted on account of their judicial
decisions.[31]

But attacks on federal judges extend far beyond—and much deeper—than the
Schiavo case. First, Congress has increasingly used its legislative power to strip the
federal courts of selected jurisdiction. These jurisdiction-stripping provisions typically prevent judicial review of particular administrative decisions. For example,
a spending bill in 2002 prevented the courts from reviewing Agriculture Department decisions about forest thinning in certain Colorado forests.[32] As Figure 3-7
suggests, the number of jurisdiction-stripping laws enacted by each Congress has
increased over the past half-century, roughly tracking the degree of partisan polarization. Although it would be preferable to control for a range of court-related factors that might affect Congress's interest in stripping jurisdiction, it seems quite
plausible that partisan differences over the courts could prompt an aggressive
majority to pursue opportunities to remove court review. Certainly some of the
most contentious issues dividing the parties have been the target of congressional
Republicans' recent efforts to strip jurisdiction from the courts.[33]

Second, in 2003 Congress enacted the PROTECT Act, an anticrime measure
intended to bolster the government's ability to investigate and prosecute those
responsible for violence against children. Embedded in the act was a provision limiting judges' ability to depart downward from federal sentencing guidelines for
crimes against children. The act also required the Department of Justice to report
to Congress any sentencing guideline departures by individual federal judges.
Rehnquist observed at the time that the provisions "could appear to be an un-
warranted and ill-considered effort to intimidate individual judges in the performance of their judicial duties."[34]

Third, although the provisions of the PROTECT Act affecting sentencing
guidelines were essentially made moot by the Supreme Court's 2005 decision that
made the guidelines advisory rather than binding, efforts by conservative Repub-

31. Ted Barrett and Ed Henry, "DeLay Apologizes for Comment about Judges," CNN.com, May
28, 2005 (www.cnn.com/2005/POLITICS/04/13/delay.apology).
32. See Chutkow (2006).
33. Some such efforts have failed, such as the move to bar the courts from reviewing constitutional challenges to the Pledge of Allegiance and to the House-passed Defense of Marriage Act.
Others have thus far succeeded, such as the move in the Military Commissions Act of 2006 to bar
detainees at Guantanamo Bay from challenging their detention in federal court.
34. Rehnquist (2004).

Figure 3-7. *Jurisdiction Stripping by Congress, 1947–2004*

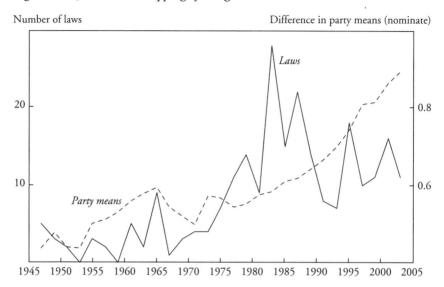

Number of laws   Difference in party means (nominate)

Source: Data on the number of laws enacted each Congress appears in Chutkow (2006, appendix p. 19). Difference in party means is based on DW-nominate scores from www.voteview.com.

licans to aggressively oversee federal judges' sentencing decisions continued while they held control of the House. Most notably, Representative James Sensenbrenner (R-Wisc.), chairman of the House Judiciary Committee in the 109th Congress (2005–06), tried to force a Seventh Circuit Court of Appeals judge to change his panel's sentencing decision because Sensenbrenner believed it was not harsh enough.[35]

Polarization has, at least indirectly, made possible such congressional intrusion into judicial affairs. This indirect effect was observable in the process used to secure enactment of the PROTECT Act's provisions. Majority-party efforts to limit minority-party participation and floor deliberation—a direct consequence of polarized parties in the House—played a major role in allowing the measure's sponsors to circumvent opposition from Democrats and from the Senate.[36] Majority-party leaders used their control over the House Rules Committee—and

35. See Maurice Possley, "Lawmaker Prods Court, Raises Brows," *Chicago Tribune*, July 10, 2005.
36. See "2003 Legislative Summary: Crimes against Children," *CQ Weekly*, December 13, 2003.

thus their ability to shape the floor agenda—in two consequential ways. First, committee and party leaders limited consideration of any amendments that would have challenged the sentencing provisions, which were themselves offered as a floor amendment. Second, and probably more important, they packaged the controversial provisions with broadly popular measures to combat child pornography and violence against children. The original Senate bill had been a stand-alone effort to expand the use of AMBER alerts after the March 2003 rescue of Elizabeth Smart, a Utah teenager who had been abducted nine months before. Once the controversial judicial provisions were packaged with popular anticrime measures, opponents of the provisions were essentially left with no choice but to vote in favor of protecting kids from violence. Chief Justice Rehnquist's pointed remarks about those provisions are strong evidence that polarization has had troubling consequences for judicial independence. Bad process in this case does seem to have produced bad policy.

Stalemate over Judges' Pay

Beyond attacks on judicial independence, do party differences have a broader impact on Congress's interactions with the federal courts? One likely indication is the stalemate over judicial pay that has resulted in the erosion of judges' salaries.[37] Since enactment of a major congressional ethics and congressional pay package in 1989, increases in judges' pay have been linked to increases in congressional salaries. On several occasions over the past decade, Congress has prevented a cost-of-living adjustment (COLA) for judges when it has acted to block its own pay raises. Even if Congress were to grant itself a COLA (and, thus, a COLA for judges), a 1981 law made salary increases for Article III judges contingent on explicit congressional authorization. In other words, Congress requires an affirmative vote to waive what is known as section 140 in order for judges to receive any increases in their pay.[38] Given the erosion in the value of judicial salaries over the past decades, Chief Justice John Roberts, in his first year-end report on the judiciary, lobbied Congress for a major increase in judges' salaries, as Chief Justice Rehnquist had done for many years before him.[39]

Could congressional reluctance to raise judges' pay flow from ideological disputes over the proper role of federal judges and their judicial actions? It is tough

---

37. The history and politics of judicial pay are explored in Wheeler and Greve (2007).
38. Gressle (2003).
39. Roberts (2006).

to draw such a direct connection between the two, as Congress certainly has an incentive to reduce the traceability of its votes to raise its members' pay. Thus it is hardly surprising that in 1989 Congress moved to link all federal salaries to provide some cover when it came to raising members' own pay. But Congress has gone out of its way to make it even more difficult to raise judges' pay: in 2001 Congress made section 140 permanent after the provision had been challenged in a federal suit by a cohort of federal judges. Congressional ire toward raising judicial salaries might be a reflection of the preferences of conservative Republicans, given their animosity toward activist judges, rather than a reflection of the stalemate that often emerges between polarized parties. Still, numerous members from both sides of the aisle have advocated reforming the process for raising judges' pay, but such centrist proposals have made little headway over the past several years. The reluctance of an off-center majority to raise the pay of judges it at times derides as activist certainly suggests that partisan polarization has an indirect impact on the federal bench.

Conclusions

In his "2004 Year-End Report on the Federal Judiciary," Chief Justice William Rehnquist bemoaned what he perceived to be a dramatic increase in congressional criticism of federal judges. Although he recognized that "criticism of judges and judicial decisions is as old as our republic," Rehnquist warned that criticizing judges for their judicial acts puts at risk the courts' ability to "command sufficient public respect to enable them to survive basic attacks on . . . judicial independence."[40] Rehnquist's conservatism and Republican pedigree give him credibility, as it were, to declare such criticism by off-center legislators as breaching the line of acceptable congressional behavior with respect to the courts.

Leaving aside such debates over congressional treatment of the courts, it does seem incontrovertible that partisan polarization has seeped into elite debates and behavior over both the composition and the role of the federal courts. Attacks by House Republicans on judges and their decisions, the refusal to bring judicial pay in line with professional salaries, and intense, partisan debates over presidential nominations to the federal bench—these and other trends have eroded the norm of judicial independence under which judges are granted the room to decide legal and political questions without fear of retribution from Congress. Public

40. Rehnquist (2005).

awareness of the stakes associated with new court appointments is surely valuable. But partisan conflict over the views and values of potential new judges risks the creation of a partisan and far less legitimate judiciary.

Are correctives in order for judicial selection that might prevent the seepage of partisanship into the politics of advice and consent? If so, what reforms would be desirable? Some advocate a formal move to require supermajorities for confirmation of lower court nominees. The basic premise of this reform is a sound one: if supermajorities are required for confirmation, then presidents should be unable to place ideologues on the bench. Requiring support from across the ideological spectrum makes confirmation of off-center judges less likely (except in times of very oversized Senate majorities). My hunch, however, is that the unintended consequence of requiring supermajorities for confirmation would be an increase in the likelihood of gridlock in the appointment of federal judges. Rather than encouraging nomination of centrist judges, supermajority rules might still give presidents the incentive to nominate off-center candidates and then to blame the opposition party for blocking confirmation. As long as the federal courts remain a central venue for contests over issues of importance to the parties, activists on both ends of the ideological spectrum will have an incentive to exploit the practices of advice and consent for party purposes.

To address the proclivity of presidents to nominate immoderate candidates during periods of polarization, it makes some sense to explore reforms of the selection process rather than reforms of the confirmation process.[41] Some states have experimented with bipartisan selection commissions as a way of generating a list of judicial candidates acceptable to legal and political elites in both parties at the state level. Presumably centrist candidates have an edge over more ideological candidates. If so (and this remains to be evaluated), then encouraging senators to set up bipartisan selection commissions and encouraging the president to choose from among those recommended candidates would go a long way toward depolarizing judicial selection in the Senate. And how might presidents be encouraged to select nominees from such commissions? One solution would be to grant such nominees a confirmation "fast track," barring judicial filibuster and ensuring a reasonably expeditious up-or-down vote on the Senate floor. Linkage of selection and confirmation incentives might allow moderate judges to be confirmed without formalizing new supermajority requirements for advice and consent.

---

41. The following discussion of selection reforms is drawn from Maltzman (2005).

Do legislators care enough about judicial independence to reform judicial selection? Ultimately, legislators are unlikely to give up their efforts to mold the courts to their party's advantage as long as the courts remain central policymakers in the political system, the parties remain deeply opposed over key policies, and Senate rules and practices allocate veto rights across the chamber. Perhaps the vociferous reaction by conservative Chief Justices Rehnquist and Roberts to congressional attacks on the courts will be sufficient to dampen efforts to hold judges accountable for their acts in office. If not, intense partisan criticism of federal judges may undermine the public's views about the courts—to the perhaps lasting detriment of the unelected branch.

Comments on Chapter Three

COMMENT

Martin Shapiro

Judicial nomination politics, particularly relating to Supreme Court nominations, present a grave challenge for social science analysis, one which Sarah Binder has accepted with some success. The challenge has a number of dimensions. First, the total number of cases is small and spread over a long period of time during which all sorts of variables intervene. Second, sequencing may be a key variable, rendering each nomination unique or noncomparable on a crucial dimension. Whom the president nominated last and what happened to that nomination may be a key factor in whom he nominates next and what happens to that nomination. Third, Binder notes that judicial nominations present senators with yes-no, all-or-nothing votes. Rather than confronting the minority party with such yes-no situations, proposals for legislation made by the majority party are subject to amendments by the minority that may produce legislative compromises to which both parties can agree. Thus she concludes that nominations are more likely to produce confrontations than are legislative proposals. In reality, however, presidents nominate compromise judicial candidates that have at least some appeal to both parties and so reduce the potential for confrontation. For instance, Binder chooses the nomination of Stephen Breyer to the First District Court of Appeals in 1980 to illustrate ease of confirmation when the Senate is centrist. But the ease of consent to Breyer might equally well be explained as based on compromise between Republican and Democratic goals. Breyer was closely associated with liberal Senator Edward Kennedy (D-Mass.) in his efforts to push a deregulatory agenda favored by conservative Republicans. So even if the Senate at the time had been deeply polarized, Breyer might well have garnered the support of both poles.

Finally, all the usual problems of covariance that plague social science analysis are present here. During the period under examination, through a tragic miscalculation by the Court, abortion issues—characterized by at least one side as not having centrist solutions—became central to Supreme Court nomination politics. Moreover, by accident more than calculation, the Court came to be almost evenly split on abortion questions so that each new nomination raised the specter of—if not the actual opportunity for—radical policy change. At the level of the courts of appeals, judges deliberately chose, over a time period beginning in the 1960s, to become extremely active, major policymaking participants in issues relating to health, safety, the environment, and regulation of business. The judges could have stayed out, but they chose to be in. Whether or not the Senate was polarized, a judiciary that chose to interject itself into policy areas involving billions of dollars and dozens of hyperactive interest groups might reasonably expect to generate some heat surrounding its selection and confirmation.

During this same period, for reasons that had almost nothing to do with the judiciary, crime became a major social and political focus in the United States. Being tough on crime became a political asset. A massive shift in popular and even in informed thinking occurred from rehabilitation to incarceration as the aim of criminal justice. And judges (in my view quite rightly) were seen as significant laggards in this shift. In California, where a lawless Supreme Court defied the constitutionally expressed will of the voters to reinstate the death penalty, the voters unelected the defiant judges.[1]

Behind the abortion and crime issues obviously lies the broader and deeper "rights revolution" that is widely perceived as having been achieved by the Warren Court. That Court's rights-of-accused decisions certainly did materially change U.S. criminal justice practices and were viewed by many, rightly or wrongly, as hampering the struggle against a then-growing crime rate. The Court was perceived, mostly wrongly, as also having protected communists by its freedom of speech decisions and to have taken aim against religion, all this in the midst of a cold war against "godless communism." Most importantly, it had taken the lead in a civil rights movement that became central to American politics in general and the electoral fate of the political parties in particular. It is hard to see how the Court could have avoided *Brown* v. *Board of Education* in 1954 or deciding it the way it did, but it could hardly expect to be "out of politics" once it did. And along the way, it had discovered that the state legislatures were unconstitutional. Subsequently, the Burger Court not only failed to undo the revolution but, by a stupendous leap of judicial imagination, managed to discover a constitutional right to abortion. Just how much "judicial independence" can people who believe in electoral democracy be expected to take? And why shouldn't they seek out one of the few avenues of democratic control available to them—the confirmation process?

Adopting a relatively long time frame helps to reveal what is probably the overdetermination of falling confirmation rates. Acquiescent courts are not necessarily neutral, independent courts. By the late 1940s, the cycles of life span and elections had left a New Deal legislature facing a New Deal president, a New Deal

1. See Stolz (1981) for an account of the 1979 investigation of Chief Justice Rose Bird and the California Supreme Court. Bird was recalled by voters in 1986.

federal bureaucracy, and a New Deal judiciary. New Deal judges reviewing New Deal government could easily proclaim and practice judicial self-restraint. (After all, they were simply approving whatever the rest of the New Deal government did.) When Republicans began to reacquire the presidency, they inherited a career civil service that was supposed to be neutral but was not. Republicans responded by seeking to "reform" the federal bureaucracy through the Hoover Commission studies, the creation of an executive service, and other such devices. More recently, these efforts have taken the forms of shifting decisionmaking from career people to political appointees and suppressing, ignoring, or lying about what the career people have to say, although that is now because the career people are loyal to science or environmentalism or honesty rather than loyal to the New Deal.

It is little wonder, then, that Republicans should have adopted a hostile stance toward the New Deal judiciary they inherited. A small part of such a stance could be built up by statutory limitations on judicial jurisdiction or judicial discretion (sentencing guidelines, for instance). Limiting the courts' jurisdiction or the standing of citizens to reach them is, however, a kind of head-on attack on "constitutional values" that is likely to have high political costs. Intervals of Democratic government had yielded environmental, health, and safety statutes with very broad standing provisions, and these measures proved too popular to attack directly. Thus appointments became the principal vehicle for eroding the New Deal judiciary's policy influence. Subsequently, neoconservatives could move on from diluting New Deal courts to the dream of a true right-wing judiciary with visions of *Lochner* dancing in their heads—or at least courts that did not invent new rights and entitlements at the drop of a "public interest" lawsuit.[2]

Indeed, a major contributor to the increased heat of the *confirmation* process has been the polarization of the *selection* process. Either because of the direct influence of neoconservatives or because judicial nominations are a relatively easy way to recruit and sustain right-wing support, recent Republican administrations seem to have pursued a rather conscious policy of nominating judges who are, or are perceived to be, far to the right of center.[3] One current product of the earlier mode of confirmation politics is Republican lauding of previous judicial experience as a qualification for higher judicial office. Thus many Republican nominees to higher courts are serving judges. One consequence is that unlike former practitioners— who can claim, with some justification, that their on-the-record positions were

2. The 1905 *Lochner* v. *New York* decision supposedly enshrined laissez-faire antagonism to government interference with free markets in the due process clauses of the Constitution.

3. See Law and Solum (2006).

mere advocacy for their clients—serving judges have opinion and voting records that open them up to close, partisan political scrutiny. Moreover, each Republican nomination to a district or circuit court can be seen as a preparatory move toward qualifying that person for a later higher-level judicial appointment, thus raising the partisan stakes of the lower-level appointments.

It has been perfectly reasonable for conservatives to engage in a consistent, calculated drive to move the ideology of the federal bench far to the right, given federal judges' propensity to engage in policymaking. It is, therefore, perfectly reasonable for the center and left to consistently and calculatingly attempt to counter it. Even if the Senate were to be controlled by moderate Republicans and Democrats, considerable opposition to a stream of decidedly far-right nominations would be anticipated.

In short, the hyperdominance of American politics by the New Deal obscured the political role of the American judiciary. The Republican revival—plus civil rights, abortion, and crime—ultimately cast a light on that role. If judges make a lot of public policy, or can choose not to make it, and judges carry their party allegiances onto the bench, why shouldn't judicial confirmations become politically contested? And if contested, then confirmation rates might well be expected to drop, especially in periods of divided government, even if both parties are controlled by their relatively moderate wings. The difficulty is that during the same time period that congressional polarization is occurring, there is also an increasing propensity of the judiciary (on both the statutory interpretation and constitutional fronts) to interject itself into the policymaking process. Losers in various policy arenas have tended to exaggerate the extent of policy judicialization, but it is there both in reality and public perception.

Ultimately pleas for "judicial independence" often turn out to be yearnings for the voters to remain in a state of naive ignorance about what judges really do. The claim that in a democracy law (public policy) ought to be made by people responsible to the electorate is not an entirely benighted one. As American voters have become more aware of how much public policy federal judges make, the political heat surrounding presidential judicial nominations might reasonably be expected to increase, and that response might reasonably be applauded, whether or not the Senate was more or less politically polarized.[4]

4. This is not to discount in any way the relevance of the question of whether Senate polarization has influenced the shape and temperature of the flame. That is an important question for a positive political science. I find Binder's analysis quite convincing on the point that Senate polarization, particularly in periods of divided government, tends to drive down confirmation rates, but I also believe that the decline in confirmation rates has been highly overdetermined by a whole series of concomitant causes.

Judicial independence turns out to be a particularly murky concept because it is so often applied to situations improperly. The essence of judicial independence is that no fourth party shall seek to influence the outcome of a *particular* litigation. We believe in judicial independence at retail but not at wholesale. At wholesale (that is, when considering how courts should deal with litigation in general), we believe in the very opposite of judicial independence. Courts are courts of law. Rather than being independent, they are to be the absolutely obedient servants of the statutes enacted by the legislature. Both the bureaucracy and the judiciary serve for life or good behavior, so that they will be neutral implementers of the statutory law (that is, obedient rather than independent).

The rub, of course, comes because even the most obedient statute implementer necessarily and inevitably must interpret the statute in order to implement it, and some quantum of lawmaking is unavoidable in the process of interpretation. Here again judicial independence means that no fourth party shall seek to determine the judicial statutory interpretation-cum-lawmaking that occurs in a particular case. Surely, however, by judicial independence we do not mean that judges should be free of any general responsibility to outsiders for the law they make.

In a democracy, the law ought to be made by the elected representatives of the people. We properly may respond to the inevitability that both the administrative and judicial implementers of law must necessarily make some law themselves by seeking to ensure their neutrality or nonpartisanship by giving them life tenure but surely not by ensuring their independence. Rather, we make them dependent on appointment by elected government officials (when we don't subject them to some kind of periodic election process, as with most state judgeships). Political appointment is one of the few means available for resolving the potential conflict between judicial independence and the need to subject judicial lawmaking to some democratic control.

Of course, leaving constitutional cases aside, the principal mode of holding judicial lawmaking democratically accountable is to insist that judges obey the law and that legislatures "correct" judicial "misinterpretations" by amending the statutory language. Observers of courts have long known that the less efficient legislatures were at passing laws, the more independent judiciaries could be in their lawmaking by interpretation. In terms of democratic responsibility, this ought to mean that the less efficient the legislature, the more it ought to rely on the appointment process to bring judges to heel, given that it could not place much faith in its own powers to correct judicial interpretations by amending the statutes interpreted. Thus, if the U.S. Congress indeed suffers from polarization that makes it more difficult to pass legislation (which I assume is still an open question), then it would be wise to invest more, not less, attention in the confirmation process.

Yes, it is true that a heated confirmation process is a threat to judicial independence, but it is a threat to precisely the kind of judicial independence we do not want—irresponsible judicial lawmaking. That is why the abortion "litmus test" causes such alarm. Given the close balance on abortion that has emerged on the Supreme Court subsequent to the *Roe* v. *Wade* decision in 1973, keying confirmation to a nominee's anticipated vote in future abortion cases moves very far in the direction of using the confirmation process to determine the outcome of a particular case rather than ensuring the general political responsibility of the judiciary in a democracy.

The issue of abortion brings us to *constitutional* as opposed to *statutory* interpretation. It is axiomatic that the more general the language of the legal text and the more difficult it is to amend, the more lawmaking capacity resides in the authorized interpreter. Thus constitutional courts have the greatest potential for judicial lawmaking and present the greatest judicial problem for democracy. European courts, which Binder comments on briefly in her introductory remarks, provide an instructive comparison. As Europeans established constitutional judicial review, they deliberately established it in separate constitutional courts. They did so because they recognized that constitutional decisions, particularly decisions about "rights," were necessarily and unavoidably highly discretionary, essentially political decisions. Through the establishment of constitutional courts separate from the regular courts, special, highly politicized modes of appointment to those courts could be and were introduced. As first in the field (and so without the benefit of hindsight), the United States vested constitutional review in its courts of general jurisdiction. Thus, if we are to respond to the grave dangers to democracy posed by constitutional judicial review, we must do so in ways that also impinge on more routine judicial activity. Unlike the Europeans, we cannot concentrate the political aspects of confirmation on constitutional courts alone.

Ultimately that may be a good thing. Over the last forty years or so, Congress has enacted a number of civil rights, health, safety, and environmental statutes that combine sweeping, aspirational language with long, complex, highly detailed provisions, much delegation to administrative agencies, and generous judicial review provisions. Such statutes invite both administrative and judicial statutory interpretation that comes very close, in both scope and leeway, to constitutional interpretation. To a relatively high degree, we can control administrative statutory interpretation through presidential elections, piecemeal congressional hearings, and appropriations processes instead of major—and difficult to achieve—correcting

amendments. About the only means we have of controlling judicial statutory interpretation in this realm is a politicized appointment process on behalf of both the
president and the Congress.

Perhaps the best route to achieving popular perceived legitimacy for our governing institutions might be to tell the truth about them, and for them to tell the
truth about themselves. Or perhaps one good route toward healthy limits on government power is for government institutions to feel compelled to act in such a
way as to maintain the myths about themselves. If it is, for some reason, a good
idea to lower the heat of judicial confirmation politics that is generated by partisan polarization, the Supreme Court and the lower federal courts could themselves
follow a number of paths.

Abortion is obviously one—and probably the greatest—of the temperature
raisers. To get itself at least part way out of the kitchen, the Court can persist in
Justice Sandra Day O'Connor's "undue burden" test, using it in particular cases
to allow the states as much variation as they want, down to a minimum of protecting medically certified "health of the mother" abortions. This could have the
effect of partially returning the issue to state legislatures, from which the Court
transferred the heat to itself with *Roe* v. *Wade*.

Civil rights probably cannot be cooled off entirely, and prospective nominees
no doubt will continue to be carefully vetted for "insensitivity" and so on. Affirmative action is the really hot issue. The Court's current position on affirmative
action generally and racial gerrymandering (namely, that you can take race into
account but not too much and not too obviously) probably sufficiently reduces
the heat.

The Court has already whittled back its rights-of-accused jurisprudence sufficiently that toughness on crime is unlikely to be a highly salient confirmation
issue. Popular ambivalence about the death penalty also means that capital pun-
ishment will not likely become a significant confirmation issue no matter what the
Court does. Nevertheless, Justice Breyer and like-minded judges might temper
their displays of erudition and stop antagonizing an increasingly ethnocentric
public by pointing to Nigerian or Lithuanian jurisprudence as a guide to American constitutional interpretation.

Indeed, the really key stakes lie not in the constitutional but the statutory realm.
The George W. Bush administration has used every imaginable device of administrative statutory interpretation to avoid full implementation of a host of regulatory statutes enacted by previous mostly Democratic regimes. If the Democrats win
the presidency in 2008, they are still likely to face relatively narrow margins in Congress and find legislation difficult. They are likely to resort to new administrative

reinterpretations to counter recent Republican reinterpretations. Many of these "new rules to get back to old rules" will be challenged in court, mostly in the D.C. Circuit, and judicial attitudes could have a good deal to do with agency success in such cases. The devil here, however, is usually in the details, and there are dozens of diverse issues. Except for nominees who have had very close and extended ties with particular regulated industries or pro- or antiregulatory nongovernmental organizations, it is not easy to dramatize these matters for confirmation hearings. So, short of extraordinarily bold and one-sided judicial lawmaking, court decisions in these areas are unlikely to generate much heat during confirmation hearings.

In short, most concerns about judicial independence mistake the values involved and the problem, which is judicial lawmaking. And if Senate polarization threatens more confirmation heat, and confirmation heat is somehow a bad thing, the courts could easily respond by doing less judicial policymaking.

COMMENT

Benjamin Wittes

I have broad sympathy for the major propositions in Sarah Binder's discussion of the consequences of political polarization for the relationship between Congress and the courts. Increased polarization undoubtedly contributes to contentiousness in judicial confirmations. I have little doubt as well that these battles undermine public confidence in judicial impartiality and, indeed, in law as a discipline independent of politics. Furthermore, Binder's hypothesis of a link between judicial confirmation fights and a wider array of affronts to the independence of the courts dovetails considerably with my own work on the subject. I will not detain the reader with a discussion of our considerable areas of agreement.

Binder advances one significant argument, however, of which I remain unconvinced and which merits close scrutiny. She contends that polarization increases the likelihood of presidential advancement of nominees she describes as "off-center," "immoderate," or "ideologically extreme." She takes as evidence of this trend the changing partisan composition of the Senate coalitions voting to confirm nominees over the years—using the confirmation coalition as a kind of proxy for the ideology of the nominee. In other words, Binder suggests that a nominee who wins confirmation by a nearly party-line vote is likely to be more extreme than one confirmed on a broadly bipartisan basis. I suspect Binder's underlying hypothesis here is incorrect—that is, I doubt that polarization generally is increasing the extremity of nominees. And, in any event, her very interesting data do not clearly support this thesis. While they do illuminate the effect of polarization on judicial confirmations, they seem to say less about nominee ideology than about senatorial tolerance for nominees of the opposite party.

Let me start with a preliminary word about terminology. As Binder acknowledges, we have no direct measure of a nominee's ideology—nor, to be frank, can the literature even claim a stable and consistent definition of judicial ideology itself. We use "ideology" as a catch-all term to situate judges on a left–right spectrum, a spectrum that describes the judicial world less comfortably than it does the political world. The term has to carry a great deal of weight, making reference all at once to a judge's jurisprudential approach and to his or her philosophical, political, and even partisan views. To say that a judge (or a would-be judge) is conservative, liberal, ideological, mainstream, or off-center can mean any number of utterly distinct things—or just about any combination of them. These terms are inherently impressionistic and, as such, of limited analytical value. The search for any kind of objective measure of ideology necessarily leads down a rabbit hole.

So, I suspect, does the search for a proxy for nominee ideology. Binder's choice—the group of senators who choose to support confirmation—is as good a stab as I can imagine. But it does not work. Consider two nominees to the D.C. Circuit Court of Appeals who became controversial during the George W. Bush administration: Janice Rogers Brown and Miguel Estrada. According to Binder's proxy, they would both be ideologically extreme. Both received support almost exclusively from Republicans and were filibustered by Democrats.[5] Yet Brown had given speeches outlining a genuinely unusual view of jurisprudence and the judicial function, one that embraced long-discarded Supreme Court doctrines on property rights and constitutional restraints on regulation.[6] Estrada, by contrast, had never articulated any unconventional views of judging—nor could Democrats point to much evidence to back up their charge that he was "extreme."[7]

5. Estrada's nomination never came to a vote, though a few Democrats declined to support the filibuster against him. In the roll call vote on Brown's nomination, only one Democrat—Nebraska senator Ben Nelson—crossed party lines to support her.

6. Two of Brown's speeches, in particular, drew fire. See Janice Rogers Brown, " 'A Whiter Shade of Pale,' Sense and Nonsense—the Pursuit of Perfection in Law and Politics," presented to the Federalist Society, University of Chicago Law School, April 20, 2000 (www.constitution.org/col/jrb/00420_jrb_fedsoc.htm); "Fifty Ways to Lose Your Freedom," speech presented at the Institute for Justice, Washington, August 12, 2000 (www.communityrights.org/PDFs/8-12-00IFJ.pdf).

7. The Democratic complaint against Estrada, in fact, was that he refused to articulate views that they could subsequently use to tag him with extremity. In their January 29, 2003, letter of opposition to Estrada's appointment, People for the American Way complained, "Mr. Estrada refused to

While Estrada is undoubtedly a strong conservative, there is simply no basis on which one can claim objectively that he was as far from the norm as Brown—or even outside of the normal range at all. The most that these data can show is that he was *perceived by Democrats* to be as conservative as she was *perceived* to be. But the data do not even really show that. There are many reasons, other than nominee ideology, why nominees become targets. One of the most important is that the opposition party perceives them as likely candidates for elevation to the Supreme Court; this was a big part of Democratic anxiety about Estrada from the time Bush nominated him.[8] A method that converts the degree of partisan opposition to a nominee into a commentary on that nominee's ideological extremity risks conflating the observed fact of political polarization with its supposed effects.

Binder's own example—the contrasting votes to confirm Judge Brown in 2005 and Stephen Breyer to be a judge on the First Circuit Court of Appeals in 1980—seems at first glance to validate her choice of proxies. In contrast to Brown's unconventional stances on jurisprudential matters and the ensuing strongly partisan confirmation vote, Breyer is the personification of a moderate liberal judge—and he received a strongly bipartisan vote. Yet the power of this example is skin deep. Twenty-five years elapsed between these two votes, and in the history of judicial confirmations, these are twenty-five very important years—the very period in which political polarization fundamentally altered the confirmation process. We have no way of knowing whether a Breyer confirmation in 2005 would have looked a lot more like Brown's, or whether in 1980 more senators might have

---

reveal his jurisprudential views on these and other subjects in response to questions by Senators. . . . [H]e refused to answer questions concerning his view of *Roe* v. *Wade* and of recent Supreme Court decisions curtailing Congress' power. He declined to state his jurisprudential views concerning the role of government in balancing the protection of the environment with property rights, concerning secrecy orders in products liability cases, and concerning recent federal court rulings on the death penalty. He would not answer questions on affirmative action, including even a question about the propriety of broad outreach to increase diversity, despite serious concerns about his views on affirmative action according to published reports." The full text of the letter can be found at www.pfaw.org/pfaw/general/default.aspx?oid=8077.

8. In an essay published shortly after Estrada's nomination, Peter Beinart wrote, "The fight over Bush's federal court nominees is about establishing parameters for Bush's Supreme Court picks. And knocking off [Judge Terrence] Boyle doesn't set a meaningful precedent for that fight, because when a Supreme Court seat opens up, Bush won't appoint someone like him. The days of Republican presidents naming white, male, right-wing Supreme Court nominees are probably over. Just as the conservative movement realized years ago that its anti-feminist spokespeople had to be women, the Bush administration has realized that its right-wing judges had better be minorities or female. . . . Which is why the Democrats should go after a different Bush federal court nominee: Miguel Estrada." Peter Beinart, "No Appeal: Liberal Multiculturalism Comes Home to Roost," *New Republic,* May 28, 2001.

tolerated Brown. In fact, both of these counterfactual scenarios, particularly the latter one, seem likely.

Binder frankly recognizes this problem. But despite the concession, she consistently treats the extremity of the confirmation coalition as all but interchangeable with the extremity of the nominee. From this basic assumption, she interprets the increasingly partisan nature of the votes over nominees in the postwar era as evidence of the increasingly ideological nature of the nominees themselves: "The average nomination to the federal courts is increasingly likely to be off-center over the course of the postwar period."

This seems wrong to me; a few examples will illustrate why. According to Binder's interpretation, the most ideological nominees of the postwar era were sent to the Senate by President Bill Clinton during his six years facing a Republican Senate (based on the average extremity of senators voting to confirm; see figure 3-6). The least ideological nominees among the last five presidents were put forth by Ronald Reagan and Jimmy Carter. These suggestions simply defy the everyday experience of lawyers and scholars who study and practice before the federal courts. Reagan came into office with very public ambitions to move the courts away from the liberal enthusiasms of the Warren and Burger Court eras.[9] He made judicial nominations a priority, and officials of his administration discussed them in overtly philosophical terms. Clinton, by contrast, mostly eschewed the aggressively liberal nominees of prior eras. His nominees were by most accounts more moderate on average than, for example, Carter's. If Reagan's commitment to opposing liberal judicial activism defined the terms of the modern war over the courts, Clinton's nominees blurred rather than sharpened the battle lines.

Nor does it make intuitive sense that greater polarization should make confirmation of extreme judges more, rather than less, likely. Binder's explanation for this phenomenon is that in periods of lesser polarization, presidents have to play to the strong center, whereas in periods of high polarization, they have to play to their political bases. The relatively few moderates, she argues, will tend to support

9. Reagan, in fact, promised as early as his 1980 campaign to appoint a different breed of judge, and liberals at the time noticed the promise with alarm. *New York Times* columnist Anthony Lewis, for example, warned that "if Reagan becomes President . . . he would . . . surely—and quite properly—try to pick nominees who share his view of the Court's function and of the country's 'values and morals.'" Reagan's model, Lewis correctly predicted, would be then associate justice William Rehnquist, whom he described as "a judicial ideologue of the right, the most predictable conservative appointed to the Court in fifty years." See Anthony Lewis, "Reagan and the Court," *New York Times*, October 9, 1980.

extreme nominees because the alternative is to "accept the status quo of a vacant judgeship." I believe very nearly the opposite phenomenon is more the norm: presidents in periods of high polarization consider the possibility of nomination failure a very real constraint on their power to appoint judges. The White House under both Clinton and George W. Bush spent a lot of time negotiating with individual senators, including opposition party senators, to find mutually acceptable combinations of nominations. Nor have I seen many instances in which senators appeared deeply moved by the possibility of leaving a judgeship vacant; to the contrary, senators have often shown great willingness to hold judgeships open by way of extracting concessions from the White House on nominations or unrelated matters.[10] Polarization surely makes the battle lines clearer over judges and increases the executive's desire to appoint nominees who will excite the president's party (and upset the opposition). But it makes confirmation of judges harder, in general, not easier. And it forces presidents to think hard about the possible roadblocks that ideological opposition to nominees can place in the president's way.

Presidents respond to this constraint differently. Clinton took a fairly consistent posture of conciliation with Republican senators. He tended to nominate moderates both as a reflection of his own ideological stance and out of a desire not to invest political energy in nomination fights. He struck several deals with Republican senators to get people through, and he never made confirmations a high political priority of his own agenda. George W. Bush, by contrast, has sought more consistently to nominate strong conservatives, stood his ground more of the time, invested considerable political energy in confirmations, and tried—often successfully—to make a political issue out of the mistreatment of his nominees. But I doubt very much that either man would have nominated *more* moderate people had they needed to contend with *less* ideological opposition.

How should we understand Binder's data then, if not as evidence of presidents' nominating ever more extreme people to the bench? I suggest that the rather strik-

10. Prominent examples of this were efforts by Senator Jesse Helms (R-N.C.) during the Clinton administration to force Clinton to nominate Judge Terrence Boyle to the Fourth Circuit Court of Appeals in Richmond. Helms prevented the confirmation of several judges to the court, demanding that Clinton renominate Boyle, whose nomination had lapsed when Clinton came into office. Similarly, when President Bush took office, Michigan's Democratic senators held up his nominations to the Sixth Circuit Court of Appeals in Cincinnati in an effort to force Bush to make amends for the fact that Clinton's nominees had never received a vote. Perhaps the most prominent example of such senatorial extortion is the refusal of Republican senators to confirm Clinton's nominee to the Ninth Circuit Court of Appeals, William Fletcher, until Fletcher's mother—who served on the court already—took senior status.

ing effect she demonstrates is a vivid illustration of the impact of polarization on the presidency's institutional capacity to get nominees confirmed. Along with the declining confirmation rates Binder also cites, it illustrates that our political system is more prone to fight about judges than it used to be and that it is more likely to do so in a partisan fashion. This depiction is fully consistent with many other indicators. The time it takes to confirm the average nominee has skyrocketed since the late 1980s. Roll call votes, once the exception in judicial confirmations, have become the norm. We now routinely see the kind of battles over nominations to the appeals courts that were once reserved for nominees to the Supreme Court.[11] None of this should be taken as evidence that the nominees themselves are more extreme—merely as evidence that the political system, alarmed by the increasing power of the courts, has decided to mind the gates more closely.

This leaves a question I do not believe we can answer quantitatively, only qualitatively: are judicial nominees becoming more extreme or not? I can think of no coherent methodology for addressing this question, but I think the best impressionistic answer is that, at least so far, they are not.

It is certainly true that the parties have more defined judicial philosophies than they used to. The parties used to be less ideological and more patronage based than they are now. As a consequence, the ideological divide in America did not neatly track the partisan divide at all. There were Republican and Democratic liberals, Republican and Democratic conservatives. As the shift toward more ideological parties has taken place, ideological divisions among judges have tended to come into greater alignment with partisan divisions—that is, the more conservative flanks on courts have tended to become more Republican and the more liberal flanks have tended to become more Democratic.[12] The differences between Lyndon Johnson's and Richard Nixon's lower-court nominees, for example, are trivial compared to the differences between Carter's and Reagan's. This effect, too, is a creature of polarization.

It is also true that Republican presidents are considerably more likely today to appoint conservative judges than Republican presidents were before the Reagan revolution. The courts have become a rallying point for conservatives, largely because of social issues, and conservatives have invested great political energy in them. Republican elected officials, including presidents, have proven responsive.

11. For a fuller portrait of the changes in the judicial confirmation process, see Wittes (2006).

12. This trend is difficult to demonstrate empirically, for the simple reason that ideology is so difficult to measure. Yet most judges I have spoken with have no doubt of its truth. For a good discussion of the shift, see Scherer (2005).

In that sense, I suppose, one can say that Republican judicial nominees have become more extreme.

The trouble is that a liberal president is also likely to appoint more conservative judges than would his liberal predecessors, as evidenced by the difference between Carter's nominees and Clinton's. Liberal jurisprudence in general is not as free-wheeling as it used to be. It has been influenced a great deal by visions of judicial restraint commonly associated, until recently, with conservatism. While liberal groups, too, have invested a great deal of political energy in judicial nominations, they did not win nearly the same success from Clinton that conservatives—whose philosophical posture is clearer and more cohesive—have won from recent Republican presidents. The left flank of the Supreme Court today has at least as much in common with the conservative flank, for example, as it does with those lions of liberal activism, William O. Douglas and William Brennan. While such figures remain iconic in the liberal imagination, the aspirations of liberal jurisprudence have ebbed considerably from their day. Clinton, very notably, did not seek such a figure in either of his two Supreme Court appointments. Rather, he quite self-consciously sought people who would have been far to the right of Brennan and Douglas, had they served on the Court contemporaneously with them. In other words, it is perhaps less accurate to suggest that nominees are becoming more extreme as a consequence of political polarization than to say that the judicial culture in general is becoming more conservative.

These two trends—the increasingly partisan alignment of attitudes toward the judicial function and the increasing judicial conservatism of both political parties—seem at odds with one another. One, after all, implies a polarization of partisan attitudes toward the courts, the other a kind of partisan convergence. Yet both trends clearly exist, and they interact in complicated ways. On some courts, partisanship has intensified over the past decade. On others, particularly on the D.C. Circuit—which has seen many of the worst and most partisan confirmation battles—it has diminished dramatically.[13] I do not purport to have any kind of unified field theory to explain these effects or their interactions; I suspect the most important variable is the individual personalities of the judges. And I certainly do not dismiss the possibility that political polarization will, in the long run, tend to create more distinct party caucuses on the courts themselves. But at least for now, I do not see clear evidence that nominees are generally growing more extreme.

Finally, the assumption that having more off-center nominees necessarily represents a bad thing—one that justifies policy intervention to avert—warrants brief

13. See Edwards (2003).

examination as well. American legal history has treated "out-of-the-mainstream" judges very kindly, sometimes even heroically. Our paradigms of legal courage tend to be justices in sometimes lonely dissent—John Marshall Harlan's famous dissent from *Plessy* v. *Ferguson*'s upholding of the doctrine of "separate but equal," for example. The judiciary has powerful institutional defenses against radicalism. Appellate judges, after all, never sit alone. At a minimum, they need to persuade one of their colleagues that they are correct in order to get anything done, and even then, they are always subject to reversal. The judiciary, however, has limited defenses against conformity. Huge doctrinal edifices can grow up unchallenged and become prohibitively difficult to dismantle. It sometimes takes someone outside the mainstream to declare that the emperor has no clothes. For those of us who admire the contributions made by justices at the extremes—who are, say, unwilling to give back either Justice Brennan or Justice Scalia—the goal of limiting the ideological diversity of the courts is not all that attractive. The goal, rather, should be to preserve philosophical diversity while somehow at once resisting the sort of partisan polarization that genuinely threatens to undermine the dream of impartial justice.

References

Bailey, Michael A. 2007. "Comparable Preference Estimates across Time and Institutions for the Court, Congress and Presidency." *American Journal of Political Science* 51 (3): 433–48.

Baird, Vanessa A., and Amy Gangl. 2006. "Shattering the Myth of Legality: The Impact of the Media's Framing of Supreme Court Procedures on Perceptions of Fairness." *Political Psychology* 27 (4): 597–614.

Binder, Sarah A. 2003. *Stalemate: Causes and Consequences of Legislative Gridlock.* Brookings.

Binder, Sarah A., and Forrest Maltzman. 2002. "Senatorial Delay in Confirming Federal Judges, 1947–1998." *American Journal of Political Science* 46 (1): 190–99.

———. 2005. "Congress and the Politics of Judicial Appointment." In *Congress Reconsidered,* 8th ed., edited by Lawrence C. Dodd and Bruce I. Oppenheimer, pp. 297–318. Washington: CQ Press.

———. 2005. "Half-Empty or Half-Full? Do Vacant Federal Judgeships Matter?" Paper prepared for the annual meeting of the Midwest Political Science Association, Chicago, April 7–10.

Brody, Richard. 1991. *Assessing the President: The Media, Elite Opinion and Public Support.* Stanford University Press.

Chutkow, Dawn M. 2006. "Jurisdiction Stripping: Ideology, Institutional Concerns, and Congressional Control of the Courts." Cornell University, Department of Government.

Edwards, Harry T. 2003. "The Effects of Collegiality on Judicial Decision Making." *University of Pennsylvania Law Review* 151 (May): 1639–90.

Ferejohn, John. 2002. "Judicializing Politics, Politicizing Law." *Law and Contemporary Problems* 65 (3): 41–68.

Gressle, Sharon S. 2003. "Judicial Salary-Setting Policy." Report RS20278. Congressional Research Service, Library of Congress.

Law, David S., and Lawrence B. Solum. 2006. "Judicial Selection, Appointments Gridlock, and the Nuclear Option." *Journal of Contemporary Legal Issues* 15 (1): 51–104.

MacKenzie, G. Calvin. 2001. *Innocent until Nominated: The Breakdown of the Presidential Appointments Process.* Brookings.

Maltzman, Forrest. 2005. "Advice and Consent: Cooperation and Conflict in the Appointment of Federal Judges." In *Institutions of American Democracy: The Legislative Branch,* edited by Paul J. Quirk and Sarah A. Binder, pp. 407–31. Oxford University Press.

Mann, Thomas E., and Norman J. Ornstein. 2006. *The Broken Branch: How Congress Is Failing America and How to Get It Back on Track.* Oxford University Press.

McCarty, Nolan, Keith T. Poole, and Howard Rosenthal. 2006. *Polarized America: The Dance of Ideology and Unequal Riches.* MIT Press.

McCarty, Nolan, and Rose Razaghian. 1999. "Advice and Consent: Senate Responses to Executive Branch Nominations, 1885–1996." *American Journal of Political Science* 43 (4): 1122–143.

Price, Vincent, and Anca Romantan. 2004. "Confidence in Institutions Before, During, and After 'Indecision 2000.' " *Journal of Politics* 66 (3): 939–56.

Rehnquist, William H. 2004. "2003 Year-End Report on the Federal Judiciary." *Third Branch* 36 (1).

———. 2005. "2004 Year-End Report on the Federal Judiciary." *Third Branch* 37 (1).

Roberts, John G., Jr. 2006. "2005 Year-End Report on the Federal Judiciary." *Third Branch* 38 (1).

Scherer, Nancy. 2005. *Scoring Points: Politicians, Activists, and the Lower Federal Court Appointment Process.* Stanford University Press.

Sinclair, Barbara. 2006. *Party Wars: Polarization and the Politics of National Policy Making.* University of Oklahoma Press.

Spriggs, James F., and Paul J. Wahlbeck. 1995. "Calling It Quits: Strategic Retirement on the Federal Courts of Appeals, 1893–1991." *Political Research Quarterly* 48 (3): 573–97.

Stolz, Preble. 1981. *Judging Judges: The Investigation of Rose Bird and the California Supreme Court.* New York: Free Press.

Sunstein, Cass R., and others. 2006. *Are Judges Political? An Empirical Analysis of the Federal Judiciary.* Brookings Institution Press.

Wheeler, Russell R., and Michael S. Greve. 2007. "How to Pay the Piper: It's Time to Call Different Tunes for Congressional and Judicial Salaries." *Issues in Governance Studies* (April): 1–18.

Wittes, Benjamin. 2006. *Confirmation Wars: Preserving Independent Courts in Angry Times.* Lanham, Md.: Rowman & Littlefield.

4

When Politics No Longer Stops at the Water's Edge: Partisan Polarization and Foreign Policy

Peter Beinart

I magine if Harry Truman's aid to Greece and Turkey, or the Berlin Airlift, or the Korean War had been conducted in such a partisan manner—and turned into such a historic catastrophe—that it polarized Americans on the very notion of a "cold war." That is what has happened to American foreign policy since the war in Iraq. After the September 11 attacks, President Bush offered Americans a new framework for seeing the world—the "war on terror"—which they overwhelmingly embraced. At first, when the war on terror meant war in Afghanistan, the bipartisan consensus held. But when the target became Iraq, Democrats grew visibly uncomfortable. Then, beginning in roughly 2004, when the war began to go sour, Democrats (and some independents) began turning against Bush's entire conceptual framework.

Today, the war on terror is a partisan idea. When Republicans think of foreign policy, they think of military threats, especially from terrorists or terror-associated regimes. And when asked how to address them, they suggest coercive, unilateral responses. Democrats, by contrast, see a different world, marked by economic and humanitarian dangers: outsourcing, AIDS, and global poverty. Their favored responses are more multilateral and less militaristic. Indeed, they generally see the Bush administration's aggressive military posture less as an antidote to terrorism than as an invitation to it.

These different perspectives did not emerge de novo. They are rooted in each party's foreign policy tradition, and it was probably inevitable that when national security retook center stage after September 11, those different traditions would make harmony impossible. But it was not inevitable that foreign policy would become, as it has, the single most polarizing aspect of American politics. That must be laid primarily at the feet of George W. Bush and his decision to invade Iraq, to do so incompetently, and to use foreign policy as a wedge issue in the 2002, 2004, and 2006 elections.

Largely as a result, the United States today enjoys no basic foreign policy consensus—either on threats or on responses—as it did in the first two decades of the cold war. That by itself does not make foreign policy bipartisanship impossible: there are cross-cutting issues where Democratic and Republican perspectives might intersect. But it means that in the years to come the two parties will likely disagree fundamentally about America's role in the world, and bipartisanship will be more the exception than the rule.

The Early Cold War

At first the cold war was highly polarizing—not between the parties but within them. When Harry Truman made confrontation with the Soviet Union the centerpiece of his foreign policy in 1947, many Democrats—led by Henry Wallace, who had preceded Truman as Franklin Roosevelt's vice president—accused him of betraying Roosevelt's pro-Soviet legacy. And when Thomas Dewey and then Dwight Eisenhower largely endorsed Truman's confrontational approach, fellow Republicans such as Senator Robert Taft of Ohio accused them of betraying the GOP's prewar skepticism of foreign entanglements. But by the early 1950s, Wallace Democrats and Taft Republicans were virtually extinct. And from 1948 to 1968, a wide bipartisan consensus embraced the cold war as America's foreign policy prism and containment as its foreign policy strategy.[1]

At the margins, partisan differences remained. Impelled by a particularly Republican fear of budget deficits, Eisenhower practiced a cheaper brand of containment,

1. Studying congressional voting on foreign policy issues between 1945 and 1964, Ole R. Holsti and James N. Rosenau (1984, p. 218) concluded that "a substantial foreign policy consensus" did exist during the early cold war. James M. McCormick and Eugene R. Wittkopf (1990, p. 1084) found that the high point of cold war bipartisanship in the House was the 86th Congress (1959–60), when Eisenhower enjoyed majority support from members of both parties 80 percent of the time. The high point in the Senate was the 80th Congress, when Truman received majority bipartisan support 75 percent of the time.

centered on covert action and the threat of massive nuclear retaliation to deter Soviet aggression. Truman, and then Kennedy, supported larger defense budgets and more extensive foreign deployments, which gave the United States the flexibility to check Soviet advances without going to DEFCON 1. On the whole, Democrats also proved more sympathetic toward foreign aid, as manifested by Truman's Marshall Plan and Kennedy's Alliance for Progress, in part because they were less concerned about deficits but also because they had more faith in government intrusion into the free market, both abroad and at home. And in general, Democratic elites (especially outside the South) proved somewhat more supportive of the United Nations than their Republican counterparts, who more jealously guarded American sovereignty.

Under the surface lurked more fundamental divisions. While Republican policymakers practiced containment, in political campaigns they often denounced it. From John Foster Dulles in 1952 to Barry Goldwater in 1964, Republicans extolled "liberation," the rolling back of Soviet power.[2] And the emerging postwar conservative intelligentsia—headquartered at the *National Review*—developed a critique of containment and deterrence that would bear partisan fruit decades later.

Even more important, containment itself was a broad church, encompassing disparate foreign policy strategies. Within the Truman administration itself, as historian John Lewis Gaddis has detailed, key advisers such as George Kennan and Paul Nitze differed about whether the United States should contain international communism or merely the Soviet Union (and about whether one could reasonably distinguish the two).[3] From the late 1940s, the Republican Party generally inclined toward the former view, with many Republicans attacking the Truman administration for not moving more aggressively to prevent a communist takeover in China.[4] While such critiques had little impact on Eisenhower, it is worth remembering that from the perspective of the embryonic conservative movement that would eventually take over the GOP, Eisenhower was no better than Truman. In fact, as political scientists James M. McCormick and Eugene R. Wittkopf have

---

2. After Truman fired General Douglas MacArthur in April 1951, effectively renouncing the liberation of North Korea as an American goal, Truman's foreign policy support among Republicans in Congress substantially dropped. See McCormick and Wittkopf (1990, p. 1086).

3. Gaddis (2005, pp. 88–96).

4. For instance, Republican senator Arthur Vandenberg, a critical figure in the postwar bipartisan consensus on containment in Europe, attacked Truman bitterly for his stance on Asia. See McCormick and Wittkopf (1990, p. 1085).

noted, Eisenhower's foreign policies enjoyed significantly more support from liberal and moderate Republicans in Congress than from conservatives.[5]

The containment consensus, in other words, concealed very different visions. Those visions were easier to paper over when U.S. foreign policy was oriented largely toward Europe, where communism and Soviet power seemed one and the same. But from the very beginning, applying containment to the postcolonial world, especially Asia, revealed deep fissures that often traced partisan lines— fissures that would burst into public view during Vietnam.

Vietnam

Vietnam cut to the heart of the argument between Kennan and Nitze, and made it the defining foreign policy cleavage between the two parties. For Kennan himself, and the liberals and realists who took power in the post-1968 Democratic Party, Vietnam exposed the absurdity of trying to contain every communist movement in the world. Containment, they argued, had aimed to prevent the Soviet Union from controlling powerful industrial centers, not strategically insignificant, preindustrial backwaters such as Vietnam. Moreover, they argued, a communist triumph in Vietnam did not necessarily extend Soviet power. By the late 1960s, Tito and Mao had long since proved that communist governments were not mere agents of Moscow. To the contrary, they often proved intense adversaries. Asian and African nationalism, argued the liberals and realists, could not be controlled by either superpower, and certainly not by force. In fact, the rise of postcolonial nationalism rendered a bipolar view of the world anachronistic. Global anticommunism, they insisted, offered no answer to the new set of foreign policy challenges—from human rights to environmental degradation to the threat of nuclear war—that would confront the United States in the post-Vietnam age.

For conservatives, by contrast, Vietnam and its aftermath made global anticommunism all the more essential. The failure of containment, they argued, was a failure of American will. And while liberals were cheerfully declaring the era of superpower competition over, the Soviets were taking the offensive throughout the third world. While the United States was using détente as an excuse to ratchet back defense spending, Moscow was pursuing military superiority, with the aim of cowing Western Europe into submission and potentially even enabling a Soviet nuclear first strike.

5. McCormick and Wittkopf (1990, p. 1094).

Over the course of the 1970s, this ideological division became a clearly partisan one. After 1968—and particularly after the 1974 midterm elections, which ushered a new generation of post-Vietnam liberals into Congress—Democrats moved sharply away from global, military-oriented anticommunism. But as late as 1976, when Senator Henry "Scoop" Jackson (D-Wash.) won the Democratic presidential primaries in Massachusetts and New York, the party still boasted a powerful cold war liberal (or more pejoratively, neoconservative) wing. And as late as the mid-1970s, the GOP was still headed by Eisenhower-style foreign policy moderates such as Richard Nixon and Gerald Ford, who brought America the détente with the Soviet Union that Jackson so bitterly loathed.

As James Meernik of the University of North Texas showed in his tally of congressional roll call votes, the big drop in bipartisan cooperation—the true end of the containment consensus—came in 1976, with the election of Jimmy Carter.[6] It was Carter who brought the ideological and the partisan cleavages into line. Not only did he give détente a Democratic face, but he proposed human rights as a new foreign policy imperative, implying that the Soviet bloc and the "free" (anticommunist world) were no longer adequate moral categories. For Scoop Jackson protégés such as Jeane Kirkpatrick and Richard Perle, Carter was the last straw. And in their despair, they reached out to a Republican Party being taken over by the very movement conservatives who had been pushing militant, global anticommunism since the 1950s.

By the time Ronald Reagan took office, foreign policy was thoroughly polarized along party lines. Reagan's foreign policy fell somewhere between global containment and that even grander conservative dream, rollback. He aided anticommunist governments and rebels from Central America to Afghanistan to Angola. By launching a massive defense buildup, he rejected détente, and by launching the Strategic Defense Initiative, he edged away from the logic of deterrence. In response, the antiwar movement—by this point thoroughly entrenched within the Democratic Party—sprang back to life in opposition to Reagan's policies in El Salvador and Nicaragua, and in support of a nuclear freeze.

In the foreign policy struggles of the early to mid-1980s, one can glimpse the different worldviews bequeathed to the two parties by Vietnam. For Reagan and the GOP, communism—directed from Moscow (often via Havana)—was on the march across the developing world, including the Central American backyard of the United States, and could be stopped only by force of arms. For Democrats, by

6. Meernik (1993).

contrast, third world communism was a by-product of anti-imperialist national-ism, and trying to contain it militarily was not only ineffectual, but immoral—likely to threaten the human rights of those concerned.[7] On nuclear policy, Reagan and the GOP regarded Soviet deployments as an attempt to bully West-ern Europe into neutralism and thereby destroy the NATO alliance. For Demo-crats, however, Reagan's decision to respond with bellicose rhetoric and a massive military buildup brought the world closer to the holocaust of nuclear war. In 1980, influenced by Jimmy Carter's support for deploying intermediate-range missiles to Western Europe, the Democratic platform had quietly rejected a nuclear freeze. But when Reagan began instituting those deployments, partisan and ideological divisions snapped into alignment. By 1984 the freeze enjoyed the support of six of the seven major Democratic candidates for president.[8]

The Post–Cold War Era

The 1991 Gulf War, occurring the same year that the Soviet Union disappeared, proved the last gasp of cold war foreign policy polarization. In the House, Repub-licans backed the war 164-3, and in the Senate, 42-2. By contrast, Democrats, still deeply influenced by Vietnam, opposed it 180-86 in the House and 45-10 in the Senate (where, ironically, they were strongly influenced by Sam Nunn of Georgia, a Southern hawk who opposed the war largely because of opposition within the military).[9]

   Then the debates grew muddled. Bipartisan consensus did not return in the 1990s. To the contrary, as James M. McCormick, Eugene R. Wittkopf, and David M. Danna show, foreign policy bipartisanship in Congress decreased dur-ing George H. W. Bush's presidency and Bill Clinton's first term (before rising slightly in Clinton's second term).[10] But the terms of disagreement changed. After the cold war, national security became vastly less important to American politics. As a result, foreign policy was partially colonized by domestic policy. Compared to the cold war era, foreign policy roll call votes in the 1990s were more likely to

---

7. A 1987 Pew Research Center poll found Republicans far more likely to support aid to the Nicaraguan Contras; attribute Central America's problems to communism, not poverty; back greater military spending; and oppose arms control. See Ornstein, Kohut, and McCarthy (1988, pp. 41–47). When Congress voted in 1984 on Reagan's request for military aid to the anticommunist govern-ment in El Salvador, 78 percent of Republicans voted yes while 95 percent of Democrats voted no. See Souva and Rohde (2007, p. 15).

8. For more on this, see Beinart (2006, especially pp. 64–65).

9. Souva and Rohde (2007, p. 3).

10. McCormick, Wittkopf, and Danna (1997). See also Trubowitz and Mellow (2007).

concern trade, the environment, or cultural issues such as abortion and birth control—which were virtual corollaries of domestic debates.[11] In an era devoid of clear national security threats, domestic polarization extended more easily beyond the water's edge.

On national security itself, both Democrats and Republicans struggled to rediscover their core principles beyond the familiar context of the cold war. Those principles, it turned out, could largely be plotted on two axes: national interest and military force. In a one superpower world, in which the United States faced no clear foreign menace, Republicans defined America's foreign concerns quite narrowly. The very concept of national interest, many on the right argued, was being threatened by a growing globalist ethic, in which America expended blood and treasure not on its own behalf but in support of an illusory "international community." Older, pre–cold war fears about American sovereignty returned with new force. Democrats, by contrast, generally embraced stronger international institutions—whether through United Nations peacekeeping, International Monetary Fund bailouts, or the International Criminal Court—as essential to prosperity and human rights in a globalized age.

When it came to military force, Republicans remained somewhat more supportive in the abstract. A Pew Research Center survey conducted in 1999, for instance, found that Republicans were 16 percentage points more likely than Democrats to agree with the idea that military strength, rather than diplomacy, was the best way to keep the peace.[12] But in practice the national interest divide often trumped the divide between hawk and dove. Over time, the Clinton administration grew increasingly willing to employ military force in the service of humanitarian goals (proving, surprisingly, that the Democrats' post-Vietnam allergy to military force was less enduring than its post-Vietnam focus on human rights). A 1994 Pew poll found Democrats more supportive than Republicans of military intervention in Haiti, a country Republicans dismissed as strategically irrelevant but Democrats embraced because of the humanitarian horror being perpetrated by its military leader, Raoul Cedras.[13] In Bosnia in 1995, and four years later in Kosovo, the Clinton administration launched air wars to stop Serbian ethnic cleansing—winning praise from a new generation of Democratic human rights hawks but criticism from realist Republicans who thought those conflicts none of America's business.

11. McCormick, Wittkopf, and Danna (1997).
12. Pew Research Center (2005).
13. Times Mirror Center for the People and the Press, "The People, the Press and Politics: The New Political Landscape," September 21, 1994 (people-press.org/reports/pdf/19940921.pdf).

The September 11 Terrorist Attacks

At first George W. Bush's war on terror seemed like an even better candidate for bipartisan consensus than the cold war had been a half-century earlier. (After all, no group of Americans felt any ideological proclivity toward the new, jihadist enemy, whereas a significant portion of the American left had felt at least modest sympathy for communism in the 1930s and 1940s.) Polls conducted shortly after September 11 found virtually no partisan difference over how seriously Democrats and Republicans took the terror threat and whether they considered America to be at war. To get Republicans and Democrats to *disagree,* pollsters had to hypothesize that American retaliation would produce significant civilian casualties, thus forcing Democrats to choose between their traditional inclination toward human rights and their growing comfort with military force. But even here, while Democrats were 10 to 15 percentage points less likely than Republicans to endorse a retaliatory response, they still endorsed it by margins of three or four to one.[14]

The first campaign in America's war on terror—Afghanistan—was tailor-made for bipartisan consensus. It could be justified as self-defense. It was consistent with an unsentimental concern for the national interest, which appealed to Republicans, and yet it also enjoyed multilateral support, which appealed to Democrats. And if the potential for civilian casualties gave Democrats mild pause, the horror of the Taliban's rule in Afghanistan also made it a war for human rights, in the tradition of Bosnia and Kosovo. When Congress voted to authorize the use of military force three days after September 11, every single Republican and every Democrat except one voted yes.

Had the United States never invaded Iraq, one can imagine the war on terror playing out somewhat as the early cold war did, with a broad bipartisan consensus concealing differing partisan emphases. Democrats might have stressed multilateral cooperation (on Afghanistan, some criticized the Bush administration for not granting NATO a more prominent role) and economic development as antidotes to jihadist terror. Republicans might have proved more unilateral and more skeptical of foreign aid as an instrument in the war on terror. But the two parties would not have fundamentally diverged on the centrality to U.S. foreign policy of combating terrorism or on the extent of the country's involvement in the rest of the world. When, in June 2002, the Pew Center asked whether the United States should

14. *Los Angeles Times* Poll, "Terrorism in America," September 13–14, 2001 (www.latimes interactive.com/pdfarchive/stat_sheets/la-timespoll462ss.pdf). See also McCormick, Wittkopf, and Danna (1997).

increase its military presence overseas to combat terrorism, Republicans were 17 percentage points more likely than Democrats to assent, but more Democrats still said yes than no. And when the question switched from military engagement to American engagement in general, the partisan difference disappeared altogether.[15]

Of course, there was no guarantee that the terrorism framework would have remained as all-encompassing as the cold war. The Soviet Union was a fixed star on the geopolitical horizon, constantly reminding Americans of its presence. Jihadist terrorism, by contrast, is more subterranean and more episodic. From the beginning, how enduring the war on terror would be as a foreign policy prism depended on a grisly but simple calculus: whether America—or its close allies— were hit again, and how hard.

Iraq

But if the war on terror had faded from public concern simply through an absence of jihadist terror, the decline would have been largely bipartisan, and U.S. foreign policy might today look more like the ideologically muddled 1990s. Instead, the war on terror was redefined by the war in Iraq in ways that turned a bipartisan foreign policy vision into a deeply partisan one. As a result, U.S. foreign policy debates today resemble the highly polarized debates of the early Reagan era—only more so.

The October 2002 vote granting President Bush the authority to overthrow Saddam Hussein was far more bipartisan than the Gulf War vote eleven years earlier, largely because more Democrats voted yes. But the bipartisanship was more tenuous than it appeared on paper. The Democrats who backed the war generally represented swing states or districts, or harbored national ambitions— leading to the widespread suspicion among fellow Democrats that their votes did not stem from conviction. Democrats without presidential plans, or from safe seats or districts, by contrast, overwhelmingly voted no. (This helps explain why in the Senate, Democrats backed the war 29-21, but in the House they opposed it 126-81). And that skepticism was shared by Democrats around the country. According to a fall 2002 poll, 79 percent of Republicans supported the idea of going to war against Iraq, compared with only 50 percent of Democrats.[16]

And although the Iraq war initially enjoyed more bipartisan support than the Gulf War, it has proved far more politically divisive. George H. W. Bush

15. Pew Research Center for the People and the Press, "Diminished Public Appetite for Military Force and Mideast Oil," September 6, 2006 (people-press.org/reports/display.php3?ReportID=288).

16. Data from a *Washington Post*/ABC News poll cited in Dan Balz, David S. Broder, and Helen Rumbelow, "Poll: War Tops Economy in Voters' Minds," *Washington Post,* September 29, 2002.

scheduled the Gulf vote after the 1990 midterm elections, and because the war ended so quickly, it did not centrally figure in his 1992 reelection campaign. Iraq, by contrast, has been at the heart of three bruising political campaigns, with the Bush administration repeatedly using the war to contrast its foreign policy vision with that of the Democrats. That effort has largely succeeded: to a stunning degree, Iraq now frames how both Democrats and Republicans see the world.

By putting Iraq (and, increasingly, Iran as well) at its center, George W. Bush has expanded the scope of the war on terror. Just as containment was relatively noncontroversial when applied only to Europe but became highly divisive when extended to Asia and Central America, the war on terror has grown more polarizing as it has expanded beyond al Qaeda. In Bush's view, the United States is engaged in a struggle against all anti-American, terror-sponsoring organizations and regimes (even if that terror is directed against Israel, not the United States)— particularly if they are pursuing nuclear weapons. And among Republicans, this definition of the war on terror has stuck. Asked by the Security and Peace Institute in a January 2005 survey to name their three top foreign policy priorities, Republicans answered: keeping nuclear weapons from hostile groups and countries, destroying al Qaeda, and preventing nuclear proliferation in general.[17]

Furthermore, Republicans not only endorse Bush's definition of the war on terror, they generally endorse his methods of fighting it. In the 1990s, Republicans were modestly more sympathetic than Democrats to the use of force. Today, they are vastly more sympathetic. According to Pew, the partisan gap over whether military force, rather than diplomacy, best keeps the peace, grew from 16 percentage points in 1999 to 44 points in December 2004.[18] In November 2005, an MIT poll found that 95 percent of Republicans would back military action to destroy a terrorist camp, 38 points higher than Democrats.[19] And according to a June 2006 German Marshall Fund survey, 70 percent of Republicans would support military action as a last resort to prevent Iran from getting a nuclear weapon, compared to only 41 percent of Democrats.[20] As a Pew report put it in May 2005, "Foreign affairs assertiveness now almost completely distinguishes Republican-

17. Security and Peace Institute, "American Attitudes toward National Security, Foreign Policy and the War on Terror," January 23–27, 2005 (www.tcf.org/Publications/InternationalAffairs/americanattitudes.pdf).
18. Pew Research Center (2005, p. 15).
19. MIT Public Opinion Research Training Lab, "When Should We Fight?" *Boston Review*, January–February 2006.
20. German Marshall Fund of the United States (2006, p. 94).

oriented voters from Democratic-oriented voters; this was a relatively minor factor in past typologies. In contrast, attitudes relating to religion and social values
are not nearly as important in determining party affiliation."[21] In other words,
America's red-blue divide is no longer chiefly between churched and unchurched.
It is between hawk and dove.

Republican support for Bush's war on terror manifests itself not merely in sympathy toward the use of military force but also toward international engagement
more generally. In the 1990s, while Republicans were mildly more hawkish than
Democrats, they were also more isolationist. (The signature Republican foreign
policy initiative of the era was missile defense, which blended the two instincts.)
But today Republicans are strikingly more internationalist. A Democracy Corps
poll in the summer of 2006 found Republicans 35 percentage points more likely
than Democrats to declare American power a force for good in the world, and
according to a December 2006 CBS poll, Democrats were 34 points more likely
to say the United States should mind its own business around the world. In a historic shift, some polls even find Republicans more supportive than Democrats of
foreign aid.[22]

Perhaps the most dramatic illustration of how Iraq has reshaped the foreign
policy debate comes in response to the question of whether the United States
should promote democracy overseas. Throughout the 1990s, and culminating in
George W. Bush's 2000 presidential campaign, Republicans criticized the Clinton
administration for its excessively Wilsonian efforts to inculcate democracy in
Haiti, the Balkans, and other bleak corners of the globe. Polling in 2005 and
2006, however, shows Republicans far more likely (by 25 to 30 percentage points)
to say that the United States should try to change dictatorships to democracies,
even when the question does not mention military force.[23] And when the German
Marshall Fund asked about nonviolent forms of democracy assistance such as election monitoring, supporting dissidents, and imposing sanctions—the kinds of

21. Pew Research Center for the People and the Press, "Beyond Red vs. Blue," May 10, 2005
(people-press.org/reports/display.php3?ReportID=242).

22. Democracy Corps, "National Security Survey," August 23–27, 2006 (www.democracycorps.
com/reports/surveys/Democracy_Corps_August_23-27_2006_Survey.pdf); CBS News Poll, "War
in Iraq: Going Badly and Getting Worse," December 8–10, 2006 (www.cbsnews.com/htdocs/
CBSNews_polls/dec06iraq.pdf).

23. Security and Peace Institute, "American Attitudes toward National Security, Foreign Policy
and the War on Terror," January 23–27, 2005 (www.tcf.org/Publications/InternationalAffairs/
americanattitudes.pdf). See also German Marshall Fund (2006, p. 110); CBS News Poll, "War in
Iraq: Going Badly and Getting Worse," December 8–10, 2006.

things conservatives once derided in foreign policy as "social work"—Republicans still expressed substantially more support than did Democrats.[24]

Republicans and Democrats, in other words, do not merely disagree on Iraq. As a result of the war in Iraq, they see the world in vastly different ways. To an extent not seen since Reagan's first term (and perhaps not even then), both parties have embraced the further reaches of their ideological traditions. They have become caricatures of themselves. Evidence that Democrats no longer see the world through the prism of the war on terror is legion. For starters, the war on terror implies a political environment in which foreign policy is king. But for Democrats it is not. In January 2005, only 29 percent of Democrats said that foreign, rather than domestic, policy had determined their vote for president—half that of Republicans.[25] When the *New York Times* polled delegates to the 2004 party conventions, 46 percent of Republicans said Iraq, terrorism, war, defense, or homeland security was the biggest campaign issue in their state. Among Democratic delegates, by contrast, the figure was 18 percent.[26] And when Democrats do think about foreign policy, they do not equate it with the war on terror or even national security. The 2005 Security and Peace Institute poll, which determined that Republicans' top foreign policy priorities were stopping nuclear proliferation and destroying al Qaeda, found that the top three for Democrats were withdrawing troops from Iraq, stopping the spread of AIDS, and improving relations with America's allies.[27]

On questions relating specifically to the war on terror, Democrats are strikingly dovish and isolationist—far more than they were several years ago. Polling in August 2002 found members of the two parties nearly indistinguishable on whether the United States should reduce its international involvement as the best strategy against terrorism. By August 2006, however, the gap was 15 percentage points.[28] In November 2005, only 59 percent of Democrats still endorsed the war

24. See German Marshall Fund (2006, pp. 116, 120, 122, 124).

25. From survey data in Security and Peace Institute, "American Attitudes toward National Security, Foreign Policy and the War on Terror," January 23–27, 2005 (www.tcf.org/Publications/InternationalAffairs/americanattitudes.pdf).

26. *New York Times*/CBS News Poll, "2004 Republican National Delegate Survey," August 3–23, 2004 (www.nytimes.com/packages/html/politics/20040829_gop_poll/2004_gop_results.pdf).

27. Security and Peace Institute, "American Attitudes toward National Security, Foreign Policy and the War on Terror."

28. Pew Research Center for the People and the Press, "Diminished Public Appetite for Military Force and Mideast Oil," September 6, 2006 (people-press.org/reports/display.php3?ReportID=288).

in Afghanistan and only 57 percent endorsed the hypothetical use of military force against a terrorist camp, remarkably tepid numbers given how uncontroversial those positions were after September 11.[29]

But just because Democrats exhibit isolationist and dovish sentiments on the war on terror does not make them isolationist and dovish about everything. It is a mistake to see Democratic views on the war on terror as the sum total of their foreign policy perspective because for Democrats, unlike Republicans, the war on terror is not—or should not be—the core of U.S. foreign policy. Democrats are far more worried than Republicans about global warming, bird flu, global poverty, AIDS, and the outsourcing of jobs overseas.[30] They worry less about military threats and more about economic and humanitarian ones, less about national security and more about what has been dubbed "human security." Democrats are 19 percentage points more likely than Republicans to say economic power matters more in the world than military power.[31] And while Republicans worry about China primarily as a military threat, Democrats worry about it primarily as an economic threat.[32] It is worth remembering that in the final stages of the 2004 Democratic presidential primaries, when the remaining competitors were John Kerry and John Edwards, the foreign policy issue that garnered the most discussion was not terrorism or even Iraq. It was trade.

When one moves beyond the war on terror, Democrats regain some of their internationalism and even show traces of the humanitarian hawkishness of the 1990s. For instance, as mentioned above, polls find Democrats highly allergic to the idea of democracy promotion while Republicans are quite supportive, suggesting that the two parties have polarized along a realist-idealist or relativist-universalist divide. Yet when "democracy" is replaced with "human rights," things change dramatically—and it is Democrats who say the United States should aggressively promote its values around the world.[33] (The increasingly partisan connotations of the terms "democracy" and "human rights" represent an intriguing

29. MIT Public Opinion Research Training Lab, "When Should We Fight?" *Boston Review,* January–February 2006.

30. Security and Peace Institute, "American Attitudes toward National Security, Foreign Policy and the War on Terror," January 23–27, 2005 (www.tcf.org/Publications/InternationalAffairs/americanattitudes.pdf); German Marshall Fund (2006, pp. 56, 60, 74, 78).

31. German Marshall Fund (2006, p. 128).

32. German Marshall Fund (2006, p. 86).

33. Security and Peace Institute, "American Attitudes toward National Security, Foreign Policy and the War on Terror."

throwback to the Carter-Reagan debates of the late 1970s and early 1980s.) In fact, it is Republicans, despite supporting the promotion of democracy overseas, who are more likely to say Islam is incompatible with it.[34] For many Republicans, the war on terror seems to be a democratic crusade *and* a clash of civilizations, while for Democrats it is neither.

Democrats also become markedly more internationalist when the means of engaging the world are multilateral. They are far more supportive of the United Nations than Republicans, and even somewhat more sympathetic to NATO.[35] And when Democrats feel that the means are multilateral and the ends humanitarian, they start sounding less like George McGovern and more like Tony Blair. Democrats are a little more likely than Republicans to support sending U.S. troops into Darfur, and self-described liberals are 10 percentage points more likely than self-described conservatives to back military intervention to stop genocide.[36] Similarly, Democrats are more inclined than Republicans to deploy U.S. troops in UN peacekeeping missions and in support of international law.[37]

The only area where Democrats are significantly less multilateral is trade, where they oppose the North American Free Trade Agreement at twice the rate of Republicans (though even among Republicans, the treaty has more opponents than supporters).[38] But what bothers Democrats is the content of the trade deals, not their multilateralism. Unlike the nationalist right, Democrats do not oppose international agreements on principle because they infringe upon U.S. sovereignty. Were trade deals to contain stringent environmental and labor standards, Democrats might well embrace them.

34. German Marshall Fund (2006, p. 106).

35. German Marshall Fund (2006, pp. 20, 22). See also Democracy Corps, "National Security Survey," August 23–27, 2006 (www.democracycorps.com/reports/surveys/Democracy_Corps_August_23-27_2006_Survey.pdf).

36. Program on International Policy Attitudes, "The Darfur Crisis: African and American Public Opinion," June 22–26, 2005 (www.pipa.org/OnlineReports/Africa/Darfur_Jun05/Darfur_Jun05_rpt.pdf); Security and Peace Institute, "American Attitudes toward National Security, Foreign Policy and the War on Terror," January 23–27, 2005 (www.tcf.org/Publications/InternationalAffairs/americanattitudes.pdf).

37. Security and Peace Institute, "American Attitudes toward National Security, Foreign Policy and the War on Terror." See also MIT Public Opinion Research Training Lab, "When Should We Fight?"

38. Democracy Corps, "National Security Survey." See also German Marshall Fund (2006, p. 86).

The Future

All of which is to say that, for the moment, the prospects for foreign policy bipartisanship look dim. Part of the reason is President Bush himself, who Democrats believe will never partner with them in good faith. In 2002 it would have been easy to imagine a highly respected Democrat accepting a top foreign policy post in the Bush cabinet (as Republicans Henry Stimson and Frank Knox did in 1940, when they became Franklin Roosevelt's secretaries of war and the navy, respectively). In 2004 it was harder to envision but still conceivable. Today any Democrat who accepted such a position would likely be viewed as a pariah. In 2004 Democratic presidential candidate John Kerry reportedly asked Senator John McCain (R-Ariz.), who had contested for the Republican presidential nomination just four years earlier, to serve as his running mate, with no significant outcry from the Democratic base. Given how polarized the Iraq debate has grown since then, however, such a courtship today would be unthinkable.

The difficulty of bipartisanship on Iraq was nicely illustrated by the Iraq Study Group, which contained eminences from across the aisle, but whose report was politically orphaned nonetheless. And the war in Iraq will likely cast a shadow over the U.S. foreign policy debate for years, if not decades, to come. It will almost certainly make Democrats (and many independents) more hostile to the idea of military intervention—especially if it lacks multilateral support. Not long ago, it was considered politically shrewd for Democrats with national ambitions to try to get to Bush's right on Iran, but today such a gambit would produce revulsion among the Democratic grassroots. It is no longer conceivable that U.S. military action against Iran could enjoy anything but purely partisan Republican support. Nor is it easy to imagine a post-Bush Democratic president continuing large-scale troop deployments in Iraq for years to come. Indeed, one could even imagine Afghanistan losing its bipartisan sheen, especially if NATO stood down and Afghan public opinion turned strongly against a foreign presence. If a Republican held the White House under those circumstances, it is not impossible to imagine Democrats supporting a U.S. withdrawal. After all, only 59 percent of Democrats still approved of the Afghan war in 2005.[39]

In many ways, the looming questions are largely on the Republican side. Among Democrats there is no question that Iraq will be seen, like Vietnam, as an

39. MIT Public Opinion Research Training Lab, "When Should We Fight?" *Boston Review,* January–February 2006.

unwinnable mistake. Less clear is whether most Republicans will decide, à la Vietnam, that the United States lost because it fought with a hand tied behind its back—either because the Bush administration failed to initially send sufficient troops, as McCain has argued, or because the Democrats prematurely ended the war. (The latter assessment will probably be increasingly likely if a Democrat gains the White House in 2009.) If most Republicans see Iraq as having been lost in Washington rather than Baghdad, the Iraq war may not seriously impair GOP hawkishness, even as it pushes Democrats in a dovish direction. If McCain's view does not take hold, however, and Republicans see Iraq as an example of the limits of military force, the divide between the two parties on military force could narrow. Indeed, there is evidence that the partisan foreign policy divide has narrowed since 2006, as some Republicans have moved in a more multilateral, dovish direction. But I suspect this will prove temporary. Already Republicans exhibit significantly more hawkish instincts on China than do Democrats. And given the likelihood that competition—and potentially confrontation—with Beijing will powerfully shape U.S. foreign policy well into the future, China could be the stage on which Republicans and Democrats rehearse their hawk-dove arguments in the years to come.

Foreign policy bipartisanship, of course, is not a good in and of itself. If the Marshall Plan and the creation of NATO were bipartisan, so was the Tonkin Gulf Resolution and, to some degree, the vote to authorize the war in Iraq. Generally, we think of bipartisanship in terms of postwar internationalism. But isolationism can also enjoy bipartisan support, as it did in the 1920s.

Were bipartisanship to revive in the years to come, it could take either internationalist or isolationist forms. A bipartisan internationalism might require a renewed U.S. effort to reform and strengthen the United Nations, the International Monetary Fund and World Bank, the World Trade Organization, NATO, and other international institutions. The more multilateral American foreign policy becomes, the more Democratic internationalism will rebound from Iraq. This is especially true on the use of military force. Kosovo remains an attractive model, especially to Democratic foreign policy elites, and even in the wake of Iraq, many Democrats look favorably upon NATO military action in Darfur. In the radically unlikely event that the United States gained the support of the UN Security Council or NATO for an attack on Iran, Democratic thinking on that subject might change too.

The slide in Democratic support for military intervention, for democracy promotion, and even for foreign aid, could be partially halted if those efforts were legitimized through empowered international institutions. And while Republicans remain generally skeptical of such institutions, they might come to see them as the only way to maintain the interventionism that they embraced under Bush. John McCain, in particular, while every bit as hawkish as Bush, is less instinctively uni-lateral, as evidenced by his position on torture and his support for the Kosovo war. On Iran and North Korea, Condoleezza Rice has moved U.S. policy in a more multilateral direction. And it is worth noting that one of the few public figures who retains some prestige among both Democrats and Republicans is Tony Blair, whose foreign policy vision might be characterized as humanitarian, multilateral, and hawkish.

An isolationist-leaning bipartisanship would look very different. The point of intersection might come if Republicans abandoned their Wilsonianism in the wake of Iraq (and there is some survey evidence that they are doing so).[40] Repub-lican foreign policy might then look more like it did in the 1990s: hawkish on national security threats but not on humanitarian interventions and extremely jealous of American sovereignty. Clearly, the Republican revolt against the Bush administration on the Dubai Ports deal in early 2006 and growing Republican anxiety about immigration suggest that the GOP may move in a more inward-looking direction. Similarly, while Democrats retain streaks of humanitarian internationalism, the party has grown more realist and more isolationist since Iraq. And if Republicans are growing more hostile to unfettered immigration, Demo-crats are growing more hostile to unfettered trade. While elites are more likely to envision a bipartisanship that embraces globalization, it is politically easier to imagine a Lou Dobbs–style bipartisanship (or perhaps antipartisanship) that rejects globalization.

If Americans do come together across party lines on foreign policy in the years to come, it will more likely be to retrench America's commitments overseas than to extend them. Just five years ago that would have seemed bizarre. But such is the fateful impact of the war in Iraq.

40. CBS News Poll, "War in Iraq: Going Badly and Getting Worse," December 8–10, 2006 (www.cbsnews.com/htdocs/CBSNews_polls/dec06iraq.pdf).

Comments on Chapter Four

COMMENT

James Q. Wilson

The chief problem with political polarization is its effect on America's foreign and military policy. There are two reasons for this view. First, when the United States engages an enemy or friend abroad, its chances of success are heightened by coherent political support at home. But when our nation appears divided, our friends discount our promises and our enemies anticipate our weaknesses. The North Vietnamese understood this perfectly: their armies could not defeat us in battle, but our critics could defeat us at home.

Second, the American people are heavily influenced by elite opinion on matters about which they are personally uninformed. Elite opinions are largely irrelevant when it comes to issues such as crime, inflation, and unemployment; Americans know firsthand about these things. But elite views can be very influential when it comes to foreign and military policy since, except for the families of combat personnel, Americans have little knowledge about what the government does, or might do, overseas and even less about the countries where these actions could occur. The opinions of Americans will change, of course, when the country is attacked, as it was on December 7, 1941, and September 11, 2001. But public support for what the nation does in response to such attacks—or in response to some other kind of international crisis—is heavily influenced by elite opinion.

The central issue in judging the effect of political polarization on foreign and military policy is to assess the size of the elite and what it has to say about the country's foreign and military efforts. During the Second World War, the elite consisted of political and military leaders and the editors of newspapers, magazines, and radio broadcasts, and they all spoke with one voice: it was a war that had to be won even though early on the United States and its allies suffered heavy losses in Europe, Asia, and North Africa.

In his essay, Peter Beinart expresses a belief, which I share, that this nation needs a bipartisan foreign policy and one that is internationalist and not isolationist. Though bipartisanship existed in the 1940s, its likelihood today seems close to zero. Between the 1940s and the present, bipartisanship declined, but not until the Iraq war did it utterly collapse. In the 1950s and 1960s, there was cer-

tainly elite disagreement about the wars in Korea and Vietnam, but that disagreement had only a modest effect on public opinion.

In his comments in the first volume of *Red and Blue Nation?* Carl Cannon of
the *National Journal* examined surveys of public opinion during these earlier conflicts. When people were asked in 1951 whether the war in Korea was "a mistake,"
43 percent of Democrats and 55 percent of Republicans said it was.[1] Note that
even though U.S. involvement in the war was the product of a Democratic president, Democratic opposition among those polled was only 12 percentage points
less than that of Republicans.

This modest gap did not exist because of elite unity. On the contrary, Democratic and Republican members of Congress were deeply divided. Many congressional Republicans blamed the Democrats for the "loss" of China to Mao Zedong.
Senator William Jenner (R-Ind.) called George Marshall, the secretary of defense,
a "front man for traitors" and "a living lie." Senator Joseph McCarthy (R-Wis.)
called Marshall "completely incompetent" and published a book in which he
accused Marshall of being part of a "conspiracy so immense and an infamy so
black as to dwarf any previous such venture in the history of man."[2] Senator
Richard Nixon (R-Calif.) called for Truman's impeachment. After Truman fired
General Douglas MacArthur, the general received the biggest ticker tape parade
in the history of New York City; he then gave an emotional defense of himself to
a joint session of Congress, leading the Senate Republican Policy Committee to
vote unanimously for a manifesto indicting Truman, Marshall, and Secretary of
State Dean Acheson for a "super-Munich in Asia."[3] Yet despite all of this, more
than a third of all Republican voters (and 40 percent of independents) told pollsters that the war in Korea was *not* a mistake.

Elite opinion was similarly divided over the war in Vietnam, at least after 1968.
Senator J. William Fulbright (D-Ark.), chairman of the Foreign Relations Committee, held hearings featuring witnesses who denounced U.S. efforts in Vietnam.
Reporting from young journalists who covered the war there was overwhelmingly
negative. The *New York Times's* David Halberstam, one of the leading writers, later
said that the pessimistic stories that he and others filed were justified because "there
was something terribly wrong going on over there."[4] When North Vietnamese

1. The data Cannon reviews are from Gallup polls cited in Carl M. Cannon, "Administration:
A New Era of Partisan War," *National Journal,* March 18, 2006.
2. Quoted in Stoler (1989, pp. 182, 188–89).
3. Stoler (1989, p. 188); Cray (2000, pp. 708–14).
4. Quoted in James Q. Wilson, "The Press at War," *City Journal,* Autumn 2006.

forces were defeated during the Tet Offensive in early 1968, the press almost universally reported that it was instead a defeat for American forces. Shown evidence that it was the North Vietnamese, not the Americans, who had lost, a key television news producer for NBC rejected the idea of issuing a correction on the grounds that Tet was already "established in the public's mind as a defeat, and therefore it was an American defeat."[5] But when Americans were polled after the Tet Offensive, one third of Republicans, Democrats, and independents said the war "was not a mistake." Political party affiliation made no difference in their perceptions.

Now we come to Iraq. Elite opinion has been divided about this war as well, but now elite divisions are almost precisely mirrored in public divisions. In February 2006, a CBS News poll asked Americans whether the United States "did the right thing in taking military action against Iraq or should the U.S. have stayed out." Among Democrats 76 percent said the United States should have stayed out; only 25 percent of Republicans said that. (Independent voters were split down the middle.)[6] This is a stark contrast with public opinion during the Vietnam era, when Democrats and Republicans held roughly similar views of the war until well after the Tet Offensive (and even then their views differed only slightly). During the Iraq war, Democrats and Republicans differed from the outset, with the gap widening as the war went on.[7]

Something, then, has changed. Both the Korean and Vietnam wars were controversial, and each was an important element in a presidential campaign (Korea in 1952, Vietnam in 1972). But unlike the situation today with regard to the Iraq war, Democrats and Republicans were not then almost entirely on opposite sides. And the current split over the war is mirrored in many other aspects of foreign and military policy. Republicans, for instance, believe military strength is more important than diplomacy in advancing U.S. interests; Democrats have the opposite view. Republicans define America's international obligations as resisting nuclear proliferation and opposing terrorism; Democrats define it as bringing troops home, fighting AIDS, and improving relations with U.S. allies. If the overseas mission of the United States is defined as expanding democracy, Republicans favor it and Democrats oppose it; if it is defined as enhancing human rights, Democrats support it and Republicans question it.

5. Epstein (1975, p. 225).

6. CBS News Poll, "President Bush, the Post, and Iraq," February 22–26, 2006 (www.cbsnews.com/htdocs/pdf/poll_bush_022706.pdf), cited Carl Cannon's comment in the first volume of the *Red and Blue Nation?* study.

7. Michael Dimock, "The Iraq-Vietnam Difference," Pew Research Center for the People and the Press, May 16, 2006 (pewresearch.org/pubs/25/the-iraq-vietnam-difference).

One reason for this divide is partisanship. In the 1990s, Democrats and the liberal media favored a United Nations intervention in Bosnia and Kosovo. The *New York Times* editorial page strongly criticized President George H. W. Bush for having ignored the creation of concentration camps in Bosnia, and it supported U.S. bombing raids in Kosovo. It urged its readers not to worry about air attacks that inadvertently killed innocent civilians, even though our interventions there were not authorized by the UN. Prominent Democratic senators Barbara Boxer (Calif.), Carl Levin (Mich.), and Paul Wellstone (Minn.) supported U.S. actions in Bosnia and Kosovo; Republican senators Don Nickels (Okla.) and John Warner (Va.) and Republican representative Dan Burton (Ind.) opposed them. Ten years later, on the issue of invading Iraq, the positions of the *New York Times,* the parties, and these legislators were reversed.

One can imagine certain explanations for this reversal. Possibly Democrats believed that Europeans were more important than Middle Easterners, or that it was safe to conduct a war in which U.S. planes dropped bombs from above 15,000 feet but not one in which troops fought on the ground. Republicans may have thought the oil-rich Middle East is more important than the remnants of Yugoslavia and that boots on the ground are more effective than air strikes. But this is not just routine partisanship. If it were, the public would not follow elite leads so closely today when they followed them only slightly during the fighting in Korea and Vietnam.

A second reason for the collapse of bipartisanship is the growth of a sectarian mass media that no longer works as hard as it once did to attract a mass audience and to maintain moderate or equivocal opinions. Owing to the multiplication of cable outlets, news programs are becoming more like magazines that target committed followers (much as *Yachting* and *Road & Track* do) and less like entities seeking a mass audience. The number of viewers of network broadcast news has been dropping sharply for years while the audience for cable outlets has been growing. The demise of the FCC's fairness doctrine has meant that controversial political talk shows are now commonplace. The thirty-minute *Huntley-Brinkley Report* has been replaced by a left-wing CBS News and a right-wing Fox News Channel, a left-leaning Al Franken and a right-leaning Rush Limbaugh. Some may note that the top cable programs draw only a few million viewers, but they should remember that the *Rush Limbaugh Show* draws 13.5 million a week.[8]

The nonpartisan Center for Media and Public Affairs found that during the active and swift war against Saddam Hussein, 51 percent of network news stories

8. Project for Excellence in Journalism (2004).

were critical of the American role. Six months after that fighting ended, 77 percent were negative. By the spring of 2006, 94 percent of reports on Bush's foreign
policy were negative.[9] And for those media outlets that still strive for a mass audience, economics has led them to shift their focus. As economist James Hamilton
has argued, their rational strategy is to take older (and generally more conservative) viewers for granted and struggle hard to win younger (and generally more
liberal) viewers.[10] Young females, disproportionately liberal, are the key marginal
viewer; it is they, network executives believe, who make the purchasing decisions.

A third factor explaining the partisan divide is the growth of higher education,
especially at the postgraduate level. U.S. colleges and universities award more than
40,000 Ph.D.'s each year. Though college graduates tend to be centrists, those
with postgraduate education are strongly liberal. (Half of all Democrats with a
postgraduate education supported John Kerry for president in 2004; less than a
third of postgraduates supported President Bush.)[11] The growth in postgraduate
education has not necessarily made people more knowledgeable about the world,
but it has surely put them more closely in touch with political agitation.

All of these factors reinforce what political scientist John Zaller has shown
regarding the relationship between elite and mass opinions: when elites agree on
a matter, the public goes along with them; when they disagree, as they did over
the first Persian Gulf War, the people divide.[12] And the greatest division occurs
among people who read or watch the media the most.

All national leaders will make mistakes. Republicans made them in how they
mismanaged their occupation of Iraq and currently make them with their short-
sighted view on immigration. Democrats make them by wishing to expand
human rights without insisting that exporting democracy is essential to such
rights. But for the country, mistakes seem to be less important than ideological
orientation—and that orientation has diverged greatly.

9. See Center for Media and Public Affairs, *Media Monitors* (July–August 2003, November–
December 2003, November–December 2004, and Spring 2006).

10. Hamilton (2004, pp. 72, 85, 93, 104–05).

11. Pew Research Center for the People and the Press, "Slight Bush Margin in Final Days of Campaign," October 31, 2004 (people-press.org/reports/display.php3?ReportID=232).

12. Zaller (1996).

Jonathan Rauch

As a concise history of elite opinion on foreign policy in the postwar era, Peter Beinart's chapter commands unreserved admiration and endorsement. It also offers provocative insights on where foreign policy may be headed in the future. Where the present is concerned, however, I want to use this comment to demur. Beinart's thesis, as I understand it, is that George W. Bush's presidency and the Iraq war have taken partisanship in U.S. foreign policy to a new level, and that hyperpartisanship will be a fact of political life for some time to come. Perhaps. But there is evidence that America's rank-and-file partisans agree on much more than the conventional wisdom would suggest. A look at political fundamentals, in the form of public opinion in both parties, hints that polarization may have already peaked and that President Bush's departure from the scene may bring rapid bipartisan movement toward a more multilateralist, less confrontational foreign policy.

Let me begin, however, with some important points of agreement. The broad story that Beinart tells as he looks back over the past several decades is unquestionably correct. Partisans' opinions on foreign policy grew both more intense and more ideologically polarized in the years from Truman through Reagan. The 1990s brought a more muddled kind of partisanship, with differences still pronounced but organized less around ideology than around personal and situational politics. The George W. Bush era has brought a third period, this one marked by extreme partisanship. The trend, then, toward heightened partisan polarization on U.S. foreign policy is not in doubt.

Beinart is also right to emphasize the importance of two wars—first Vietnam, then Iraq—in driving a wedge between the parties. At least in passing, however, it is worth noting that the causality flowed not just from foreign policy disagreement to party polarization but also the other way around. One of the best-documented changes in the structure of twentieth-century U.S. politics has been the ideological sorting of the parties. The liberal northeastern Republicans and conservative southern Democrats who were common in the pre-Vietnam years are now all but extinct; the two parties are much more ideologically homogeneous than in the 1950s and 1960s, and much more reliably opposed to each other. The result has been to heighten partisan polarization up and down the line, not just on foreign policy but on social issues, economic issues, and everything else. That, of course, does not make Beinart's story wrong; it merely serves as a reminder not to view the foreign policy debate in isolation—and that the parties have been more rapidly and thoroughly polarized than the public.

Beinart is also correct about what is generating the increasing partisan disagreement. Intensely partisan members of each party have different theories of how to achieve peace. Republicans believe peace comes from American strength, wielded vigorously and, if necessary, unilaterally and preemptively. Democrats believe peace comes from international cooperation, which the United States should take the lead in organizing. Americans have always differed over the relative utility of strength versus cooperation; what is new is that the two schools are now roughly congruent with the two parties. That will likely sharpen and intensify the foreign policy debate for years to come.

Even so, it is easy to overstate how far apart the parties actually are—particularly if one focuses primarily, as Beinart does, on opinion among partisan elites, who are both more ideological and more polarized than are rank-and-file partisans and (especially) the broad public. Beinart argues that "America's red-blue divide is no longer chiefly between churched and unchurched. It is between hawk and dove." That may be true, or largely true, of *Washington's* red-blue divide, but I am not convinced it is true of *America's* red-blue divide. "As a result of the war in Iraq," Beinart writes, Republicans and Democrats "see the world in vastly different ways." He reads the Iraq war as a political rupture, emptying the center and turning both parties into ideological "caricatures of themselves." Again, that may be true of many polarized partisans and activists in Washington, but the evidence on the public as a whole is that the Iraq war is less a permanent rupture than a temporary overshoot—with a centrist correction already under way.

To understand the difference in our views, recall a fact often overlooked: the red-blue opinion gap on any given subject may widen significantly *without producing actual disagreement.* Instead, a widening gap can indicate *weaker agreement* across party lines. For instance, in a January 2007 article arguing that hawks-versus-doves has become "the real divide in American politics," one political writer noted that "the partisan difference on expanding defense spending increased by 10 percentage points between 1998 and 2004."[13] Perhaps, but according to a December 2006 poll by the University of Maryland's Program on International Policy Attitudes, 61 percent of Republicans *agreed* with 83 percent of Democrats that defense spending should not be increased. (Those respon-

---

13. Matthew Continetti, "The Peace Party vs. the Power Party," *Weekly Standard,* January 1, 2007.

dents said defense spending should be cut or kept the same.)[14] This distinction between *softened consensus* and *outright disagreement* is a crucial one because partisans in the general public turn out to agree on quite a lot. In fact, they agree on what they want: a less confrontational foreign policy than the one the Bush administration pursued.

In an effort to look beyond the partisan hothouse of Washington, I gathered nine polls on foreign policy taken over the course of 2006 and assembled responses to sixty-two questions. The results are shown table 4-1. Questions on which majorities of both parties expressed agreement are highlighted in gray. The sample of poll questions is neither scientific nor representative; I chose them subjectively, for diversity and quality, and so nothing in particular can be learned by counting up responses on one side or another. Nonetheless, those who assume that the country is riven by partisanship on foreign policy may be surprised by the results.

Questions about President Bush's performance were polarizing, with partisans rushing to their respective corners, as might be expected given the strong feelings Bush engenders among partisans. Backward-looking, evaluative questions on the Iraq war (all of which were asked before the administration's 2007 "surge" of additional troops into Iraq) were also polarizing, with Republicans refusing to see U.S. failure in Iraq and Democrats refusing to see success.

Yet when surveys turned to forward-looking strategies for Iraq, majorities of Republicans and Democrats agreed on favoring a major international conference and talks with Iran and Syria (steps that had met with resistance from the Bush administration), abjuring the retention of U.S. bases in Iraq, withdrawing most American forces by early 2008, and even putting the whole operation under United Nations command if doing so would obtain more foreign troops. Democrats were more enthusiastic about all of those measures than Republicans, but the overall agreement on courses of action rejected by the Republican leadership in Washington was striking.

The hawks-versus-doves analysis focuses on attitudes toward the use of force as the fulcrum of disagreement between the parties. On that score, Republicans were clearly more hawkish than Democrats, but the accent is on the "ish." Majorities in both parties saw economic power as more important than military power, opposed making regime change an explicit goal of policy, favored using U.S. troops to stop genocide, thought the United States should put more emphasis on

<hr />

14. Program on International Policy Attitudes, "Opportunities for Bipartisan Consensus—2007: What Both Republicans and Democrats Want in U.S. Foreign Policy," December 6–12, 2006 (www.worldpublicopinion.org/pipa/pdf/jan07/Bipartisan_Jan07_rpt.pdf).

Table 4-1. *Shades of Agreement*

Percent of respondents who agree

Questions on which majorities of both parties expressed agreement are highlighted in gray.

Survey categories and questions	Republicans	Democrats	Independents
President Bush			
Bush has decreased goodwill toward United States[a]	64	89	76
Bush's foreign policy has increased likelihood of terror attack on United States[a]	27	80	70
Bush is too quick to involve U.S. military forces[a]	29	91	74
Use of force			
Favor using U.S. troops to stop genocide[b]	74	72	64
Oppose using U.S. troops to replace dictatorship with democracy[b]	65	69	64
Maintaining superior military power: very/somewhat important[b]	96	89	86
Do not announce goal of removing problem government[c]	67	78	68
Economic power is more important than military power[d]	62	81	74
Countries have right to war on strong evidence of weapons of mass destruction[b]	72	53	53
Iraq war should increase caution on using force against rogue states[b]	55	75	68
Do not increase defense spending ("cut" plus "keep the same")[c]	61	83	72
War sometimes necessary to obtain justice: agree strongly/somewhat[d]	93	70	74
Increase emphasis on diplomatic and economic methods (versus military)[a]	52	77	74
Oppose military force to remove authoritarian regimes[d]	37	65	60
Maintaining superior military power: very important[b]	72	44	45
Foreign leaders' fear of U.S. military force aids U.S. security[c]	53	20	29
War sometimes necessary to obtain justice: agree strongly[d]	63	30	38
Must address sources of hostility, not just destroy terrorists[c]	41	76	60
Iran			
Military strike only with allies and UN authorization[b]	57	65	49
Use troops to stop Iran from obtaining nuclear weapons[b]	73	57	54
Try to build better relations (versus implying threats of force)[c]	56	88	80

Table 4-1. *Shades of Agreement (continued)*
Percent of respondents who agree
Questions on which majorities of both parties expressed agreement are highlighted in gray.

Survey categories and questions	Republicans	Democrats	Independents
No preconditions for talks[c]	36	62	49
U.S. military action if other options would not stop nukes[d]	70	41	54
Iraq			
Hold major international conference on Iraq[c]	79	80	77
Talk with Iran to stabilize Iraq[c]	72	81	71
Talk with Syria to stabilize Iraq[c]	72	82	69
No U.S. bases in Iraq[c]	53	77	70
Withdraw almost all U.S. troops by early 2008[e]	62	88	62
Put operation under UN command if this obtains more foreign troops[f]	60	86	67
Iraq war will not spread democracy in Middle East[b]	48	80	62
War has not reduced threat of terrorism[b]	44	78	60
Withdraw according to timetable[c]	35	78	56
War will be another Vietnam[g]	23	67	53
U.S. forces provoke more conflict than they prevent[c]	27	85	60
Multilateralism			
Participate in biological weapons convention with inspections[b]	91	89	86
Participate in nuclear-test-ban treaty[b]	86	88	83
Participate in treaties on detainee treatment[h]	85	89	76
International problems: United States should solve with other countries[a]	72	77	67
Participate in International Criminal Court[b]	68	73	69
International problems: United States should withdraw from efforts to solve[a]	11	18	21
Critical to act together with closest allies[d]	60	68	68
Approve of treaty prohibiting torture[h]	81	90	68
Coordinate with other countries (versus use power in U.S. interest)[a]	75	84	77
United States should comply with adverse World Trade Organization rulings[b]	67	78	74
International problems: United States should be preeminent world leader in solving[a]	16	5	6
United States should not go its own way in international matters[a]	62	81	71
United States should participate in Kyoto global warming treaty[b]	59	79	70
Change Guantanamo practices in accord with UN prescriptions[i]	51	73	58
Increasingly necessary to work through international institutions[a]	55	81	68

(continued)

Table 4-1. *Shades of Agreement (continued)*
Percent of respondents who agree
Questions on which majorities of both parties expressed agreement are highlighted in gray.

Survey categories and questions	Republicans	Democrats	Independents
United Nations			
Favor UN marshal service to arrest genocidal leaders[b]	73	77	72
Favor standing peacekeeping force under UN command[b]	64	80	68
Important to strengthen UN[b]	66	91	79
Favorable opinion of UN[d]	48	76	63
Work more within UN, even if this means compromising[a]	41	77	62
Other			
Preventing spread of nuclear weapons very important[b]	77	75	66
Eventually eliminate all nuclear weapons as per nonproliferation treaty[c]	73	87	84
Talk to U.S. adversaries (versus isolate)[c]	71	89	85
No torture even to save innocent lives[b]	56	75	70
North Korea: United States should be willing to agree to nonaggression pact[c]	61	82	66
Favor limits on U.S. greenhouse gas emissions[e]	61	82	57
No preconditions on talks with U.S. adversaries[a]	47	60	56
U.S. role to help establish democracy in other countries[d]	64	35	41

Source: Author compilation from nine polls, as indicated below.

a. Program on International Policy Attitudes, "What Kind of Foreign Policy Does the American Public Want?" October 6–15, 2006 (www.worldpublicopinion.org/pipa/pdf/oct06/SecurityFP_Oct06_rpt.pdf).

b. Chicago Council on Global Affairs, "Global Views 2006: The United States and the Rise of China and India," October 11, 2006 (www.thechicagocouncil.org/UserFiles/File/GlobalViews06Final.pdf).

c. Program on International Policy Attitudes, "Americans Assess U.S. International Strategy," November 21–29, 2006 (www.worldpublicopinion.org/pipa/pdf/dec06/USIntlStrategy_Dec06_rpt.pdf).

d. German Marshall Fund (2006).

e. Program on International Policy Attitudes, "Opportunities for Bipartisan Consensus—2007: What Both Republicans and Democrats Want in U.S. Foreign Policy," December 6–12, 2006 (www.world publicopinion.org/pipa/pdf/jan07/Bipartisan_Jan07_rpt.pdf).

f. Program on International Policy Attitudes, "Americans on Iraq: Three Years On," March 1–6, 2006 (www.worldpublicopinion.org/pipa/pdf/mar06/USIraq_Mar06_rpt.pdf).

g. Pew Research Center for the People and the Press, "Baker-Hamilton Report Evokes Modest Public Interest," December 12, 2006 (people-press.org/reports/display.php3?ReportID=297).

h. Program on International Policy Attitudes, "Americans on International Courts and Their Jurisdiction over the U.S.," April 18–24, 2006 (www.worldpublicopinion.org/pipa/pdf/may06/Tribunals_May06_rpt.pdf).

i. Program on International Policy Attitudes, "American and International Opinion on the Rights of Terrorism Suspects," June 27–July 2, 2006 (www.worldpublicopinion.org/pipa/pdf/jul06/TerrSuspect_Jul06_rpt.pdf).

diplomacy than force, and saw Iraq as inspiring caution about the use of force against rogue states. On whether to use force to replace dictatorships, Republicans wavered, switching sides depending on how the question was asked; they appeared to be half-hearted neoconservatives at best.

On Iran, Republicans were more willing to use force (as the hawks-versus-doves theory would predict), but they nonetheless sided with Democrats on preferring efforts to improve relations. More surprising, both parties said that force should be used only with the support of allies and with United Nations authorization.

In a similar vein, more Democrats than Republicans liked and trusted the United Nations, but both parties wanted to strengthen it, even to the point of granting it coercive powers that would appall neoconservatives. On what might be called "tough versus tender" diplomacy, the parties differed on whether to talk to adversaries without preconditions (both generically and in the specific case of Iran), but they agreed on favoring talking to adversaries over isolating them (another implicit rebuke to neocons).

Any lingering doubts that both parties, not just Democrats, would prefer a softer touch are dispatched with a look at the questions relating to multilateralism—a sea of consensus. Democrats were assuredly more avidly for multilateralism than Republicans, but both parties loved all kinds of treaties, including ones that the Bush administration has rejected (global warming, nuclear test ban, and biological weapons inspections). In fact, partisans were generally more pro-treaty than were independents, whose libertarian streak showed in their greater suspicion of foreign entanglements. Both parties strongly preferred cooperation to both unilateralism and withdrawal from global affairs; strikingly, Republicans hardly differed from Democrats in preferring cooperation to U.S. preeminence in solving global problems.

In sum, not only the public as a whole but even rank-and-file Republicans say they want a foreign policy well to the left of the one pursued by the Bush administration. The sharply polarized debate between partisans in Washington does not fully or accurately reflect the mood of partisans in the rest of the country. The question, then, is: why the apparent disconnect between public preferences—even partisan preferences—and the Republican-led foreign policy of the Bush years?

Among many possible explanations, one that enjoys some empirical support is that the Bush period concentrated Republican power in the hands of a distinctively hawkish faction of Republicans. Consider the data presented in Figure 4-1. In a 2004 paper published by the German Marshall Fund of the United States, Ronald Asmus, Philip Everts, and Pierangelo Isernia used a two-question matrix

Figure 4-1. *Where Hawks Squawk: Percentage Distribution of Foreign Policy Typologies by Party*[a]

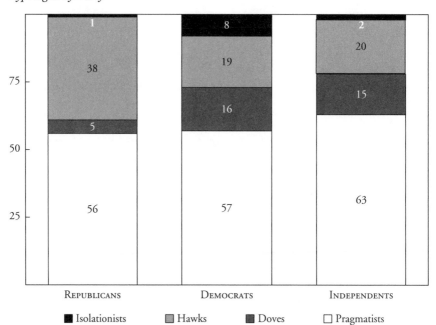

Source: Asmus, Everts, and Isernia (2004, p. 4).

a. Survey respondents were asked whether they agreed or disagreed with the following statements: "Under some conditions war is necessary to obtain justice," and "Economic power is becoming more important in the world than military power."

to sort Democrats, Republicans, and independents into four types.[15] If respondents agreed that war is sometimes necessary to obtain justice and that military power is more important than economic power, they were classified as hawks; if they disagreed on both questions, they were classified as doves. Respondents who split on the two questions were classified as "pragmatists" (war is sometimes necessary, but economic power is more important) and "isolationists" (war is not necessary, and military power is more important). As the chart shows, pragmatists form majorities of Democrats, Republicans, and independents. Isolationists are more common among Democrats than among Republicans or independents, but they are scarce in all parties. The largest difference is the one that sets Republicans apart: their hawkish contingent is a much larger minority—twice as large as in either of the other two partisan groupings.

15. Asmus, Everts, and Isernia (2004, p. 4).

Figure 4-2. *The Republican Coalition*[a]

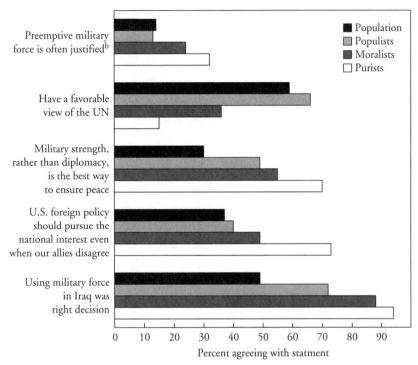

Source: Pew Research Center for the People and the Press, "Beyond Red vs. Blue," May 10, 2005 (people-press.org/reports/display.php3?ReportID=242).

a. Pew uses the type names "enterprisers" (purists), "social conservatives" (moralists), and "pro-government conservatives" (populists).

b. The survey's specific wording of this statement was, "Using military force against countries that may seriously threaten our county, but have not attacked us, [is] often justified."

And what do Republican hawks believe? A different typology offers some insight, although it is not directly comparable to the one used by Asmus and colleagues. In 2005 the Pew Research Center sorted Republicans into three groups, which I will call purists, moralists, and populists.[16] As figure 4-2 shows, foreign policy purists sound a lot like Dick Cheney–style hawks. Specifically, they are more

16. See Pew Research Center for the People and the Press, "Beyond Red vs. Blue," May 10, 2005 (people-press.org/reports/display.php3?ReportID=242). I thank Pietro Nivola of Brookings for the terms "purists," "moralists," and "populists." The Pew Research Center, the original source, uses the terms "enterprisers" (purists), "social conservatives" (moralists), and "pro-government conservatives" (populists).

supportive than other Republicans of using military force, both preemptively and to ensure peace; they take a dimmer view of the United Nations; they are more willing to pursue the national interest unilaterally; and they are staunchest in their support for the Iraq war. They are also consistently keener on force and unilateralism than is the public as a whole. Indeed, on unilateralism, the larger divide is not between Republicans and the public but between Republican purists and other Republicans. Republican purists, in short, wholeheartedly embrace neoconservative and unilateralist attitudes that many other Republicans, let alone the public, regard with much less enthusiasm.

So how did this hawkish perspective come to dominate the Republican Party? Republican hawks (purists, neocons, or whatever one chooses to call them) developed, in the Clinton years, good political connections, powerful advocacy skills, and, most important, a coherent foreign policy worldview that was ready to be taken off the shelf when an opportunity arose. The terrorist attacks of September 11, 2001, brought just such an opportunity. With realism suddenly seeming part of the problem and multilateralism seeming inadequate as a solution, Republican hawks stepped forward to grasp an unmanned tiller.

The support of Bush and the Republican establishment, the effective collapse of Democratic opposition, the public's hunger for decisive action, and the strength of their own arguments gave the hawks their head on foreign policy. They used it to shape policy decisively in Bush's first term. But, in doing so, they pushed U.S. foreign policy well to the right of where the public, and even many Republicans, thought it should be. The result was bitter polarization, followed by an emergent backlash.

If that story is wholly or even partly true, it suggests that domination of foreign policy by a minority faction of hawks cannot continue forever. And that brings us to the future. Beinart suggests that "the prospects for foreign policy bipartisanship look dim." He conjectures that post-Iraq syndrome among Republicans will be temporary, after which hawks' confidence and dominance will return. I suspect that the contrary may be more likely: that it is the hawks' dominance that will prove transitory, if only because their public support is so thin. Indeed, even before the 2006 elections rebuked Republicans, a centrist correction in Bush's foreign policy was already well under way. By August 2006, nearly half of *Republicans* said they were concerned that "if Republicans keep the majority they will get the U.S. involved in too many military operations."[17]

17. Pew Research Center for the People and the Press, "American Attitudes Hold Steady in Face of Foreign Crises," August 17, 2006 (people-press.org/reports/display.php3?ReportID=285).

Beinart suggests that bipartisanship, if revived, might take either internationalist or isolationist forms. Judging from public opinion, an isolationist convergence seems unlikely: the public unambiguously rejects the idea of U.S. hegemony, but it equally shuns withdrawal from world affairs. Bipartisan movement toward a less confrontational, more internationalist foreign policy thus looks like a strong possibility.

The point is not that all will be sweetness and light between Washington's partisans when Bush and the Iraq war are out of the way. Nor is it to predict that pigs will grow wings and fly, which is equally unlikely. The point, rather, is that hyperpartisanship in foreign policy may give way to something more like the muddled partisan sniping of the 1990s. The post-Bush period could end up looking less like the Bush era than the Clinton era.

References

Asmus, Ronald, Philip P. Everts, and Pierangelo Isernia. 2004. "Across the Atlantic and the Political Aisle: The Double Divide in U.S.-European Relations." Washington: German Marshall Fund of the United States.

Beinart, Peter. 2006. *The Good Fight: Why Liberals—and Only Liberals—Can Win the War on Terror and Make America Great Again.* New York: HarperCollins.

Cray, Ed. 2000. *General of the Army: George Marshall, Soldier and Statesman.* New York: Cooper Square Press.

Epstein, Edward Jay. 1975. *Between Fact and Fiction: The Problem of Journalism.* New York: Vintage.

Gaddis, John Lewis. 2005. *Strategies of Containment: A Critical Appraisal of American National Security Policy during the Cold War.* Oxford University Press.

German Marshall Fund of the United States. 2006. *Transatlantic Trends 2006.* Washington.

Halberstam, David. 1965. *The Making of a Quagmire.* New York: Random House.

Hamilton, James T. 2004. *All the News That's Fit to Sell: How the Market Transforms Information into News.* Princeton University Press.

Holsti, Ole R., and James N. Rosenau. 1984. *American Leadership in World Affairs: Vietnam and the Breakdown of Consensus.* Boston: Allen & Unwin.

McCormick, James M., and Eugene R. Wittkopf. 1990. "Bipartisanship, Partisanship, and Ideology in Congressional-Executive Foreign Policy Relations, 1947–1988." *Journal of Politics* 52 (4): 1077–100.

McCormick, James M., Eugene R. Wittkopf, and David M. Danna. 1997. "Politics and Bipartisanship at the Water's Edge: A Note on Bush and Clinton." *Polity* 30 (1): 133–49.

Meernik, James. 1993. "Presidential Support in Congress: Conflict and Consensus on Foreign and Defense Policy." *Journal of Politics* 55 (3): 569–87.

Ornstein, Norman, Andrew Kohut, and Larry McCarthy. 1988. *The People, the Press and Politics: The Times Mirror Study of the American Electorate.* Reading, Mass.: Addison-Wesley.

Pew Research Center. 2005. *Trends 2005.* Washington.

Project for Excellence in Journalism. 2004. *The State of the News Media 2004: An Annual Report on American Journalism.* Washington.

Souva, Mark, and David Rohde. 2007. "Elite Opinion Differences and Partisanship in Congressional Foreign Policy, 1975–1996." *Political Research Quarterly* 60 (1): 113–23.

Stoler, Mark A. 1989. *George C. Marshall: Soldier-Statesman of the American Century.* Boston: Twayne.

Trubowitz, Peter, and Nicole Mellow. 2007. "Foreign Policy and Bipartisanship: The Electoral Connection." University of Texas at Austin, Department of Government.

Zaller, John. 1996. "The Myth of Massive Media Impact Revived: New Support for a Discredited Idea." In *Political Persuasion and Attitude Change,* edited by Diana C. Mutz, Paul M. Sniderman, and Richard A. Brody, pp. 17–78. University of Michigan Press.

5

Polarization and Public Policy: A General Assessment

David W. Brady
John Ferejohn
Laurel Harbridge

In the first volume generated by the Brookings–Hoover study on polarization in American politics, William Galston and Pietro Nivola correctly state that polarization is a serious concern if it "can be demonstrated to imperil the democratic process or the prospects of attending to urgent political priorities."[1] Their essay draws attention to a number of areas where it is alleged that polarization has negative consequences, including endangering the health of vital public institutions such as Congress, the courts, and the news media; reducing the responsiveness and accountability of the political process and the government to the citizenry; gridlock over major national priorities such as balanced budgets and sustainable social insurance programs; and the rise of incivility, which threatens pragmatic accommodation.

Galston and Nivola's discussion of possible consequences provides a balanced, judicious assessment of the likelihood that the various claims about polarization are more or less correct. In regard to accountability and representation, they cite Jacob Hacker and Paul Pierson's recent book, *Off Center,* but they cast doubt on

The authors wish to thank Mandy MacCalla for her help in the editing process and Andrea Campbell, Eric Patashnik, and Nolan McCarty for their comments and suggestions. Any remaining errors are our own.
1. See chapter 1 in the first volume of *Red and Blue Nation?*

some of the strong claims made in the book.[2] Galston and Nivola view policy grid-lock as a potentially more serious problem; however, they also assert that a large amount of centrist policy has been made law over the last decade. Their discussion of Congress as "Hell's Kitchen" is likewise balanced, with examples from both sides of the debate. They conclude by asserting correctly that increased polarization of the parties carries some risks. Specifically, polarization can complicate the task of addressing long-term problems; hinder the ability to have a steady, resolute foreign policy; damage vulnerable institutions; and erode public trust in government.

This chapter deals with many of the domestic policy issues raised by Galston and Nivola. First, the relationship between polarization and citizen trust in government is evaluated. Then we turn to the issue of decreased accountability and responsiveness, where we find little, if any, support for Hacker and Pierson's claims. That discussion is followed by analyses of gridlock and the use of restrictive rules as a congressional tactic. Here we find reasonable levels of support for asserting a relationship between polarization and both of these consequences.[3] In each of these areas we bring data to bear on some part of the issue. In the final section, we deal with the broader issues raised by Galston and Nivola, especially the inability of government to deal with long-range problems.

However, before we begin the analysis of the empirical relationship between polarization and the aforementioned policy consequences, let us go on what seems a tangent and describe some manifestations of how polarization might work. We say "what seems a tangent" because depending upon how the actual mechanism and manifestations of polarization operate, different policy implications arise. That is, given that our analysis of Galston and Nivola's agenda shows mixed support for the relationship between polarization and policy consequences, these different levels of support could be accounted for by how polarization manifests itself.

Our intention is not to assert that we know how polarization works; rather, it is to describe several alternatives and leave them on the table as possible explanations for our actual results. In other words, *how* the country is polarized matters. An unpolarized centrist electorate would surely, over time, become disenchanted

---

2. Hacker and Pierson (2005).

3. There are, of course, other possible policy consequences of polarization, but our point is not to endlessly elaborate but rather to examine with data those consequences put forth in the Galston and Nivola essay. Thus our intent here is to take an independent variable, polarization, and examine or trace its effects over an array of political outcomes, not to examine a series of dependent variables where polarization is one of many independent variables.

with extreme rhetoric and policy proposals. Such disenchantment would result in parties and candidates choosing centrist policies in order to be electable. Indeed, some interpretations of the 2006 congressional election and its potential conse-quences draw exactly this conclusion.[4] There are, of course, many explanations for the 2006 election results that do not feature a reaction to polarization as a reason. Our intention in discussing several variants of the structure and mechanics of polarization is not to claim to know the answer but rather to suggest that the form of polarization matters because in different policy areas, there could exist differ-ent variants of polarization, each entailing different policy consequences.

If polarization were a stark and pervasive bimodal distribution of opinion, then parties would have little choice but to be polarized over issues. Such a manifesta-tion would surely result in absolute party voting and likely generate acrimonious, uncivil behavior in both elections and congressional rules and relations. Voters centrally distributed but not particularly attentive to a polarized, passionate elite would create an interesting mixed scenario: on issues of little concern to such vot-ers, elites could act on their polarized beliefs; but on key issues where voters pay attention, the elites would also have to be attentive and take a more centrist stance. In short, this and other variants on polarization could explain mixed results on polarization and policy as a result of a public attentiveness variable.

Polarization manifested through campaign contributions or low voter turnout in primary elections would also be able to explain mixed results, but surely the issues and specifics of these explanations would differ from those of the voter attention factor. However, our purpose is not to lay out such scenarios for their own sake but simply to put these and other scenarios on the table as possible expla-nations for the results presented below.

Trust in Government and Polarization in Congress

Galston and Nivola suggest that polarization may alienate ordinary citizens and that the quarrelsome nature of Congress can erode the public's trust in its gov-erning institutions. The issue of trust in government is not easily established, as on the one hand it, seems clear that Americans do not like the confrontational nature of politics—especially, perhaps, congressional politics.[5] A leading scholar on trust in government, Jack Citrin of the University of California at Berkeley, has documented the difficulty of assessing trust in government. In 1974 he

4. See Joe Klein, "Reaching for the Center," *Time,* November 20, 2006.
5. See Hibbing and Theiss-Morse (1995).

showed that high levels of pride in our form of government can and do coexist with widespread public cynicism about the "government in Washington" and the people running it.[6] Moreover, he found that disagreement with the policies of incumbent authorities is related to judging them. In short, trust in government comprises numerous parts, including judgments about present authorities. In 1986 Citrin and Donald P. Green of Yale showed that trust in government increased significantly under Ronald Reagan, suggesting that trust may be very strongly related to presidential personas.[7] In the same article, Citrin and Green concluded that even when trust in government was low, "pride in the American 'form of government,' rejection of alternative systems of rule and commitment to the values comprising . . . the 'American creed' remained firmly entrenched, even among the cynical segments of the public."[8] Nonetheless, trust in government has potentially important consequences: research suggests that low levels of trust can affect voting in presidential elections, support for government policies in which the public perceives little direct benefit but sees a direct cost (affirmative action, for example), and the ability of government to solve political problems.[9]

Trust in government is a complicated issue, and we do not attempt to fully explain how polarization and trust interact with other factors such as ideology; this is explored in depth in this volume by Marc Hetherington.[10] Rather, we focus on the grand claim about the relationship over time between polarization and trust in government by tracing citizens' responses to surveys from 1964 through 2006.[11] The relationship between polarization and trust in government as well as the relationship between polarization and public confidence in Congress are plotted in figure 5-1. Polarization is measured as the difference between the mean Democrat and Republican in the House, based on Americans for Democratic Action (ADA) scores.[12] The general trust in government time series

6. Citrin (1974).
7. Citrin and Green (1986).
8. Citrin and Green (1986).
9. Hetherington (1998, 1999); Hetherington and Globetti (2002).
10. See chapter 1.
11. Based on a combination of data from the University of Michigan Survey Research Center (Miller [1974]) as well as yearly survey data from the Roper iPoll for 1973–2006 (www.ropercenter. uconn.edu/data_access/ipoll/ipoll.html). Trust in government is measured as the sum of those who trust government in Washington to do the right thing always or most of the time. For years where this question was asked multiple times, we took an average.
12. For raw ADA scores, see Americans for Democratic Action, "ADA Voting Records" (www. adaction.org/votingrecords.htm). To make the scores comparable across years, the interest group's scores were adjusted with the Groseclose, Levitt, and Snyder (1999) algorithm (adjustments done by

Figure 5-1. *Effect of Polarization on Trust and Confidence in Government, 1964–2006*[a]

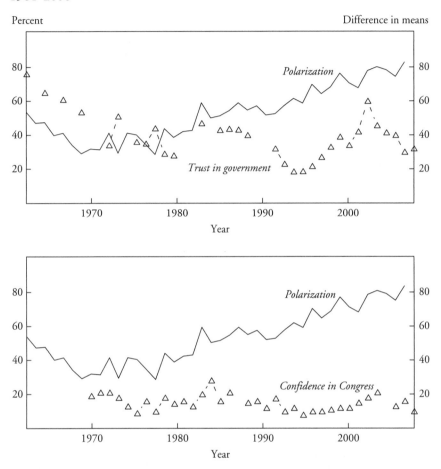

Source: Data from University of Michigan Survey Research Center (Mille [1974]), Roper iPoll, Harris Interactive polls, and Americans for Democratic Action (ADA) scores for difference in means.

a. Top panel: percent of respondents who state they trust the government all or most of the time. Bottom panel: percent of respondents who have a great deal of confidence in Congress.

Note: Data are discontinuous in the earlier period because surveys were not done yearly with the same question.

Sarah Anderson). Throughout this chapter, we use House measures of polarization, but the substantive results are the same for Senate measures since polarization in the House and Senate is highly correlated.

begins high and then, with a few exceptions, falls until the Reagan administration. At that point it rises slightly, falls, rises again from the mid-1990s to 2002, and then falls again. The polarization measure does not track well with this, because after a gradual decline from the initial starting point, the measure essentially increases over the entire period.[13] The relationship between polarization and confidence in Congress is likewise not strong because with very few exceptions, the Congress has not inspired a great deal of confidence in more than 15 to 20 percent of citizens. Since confidence in Congress is a variable with little upward or downward trend, it cannot be strongly associated with polarization, a variable that is consistently increasing over time.

There is certainly some relationship between increasing polarization and decreasing trust in government, but it is likely complicated by other variables such as presidential approval, ideology, and, potentially, which groups of society have their interests met by policy outputs. Nevertheless, given these general results, it does seem commonsensical that if citizens do not like the quarrelsome nature of politics, they might show appreciation or support for a less publicly quarrelsome federal institution, such as the Supreme Court, during times of high polarization. Figure 5-2 shows the percentage of Americans expressing a great deal of confidence in the Supreme Court plotted alongside polarization in Congress. Here the results are stronger: trust in the Court increases as polarization increases. This is the opposite of the results for trust in government and confidence in Congress. The correlation between polarization and trust in government is −0.17 while the same figure for confidence in Congress is −0.15. That means there is a slight negative relationship between polarization and trust (that is, as polarization increases trust slightly decreases). In contrast, confidence in the least publicly quarrelsome institution, the Supreme Court, is positively related to polarization (0.38). Thus, as polarization increases, it appears that trust in the more contentious American institutions decreases while trust in our least contentious or quarrelsome institution increases.[14]

13. See Rohde (1991).

14. Using congressional term averages of trust and either ADA scores or nominate scores by Congress produces similar results. If the difference in means of ADA scores is used, the correlation with trust in government is −0.19, the correlation with confidence in Congress is −0.20, and the correlation with confidence in the Supreme Court is 0.60. If the difference in means of nominate scores is used as the measure of polarization, the correlation with trust in government is −0.42, the correlation with confidence in Congress is −0.29, and the correlation with confidence in the Supreme Court is 0.54. Although the magnitude of the correlation varies depending on the measure of polarization and whether the data are aggregated by year or by Congress, the direction of the relationship is consistent.

Figure 5-2. *Polarization and Confidence in the Supreme Court, 1964–2006*[a]

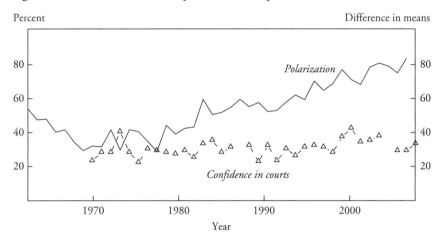

Percent   Difference in means

Source: Data from Roper iPoll, Harris Interactive polls, and ADA scores.
a. Percent of respondents who have a great deal of confidence in the courts.
Note: Data are discontinuous in the earlier period because surveys were not done yearly with the same question.

The findings in general show that while there is not a strong relationship between congressional polarization and trust in government, the relationship is in the correct (hypothesized) direction, and when we tested for trust in the Supreme Court as an opposite reaction to polarization, the results were encouraging. That is, an institution that does its job without public (and private) bickering seems to be more highly respected and trusted during times of polarization. In sum, there is some support for a relationship between polarization and trust in government institutions, albeit one that might be complicated by variables such as presidential popularity and ideology.

Unrepresentative Policy and Decreased Accountability

The essential claim regarding polarization and the lack of representative or accountable policy is that extremists in a party push for *and pass* policies that are not in accord with what citizens want. Determining what citizens want is the fly in the ointment here because American politics is replete with examples where surveys show the public favors policies that are not passed or opposes policies that are passed. Long before polarization was an issue, majorities of Americans supported gun control legislation and an end to tobacco subsidies. The lack of gun control legislation and no end to tobacco subsidies was easily explainable through group theory. Thus polarization would not be seen to account for the general phenomenon of special interest legislation. In addition to this, it is hard to say that because Americans favor some policy in a public opinion poll, it means they *really* favor it. Free public goods are always favored in polls, but when the costs are brought to bear, policy preferences often change. About two-thirds of Americans at any time favor a balanced budget, more government spending, and a reduction in taxes—a combination of policies never encountered save for perhaps in the administration of Andrew Jackson.

Although it would be nice to know whether policies reflect the will of the people, that is beyond the scope of this chapter, and thus the better and more testable case is that polarized conditions in Congress allow the extremes of the majority party to pass policy not representative of the median voter in Congress. This is essentially the claim of Hacker and Pierson in *Off Center*.[15] The authors make much of the Bush tax cuts of 2001 and 2003, citing them as prime examples of policies out of touch with the public (that is, as unresponsive *and* unaccountable). However, an analysis of these tax cuts, testing a median congressional voter model, indicates that they fit a standard model of politics and policymaking.[16] Although it is difficult, if not impossible, to map the preferences of the median congressperson back to the preferences of the public, showing that policy outcomes are at the position of the median congressional voter, who is a moderate, would cast doubt on Hacker and Pierson's claim.

The 2001 Bush tax cut proposal totaled $1.6 trillion and had several components, including reduced rates; reduced, then repealed, estate taxes; and tax breaks for savings, married people, and children. In 2002, after the September 11 terror attacks, the parameters changed to include business investment tax breaks. After the 2002 Republican electoral victory, the 2003 cuts reduced dividend and capital gains taxes and accelerated the timelines for the 2001 tax cuts to take effect. In the following discussion, we highlight the compromises that allowed these tax cuts to take place *with the support of the median member of Congress*.

The Democratic leadership in Congress opposed the 2001 Bush tax cuts because of its magnitude, both in terms of money and breadth of taxes cut. The leaders, however, were unwilling to let the president portray them as "tax-and-spend Democrats." (Indeed, as the Democratic Party's presidential candidate in

---

15. Hacker and Pierson (2005).
16. See Brady and Volden (2006); Krehbiel (1998).

2000, Al Gore had proposed a $700 to $800 billion middle-class tax cut.) Thus the Democrats proposed a $300 billion cut that did not decrease rates in the highest bracket, making the distributional consequences more acceptable to the leadership. The decline in the U.S. economy over the next two months and the president's campaign for the cuts caused the Democratic leaders to move to a Gore-like cut of $700 billion (both in income and other tax cuts). The more polarized and conservative House passed the various parts of the Bush tax cuts by early April.

In the Senate, where the distribution of preferences was not as conservative as the House (and where sixty, not fifty, votes are often needed to pass legislation), the House bill ran into trouble. The compromise solution was written by Max Baucus (D-Mont.) and Charles Grassley (R-Iowa) after the House bill had failed when moderate Republican senators like Olympia Snowe and Susan Collins, both of Maine, voted against the original proposal. The compromise used reconciliation procedures and reduced the amount of the cuts, made a slight move toward middle-income taxpayers and, most important, phased in the cuts over ten years and then reverted taxes back to the 2000 status quo. In the midst of these deliberations, Senator Jim Jeffords of Vermont announced that he was leaving the Republican Party to become an independent, making the Democrats the majority party in the Senate. Many in the press and elsewhere saw this as an opportunity to turn back the Baucus-Grassley compromise. However, consistent with a story of induced preferences irrespective of party, Senator Jeffords declared on May 22, 2001, that he would leave his party but waited to switch until after the tax bill passed, with Jeffords voting for the $1.3 trillion tax cut.

The 2002 and 2003 tax cuts follow essentially the same story. In 2002 President Bush and the Congress agreed to broaden business deductions but not to give the president a new large tax cut. The Republican victory in 2002 emboldened the president, and he immediately proposed a $730 billion tax cut to be phased in over the next decade, in addition to accelerating the 2001 tax cuts. The 2001 bill had passed under conditions of a surplus whereas in 2003 there was a deficit and an expensive war in Iraq. Republican senators Snowe and George Voinovich (Ohio) signed a pledge to oppose any cut over $350 billion. Analysis of the senators shifting their votes from nay on the original Bush proposals in 2001 and 2003 to supporting compromises such as reduced tax cuts, time tables, and reversion to the pre-2001 status quo shows that both the Democratic and Republican senators who switched their votes were located, ideologically, near the median of the chamber. Democrats who voted no to *any* cut had average ADA scores of 88.0; Republicans voting yes on any cut were at the opposite extreme (12.0). Democrats who switched had an average ADA score of 72.5, while Republicans were at 52. The same results are obtained for the House: tax cutters had an average ADA score of 7.5 and stalwart opponents had an average score of 88.0. The average score for vote switchers in the House was 22.0 for the Republicans and 44.0 for the Democrats.[17] The switching story is consistent with House-Senate differences in preferences, and no set of rules could get the president's original tax proposal passed.

Across a wide range of issues such as education and Medicare, the proposed policies were left of the House Republican core, while in areas such as energy, campaign finance reform, and faith-based initiatives, the original proposals were to the right of the median senator. Yet irrespective of the original left or right position of the proposal, the final policies were approximately at the median. On education, Bush gave up vouchers and tough standards on student evaluation in order to get a bill supported by Democrats such as Senator Edward Kennedy (D-Mass.). The Medicare prescription drug bill arose because the president and his party did not want to give Democrats an issue to hold over them in the 2004 elections. From the start the bill was not popular with conservative Republicans, causing Representative Jeff Flake (R-Ariz.) to fume that "the enormous cost of this bill will only hasten Medicare's insolvency."[18] The passage of the bill was summed up by Senator John Breaux (D-La.) when he said, "This is a great victory for a coalition built from the center out. People on the far left and the far right were not necessarily part of the team."[19]

Campaign finance reform was not favored by the core of the Republican Party nor by President Bush. However, the president saw that opposition to it would be costly, so he took a hands-off approach, letting congressional Republicans know that he would not veto the bill if it came to his desk. The House and Senate Republicans would have to defeat the bill themselves, and they could not do it. Legislation for faith-based initiatives passed the House several times but failed in the Senate through the first Bush Congress. A bill passed the Senate in 2003, but the version was so different from the House bill that no compromise was possible. Thus in 2004 the president chose to pursue the policy through administrative means. Similarly, the administration's energy bill could not pass the Congress for four years, and the final legislation occurred only after the Republicans

17. For an extended analysis, see Brady and Volden (2006).
18. Robert Pear and Robin Toner, "Medicare Plan Covering Drugs Backed by AARP," *New York Times,* November 17, 2003.
19. Robert Pear, "A Final Push in Congress: The Overview; Sweeping Medicare Change Wins Approval in Congress; President Claims a Victory," *New York Times,* November 26, 2003.

widened their Senate margin to 55 and used reconciliation to get a less conservative bill passed.

Legislation passed (and some not passed) during President Bush's first three Congresses seems, in general, to meet the criteria of policy forced to attract the median voter in the House and Senate. The tax cuts clearly meet this standard, as in both 2001 and 2003 the major players included Senators Baucus, Jeffords, and Snowe, none of whom could be considered anything but centrist. Passage of the Medicare Prescription Drug Act was indeed a center-out coalition, as Senator Breaux asserted. The failure of the faith-based initiative and the original energy legislation signals that the right in the Republican Party did not control Congress. Likewise, passage of the PATRIOT Act, the McCain-Feingold campaign finance reform, the No Child Left Behind Act, the Sarbanes-Oxley Act, and creation of the Department of Homeland Security were all characterized by bipartisan coalitions, making it hard to conclude that policymaking in the Bush presidency was any more unresponsive and unaccountable than in the past. In sum, we agree with Galston and Nivola that across a wide variety of legislation, "there has been enough partisan convergence (albeit selective, tenuous, opportunistic, or episodic) to secure key pieces of legislation." In fact, our conclusion is even less qualified in that we would leave out the "selective, tenuous, opportunistic, or episodic" part of the quote to state that the policies passed represent at least the median congressional voter. It is surely true, however, that over time elections have increased polarization in Congress—with the result that there are ever-fewer moderates in both bodies of Congress.

Gridlock

In contrast to the issues discussed thus far, we find stronger evidence to support the relationship between polarization and policy gridlock. The gridlock hypothesis states that as polarization of the congressional parties increases, Congress will be less able to sustain the coalitions needed to pass legislative changes, leaving policy "gridlocked." Sarah Binder of Brookings defines gridlock (or stalemate) as "Congress's relative inability over time and issues to broach and secure policy compromise on issues high on the national agenda . . . [It] is best viewed as the share of salient issues on the nation's agenda that is left in limbo at the close of a Congress."[20] As noted by Galston and Nivola, polarization may prevent government from accomplishing much. They note that in the presence of polarization,

20. Binder (2003).

there has been gridlock over many major policies, including those concerning budgetary balance, the environment, and immigration; but they also concede that there have been many milestone achievements under polarized governments. We attempt to assess this claim using existing work in the field as well as our own research on budgetary gridlock.

The idea behind the gridlock hypothesis is that as parties become polarized, they are less likely to be able to make policy coalitions with the requisite numbers to beat filibusters or to override presidential vetoes. This problem may be exacerbated by divided government or very narrow majorities. A variety of approaches to measuring gridlock has produced results suggesting that polarization leads to increased gridlock. Measuring gridlock as the percentage of agenda items that failed to become law by the end of the Congress (where the agenda is determined by *New York Times* editorials), Binder finds that polarization (measured as issue partisanship on a bill) negatively affects the likelihood that an agenda item will become law.[21] Similarly, Princeton University political scientist Nolan McCarty finds that polarization is associated with lower numbers of important legislative enactments, both excluding and including the mass of post–September 11 legislation.[22] McCarty also examines data on legislative output in the late nineteenth and early twentieth centuries that confirm the negative effects of polarization on output.

As suggested earlier, the presence of divided or unified government may also matter, not just polarization alone. McCarty, Keith Poole, and Howard Rosenthal examine state Temporary Assistance to Needy Families (TANF) benefits in polarized governments and find evidence to suggest that there is gridlock (as indicated by a decline in the real value of benefits) only when governments are divided as well as polarized.[23] Under unified governments, in contrast, polarization could increase the ability of government to pass important legislation.

Our analysis does not rely on broad, general measures but instead uses budget data to focus on specific policy areas. Scholars and politicians agree that the budget is one of the most important indicators of public policy. However, the size and complexity of the federal budget, changes in fundamental accounting procedures, and the omission of supplemental spending have limited scholars' ability to do time series analysis with budget data. The data set of appropriations from 1955 to 2002 created by John Cogan, former deputy director of the

21. Binder (2003).
22. McCarty (2007).
23. McCarty, Poole, and Rosenthal (2006).

Office of Management and Budget, allows comparison of federal spending by policy area across time.[24] In addition to solving the aforementioned problems, these data account for whether spending was mandatory or permanent. Although budget decisions are generally reported by fiscal year, this data set enables us to measure current discretionary budget authority by calendar year, thereby making it comparable with our measures of polarization and other control variables. Additionally, we correct for inflation, putting the values in constant 1982–84 dollars.[25]

The hypothesis proposed here asserts that as the parties polarize, the normal result should be fewer changes in appropriations from the previous year. This occurs because policy can be shifted far to the left or the right only if a majority party can cover the minority party's filibuster pivot and has party control of the presidency. The recent period of polarization in Congress has no instances of the majority party covering the minority filibuster, which would lead to the prediction of gridlock, as evidenced by relatively little change in policy.[26] Using the discretionary budget authority numbers, we interpret gridlock as the inability to make large year-to-year changes—either increases or decreases—to the budget.[27]

In the existing literature on budgetary policy, there are conflicting views about the measurement of gridlock and, at a broader level, what consequences to expect from dissensus in government. One possibility is that consensus is associated with incrementalism, whereas dissensus is associated with large year-to-year budget changes.[28] An alternative possibility, and the one we follow in this analysis, is that political dissensus (what we predict polarization leads to) is associated with classic gridlock, in which policy moves little from year to year. Bryan Jones, James True, and Frank Baumgartner test these competing theories for the 1948–95 period and find that divided government leads to increased budget volatility when they control for a time trend.[29] However, using polarization (measured only from 1962 to 1995) as their measure of dissensus, they find a negative relationship with budget volatility, more consistent with the

24. Cogan (2002).

25. Both the Office of Management and Budget and the Congressional Budget Office have collaborated on the construction of the data set and assure the accuracy of the data.

26. This approach is consistent with the work of Alt and Lowry (2000).

27. Although the budget is technically protected from filibusters and, as such, only needs a simple majority to pass, given legislative intricacies we still predict that polarization will lead to increased disagreement and gridlock over changes in budgetary spending.

28. Wildavsky (1992).

29. Jones, True, and Baumgartner (1997).

gridlock hypothesis.[30] The problem in disentangling these effects is the high degree of colinearity between polarization and their time trend, such that when all variables are included in the analysis, only divided government remains significant. Although both theories of how dissensus in government influences budgetary policy are plausible, we focus on the traditional gridlock hypothesis, which is consistent with the work of James E. Alt of Harvard and Robert C. Lowry of the University of Texas at Dallas, as well as with a pivotal politics framework.[31] Within the definition of budgetary gridlock, there are two possible benchmarks for the reversion point, the policy we would expect if gridlock exists. The first is $0 in appropriations (which suggests that it is impossible to have gridlock in budgetary policy). The second interpretation of gridlock is last year's nominal funding. We take the later approach, measuring gridlock as the absolute value of the percentage change in spending between this year and last year, adjusted for inflation.

To assess the relationship between polarization and changes in budgetary policy, we chose areas where we expected ideological distance between the parties to be significant (environmental and energy policy) and two areas characterized by pork barrel reelection politics (agriculture and highway spending). The argument is straightforward. The Democratic Party generally favors increasing Corporate Average Fuel Economy (CAFE) standards, alternative fuel supports, no drilling in Arctic National Wildlife Refuge (ANWR), and fewer, in any, subsidies for oil interests. Republicans meanwhile favor more exploration for oil, including in ANWR, no increases in CAFE standards, and so on. On environmental issues, there are similarly large ideological gaps between the parties; thus we expect the gridlock hypothesis to be borne out in these areas. In contrast, Republican and Democratic representatives and senators from rural areas favor agricultural subsidies; likewise, all representatives and senators have highways in their district or state and do not see why their roads should not be as good as everyone else's. Thus we expect that in these areas, the gridlock hypothesis will not work because both parties will support some level of pork spread relatively equally across districts and states. In all four of these areas, we looked at discretionary spending both as the

30. To assess the plausibility of the argument by Jones, True, and Baumgartner that dissensus leads to increased volatility, we analyzed thirty discretionary budget categories within our data set and did not find support for this argument. Using just a time trend and a divided-government indicator to explain the log of the absolute value of percentage change in budget authority, we found the effect of divided government to be either insignificant or negative. This difference in results may be attributable to either the additional years in our data set, the difference in the measurement of volatility, or our way of accounting for supplemental spending. In our data set, we adjust for supplemental spending to get our dependent variable as all budget authority voted on in a given calendar year.

31. Alt and Lowry (2000).

percentage change from the previous year and as the percentage change in the proportion of the budget from the previous year.[32] The same patterns result regardless of the specification of policy change.

The following set of figures shows the relationship between polarization and percentage change in the budget from the previous year for selected policy areas.[33] Although we find evidence of gridlock in some policy areas as polarization increases, we also find that there are pork barrel policy areas in which there is no apparent relationship, and thus relatively large budgetary changes occur both under low and high polarization.

Figure 5-3 shows the two instances—environmental policy and energy policy—where the gridlock hypothesis is supported. That is, as polarization increases (shown by the increasing difference in party means using ADA scores), the magnitude of the percentage change in spending from year to year decreases. The plots are restricted to the same scales for ease of comparison, but it does mean that some values of extreme shifts in policy are larger than the range of the graph. The vertical line denotes the breakpoint between high and low polarization (using the assumption that polarization is relatively high beginning in 1980). This line separates the data into two eras: the period of low polarization, where we expect large year-to-year changes to the left of the vertical line, and the high-polarization period to the right of the line, where the magnitude of change is lower, suggesting policy gridlock.[34] Looking at the correlation between the absolute value of the percentage change in spending and polarization, we find that for both of these policy areas, the relationship is relatively strong and in the expected direction—negative because increasing polarization is associated with a decrease in changes to spending. For environmental policy the correlation is −0.44, and for energy policy the correlation is −0.33, indicating support for the hypothesis that increased polarization has made it more difficult for Congress to make changes to policy.[35]

32. Discussions of what programs are included in these policy areas as well as how much budgetary levels changed is included in appendix A.

33. The same results hold regardless of whether we examine the percentage change in the budget between year t and t − 1 or the percentage change in the proportion of the budget between year t and t − 1.

34. For clarity of presentation, we restrict the graphs to the post-1970 time period. However, in the regression analysis, we use all of the data back to 1955.

35. The strength of the relationship in these policy areas is robust to various regression specifications that control for changes in the public mood, changes in unemployment, the presence of divided government, presidential election years, and the size of House majority seat shares. For both the raw correlations and the regression analysis, we used the full data set of 1955–2002 data for more precise estimates.

Figure 5-3. *Polarization and Changes in Government Spending on Environmental and Energy Programs, 1970–2002*[a]

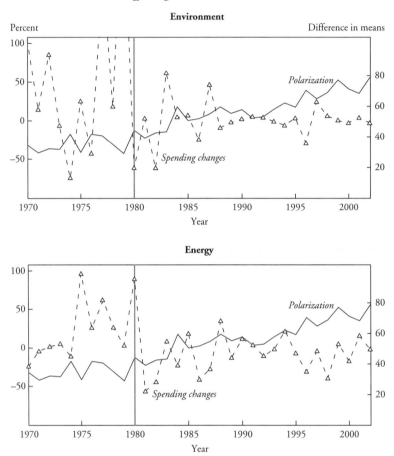

Source: Polarization measured using ADA scores; spending calculated using John Cogan's budget data set (Cogan 2002).

a. Vertical line shows breakpoint between periods of low and high polarization. Some values for extreme policy shifts (spending) exceed the range of the graph due to the use of same-size scales.

The same analysis of agriculture and highway spending does not support the gridlock hypothesis well. (See figure 5-4.) Throughout the period of our analysis, agricultural spending did not vary much from year to year, regardless of the level of polarization, and this is particularly true as polarization rose, beginning in the 1970s. Highway spending, in contrast, had much greater year-to-year variation, but again, the magnitude of the changes was not strongly associated with the level

Figure 5-4. *Polarization and Changes in Government Spending on Agriculture and Highways, 1970–2002*[a]

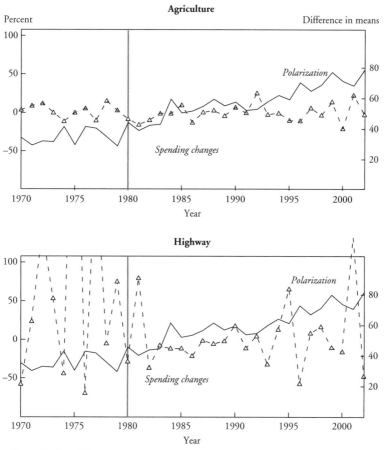

Source: See figure 5-3.
a. Vertical line shows breakpoint between periods of low and high polarization. Some values for extreme policy shifts (spending) exceed the range of the graph due to the use of same-size scales.

of polarization. As evidenced by the periods to the left and right of the 1980 breakpoint, the magnitude of percentage change in spending in both policy areas is very similar in both the pre- and post-1980s periods. Assessing the correlation between the absolute value of the percentage change in spending and polarization yields weaker relationships than for the two preceding examples, although the sign of the relationship is still consistent with the gridlock hypothesis. For

202 DAVID W. BRADY, JOHN FEREJOHN, AND LAUREL HARBRIDGE

agricultural spending the correlation was −0.25, and for highway spending the correlation was −0.09.[36] Although the difference between the agriculture and energy spending correlations (−0.25 versus −0.33, respectively) may not seem large, in the regression analysis, polarization is significant for energy policy but insignificant for agricultural policy. Thus, as expected, gridlock is related to polarization in areas where the parties differ but is not strongly related where parties see reelection opportunities.

On the whole, we find only moderate support for budgetary gridlock across a number of discretionary funding categories when we ignore the distinction between pork barrel policy and areas where the parties fundamentally disagree. To verify that our results are not an artifact of our sample of issues, we ran the regression analysis on nine additional areas where Congress has discretionary spending power. Of the thirteen policy areas we examined, polarization is associated with increased gridlock in only four: foreign aid, water projects and navigation, environmental programs, and energy. Conversely, in the other nine policy areas, polarization was not significantly related to gridlock when we controlled for the past magnitude of budgetary change, change in the unemployment rate, change in public mood, divided government, presidential election year, and majority-party seat share.[37] Given that there was no significant effect in nine of the thirteen areas, it seems unlikely that polarization could be responsible for an overall decrease in variability of budget expenditures. This outcome may be due to the budget's protection from filibusters, which reduces the minority party's ability to obstruct.

Another way that polarization might affect policy is to prohibit action in a crisis, such as the late 1970s Social Security deficit. This is an important question given that neither energy nor environmental policy faced a short-term fiscal crisis in the period of our analysis. Thus we analyze some cases in which the government was able to respond to fiscal crises despite polarization and divided government. Here, we use the term *crisis* to refer to instances when everyone believes something must be done with regard to a policy area. Possible examples include the

36. Regression analysis for both agricultural and highway spending produced insignificant effects of polarization when we controlled for changes in unemployment, change in public mood, divided government, presidential election years, and majority seat shares.

37. In addition to agriculture and highways, the other discretionary policy areas showing no significant effect were education, health services, social services, airports and airways, housing, community development financial institutions, and community development aid. Although polarization was not significant at conventional levels in any of these programs, the direction of the effect was negative (as predicted by the gridlock hypothesis) in all of the policy areas except housing and community development financial institutions.

1983 fix of Social Security, the 1986 bipartisan support for changes in tax policy, and the 1990 budget crisis. After a five-year debate and significant political struggles over tax policy, the Tax Reform Act of 1986 shocked many when it passed the Senate with a vote of 97 to 3.[38] Despite divided government and increasing polarization since Reagan's initial tax proposals, Congress was able to put aside the controversy provoked by vertical equity discussions and focus on horizontal equity, an issue where the two parties were able to find common ground. Similarly, the 1990 budget crisis, which initially appeared to be headed for gridlock, was salvaged through a compromise between liberal Democrats and moderate Republicans.[39] The initial version of the 1990 budget was voted down by the ideological wings of both parties—Democrats because they opposed the cuts in public spending and Republicans because they opposed the increases in taxes. The prospects of government shutdown and the automatic Gramm-Rudman-Hollings cuts raised the stakes of gridlock, leading to a quick restructuring of the budget that included increases in Medicare spending that would allow for its passage. (See figure 5-5.) Although fewer Republicans voted for the final version, liberal Democrats joined on, prompted by the increases in Medicare spending. Thus, despite conditions of divided government and polarization over the issue, we see policy enacted when the stakes of gridlock are high. Although Medicare is a mandatory program rather than a discretionary program like the others we examined, this example nonetheless suggests that government, even when the parties are polarized, can make necessary changes to policies if the stakes are high enough.

However, nothing of a similar nature has occurred in these policy areas since 1990, and several factors lead us to suspect that such actions are less likely today. First, over half of the increase in polarization has occurred since 1990. Second, the compromise that President George H. W. Bush made in 1990 is often cited as a reason for his defeat in 1992, and his son has certainly acted as though he would not follow in his father's footsteps. Finally, the compromises of 1990 were supported by members like Representative Bob Michel (R-Ill.), and, as often noted, the number of such centrists in the Congress has declined. This combination of factors, plus the passage of seventeen years since the 1990 budget act, suggests caution regarding the current possibility of bipartisan action over crucial long-term spending issues. With this caveat in mind, the Social Security fix, the 1986 tax cuts, and the 1990 budget battle featuring the increases in Medicare do show that bipartisan action can occur under polarized government.

38. Weiss (1996).
39. Brady and Volden (2006).

Figure 5-5. *Polarization and Changes in Medicare Spending, 1970–2002*[a]

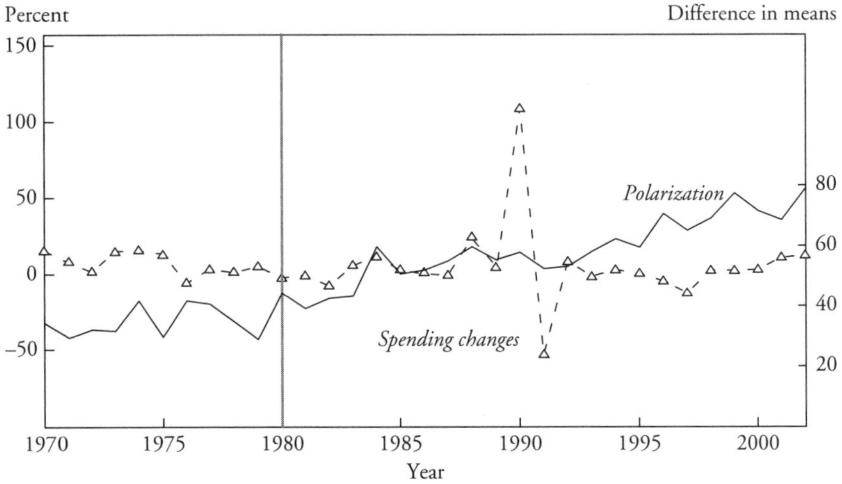

Given our findings as well as those of others, we conclude that polarization certainly increases the potential for policy gridlock but that its effect is not absolute. Policymaking is a complicated process, and no simple model can fully capture the variation across time and policy areas.[40] One might ask whether the presence of gridlock is inconsistent with our finding that important pieces of legislation are passed in accordance with the preferences of the median member of Congress; but our answer is no, that these two consequences are compatible. This conclusion rests on the relationship between policy status quo points and the distribution of preferences within the chamber. Status quo points for a policy area that are located within the gridlock region (defined by the filibuster and veto-override pivots) cannot be changed easily and thus may be susceptible to gridlock. The polarization of preferences in a given policy area may be one influence on the width of the gridlock interval since the filibuster and veto-override pivots are likely to be members of opposite parties unless the majority seat share is high. Of the policy areas we analyzed, those concerning the environment and energy are where partisan ideological differences are apparent and show signs that polarization matters, whereas agriculture and highway spending are pork-barrel areas where partisan differences, and therefore polarization, are less important. In areas where all mem-

40. Anderson (2006).

bers of either the committee or floor can benefit (as in agricultural spending and highway spending, respectively), polarization seems irrelevant to outcomes. As a result, knowing the level of partisan divergence in a policy helps us determine which policy areas we expect to exhibit gridlock.

Procedural Tactics and Restrictive Rules

The hypothesized relationship between polarization and procedural tactics has been discussed at length by Thomas E. Mann of Brookings and Norman J. Ornstein of the American Enterprise Institute. Mann and Ornstein suggest that polarization and leadership-centered policies have led to increased use of restrictive rules, backroom pressuring and deals, a decline in deliberation, and attempts to change long-standing procedures and rules to further favor the majority party.[41] Ornstein goes so far as to say the Republican use of restrictive rules and other procedural tactics in recent years "is the middle-finger approach to governing, driven by a mind-set that has brought us to the most rancorous and partisan atmosphere . . . in the House in nearly 35 years."[42] Galston and Nivola suggest that polarization may have led to a decline in deliberation, less transparency, and increased use of partisan tactics to secure partisan advantage, as well as other tactics to exclude the minority. They suggest that the use of procedural tactics can result in poor oversight, bad legislation, or both. We examine evidence for the first part of this claim, that the use of procedural tactics has increased—in particular, the use of special rules in the House. Whether this has changed the type of legislation coming out of Congress is a question left for future work.

Rules of consideration are intermediate between policy proposals and policy outcomes. The two chambers differ in their use of rules to structure their proceedings, with the House majority having the greater capacity to use formal rules to govern the way that bills are scheduled and debated. But the minority-party members do, in some circumstances, retain some capacity to obstruct the ability of the majority to work its will. And this power can be used either to stall legislation or else to extract concessions from the majority. So the majority has an interest in restricting the minority party from taking advantage of these opportunities. But restrictions on debate and deliberation may, at times, affect some members of the majority as well, so we do not expect to observe debate-restricting rules in all

41. Mann and Ornstein (2006).
42. Norman J. Ornstein, "GOP's Approach to Continuity: Not Just Unfortunate, Stupid," *Roll Call,* June 9, 2004.

circumstances. Rather, such restrictions are more likely in circumstances of polarization where the majority party is fairly homogeneous (ideologically or otherwise) and where the preferences of minority-party members are quite different from those in the majority. In such cases, the members of the majority may find it attractive to restrict their own ability to offer amendments in order to prevent the minority from obstructing their proposals.

Previous writers have offered both theoretical justifications for this expectation and empirical support for it, at least in the early days of congressional polarization.[43] For our analysis, we compiled data on earlier years plus data from Don Wolfensberger, director of the Congress Project at the Wilson Center in Washington, on special rules through the 108th Congress. As can be seen in figure 5-6, the proportion of open rules granted each year has a fairly regular relationship to the degree of polarization in the House (measured either by the ideological overlap of the parties or by the distance between the party means).[44] Except for what now looks to be a transient upturn in the early 1990s (roughly spanning the 103rd to 105th Congress), the proportion of open rules has steadily declined since the onset of polarization in the 1970s. It is not really possible, with these data, to explain why those Congresses deviated from the overall trend, but it may be related to the fact that this was a period in which party control of Congress, and the government generally, was shifting back and forth.

A more elaborate picture emerges, though one consistent with figure 5-6, if we examine the frequency with which other kinds of rules are conferred. Figure 5-7 illustrates the probability that a bill would receive an open, modified open, modified closed, or a closed rule during the 98th through 108th Congress. Evidently, the proportion of open and modified open rules generally declined from the 98th Congress onward. However, there was a difference between the 103rd and 104th Congress with respect to what kind of restrictions were placed on rules: the 103rd Congress shifted away from unfettered open rules toward modified open rules, and the 104th essentially shifted back. In the closed rules series, the results

43. Bach and Smith (1998); Smith (1989). See Rohde and Shepsle (1987) for the general argument about delegation.

44. The data on rule types come from House Calendars; see "Survey of Activities. Calendars of the U.S. House of Representatives and History of Legislation" (www.gpoaccess.gov/calendars/house/index.html). For information on special rules reported by the House Rules Committee, see Library of Congress, "THOMAS" (thomas.loc.gov) and House of Representatives, Committee on Rules (www.rules.house.gov); for earlier years, see the House Report on "Survey of Activities of the House Committee on Rules." The data are highly correlated with the aggregate figures from Davidson and Oleszek (2006).

Figure 5-6. *Polarization and Open Rule Probability, by Two Methods, House of Representatives, 98th–108th*[a] *Congress*

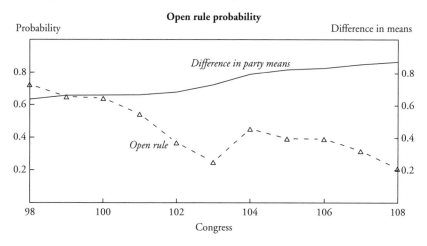

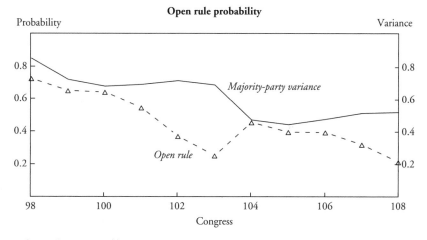

Source: See text, note 44.
a. Polarization measured using DW-nominate scores.

are a bit more consistent: the 104th Congress began to rely more on both kinds of closed rule than its Democratically controlled predecessor, and this increasing reliance on closed rules has generally continued to the present. At the time of this writing, the early stages of the 110th Congress show that the Democrats have used closed rules on both the "hundred hours" legislation as well as on all divisive legislation, suggesting that this is not merely a Republican pattern.

Figure 5-7. *Probability of Rule Types by Congress, House of Representatives, 98th–109th Congress*

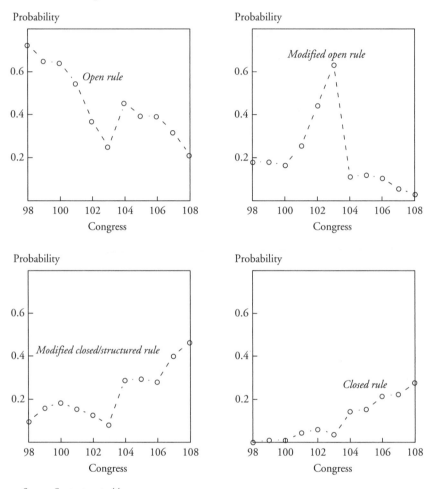

Source: See text, note 44.

To assess how polarization affects the choice of House rules, we analyze a number of regression models with fixed effects for policy areas (see appendix B). First, we look at the choice of fully open rules and find a trend against open rules over time that can be accounted for by polarization (difference in party means). Repeating our analysis with closed rules produces similar results: rising polarization increases the likelihood of closed rule consideration. The same pattern holds when we look at various combinations of rule types from open to closed, with

Figure 5-8. *Predictions of Rule Type for Different Levels of Polarization, Ordered Probit Model*

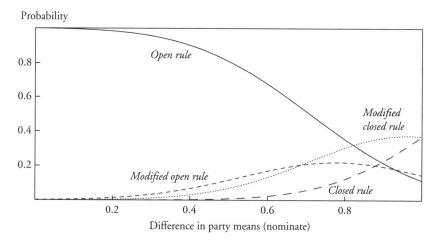

Source: See text, note 44.

modified open and modified closed as intermediate definitional categories, or when we use an ordinal measure of rule type ranging from fully open to fully closed in four categories. Figure 5-8 shows the regression predictions of rules by type as polarization—measured as the difference in party means—varies. For ease of interpretation, we omit the policy area fixed effects from the analysis and hold both majority control of the Senate and presidency at their median values, 1 and 0, respectively. The model predicts that as polarization increases, the probability of open rules declines and the probabilities of the various forms of restrictive rules increases in general but is not strictly increasing. Between the 98th and 108th congresses, actual levels of the difference in party means varied between 0.63 and 0.86.

Where significant in the ordered probit analysis, control of the Senate and presidency by the same party that controls the House has a negative effect on the likelihood of an open rule and a positive relationship with movement toward a more closed rule. This is consistent with our expectation that a polarized majority party may choose a restrictive rule to prevent obstruction by the minority since control of other branches is likely to further increase the odds that a majority party can get policy enacted into law that aligns more closely with its own preferences. Thus polarization combined with agenda control across branches appears to further increase the incentives for a majority party to pursue closed rules.

Combined, our various approaches to the analysis of the connection between polarization and the use of restrictive rules all suggest similar findings. As the two parties have separated and become more homogeneous (trends that have occurred in tandem), the use of more restrictive rules in the House has risen. This finding is true both when we compare open versus closed rules as well as when we consider intermediate categories. Unfortunately the colinearity of the two forms of polarization (separation and homogenization) prevents us from parsing out their effects separately, but both appear significantly related to the use of restrictive rules if we examine their separate or combined impact. In sum, we find strong evidence to support the claim that polarization has been accompanied by an increased use of restrictive rules.

Conclusions

Throughout this chapter we sought to bring empirical evidence to bear on the potential policy consequences of polarization as put forth by Galston and Nivola. Our results, in general, show empirical support for some of the judgments made in the Galston and Nivola essay. The claim that polarization has made the government less responsive and less accountable to the preferences of the citizenry and the median voter has little if any direct support. Although there are instances in which a polarized government has coexisted with policies that are not preferred by the majority of citizens (for example, stem-cell research or the Terry Schiavo case), this condition is not unique to polarized governments, as evidenced by the discussion of gun control and tobacco subsidies at the beginning of this chapter. Furthermore, analysis of tax policy in the Bush administration and other policy areas ranging from education to faith-based initiatives indicates that policy proposals introduced far to the left or right of the median member of Congress were moderated to an outcome consistent with the preferences of the median.

We found greater levels of support for each of the other three claims we assessed: trust in government, policy gridlock, and restrictive rules and partisan tactics. Although the empirical support for the hypothesized relationship between increased polarization and decreased trust in government is not particularly strong, the relationship is in the hypothesized direction. We find relatively strong empirical support for policy gridlock in those policy areas where partisan differences are high whereas there was little evidence of gridlock in pork-barrel policy areas, where we predicted that partisan differences would not be paramount. Finally, the claim that polarization has led to increased use of partisan tactics and restrictive rules receives considerable empirical support in our analysis. Combined, our analyses of the consequences suggested by Galston and Nivola indicate that polarization has changed the dynamic of policymaking and the range of policies that can be changed. We contend, however, that those policy areas that do see changes are reflective of the preferences of the median voter *despite* the polarization of Congress.

Given the potential for policy gridlock, particularly in those areas where partisan differences are large, there is a risk that polarization may limit the ability of the government to address long-range domestic policies, particularly those that require altering the distribution of benefits. As suggested by Galston and Nivola, bipartisan agreement is necessary to restructure entitlement programs, Social Security, and health care. Such agreement can sometimes be forged if the situation is dire, as exemplified by the Medicare restructuring in 1990, but on the surface, it appears that polarization may be particularly damaging to these sorts of domestic policy goals. Although we admit that polarization may exacerbate the situation, we speculate that much of the inability of government to address long-range policies, particularly those that require a change in the distribution of benefits, stems from electoral and institutional dynamics unrelated to polarization. The institutional structure of Congress—particularly the House, where elections are held every two years—causes members to focus on policies with short-term benefits that help them be reelected. Since voters focus on short-term changes in their income or received goods or services, members have the incentive to put off long-range problems to future generations to solve.[45] This problem, the difficulty of addressing long-term unfunded liabilities or overpromising or overpaying in the present at the expense of the future, is not unique to the United States. Many European democracies, as well as Korea and Japan, have long-term health care and retirement liabilities that are not affordable without placing unacceptable tax burdens on future generations.[46] In short, all these democracies have the same problem as the United States (and in most cases, more severe problems due to declining birth rates). Some of these democracies are polarized; some, like Japan, are not; yet none have solved the problem. The extent to which polarization may intensify the problem will surely have to be answered by a comparative study, and it should be noted that studies on polarization and long-term economic health are under way in several countries, including Korea. Thus the root cause of government's inability to deal with long-range problems is at least partly institutional

45. For an overview of how short-term changes in income and other factors influence voters, see Achen and Bartels (2004).

46. See Miles and Timmermann (1999).

rather than purely the result of polarization. Nonetheless, polarization may exacerbate the problem by reducing the likelihood of agreement across the aisle.

Our final point is that over the past thirty years, there has been a sorting in Congress, where conservative Democrats and moderate Republicans have been replaced by more ideological members of these parties—a phenomenon that has increased party-line voting at the expense of bipartisanship.[47] This polarization of the congressional parties has led to some gridlock because in the American system, a supermajority is required to cover the various veto and filibuster pivots, and unlike in the early New Deal period, no party in recent years has had a majority sufficient to cover the veto points. Thus it is clear that in order to do anything, parties have sought rule changes to solve the problem of not being able to meet the supermajority requirements. Is this polarization driven by elites, or does it come from deep in the body politic? Our view is that polarization is driven by elites and not by voters in general. We base this belief on the fact that the connections between congressional polarization and policy consequences, while present, are not always strong across all areas and are sometimes weak. Voter-driven polarization would be unlikely to yield this pattern of results. Is this definitive? The answer is no, as we have not tested this hypothesis, nor could we since several interpretations are compatible with the time series we have covered. In other words, a gradually polarizing electorate and a relatively nonpolarized electorate are both plausible explanations for our findings in 2007. Which of the many explanations is correct will be determined over time. Our view is that a centrist electorate with numerous swing voters will, over time, induce parties to present centrist candidates and policies, and government officials will ultimately work out cross-party solutions to long-term economic and social policy issues.

Appendix A

Our category of environmental policy includes programs such as wildlife refuges, land acquisition, state and tribal wildlife grants, species conservation funds, the North American Wetlands Conservation Fund, and environmental programs and management. These programs account for anywhere between 0.04 percent and 4 percent of discretionary spending or between $73 million and $16 billion, peak-

47. Han and Brady (2007).

ing in 1978. The average magnitude of percentage change from the previous year's level was 39 percent.

Energy policy includes programs such as research and development; Interstate Commerce Commission activities; nuclear waste disposal; clean coal technologies; the Federal Energy Regulatory Commission; Colorado River Basin; power, sale, and transmission of electric energy; and the Tennessee Valley Authority Fund. These programs account for between 0.2 and 6 percent of federal discretionary spending, with a peak in 1979. These percentages correspond to expenditures between $465 million and $26 billion. Across our time period of analysis, the magnitude of energy spending changed between 0.9 and 98 percent from the previous year's spending level, with an average of 23 percent.

The policy area of agriculture subsidies includes a range of federal programs including the Agricultural Marketing Act, payments to states and possessions, outreach for socially disadvantaged farmers, hazardous materials management, the Agricultural Adjustment Act, forestry incentives, and Great Plains conservation. These programs account for between 1 and 2 percent of annual discretionary spending, or between $2 billion and $7.6 billion annually. From year to year, agricultural spending varies in magnitude by 0.22 percent to 82 percent, with an average of 11 percent change from the previous year.

The policy area of highway and mass transit spending includes federal programs such as transportation research, highway safety, Interstate Transfer Grants, Appalachian Development Highway System, Federal Aid to Highways, Railway Safety, and the Urban Mass Transportation Administration Fund. Spending on these programs accounts for up to 2.3 percent of annual discretionary spending. This corresponds to yearly expenditures of up to $9.6 billion, with an average of $2.3 billion. Year-to-year variation in spending ranged in magnitude by 2.5 percent to 910 percent, with an average of 72 percent change from the previous year's budget authority.

In each of the policy areas, the seemingly large average changes in budget authority from year to year are driven in part by the few outlier values of huge positive or negative changes. Looking at the median percentage change values may be more appropriate for these cases. The median values, along with other summary statistics for percentage change, total spending, and proportion of the discretionary budget, are presented in the tables below.

Table A-1. *Summary Statistics of Percentage Change, 1955–2002*

Percent

Policy area	Minimum	First quartile	Median	Mean	Third quartile	Maximum
Environment	−73.620	−2.247	4.760	24.340	24.010	301.000
Energy	−55.600	−9.618	4.698	7.521	18.760	97.520
Agriculture	−40.870	−5.837	1.592	3.891	10.810	82.110
Highway	−910.400	−28.150	−6.176	−9.179	15.120	528.600

Source: Authors' calculations based on Cogan (2002).

Table A-2. *Summary Statistics of Inflation-Adjusted Budget Authority, 1955–2002*

Thousands of 1982–84 dollars

Policy area	Minimum	First quartile	Median	Mean	Third quartile	Maximum
Environment	73,870	1,126,000	4,062,000	3,602,000	5,184,000	1,5890,000
Energy	465,400	2,306,000	3,187,000	4,482,000	4,330,000	2,6300000
Agriculture	2,029,000	4,720,000	5,242,000	5,211,000	5,937,000	7,614,000
Highway	−1,055,000	691,500	1,717,000	2,345,000	3,232,000	9,639,000

Source: See table 5A-1.

Table A-3. *Summary Statistics of Inflation-Adjusted Budget Authority as a Proportion of Discretionary Spending, 1955–2002*

Proportion of discretionary spending

Policy area	Minimum	First quartile	Median	Mean	Third quartile	Maximum
Environment	0.000420	0.003208	0.010700	0.009668	0.014370	0.037450
Energy	0.002646	0.008031	0.009766	0.012260	0.012520	0.063520
Agriculture	0.011030	0.013150	0.015090	0.015470	0.017340	0.024640
Highway	0.000369	0.002304	0.005045	0.006224	0.008132	0.023030

Source: See table 5A-1.

Appendix B

Table B-4. *Logistic Regression of Rule Type with Fixed Effects for Policy Areas, 98th–108th Congress*[a]

	Open rule	Open or modified open rule	Closed or modified closed rule	Closed rule
Intercept	−0.631	8.56***	−8.27***	−12.3***
	(0.734)	(0.732)	(0.721)	(1.32)
Difference in party means	−2.37**	−13.8***	13.2***	14.4***
(DW-nominate)	(0.825)	(1.02)	(1)	(1.7)
House majority party	−1.13***	−0.0924	0.0565	0.277
controls Senate	(0.163)	(0.187)	(0.185)	(0.289)
House majority party	−1.11***	0.342[†]	−0.309[†]	−0.563*
controls presidency	(0.171)	(0.184)	(0.182)	(0.266)
Policy area fixed effects	Yes	Yes	Yes	Yes
N	1,438	1,438	1,438	1,438
Log likelihood	−756	−642	−650	−375

Source: Authors' calculations based on rules database (see note 44 in text).
[†]$p < 0.1$, *$p < 0.05$, **$p < 0.01$, ***$p < 0.001$.
a. Standard errors are shown in parentheses.

Table B-5. *Ordered Probit Regression of Rules, 98th–108th Congress*[a]

	Model 1	Model 2	Model 3
Intercept	−14.02***	−11.87*	−2.22**
	(1.37)	(5.26)	(0.31)
Congress	0.14***	0.12[†]	...
	(0.01)	(0.07)	
Difference in party	...	0.84	4.43***
means (DW-nominate)		(1.99)	(0.41)
House majority party	0.18*	0.21[†]	0.35***
controls Senate	(0.08)	(0.11)	(0.08)
House majority party	0.09	0.10	0.20*
controls presidency	(0.08)	(0.09)	(0.08)
Policy area fixed effects	Yes	Yes	Yes
Threshold 1	0	0	0
	...	...	...
Threshold 2	0.711	0.711	0.709
	(0.037)	(0.037)	(0.037)
Threshold 3	1.810	1.810	1.808
	(0.060)	(0.061)	(0.061)
N	1,438	1,438	1,438
Percent correctly predicted[b]			
	54.6	54.7	54.0
Log likelihood	−1,521.26	−5,121.73	−1,525.88

Source: Authors' calculations based on rules database (see note 44 in text).
[†]$p < 0.1$, *$p < 0.05$, **$p < 0.01$, ***$p < 0.001$.
a. Rules: 1, open; 2, modified open; 3, modified closed; 4, closed. Standard errors are shown in parentheses.
b. Modal outcome (open) predicts 44.2 percent correctly.

Comments on Chapter Five

COMMENT

Andrea L. Campbell

David Brady, John Ferejohn, and Laurel Harbridge test commonly heard claims that increased polarization has pernicious consequences for the policymaking process and for actual policy outcomes. They focus in particular on four possible consequences: unrepresentative policy and lack of accountability, diminished trust in government, divisive use of rules and tactics within Congress, and gridlock on issues of national importance.

The authors find little support for the unrepresentative policy argument, some support for the trust in government effect, and a fair amount of evidence for changes in the use of rules and for the policy gridlock thesis. These are largely sound conclusions, even if the empirical tests are necessarily brief. (The policy consequences of polarization deserve a book-length treatment, not merely a chapter in an edited volume.) Moreover, the hierarchy of evidence and support also makes sense, given the array of forces impinging on lawmakers. Producing unresponsive policy is something lawmakers do only at their electoral peril. Yes, they can try to hide costs and benefits in clever ways, as political scientists Jacob S. Hacker and Paul Pierson have suggested, but ultimately the violations of the median voter's desires cannot be too numerous or egregious.[1] When such violations do occur, they can often be explained by group theory and the permeability of the American system to organized interests rather than being viewed solely as a consequence of polarization. In contrast, using rules and tactics within Congress to shut out the minority party is an inside strategy that will not directly provoke voter ire and so can be utilized more frequently and cavalierly. Hence it is not surprising to find the strongest evidence for the impact of polarization in this arena. Similarly, the gridlock thesis simply makes intuitive sense, especially on issues characterized by pronounced partisan difference, as the authors find.

Whether polarization is caused by increased ideological homogeneity within the parties or by the separation of their ideological midpoints, there are fewer members who overlap with the other party, diminishing the likelihood of bipartisanship and resulting in policy sclerosis. That the amount of evidence for a

---

1. Hacker and Pierson (2005).

relationship between polarization and trust in government is somewhere in the middle also makes sense in this context. To the extent that trust in government is shaped by news of political "bickering," as the authors assert, increased polarization would surely magnify the volume of such mudslinging conveyed to the voters through the media.

My comments, then, are less a critique of the authors' basic findings than a plea for more evidence, a more thorough delineation of the mechanisms linking polarization with the observed phenomena, and a more thorough parsing of those hypothesized effects.

Unresponsive Policy

The authors find that the Bush tax cuts, rather than being an example of unrepresentative policy as Hacker and Pierson have asserted, are instead consistent with the desires of the median member of Congress.[2] In particular, the more extreme proposals from the right were rejected, chiefly by moderates in the Senate. Research that Kimberly Morgan of George Washington University and I are doing on the 2003 Medicare prescription drug reform tells largely the same story: conservatives' more extreme proposals—restricting the new drug benefit to senior citizens enrolled in private plans like HMOs and forcing traditional fee-for-service Medicare into price competition with private plans—were thwarted by moderate senators (many of whom were from rural states with few HMOs). Thus electoral reality forced the watering down of the ideological push to privatize Medicare more significantly. The surviving provisions of the legislation that were unpopular with the public—seniors in particular—can be explained through group theory. Having announced that the new drug benefit would be available only through private drug insurance plans (which did not exist at the time) and that increased senior enrollment in HMOs was sought (after HMOs had dropped the unprofitable senior sector like a hot potato over the previous half decade), Republicans had no choice but to meet the insurance companies' and private health plans' demands for generous subsidies. Moreover, pharmaceutical companies agreed to support the legislation only if government negotiating power over prescription drug prices was ruled out.[3] Lawmakers acquiesced, and this major lobby was on board.

2. Hacker and Pierson (2005).

3. Sheryl Gay Stolberg and Gardiner Harris, "Industry Fights to Put Imprint on Drug Bill," *New York Times,* September 5, 2003.

Trust in Government

The authors test the "grand claim" that there is a relationship between polarization and trust in government. Trust falls roughly as polarization rises, although the influence of factors like presidential personality interferes with the neat relationship between the two phenomena. The authors suggest in their comparison of Congress and the judiciary that the "bickering" associated with polarization diminishes trust in government (regard for the more contentious institution, Congress, falling as polarization rises, while confidence in the less contentious Supreme Court increases).

But what about the influence of policy outputs? To the degree that the public reacts to gridlock, which does seem to be a consequence of polarization, then perhaps the failure to produce policy addressing the nation's problems is the mediating factor between polarization and trust. Brady, Ferejohn, and Harbridge write that they will leave for future research the question of whether the style of policymaking under polarization changes the kind of legislation produced by Congress. But this may be key in understanding the polarization-trust linkage. That pork-barrel spending continues unabated by changes in polarization while more significant, bipartisan, large-scale policymaking (which might meaningfully address the risks and concerns faced by ordinary Americans) seems more and more a thing of the past would seem to affect trust in government. This may be difficult to test, but deserves testing against the "bickering" model.

For example, we might expect groups that have had more of their policy needs met to exhibit greater trust in government. Analysis of National Election Study data from 1958 through 2004 shows, for instance, that farmers have somewhat higher levels of trust in government than other respondents (see table 5-1 for regression results). Similarly, we might expect senior citizens—the chief beneficiaries of the American welfare state—to display higher trust as well. But contrary to expectations, they have less trust in government than younger respondents for the entire period. This is particularly the case before 1980; after 1980, when their programs were fully developed and when they had successfully beat back threats to their programs, seniors display only modestly higher levels of trust than non-seniors.[4] In addition, trust typically rises with income, as we might expect to the extent that policy outcomes favor the well-heeled.[5]

---

4. Campbell (2003).
5. Hacker and Pierson (2005).

Table 5-1. *Explaining Trust in Government, 1958–2004*

	Farmers	Seniors Overall	Seniors Before 1980	Seniors 1980–2004
Farmers	0.013*	. . .	. . .	. . .
Seniors	. . .	−0.040***	−0.033***	0.015†
Income	0.026***	0.014***	0.026***	−0.005
Education	−0.048***	−0.036***	0.008	0.006
Black	−0.057***	−0.107***	−0.033***	−0.053***
Male	0.004	0.008*	0.029***	−0.013
Age	−0.027***	. . .	. . .	. . .
Number of respondents	28,429	30,576	15,321	15,255
R^2	0.01	0.01	0.01	0.01

Source: Author's calculations based on data from the National Election Studies Cumulative Data File, 1948–2004.

†$p < 0.1$; *$p < 0.05$; **$p < 0.01$; ***$p < 0.001$.

a. Figures in cells are standardized coefficients from ordinary least squares regressions. The dependent variable is the four-item trust in government scale (variable VCF0604 in the NES Cumulative Data File).

These are modest results, but they do suggest that groups that can be identified as receiving policy benefits may have more trust in government (although the negative coefficients for education suggest that those with more exposure to "bickering" may have less trust). This is work that deserves to be pursued further.

Rules and Tactics

The authors show that during the polarization era (from the 98th through 109th Congress), the use of open rules of various kinds has declined while the use of closed rules has increased. Closed rules are especially common when there is both polarization and unified control of government; then the majority party has a particularly significant incentive to use closed rules to thwart minority attempts to block legislation.

However, the period exhibits two characteristics that may also have influenced the types of rules utilized. First, when there has been unified control during this period, it has been unified Republican control (except for the first two years of the Clinton administration). Therefore one must wonder whether these patterns of rule-making behavior are a uniquely, or mostly, GOP phenomenon. Democrats certainly allege that there is asymmetry by party, and in the aftermath of the 2006 election, some pledged not to shut out the Republican Party as they had been shut out when in the minority. Such pledges may be more for rhetorical effect than actual governing, but it would be fascinating to see whether the parties differ in their likelihood of thwarting the other party. A Democratic presidential victory in 2008, along with continued Democratic control of Congress, would allow testing of this phenomenon.

Second, we might wonder how much the change in rules and tactics is due to narrow margins rather than to polarization per se. This era, particularly in more recent years, has been marked by some of the narrowest margins in the history of Congress. Closed rules help protect slim majorities and protect against amendments, whether there is polarization or not (although the existence of polarization may increase the incentives to engage in such maneuvers).

Gridlock

That polarization causes policy gridlock makes the most intuitive sense and is the hypothesis with the most empirical support—not only from the data offered here but also from earlier examinations by Sarah Binder of the Brookings Institution and Nolan McCarty of Princeton University.[6] Here the authors analyze not counts of major-versus-minor legislation but rather variation in appropriations, with gridlock defined as the inability to foment change and measured by reduced change in spending. They cleverly show a difference between pork-barrel areas, where polarization produces little difference in year-to-year spending, and more ideologically contested areas, where the advent of heightened polarization reduces the magnitude of up- and downswings in spending.[7]

The deeper puzzle is that despite polarization, major policy has been enacted over the past two to three decades and even recently, when polarization appears to be most acute. Although beyond the scope of the authors' chapter, it is important that we know the conditions under which the effects of polarization can be overcome and major enactments are possible. Is it crisis, as the authors suggest, or the presence of political entrepreneurs with a desire to make good policy, or perhaps the salience of an issue or the size and political mobilization of the associated issue public?

6. See Binder (2003); McCarty (2007).
7. In addition, the relationship between polarization and gridlock in state legislatures would also be a fascinating area of study. Veto and filibuster points vary across states, and sometimes across issues within states (as where ballot initiatives have increased the supermajority necessary to pass tax increases).

Addressing Future Problems

Knowing the conditions for overcoming polarization is especially important since, as the authors correctly note, there are a number of profound policy challenges facing the United States in coming decades, not least of which is the long-term solvency of Social Security and Medicare as baby boomers retire.

The authors cite the 1983 Social Security Amendments, the 1986 Tax Reform Act, and the 1990 budget crisis as three instances in which crises were addressed despite polarization. In each case, there was an emergency that forced action: the stakes were "high enough" to force policy change, as the authors note.[8] They also worry that "nothing of a similar nature has occurred in these policy areas since 1990" and that polarization makes such problem solving less likely, with the loss of moderates in Congress and so on.

But the other reason no policymaking of similar magnitude has taken place is that we have not confronted a comparable crisis in these policy areas. The failure to take action has less to do with polarization than the array of short-term forces confronting elected officials. Obviously, the sooner Congress takes on long-term Social Security and Medicare financing, the less onerous the problem. But without a crisis to force action, no lawmaker wants to impose higher taxes or reduced benefits or other forms of pain today to address tomorrow's fiscal crisis. The desire to avoid inflicting pain and therefore avoid electoral retribution is something that affects democratically elected officials no matter what the particular electoral system, as evidenced by the failure of other industrialized democracies to tackle these difficult issues.

Where polarization will matter is in the mode of addressing these problems. Both the 1983 Social Security Amendments and the 1986 Tax Reform Act were hammered out in extraordinary bipartisan, closed-door sessions.[9] Historically, most major legislation has been bipartisan. The most significant consequence of polarization is that it will reduce the likelihood of such bipartisanship in the future.

My final point is something the authors do not discuss but which is nonetheless an important feature of American politics. The authors find that gridlock is most likely to occur in issue areas where partisan differences are greater. But has the number of areas with significant party differences increased over time? Two

---

8. Although I would argue that there was no particular crisis that fomented the 1986 tax reform.
9. Birnbaum (1987); Light (1985).

examples that come to mind are Social Security and taxes. For many years, because of the power of the House Ways and Means Committee, its domination by conservative Southern Democrats like long-term chairman Wilbur Mills, and its technocratic orientation, Social Security and tax policy were relatively noncontroversial. The parties agreed to agree both on the desirability of financing Social Security and the level of taxes necessary to do so, and on the nature of the American tax regime.[10] Over time, however, the parties drifted apart. Beginning in the 1970s, Republicans began criticizing social insurance and promoting private alternatives, and taxes became a more politicized and hotly contested arena with a pronounced partisan difference. The greater number of areas now characterized by profound party disagreements suggests that gridlock will become an increasing characteristic of the American political system.

Conclusion

Upon close examination, polarization does not appear to produce extreme, unresponsive policies. However, polarization does undermine the possibilities for bipartisanship—and this reduces the likelihood that elected officials will be able to pass major legislation that addresses the new and increased risks that citizens face, because such major legislation is typically forged through bipartisan means. In his comment on Barbara Sinclair's chapter in this volume, Keith Krehbiel writes that when majorities overreach, they are reined in by moderates, and currently there are enough moderates to prevent "bad legislation."[11] However, the loss of moderates in Congress may reduce the possibility that this kind of mechanism will work in the future. Some see the Democratic victories in the 2006 midterm elections as a "thermostatic" reaction to extreme rhetoric and politics and unresponsive policy, evidence that a centrist electorate can rein in excesses and that the system is self-correcting.[12] But when the reaction of electorates is to vote a number of moderates out of office, we must be concerned about future policy consequences. It remains an open question whether the 2006 election was a moderating election, or one that, with its loss of moderates, exacerbates the policy consequences of polarization.

10. See Zelizer (1998); Brownlee (2004).
11. See chapter 2 comments.
12. See Wlezien (1995) on the electorate as "thermostat."

COMMENT

Eric M. Patashnik

How much should citizens, politicians, and scholars who care about good government and the well-being of American democracy worry about the consequences of political polarization? David Brady, John Ferejohn, and Laurel Harbridge address this timely question by bringing empirical data to bear on four alleged consequences of polarization: gridlock, unresponsive policy, public mistrust of government, and the decline of bipartisan deliberation in Congress. The authors find mixed effects. Polarization leads to more gridlock and increased use of restrictive rules and partisan tactics on chamber floors. There also appears to be a relationship between polarization and declining public trust in government. Yet Congress continues to pass important laws that are broadly responsive to the preferences of the median voter in Congress.

The authors' nuanced and balanced assessment is a valuable corrective to broad claims that polarization has "changed everything." Still, important questions remain about how we should interpret their findings. If politics is so much more partisan and rancorous than in the past, why have policy outcomes remained relatively stable? If "off median" proposals frequently get moderated to a degree that brings them into the political mainstream, why so much frustration with governmental performance? If polarization leads to stalemate, what keeps the Washington establishment going?

At the outset, it is important to clarify the authors' methodological approach for answering the question of whether we should worry about polarization. They treat polarization as an "independent variable" and then examine whether it has a relationship with various political outcomes such as public trust and policy gridlock. This "independent variable" approach has certain pragmatic and methodological advantages, as it clarifies bivariate relations in the data. Still, this research design has clear limitations for an assessment of the effects of a complex phenomenon like polarization.[13] For one, it can elevate the importance of statistical associations that may in fact be much less substantive and divert attention from problems and empirical puzzles that may be more significant. More worrisome, it can strip outcomes from their larger political contexts. Without taking into

---

13. On the limitations of a focus on independent variables (as opposed to dependent variables or problems) in political science, see Laitin (2004) and Shapiro (2004).

account crucial background conditions, the true effects of polarization may be difficult to assess.[14]

The partisan debate between liberal and conservative elites in the United States today takes place not in a political state of nature but against the institutional backdrop of a massive welfare, regulatory, and administrative state in which nearly everything the federal government does has the support of the mass public or some important constituency. The political and organizational inertia from settled policy commitments and clientele expectations means that it is increasingly difficult for each party to alter the trajectory of domestic policy—whether political polarization is relatively high *or* low. The consequences of polarization therefore manifest themselves mainly in procedural breakdowns, institutional frictions, and rhetorical battles. In sum, the effect of polarization on domestic policy outcomes is often swamped by other factors, including the weight of "big government" itself. This cautionary perspective has implications for how we interpret the authors' results.

Exhibit A is national budget policy. Brady, Ferejohn, and Harbridge appropriately focus on the federal budget as one of the most important indicators of public policy.[15] The authors' central claim is that polarization leads to budgetary gridlock in areas where the parties disagree. The greater the ideological gap between the parties, the harder it is to forge coalitions to overcome the veto points built into the Madisonian system, and the less spending outcomes will change from year to year. In other words, polarization should be associated with more incremental budget changes. To test this interesting claim, the authors initially

---

14. See Pierson (2007). For all its penetrating insights into the politics of distributional fights, the assessment of the Bush tax cuts by Hacker and Pierson (2005) pays relatively little attention to certain historical factors and therefore arguably overstates the degree to which the tax cuts fundamentally reshaped the American fiscal landscape. One of the reasons why Hacker and Pierson conclude that the tax cuts constitute a dramatic policy shift is because of their sheer size. The 2001–03 tax cuts have an estimated revenue loss of more than 2 percent of GDP in 2013. Yet federal taxes had climbed to almost 21 percent of GDP at the end of the Clinton administration due to the dot-com boom and legislated tax hikes. This aggregate level of federal taxation was far above the historical average over the past forty years (18.2 percent of GDP). Viewed in historical perspective, it is not altogether surprising that a conservative Republican president would push hard to reduce federal taxes by 2 percent of GDP. More surprising is that the tax-cutting drive continued even after the costs of the Iraq war began to mount.

15. I shall restrict the bulk of my comments to this section of their analysis because I think it contains the authors' crispest and potentially most significant positive findings about the effects of polarization on actual policy outcomes (as opposed to the effects of polarization on the internal rules and procedures of the House).

examined four areas of federal spending: two where they expected the ideological distance between the parties to be large (environment and energy) and two areas characterized by "pork-barrel reelection politics" (agriculture and highways), where they expected the partisan gap to be small. Brady, Ferejohn, and Harbridge find support for the gridlock hypothesis in the first two cases: greater polarization in the environmental and energy areas is associated with smaller budget changes. In the latter two cases, however, the magnitude of spending changes was not strongly associated with the level of polarization. Thus the authors end up arguing that the fiscal effects of polarization are contingent: polarization is related to gridlock in areas where the parties differ but not in distributive areas where parties see reelection opportunities.

This is an intriguing and plausible argument, but its validity and significance are open to question. The authors make a sharp distinction between pork barrel (consensual) and non–pork barrel (prone to gridlock) categories of spending, but the empirical basis for such a dichotomy is uncertain. They tested their model on nine additional areas of the budget to verify their results, but it is unclear in which of the nine we should expect to observe budgetary gridlock. Polarization was in fact found to be empirically associated with gridlock in only two of the nine. Interestingly, the two areas where polarization was found to have an empirical effect— foreign aid and water projects and navigation—have very different reputations for pork barreling.

It would be interesting to explore the gridlock hypothesis across the entire range of spending functions. One reason why the analytic distinction between pork and non-pork spending areas might not hold up is because of the growth of earmarking. While some programs clearly have more concentrated benefits than others, committee leaders can sprinkle particularistic projects into virtually any appropriations bill to dampen partisan conflict and build winning coalitions. Pork barrel reelection politics is deeply woven into congressional life; it is not restricted to a few select areas of the budget. Indeed, the number of earmarks has exploded in recent years. In fiscal year 2005, for example, there were 13,496 earmarks totaling $19 billion. The transportation and defense departments received the most earmarks of any agencies, but appropriations bills for many other agencies (including those that administer "national" programs) featured substantial earmarking as well. The appropriations bill for the Environmental Protection Agency included 838 separate earmarks (at total cost of $464 million), the Department of Health and Human Services appropriation had 1,535 earmarks ($706 million), and the Department of Education had

1,199 ($483 million).[16] And these counts do not capture the many earmarks contained in authorization bills. The greater resort to earmarking might, of course, be a *response* to polarization and the increasing need for coalition leaders to use particularistic benefits to buy votes, but this would imply that the political system has a built-in capacity to manage the threat of budgetary gridlock and that we need not worry too much about it.[17]

Even if there is some relationship between polarization and gridlock in certain subparts of the budget, its aggregate fiscal importance is unclear.[18] Indeed, the big story is how *little* polarization seems to have mattered for overall federal spending patterns. As Brady, Ferejohn, and Harbridge acknowledge, a key secular trend in American national budgeting over the postwar era has been the declining overall volatility of budget outcomes over the years.[19] Spending changes are becoming more incremental over time. This powerful secular trend needs to be taken into account when one tries to assess the fiscal effects of polarization.

Using data from the University of Washington's Policy Agendas Project, I constructed a measure of variability in year-to-year percentage changes across all fifty-five domestic subfunctions between fiscal years 1951 and 2005. Figure 5-9 plots the intersextile range of annual percentage changes over this period.[20] It shows that year-to-year variability declined significantly between the 1950s and the

16. Appropriations earmarking data come from the Office of Management and Budget. (www.whitehouse.gov/omb/earmarks/preview-public-site/agencies742a.html?source=APP). Data on authorizations earmarks were not yet available.

17. Of course, earmarking has a cost, but it is a relatively efficient way to build majority coalitions for major general-interest legislation. See Evans (2004).

18. The statistical association between polarization and budgetary gridlock across discretionary spending categories is not overwhelmingly strong. When they examine whether polarization has contributed to the overall decrease in the variability of budget expenditures, Brady, Ferejohn, and Harbridge, in effect, treat each of the thirteen regression models as an independent test of the gridlock hypothesis. But the more statistical tests conducted on subcategories of the budget, the more likely that associations between polarization and gridlock will be discovered by chance. While it is a judgment call, a case could be made for taking into account the fact that thirteen hypotheses are, in effect, being tested at the same time. If a Bonferroni correction procedure is employed to reduce the risk of spurious positives when multiple tests are being conducted simultaneously, the polarization variable would be significant (at the $p < 0.1$ level) in only one of the thirteen spending areas (environment). I thank the authors for sharing their regression results.

19. For the pioneering analysis of this trend, see Jones, True, and Baumgartner (1997).

20. The intersextile range (a measure of variability less influenced by large outliers than is the variance) is the absolute difference between the annual percentage change in spending outcomes for subfunctions at the 16.67th percentile and the 83.33rd percentile.

Figure 5-9. *Annual Intersextile Ranges in Budget Authority for Domestic Subfunctions, Fiscal Years 1951–2005*

Annual percentage change

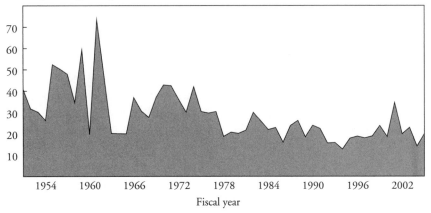

Fiscal year

Source: Author's calculations using data from the Policy Agendas Project, Center for American Politics and Public Policy, University of Washington.

mid-1980s. Since the late 1980s, budgeting volatility has largely stabilized. It is difficult to isolate the role of polarization in this story because it is confounded with the secular trend, but it seems unlikely that polarization has been the prime causal motor since the largest declines in budget volatility occurred during the period (the 1960s) when polarization was relatively stable.[21] Preliminary statistical analysis of aggregate expenditure patterns (along with the microlevel empirical findings that the authors report) casts further doubt on this claim.[22]

If polarization has not driven macrolevel budgeting outcomes, it poses a fascinating puzzle for political analysts. It is obviously not the case that federal budgeting has been isolated from the polarization of policy elites. Just the opposite.

21. Jones, True, and Baumgartner (1997, p. 1334).
22. To gain some purchase on the issue, I regressed logged intersextile ranges of percentage changes on polarization, the time counter, and a dummy variable for divided government. In general, my statistical results are similar to the original findings of Jones, True, and Baumgartner (1997). The strongest result is obtained for the time trend. It has a negative coefficient and is significant at the .01 level in all specifications. The polarization variable is insignificant (and actually has a positive coefficient) once the secular trend is controlled for. Divided government has a positive, statistically significant ($p < .01$) coefficient in a specification that controls for both the time trend and polarization.

The federal budget has been the central battleground for intense partisan conflict over the future of activist government in the United States. Over the past quarter-century, ideological polarization has led to a near collapse of the budget process. Appropriations bills have been frequently late, continuing resolutions have often been used not as stop-gap measures but to fund the entire government for months at a time, and bipartisan support for budget enforcement mechanisms has virtually collapsed. The stable budgetary equilibrium of the 1950s and 1960s is clearly a thing of the past.[23] As Bryan Jones, James True, and Frank Baumgartner point out, however, it appears that polarization has mostly affected timely passage of appropriations bills and statutory direction rather than changes in budget outcomes from year to year.[24] *The procedural manifestations of polarization and spending outcomes seem to be largely disconnected.*

I suspect that polarization is not tightly associated with overall expenditure trends because of the institutionalization of big government in the United States. The period between the 1950s and 1970s was marked by experimentation and innovation in domestic policy. New programs were being established, and the federal role in the economy was growing and rapidly changing. By the 1980s, many new programs and structures were in place, and interest group lobbies had grown up around them. Settled expectations have made budget outcomes increasingly predictable. At the same time, the pressure has increased on leaders to keep domestic programs funded. While the two parties have fought bitter battles over the budget, spending priorities have seldom changed all that much from year to year. Neither party wants the blame for reneging on existing promises.

Three issues require further attention. The first concerns the framing of fiscal policy debates. One reason why the budget process has been the setting for so much partisan rancor over the past few decades (even though budget outcomes have been quite stable) is because budget reforms have forced partisan and ideological differences out into the open. The traditional appropriations process was highly decentralized. The spending and revenue totals were simply what resulted from individual votes on the budget parts. The Congressional Budget Act of 1974, however, required members to go on record on the appropriate size of total spending, total revenues, and the budget deficit. Sharper political debates on fiscal trade-offs were now required. Conflicts over the size of budget increments can be resolved behind closed doors in committee chambers by splitting the difference.

23. Patashnik (2005).
24. Jones, True, and Baumgartner (1997).

But when the conflict is framed on the House floor in terms of an abstract contest between competing visions of government, acceptable compromises become harder to reach.[25]

A second issue is the role of countervailing institutions in reducing gridlock. President Reagan and Congress were able to agree to a Social Security rescue package in 1983 in part because the Social Security Trust Fund was then on the brink of insolvency. If quick action had not been taken, the government would have lost its legal authority to mail out benefit checks. One reason that President Bush was unable to win support for his privatization plan in 2003 is because the Social Security Trust Fund was then in surplus. Even though many experts argued that Social Security's accounting conventions were flawed and that the nation would be better off addressing the program's funding problems sooner rather than later, the surplus made it hard to convince the public that immediate action was needed. These kinds of institutional details shape the menu of feasible reform options, and they are largely exogenous to the preferences of incumbent politicians.[26]

The third and most important issue concerns the underlying elite *consensus* on domestic policy. It is certainly true that liberals and conservatives fight a great deal about public policy, and that the outcome of these fights may have important distributive consequences. Yet it is striking how much agreement there is over the size of the federal government and its role as guarantor of the public welfare. In many domestic areas, there is arguably greater ideological consensus on the legitimate purposes of government now than existed in the immediate postwar era. As Alice M. Rivlin, former director of the Congressional Budget Office, observed about changes in the national policy debate over the past half century:

> There was a time when conservatives did not want the federal government to do much of anything besides defending the borders and delivering the mail. They were for fiscal prudence, states' rights, and not much else. Reducing pollution, ensuring safe food, regulating financial markets, and paying for health care were dangerous ideas. But now it is hard to find an old-style conservative who aspires to elective office. A few intellectual libertarians hang out at places like the Cato Institute and write about all of the government programs they would eliminate if they could, but if any of them get elected they quickly find themselves voting for hugely popular government

25. Patashnik (2005).
26. Patashnik (2000).

programs like Social Security, Medicare, and Head Start—not to mention that new bridge in their district.[27]

In a similar vein, liberals no longer advocate government takeovers of private industry, recoil at the idea of using market incentives to curb pollution, or fight work-oriented welfare policies. With the crucial exception of social issues such as gay marriage and abortion, there has arguably been a convergence of views among political elites on policy tools. All this reflects the triumph of market capitalism and the collapse of central planning. At the same time, there is a strong, underlying consensus on the existence of the welfare state (if little consensus on the details of specific policies and programs). Elite polarization over domestic policy is taking place within the context of a bedrock consensus on the "regulated market."[28] Most policy debates are not about *whether* to have big government but rather about how to manage its risks and costs. As Brady, Ferejohn, and Harbridge correctly stress, much of the inability of government to deal with long-range problems such as Medicare funding stems from electoral and institutional dynamics unrelated to polarization.

None of this is to suggest that polarization lacks policy consequences. Polarization may affect agenda setting more than budgeting. It may make it more difficult for leaders to update existing policies in light of changing economic or social conditions, such as rising income inequality.[29] It may render bipartisan compromises more elusive, particularly on judicial confirmations and on social and moral issues where ideological disagreement is very high. But concerns about the policy effects of polarization should be kept in perspective. Polarization has increased, but many domestic policies have a political logic and organizational momentum of their own that have immunized them from attack by polarized partisans on Capitol Hill.

27. Alice M. Rivlin, "Is America Too Polarized to Make Public Policy?" Whittington Lecture, Georgetown Public Policy Institute, Georgetown University, September 28, 2005.
28. Shapiro (2001).
29. McCarty, Poole, and Rosenthal (2006).

References

Achen, Christopher H., and Larry M Bartels. 2004. "Musical Chairs: Pocketbook Voting and the Limits of Democratic Accountability." Paper prepared for the annual meeting of the American Political Science Association, Chicago, September 1–5.

Alt, James E., and Robert C. Lowry. 2000. "A Dynamic Model of State Budget Outcomes under Divided Partisan Government." *Journal of Politics* 62 (4): 1,035–69.

Anderson, Sarah A. 2006. *Who Matters? Testing Floor, Party, and Committee Models of Appropriations Policy Formation.* Stanford University Press.

Bach, Stanley, and Steven S. Smith. 1988. *Managing Uncertainty in the House of Representatives: Adoption and Innovation in Special Rules.* Brookings.

Binder, Sarah A. 2003. *Stalemate: Causes and Consequences of Legislative Gridlock.* Brookings.

Birnbaum, Jeffrey H. 1987. *Showdown at Gucci Gulch: Lawmakers, Lobbyists, and the Unlikely Triumph of Tax Reform.* New York: Random House.

Brady, David W., and Craig Volden. 2006. *Revolving Gridlock: Politics and Policy from Jimmy Carter to George W. Bush.* Boulder, Colo.: Westview Press.

Brownlee, W. Elliot. 2004. *Federal Taxation in America: A Short History.* 2nd ed. Cambridge University Press.

Campbell, Andrea Louise. 2003. *How Policies Shape Citizens: Senior Citizen Activism and the American Welfare State.* Princeton University Press.

Citrin, Jack. 1974. "Comment: The Political Relevance of Trust in Government." *American Political Science Review* 68 (3): 973–88.

Citrin, Jack, and Donald Green. 1986. "Presidential Leadership and the Resurgence of Trust in Government." *British Journal of Political Science* 16 (4): 431–53.

Cogan, John F. 2002. *Federal Budget Authority and Outlays: 1955–2002.* Stanford University Press.

Davidson, Roger H., and Walter J. Oleszek. 2006. *Congress and Its Members.* 10th ed. Washington: CQ Press.

Evans, Diana. 2004. *Greasing the Wheels: Using Pork Barrel Projects to Build Majority Coalitions in Congress.* Cambridge University Press.

Groseclose, Tim, Steven D. Levitt, and James M. Snyder Jr. 1999. "Comparing Interest Group Scores across Time and Chambers: Adjusted ADA Scores for the U.S. Congress." *American Political Science Review* 93 (1): 33–50.

Hacker, Jacob S., and Paul Pierson. 2005. *Off Center: The Republican Revolution and the Erosion of Democracy.* Yale University Press.

Han, Hahrie, and David W. Brady. 2007. "A Delayed Return to Historical Norms: Congressional Party Polarization after the Second World War." *British Journal of Political Science* 37 (4): 431–53.

Hetherington, Marc J. 1998. "The Political Relevance of Political Trust." *American Political Science Review* 92 (4): 791–808.

———. 1999. "The Effects of Political Trust on the Presidential Vote, 1968–96." *American Political Science Review* 93 (2): 311–26.

Hetherington, Marc J., and Suzanne Globetti. 2002. "Political Trust and Racial Policy Preferences." *American Journal of Political Science* 46 (2): 253–75.

Hibbing, John R., and Elizabeth Theiss-Morse. 1995. *Congress as Public Enemy: Public Attitudes toward American Political Institutions.* Cambridge University Press.

Jones, Bryan D., James L. True, and Frank R. Baumgartner. 1997. "Does Incrementalism Stem from Political Consensus or from Institutional Gridlock?" *American Journal of Political Science* 41 (4): 1,319–39.

Krehbiel, Keith. 1998. *Pivotal Politics: A Theory of U.S. Lawmaking.* University of Chicago Press.

Laitin, David D. 2004. "The Political Science Discipline." In *The Evolution of Political Knowledge*, edited by Edward D. Mansfield and Richard Sisson, pp. 11–40. Ohio State University Press.

Light, Paul C. 1985. *Artful Work: The Politics of Social Security Reform.* New York: Random House.

Mann, Thomas E., and Norman Ornstein. 2006. *The Broken Branch: How Congress Is Failing America and How to Get It Back on Track.* Oxford University Press.

McCarty, Nolan. 2007. "The Policy Effects of Political Polarization." In *The Transformation of American Politics: Activist Government and the Rise of Conservatism*, edited by Paul Pierson and Theda Skocpol, pp. 223–55. Princeton University Press.

McCarty, Nolan, Keith T. Poole, and Howard Rosenthal. 2006. *Polarized America: The Dance of Ideology and Unequal Riches.* MIT Press.

Miles, David, and Allan Timmermann. 1999. "Risk Sharing and Transition Costs in the Reform of Pension Systems in Europe." *Economic Policy* 14 (29): 251–86.

Miller, Arthur H. 1974. "Political Issues and Trust in Government: 1964–1970." *American Political Science Review* 68 (3): 951–72.

Patashnik, Eric M. 2000. *Putting Trust in the U.S. Budget: Federal Trust Funds and the Politics of Commitment.* Cambridge University Press.

———. 2005. "Budgets and Fiscal Policy." In *The Legislative Branch*, edited by Paul J. Quirk and Sarah A. Binder, pp. 382–406. Oxford University Press.

Pierson, Paul. 2007. "The Costs of Marginalization: Qualitative Methods in the Study of American Politics." *Comparative Political Studies* 40 (2): 145–69.

Rohde, David W. 1991. *Parties and Leaders in the Postreform House.* University of Chicago Press.

Rohde, David W., and Kenneth Shepsle. 1987. "The Transformation of American Politics: Activist Government and the Rise of Conservatism." *Congress and the Presidency* 14 (2): 111–33.

Shapiro, Ian. 2004. "Commentary: Intellectual Diversity in Political Science: A Comment on Laitin." In *The Evolution of Political Knowledge*, edited by Edward D. Mansfield and Richard Sisson, pp. 47–59. Ohio State University Press.

Shapiro, Martin. 2001. "The Politics and Policy of the Regulated Market, Efficiency-Constrained Welfare State." In *Seeking the Center: Politics and Policy at the New Century*, edited by Martin A. Levin, Marc K. Landy, and Martin Shapiro, pp. 425–38. Georgetown University Press.

Smith, Steven S. 1989. *Call to Order: Floor Politics in the House and Senate.* Brookings.

Weiss, Randall D. 1996. "The Tax Reform Act of 1986: Did Congress Love It or Leave It?" *National Tax Journal* 49 (3): 447–59.

Wildavsky, Aaron. 1992. *The New Politics of the Budgetary Process.* 2nd ed. New York: HarperCollins.

Wlezien, Christopher. 1995. "The Public as Thermostat: Dynamics of Preferences for Spending." *American Journal of Political Science* 39 (4): 981–1000.

Zelizer, Julian E. 1998. *Taxing America: Wilbur D. Mills, Congress, and the State, 1945–1975.* Cambridge University Press.

6

Toward Depolarization

Pietro S. Nivola
William A. Galston

W̶e began this project asking basic questions: In what sense are the politics of the United States "polarized"? How deep does the polarization run? How does it compare with the politics of other periods in American history? What are its causes and adverse consequences? And which remedies for it make sense?

We now have reasonably reliable answers to these queries. Two large blocs of people—amounting to as much as two-thirds of all American voters—cleave consistently to one political party or the other in presidential elections.[1] In each of these blocs, about three-quarters of the voters appear to have assembled into the opposing camps not just through force of habit but because they believe that their views are well represented by their respective parties.[2] The sorting process even has

1. Scholars have come to a consensus that these voters have undergone a sorting process, so that both parties now align partisan and ideological preferences more closely. However, some disagreement remains on *how far* apart, on average, the two groups are ideologically and *how large* the blocs of staunchly ideological voters ultimately are.

2. To the question "Would you say any of the parties represents your views reasonably well?" 93 percent of "strong" Republicans, 83 percent of "weak" Republicans, and 66 percent of independents who vote Republican answered "yes." On the Democratic side, the numbers were lower but still quite robust. Eighty percent of strong Democrats, 72 percent of weak Democrats, and 57 percent of independents who vote Democratic said "yes." See Jonathan Rauch, "Where the Missing Middle Went," *National Journal,* February 17, 2006.

some geographic manifestations; preferring to commune with their partisan soul mates, many Republican and Democratic loyalists are respectively clustering in "red" and "blue" counties, if not states or regions.

For most of the country, moreover, the partisan patterns held steady in 2006. The year's midterm election, if anything, even deepened their shades of red or blue in some regions. In the Northeast, the Republican Party suffered further losses, as the territorial sorting of the parties continued apace. When Connecticut's Christopher Shays entered Congress in 1987, he was one of nine GOP House members from New England. But by the time the electoral tide of 2006 had rolled through, only Shays managed to eke out reelection; *every* other fellow Republican remaining in the neighborhood was washed out to sea.

A convenient metric to gauge how firmly the partisan separation has taken root in much of today's political geography, in fact, is to examine the configuration of congressional districts that voted for the presidential candidate of one party and the House candidate of the other party. In 1972 there had been 192 such districts (about 44 percent of the entire House of Representatives). By 1996, the number of these split districts had dropped to 110. In 2004 it had fallen further, to a mere 59. Unsurprisingly, the 2006 midterm election showed an uptick in split districts. But it was remarkably modest: only 69 districts (just 16 percent of the House) that had last voted one way for president went the opposite way in their House races. Stated in the plainest terms, the vast majority of congressional districts appeared to stay about as predictably red or blue as they had been two years earlier.

The fusing of party preferences with ideology, not merely among the so-called political class but *within the electorate,* is more pronounced today than it was a few decades ago. This is not the same as saying that most Republicans and Democrats are spoiling for a culture war. All things considered, as Morris P. Fiorina and Matthew S. Levendusky show in this study's first volume, the ideological differences—including the "cultural" ones—between red and blue voters can seem unremarkable. Considering "all things," however, risks veiling particulars that have taken on political weight.[3] As Gary C. Jacobson and Alan I. Abramowitz stressed in their comments on the Fiorina and Levendusky narra-

---

3. When one considers the statistical distribution of attitudes among party adherents on given issues, even if the difference between their respective means or proportions remains stable or has even diminished over time, the increased "weight," or salience, attached to particular issues can still build a polarizing effect. Polarization over a given issue, in other words, might best be measured as the product of the distance between attitudinal means *multiplied* by the issue's weight. See Hetherington and Weiler (2005).

tive, real discord persists over *certain* critical issues (pro-life versus pro-choice, "soft" versus "hard" foreign policy, for or against legal status for undocumented immigrants).[4] Furthermore, what may seem to survey researchers like marginal distinctions (for example, tolerating civil unions as distinct from endorsing same-sex marriages) are not mere fine points but fundamental differences in the eyes of millions of citizens.

Coinciding with these proclivities in the public is the increasingly polarized comportment exhibited by key political institutions—the news media and the Congress, for instance. As David W. Brady and Hahrie C. Han demonstrated in the first volume of *Red and Blue Nation?* the adversarial partisanship in the contemporary Congress resembles the rough-and-tumble of the late nineteenth century more than the comparatively muted rivalry of the parties during, say, the immediate post–World War II years. That conclusion seems safe to stipulate. Less clear is whether Congress's partisan adversaries are as detached from grassroots sentiments as other strands of Brady and Han's analysis imply. The actions of a polarized Congress occur in a context, not a vacuum.

How did the reprise of intensely partisan politics happen? The impetus for it has come from both the top and the bottom of the political order: to an important degree, antagonistic elites have framed the public's perceptions and choices, but the evolving preferences of many voters have also abetted the elites' antagonisms. Exhibit A: Congress. Norms and practices there have changed over the past thirty years, gradually enabling party leaders to enforce greater party cohesion and discipline among rank-and-file members.[5] By encouraging more party-line voting on salient pieces of legislation and somewhat less need for bipartisan accommodation, the Democratic and Republican sides are separated more visibly than was common a generation ago. The effects of such institutional changes at the "top" of the system are not hermetically sealed inside the Beltway; they ultimately diffuse to a wider public, thus signaling and imparting to it a keener partisan separation.

---

4. In the 2006 election exit polls, 61 percent of Democratic voters but just 37 percent of Republican voters said they favored offering legal status to illegal immigrants. See CNN.com, "America Votes 2006," November 7, 2006 (www.cnn.com/ELECTION/2006/pages/results/states/US/H/00/epolls.0.html). Abortion remained a divisive matter. Among Republicans, 59 percent continued to oppose abortion under either any circumstance or only excepting cases of rape, incest, or when a woman's life is in danger. By contrast, only 33 percent of Democrats took so restrictive a position. See the American National Election Studies (www.electionstudies.org).

5. Among many other accounts of these changes, see Schickler (2005, especially pp. 53–54).

Polarizing pressures, however, have also emanated from the bottom. The intensified partisanship in Congress cannot be imputed solely, or perhaps even mostly, to majoritarian parliamentary procedures (or what critics have deemed the demise of "regular order") routinely practiced by the ruling party's leadership. Even such flagrant top-down manipulations of the democratic process as the gerrymandering of congressional districts explain only a small portion of the safe, one-party districts in the House of Representatives and, hence, the concomitant decline of moderate members. As Thomas E. Mann's chapter in the first volume of *Red and Blue Nation?* makes clear, the self-segregation of many voters into "red" or "blue" communities—their chosen political spaces, so to say—accounts for much more.

The fact that the nation's partisan polarization signifies more than the machinations of supercharged party activists and politicians—and reflects, to an extent, popular choices—should give pause. Inasmuch as constituents in a democracy expect, indeed demand, differing governing philosophies distinguishing candidates for elective office, a sharper partisan edge in congressional deliberations and election campaigns is no tragedy. On the contrary, it is fitting—and efforts to blunt it, through various "good government" schemes, can interfere with popular sovereignty. In short, before plumping for a big fix, reformers need to ask themselves how much of the public really shares their own disdain for polarized politics.

Four Problems

The preceding paragraph was intended to sound a note of caution. But it also invites a further inquiry: what if a plurality of Americans is tiring of Washington's partisan polemics and would prefer to see a return of less disputatious politics?[6] The 2006 election shed less light on this possibility than was widely asserted. The election was said to be a revolt of the restive center, repudiating the

6. In his comments in this study's first volume, Alan I. Abramowitz notes that the "ideological orientations of Democratic and Republican candidates and officeholders" are similar to those of the "politically engaged partisans" in the electorate, and that the latter are not "a small and unrepresentative fringe group." In 2004 they made up 46 percent of Democratic identifiers and 49 percent of Republican identifiers. Fair enough. However, Democratic identifiers overall constitute just 33 percent of all voters; Republican identifiers, only 28 percent. Thus the combined total of "politically engaged partisans" amounts to less than 30 percent of the total electorate. This leaves open the question of whether the ideologies of candidates and officeholders, however agreeable to their politically engaged partisans, might be out of step with a very large share of the voters.

"radical experiment in partisan governance."[7] Yet as Andrea Campbell notes in her entry in this book, a lot of centrist incumbents—not safely situated arch-conservatives—were ousted.[8] Perhaps the swing voters, including many presumed to be positioned smack in the political midfield, were not so hungry for moderation after all. Or, alternatively, the fluid middle of the electorate *is* truly temperate and in 2006 was fed up with an intemperate Republican majority in Congress. Yet much of the electoral upshot seemed incongruous: the most conspicuous losers in 2006 were not the perpetrators of a "radical experiment" but the GOP's *moderates*.[9]

Undiscriminating political outcomes like the latter are nettlesome. All the ingredients of a perfect storm seemed present in November 2006: an increasingly unpopular war, outrage over political scandals, an embattled presidency. Accordingly, the election saw a significant 5.5 percentage point shift in the popular vote—more or less on a par with the midterm electoral tsunamis of 1966, 1974, and 1994. Unlike those years, however, when an average of forty-nine seats changed hands in the House of Representatives, 2006 yielded a net change of only thirty. Seen in this light, whether the election was suitably responsive or, more notably, the latest display of systemic rigidity remains an open question. Put in broader terms, a robust democratic regime is attentive to its active partisans but also ought to reflect with some regularity and precision the sensibilities of the sizable, less zealous mainstream. And there, arguably, signs of misalignment abound.

Consider the results of an opinion survey conducted by the Pew Research Center in the spring of 2006. Half of the respondents had come to have an unfavorable opinion of the Republican Party. The Democratic Party, then in the minority, was viewed somewhat less negatively—though 42 percent of those

---

7. See, for instance, Joe Klein, "Reaching for the Center," *Time,* November 20, 2006. The longer-term, more probable prospect was well summarized by Gary C. Jacobson (2006, p. 51): "A pro-Democratic national tide would, by definition, shake up partisan habits, at least temporarily, counteracting the Republicans' structural advantage. But absent major shifts in stable party loyalties that lighten the deepening shades of red and blue in so many districts, after the tide ebbed the competitive environment would likely revert to what it had been since 1994."

8. See comments to chapter 5 in this volume.

9. Among the many prominent casualties in the House were such moderate icons as Representatives Jim Leach of Iowa, Nance Johnson of Connecticut, Sue Kelly of New York, and Curt Weldon and Michael Fitzpatrick of Pennsylvania. The overall loss of seats by the president's party barely approximated the historical average. Between 1902 and 2002, the president's party lost an average of 32.6 seats in the House in the sixth year of his presidency. The 2006 loss was 30.

surveyed also rated it unfavorably. To put these numbers in perspective, a dozen years earlier, only around a third of the public held so dim a view of either party.[10]

The discontent in 2006 seemed extraordinarily unsparing. The turn for the worse in the Iraq war was a major contributor, but not all objective circumstances justified so much public distress, as Carl M. Cannon's astute essay in the first volume of *Red and Blue Nation?* points out. A strong national economy, for instance, now was of almost no help to the Bush presidency and the Republican-controlled Congress.[11] By early 2007, the president's approval rating had plunged to a nadir not seen since Carter, Nixon, and Truman.[12] Meanwhile, anti-incumbent sentiment directed at Congress soared: whereas 39 percent of Americans in 2002 would have liked to see most members of Congress lose their seats, by 2006 fully 53 percent felt that vengeful. So strong was the animus toward Congress that the percentage of people who believed that the legislators were accomplishing "less than usual" had climbed from 16 percent in 2000 to more than 40 percent.[13]

Jeopardizing Trust

Quite plausibly, these attitudes (and wild misperceptions of the actual legislative record) were fueled not so much by the electorate's frustration about the general

10. Pew Research Center for the People and the Press, "Public Disillusionment with Congress at Record Levels: Anti-Incumbent Sentiment Echoes 1994," April 20, 2006 (people-press.org/reports/display.php3?ReportID=275).

11. In mid-2006 the American economy was the strongest among all major industrialized countries. During the first quarter of the year, it was surging at a rate of 5.6 percent. Unemployment (at 4.6 percent) was well below the average for each of the past preceding decades. And that was not all; many other social indicators were pointing in a positive direction. Violent crime rates, for example, were at the lowest levels since the beginning of the federal government's systematic records (1973). Welfare caseloads had plunged by almost 60 percent since 1996. The rate of abortions had reached a thirty-year low. The use of illegal drugs by teenagers had fallen by almost a fifth since 2001, and teenage pregnancies were down for the twelfth consecutive year. On the other hand, most of the economic gains in recent years have accrued to households in the upper tiers of the income distribution, while median incomes have stagnated and average Americans are reporting heightened levels of economic insecurity. As Treasury Secretary Henry Paulson acknowledged in an August 2006 speech at Columbia University, the traditional economic aggregates are not telling the full story. See U.S. Treasury, "Remarks Prepared for Delivery by Treasury Secretary Henry M. Paulson at Columbia University," August 1, 2006 (www.ustreas.gov/press/releases/hp41.htm).

12. See Roper Center for Public Opinion Research, "Comparing Past Presidential Performance" (137.99.36.203/CFIDE/roper/presidential/webroot/presidential_rating.cfm).

13. Pew Research Center, "Public Disillusionment with Congress at Record Levels," April 20, 2006 (people-press.org/reports/display.php3?ReportID=275).

TOWARD DEPOLARIZATION
241

state of the nation as by the stridently partisan quarrels of its politicians.[14] Notice that a hypothesis along these lines need not postulate that weary voters sulk at home on election day. On the contrary, as Marc J. Hetherington shows in this book, voters witnessing contentious partisanship may even participate in greater numbers.[15] But the thesis would be congruent with what political scientists have long suspected aggravates public mistrust of government. "When partisan controversy is especially acrimonious," wrote Roger H. Davidson and his colleagues nearly four decades ago, "public disaffection increases."[16]

That disaffection, it seems safe to infer, was fed by hyperpartisan antics in Congress and the White House, and contributed to the tone (if not always the results) of the 2006 midterm election. According to exit polls, revulsion with congressional scandals, corruption, and ethics violations actually exceeded the voters' despair over the course of the war in Iraq.[17] In all likelihood, many of these abuses had come to be perceived, correctly or not, as manifestations of the GOP's dogged pursuit of party supremacy.

In the end, it is hard to avoid an impression that truculent partisanship has taken a toll on trust in the Republic's core governmental institutions. Of course, how disturbing this situation really is depends on who you are. Sizable swaths of voters—those who obtain considerable customer satisfaction from their respective political parties—may deem it a price worth paying to advance their partisan ends, while a different, perhaps equally large, body of individuals in between feels

14. According to 2006 exit poll data, a majority of voters (55 percent) said the country was not headed in the "right direction." That response, however, was well below ones that stressed other concerns, such as how well Congress "is handling its job," in which 61 percent disapproved. CNN.com, "America Votes 2006," November 7, 2006 (www.cnn.com/ELECTION/2006/pages/results/states/US/H/00/epolls.0.html).

15. See chapter 1 in this volume.

16. Davidson, Kovenock, and O'Leary (1968, pp. 52–53). The thesis was revisited thoroughly by King (1997, especially pp. 174–77). For related work in more recent years, see also Jacobs and Shapiro (2000) and Hetherington (2005, pp. 23–24). Not surprisingly, levels of trust, like so many other public perceptions these days, appear to be increasingly a function of party affiliation, with distrust running most deeply among out-party voters. Still, as noted by Brady, Ferejohn, and Harbridge (chapter 5) in this volume, *overall* public trust in government has been on a clear downward slide since 2000.

17. Fully 74 percent of voters in the 2006 exit polls singled out corruption and ethics issues as either "very" (33 percent) or "extremely" (41 percent) important. Sixty-seven percent of the voters indicated that Iraq was either "very" (32 percent) or "extremely" (35 percent) important. CNN.com, "America Votes 2006."

underrepresented. No democracy can be all things to all people. Still, the more inclusive and widely esteemed it is, the better.

Deadlocking Fiscal Retrenchment

Persistence of partisan polarity also seems likely to doom long-range solutions to the nation's looming fiscal crisis. The greatest challenge for domestic policy in the twenty-first century will be to modernize the social compact between government, business, labor, and individuals to provide a sustainable measure of security for a population living longer. The extant structure of pensions, social insurance, and Medicare will buckle unless responsibly revamped.

Why does the political process keep kicking that can down the road? Just blaming fainthearted leadership is too simplistic an answer. Our last two presidents, as a matter of fact, did not flinch from expending political capital on notable initiatives. Bill Clinton gambled his on a comprehensive healthcare reform in 1994. A decade later, George W. Bush took a very long shot on partial privatization of the Social Security system. What wrecked such projects was not presidential timidity but, more basically, the absence of cooperation across party lines—the kind of cooperation among leaders that made it possible for an independent commission to propose, and the Congress to adopt, significant modifications to Social Security in 1983. The "third rail"—Social Security (or for that matter, practically any other component of the modern welfare state's assortment of entrenched entitlements)—is too dangerous to touch, let alone overhaul, without the protective buffer of bipartisanship. Indeed, just about *any* budgetary discipline has proven harder to attain amid the fissures between the political parties in recent years. As Eric M. Patashnik reminds us elsewhere in this volume, polarized Washington has presided over a relentless, even reckless, upward spiral of government spending.[18]

Encumbering Foreign Affairs

With bedrock constituencies of the two parties sharply at odds over how the nation ought to conduct its international affairs, our polarized politics also put under great strain the capacity to lead an enlightened approach to global trade, immigration, and, most notably, a resolute foreign policy.

During the summer of 2006, the House of Representatives debated the wisdom of setting a date for the withdrawal of American forces from Iraq. A resolution declaring that to pick such a date would be "arbitrary" and "not in the

18. See comments to chapter 5.

national interest" was put to a vote. Republicans went on record in favor of the resolution 214 to 3, while Democrats rejected it 149 to 42.[19] The Iraq conflict reached new heights of controversy in the ensuing months. In February 2007, the House debated another resolution, this time disapproving of President Bush's decisions to deploy additional combat troops to Baghdad. Two hundred twenty-nine Democratic members supported the resolution, while 180 Republican members and 2 Democrats rejected it; only 17 Republicans sided with the Democratic majority. A month later, a measure requiring U.S. combat forces to exit Iraq by September 2008 squeezed through the bitterly divided House. Only two Republicans went along with this Democratic Party priority, while all but fourteen Democrats voted for it.[20]

What has been the basis for this cavernous and persistent gulf between the parties?[21] Every five years, the Pew Research Center conducts an in-depth survey of the nature of the American electorate. The most recent report found something startling: Democratic and Republican voters differed more dramatically in their views about America's role in the world than about anything else. "Foreign affairs assertiveness now almost completely distinguishes Republican-oriented voters from Democratic-oriented voters," the Pew study concluded. "In contrast, attitudes relating to religion and social issues are not nearly as important in determining party affiliation."[22]

As is almost always the case with survey research, the specific wording of questionnaires can yield varying results. Jonathan Rauch writes earlier in this volume that not all survey instruments appear to confirm so wide a breach between Republican and Democratic respondents along various dimensions of international relations.[23] On the most telling issues, however, the breach has been too wide to discount from practically any vantage point. Even as the public soured on the war in Iraq, for example, fully 68 percent of Republicans in November 2006 continued to regard the U.S. military presence in Iraq as "a stabilizing force," whereas merely 14 percent of Democrats did.[24] And the exit

19. U.S. House of Representatives (2006).
20. The few Democratic dissenters, it should be noted, included a number of liberals who regarded the scheduled troop drawdown as *too slow*.
21. The following passage draws heavily on the work of Beinart (2006, pp. 186–87).
22. Pew Research Center for the People and the Press, "Beyond Red vs. Blue," May 10, 2005 (people-press.org/reports/display.php3?ReportID=242).
23. See comments to chapter 4.
24. Program on International Policy Attitudes, "Americans Assess U.S. International Strategy," November 21–29, 2006 (www.worldpublicopinion.org/pipa/pdf/dec06/USIntlStrategy_Dec06_rpt.pdf).

polls on election day found nearly three-quarters of Democratic voters demanding the withdrawal of troops, a step that three-quarters of Republican voters opposed.[25] America had been torn during the Vietnam War. But as James Q. Wilson notes in another part of this book, the divisions then defied party identification, whereas the disjuncture over Iraq, for the most part, has been along party lines.[26]

Lest it be thought that what has sundered members of the two parties is solely the Iraq war, consider the partisan divergence on the U.S. intervention in Afghanistan.[27] By late 2005, approval for it among Democrats had slid below 60 percent, while 94 percent of Republicans remained supportive.[28] Indeed, just 57 percent of Democrats—compared to 95 percent of Republicans—could bring themselves to support military action "to destroy a terrorist camp."[29] In 2006, reports Peter Beinart in his perceptive chapter about the partisan split over foreign policy, 70 percent of Republicans but only 41 percent of Democrats would support military action *even as a last resort* to cripple Iran's nuclear weapons program.[30] When the Pew researchers queried Americans whether the United States should disengage internationally—just "mind its own business"— 55 percent of Democrats said yes, whereas barely 27 percent of Republicans concurred.[31]

Few things are permanent in politics. Within both political parties, the quagmire in Iraq has plainly eroded confidence in American power. In due course, isolationist impulses may resurface in the GOP as well. Improbable as it seems, the

25. CNN.com, "America Votes 2006," November 7, 2006 (www.cnn.com/ELECTION/2006/pages/results/states/US/H/00/epolls.0.html).

26. See comments to chapter 4.

27. The divide on Iraq was, of course, most striking. A poll in March 2006, taken amid a torrent of bad news, still found 61 percent of Republicans, but just 28 percent of Democrats, willing to stay the course when asked the following fundamental question: "Do you think the United States has the responsibility to stay in Iraq until a democratic government is established, even if it takes years, or doesn't it have that responsibility?" Fox News, "Fox News/Opinion Dynamics Poll," March 14–15, 2006 (www.foxnews.com/projects/pdf/poll_031606.pdf).

28. MIT Public Opinion Research Training Lab Survey data reported in "When Should We Fight?" *Boston Review,* January/February 2006.

29. This result was consistent with an earlier MIT survey, flagged by journalist Matthew Continetti. Continetti reports that in November 2005, fully 94 percent of Republicans said the policy of regime change in Afghanistan had not been a mistake, while only 59 percent of Democrats agreed. Matthew Continetti, "The Peace Party vs. the Power Party," *Weekly Standard,* January 1, 2007.

30. See chapter 4. Italics added.

31. Pew Research Center for the People and the Press, "Opinion Leaders Turn Cautious, Public Looks Homeward," November 17, 2005 (people-press.org/reports/display.php3?ReportID=263).

two sides could even invert their stances some day, if the Democratic Party's adherents were to rediscover, say, the internationalism of the Truman era—or, more likely, if a nondelusional Democrat regains the White House and then gets mugged by the reality of world events. For now, though, the contrast of attitudes at the cores of the two parties is still stark: in the post–September 11 years, the right has remained more engaged and hawkish, while on the left, as Beinart explains, "the whole idea of focusing the nation's energies on defeating global jihad (whether you call that effort the 'war on terror' or something else) has fallen into disrepute."[32] Whether policymakers, increasingly cross-pressured by these conflicting orientations, will be able to grind out a long and costly struggle against this country's ruthless enemies is highly uncertain.

Hobbling the Judiciary

Much ink has been spilled over the negative impact of polarized parties on the legislative branch. Some critics assert that the overall productivity of Congress has been severely disrupted, others that its legislation is qualitatively worse than it used to be in recent memory, and still others that parliamentary tactics—especially the tendency of the lower chamber's majority party to steamroll the minority, and of the upper chamber's minority to obstruct majority rule—have grown more inclement. We suspect that the first of these claims is a debatable proposition, and the second is, if not a memory lapse, strained logic (for the reasons Keith Krehbiel elegantly demonstrates earlier in this text).[33] Only the last seems plainly beyond dispute.

The independent judiciary is the constitutional cornerstone most shaken by the ascent of a petulant mind-set when discharging what ought to be solemn and stately congressional responsibilities. The process of selecting and confirming court appointments has become so rancorous and protracted that the confirmation rate for appellate court nominees has slowed to a crawl, and the pool of qualified candidates willing to undergo such an ordeal may narrow.[34] Presidents have grown increasingly gun-shy about advancing nominees who have extensive paper

<hr />

32. Beinart (2006, p. 187). Strikingly, even as late as August 2006—by which time public displeasure with the Iraq war was thought to have spread across the spectrum—a *Washington Post*/ABC poll still found only 14 percent of Republican identifiers willing to assert that the war was "not worth fighting," compared to 70 percent who said so among Democrats. Peter Baker and Claudia Deane, "House Incumbents at Risk, Poll Finds," *Washington Post*, August 8, 2006.

33. See comments to chapter 2.

34. See Maltzman (2005, p. 415).

trails (for example, candidates with legislative, academic, or law practice backgrounds) and cannot readily invoke a "my-hands-were-tied-by-precedent" defense for past positions. The result is a body of jurists with less diverse professional perspectives and backgrounds.[35] At the same time, as is well known, the confirmation wars have spawned a cottage industry of advocacy groups whose main raison d'être is to shape, directly or indirectly, the federal bench or the disposition of those who sit on it. These permanent lobbies have placed Congress under added pressure to legislate statutory encroachments on the judiciary. A variety of congressional efforts to circumscribe judicial jurisdiction have been stepped up in recent years, as Sarah A. Binder observes in her illuminating contribution to this book.[36]

Up to a point, all this was to be expected. As in 1857 and 1935–36, the composition of the third branch could not escape attention, for its rulings, in the words of Archibald Cox, increasingly featured "all the qualities of social legislation: they pertain to the future; they are mandatory; they govern millions of people; they reorder people's lives in ways that benefit some and disappoint others in order to achieve social objectives."[37] Judges playing so obtrusive a role were bound to be scrutinized more assiduously, and often invidiously, by interest groups and their partisan allies in Congress. The present propensity to politicize routine recruitment to the courts, however, is rooted in more than principled debate about the proper bounds of judicial activism or restraint. Some of the controversies over judicial nominees seem phony and fabricated—crafted to be instruments for party fundraising purposes and to arouse the passions of gullible publics.

The Perils of Progressivism

The above considerations are unsettling enough to warrant a quest for correctives. But before venturing, much less championing, specific suggestions, keep in mind that political reform movements aimed at suppressing "partisanship" have had a long and less than illustrious history in this country. It is worth revisiting at least a few of the stratagems that went awry for, in light of their lessons, the recommendations sketched in subsequent sections of this chapter are offered in a spirit of humility. Reformers must remain mindful that, as in

---

35. The Supreme Court now consists entirely of former circuit court judges.
36. See chapter 3.
37. Cox (1976, p. 77).

earlier epochs, even seemingly sound remedies for the ills of our politics are best regarded as experimental cures; they could provide relief, but they also might have unforeseen side effects, including some that could turn out to be worse than the disease.

The Nonpartisan Ballot

As is well known, drastic measures to curtail the power of party organizations were adopted by American city governments during the Progressive Era. One of them was the notion of erasing, quite literally, the party identification of candidates in municipal elections. The theory behind this resort to so-called nonpartisan balloting was that it would put the voters in charge: now, presumably, they would choose directly among persons running for office rather than have their menu constrained by partisan intermediaries.

What motivated the proponents was disgust with big-city machines and party bosses, and the corruption and waste they begot. Of course, that specific complaint was not the same as the one critics level at the parties today—namely, that their elites are too polarized ideologically. In a larger sense, however, the reform ideals then and now do have something in common. The ultimate intent of the nonpartisan ballot, explained Edward C. Banfield and James Q. Wilson, was to release "the people from the shackles which the machines and bosses had fastened upon them" in order to elevate public affairs above "considerations of party interest and party advantage" and "give the democratic impulse a chance to express itself." Indeed, an overarching aim of the Progressives was to put "the electorate in the position to assert its will despite professional politicians."[38] That preoccupation has at least some parallels with current talk of a "democratic deficit"—that is, the concern that public affairs again are being dominated by professional politicians who pursue, albeit for other reasons, party interests and party advantages supposedly inconsonant with the will of average voters.

The main thing to remember about the efforts at the turn of the nineteenth century was that their principal consequence was undesirable: far from freeing people to participate more actively in electoral politics, the nonpartisan formula depressed voter turnouts. Today, more measures aimed at domesticating partisan politics and blurring party differences might appeal to battle-weary voters—or, like the nonpartisan ballot, could confuse, bore, and deactivate them. That, in

---

38. Banfield and Wilson (1965, p. 153).

turn, would not serve the cause of depolarization. The first to be weeded out by a lower turnout are the relatively apolitical voters, those who are less partisan and less intense in their attitudes toward specific issues—in short, those who are less polarized.

The Direct Primary

Among Progressivism's various political innovations, none grew more conse-quential over time than the idea of direct primary elections as the preferred means of nominating candidates. Before the diffusion of primaries, the selection of candidates was largely controlled by cadres of state and local party leaders. Their usual cast of mind, it is safe to say, lay less in any impassioned pursuit of social causes than in simply securing for the political parties material advantages such as pork and patronage. For these power brokers, therefore, anointing candidates who stood the best odds of getting elected was the first order of business. And that pragmatic imperative tended to favor office-seekers with a broad appeal.

Enter the primary system. Its purpose was to displace the role of party bosses in vetting candidates and to empower the people. Alas, not infrequently, this lat-est exercise in giving "the democratic impulse a chance to express itself" would have the perverse result of rendering U.S. elections, in a sense, less democratic. Typically, only small bands of voters bother to participate in primaries—and these motivated participants tend to be more fervid than ordinary citizens. (The effect is strongest in "closed" primaries, where only card-carrying members are eligible to vote in their party's contest—an important distinction about which we will have more to say later on.) Thus candidates find themselves campaigning for the support of unrepresentative factions. Having gained nominations that way (posi-tioning themselves outside the midfield), the contestants may then force a large part of the general electorate to swallow the political equivalent of an unappetiz-ing main course—in effect, a choice of two dishes that are at best unbalanced or, at worst, each too hot and overspiced.[39]

The party primary, in sum, risks serving up fewer moderate politicians and more ideologues. At critical junctures, it has also turned into a device for driving the remaining moderate incumbents back into the partisan fold. Recall what hap-pened to the handful of Republican House members who wavered over whether to impeach President Clinton in 1998: several were promptly threatened with the possibility of primary challenges from the right. The unmistakable effect, when

39. For a clear theoretical exposition of this argument with substantial supporting evidence, see Burden (2001).

the House came to a vote, was to press most of these holdouts into line with the rest of the party.[40]

The dynamics on the left are similar. A case in point was the impact of a primary campaign waged against Senator Joseph Lieberman in 2006. As one of a dwindling number of Senate Democrats outspokenly opposed to a precipitous U.S. retreat from Iraq, the Connecticut senator drew the ire of his party's liberal wing, which proceeded to field a strong challenger. Lieberman lost the Democratic primary. Though he ultimately retained his Senate seat by running as an independent in the general election, the intraparty uprising in Connecticut put other Democratic nonconformists on notice: toe an anti-Bush line on Iraq, or else.[41]

These examples are indicative of how little, from time to time, the influence of the primary in practice resembles its theory. Instead of attuning elective officials more directly to the prevailing inclinations of the public, the prospect of a primary can disconnect the two. Lieberman's rejection of a swift timetable for pulling troops out of Iraq and the GOP moderates who had misgivings about ousting Clinton were closer to the views of the majority of Americans (at least at the relevant points in time). Those good democratic deeds would not go unpunished, however, thanks to the long shadow cast by real or possible primary challenges. All of which suggests that, in cases like these, the primary has come to represent the reverse of what the Progressive ethos envisioned: less a dependable expression of the "democratic impulse" than a partisan instrument, used to discipline public servants whenever they distance themselves too far from the party base.

The direct primary, of course, is an invention that long predates the contemporary polarization of American politicians, so one should not blow any causal relationship out of proportion.[42] That said, the availability of the primary process

40. Among several other revealing accounts of what happened, see James Carney and John F. Dickerson, "The Big Push to Impeach," *Time,* December 14, 1998; Marc Fisher and William Claiborne, "GOP Moderates Face Consequences of Impeachment Vote," *Washington Post,* December 21, 1998; Kate O'Beirne, "Moderate Ambitions," *National Review,* December 31, 1998; Drew (1999, pp. 213–14, 224–25). On the squeezing of marginal members, see Lanoue and Emmert (1999).

41. Still, Democratic incumbents did retain considerable room to maneuver. Many—especially those in contested districts and states—refused to go along with the strict withdrawal timetable favored by their party's left wing.

42. For these and a number of other important caveats, see McCarty, Poole, and Rosenthal (2006, pp. 67–70). The following exemplifies the kind of empirical uncertainties yet to be resolved: while Burden (2001) finds that the polarizing effect of primaries is much greater for Republicans than Democrats (based on 1992 election results), McCarty, Poole, and Rosenthal find just the reverse (based on 1990 election results).

for purposes of purifying and purging candidates at almost every level and in both parties, and the pains incumbent centrists have felt compelled to take to ward off imaginable insurgencies from the parties' purists, are developments that appear to have become magnified in the past thirty or so years. One of the likely results appears to be a propensity for primaries to polarize—not something the primary system was intended to facilitate but now clearly a reality that needs to be reckoned with.

Campaign Finance Reform

It is hard to resist attaching to this discussion of political reformism the most recent offshoot of the Progressive legacy: the attempt in 2002 to restrict campaign funds flowing through the political parties. Intended to constrain the influence of the present-day analogues to the impresarios of the party machine era, the Bipartisan Campaign Reform Act of 2002 cracked down on the ability of partisan potentates to obtain (or, more precisely, shake down) large corporate and union contributions to the parties. While banning the unlimited flow of this "soft money," the new law lifted the limits for small individual contributors.[43] This combination of regulations, it was thought, would enable grassroots constituents ("the democratic impulse," once again) to ascend.

Contrary to the predictions of its opponents, the national party committees have hardly been "eviscerated" by the law.[44] (In 2004 they raised more funds than ever.) A more relevant concern is the apparent boost received by partisan polarizers, both big and small. In the 2004 election, huge sums of money dodged the ban on direct party funding and instead made their way to ostensibly independent organizations (the so-called 527s).[45] These foils, in effect, did much of the parties' dirty work with the added advantage of obscuring direct party accountability— and, as in the Swift Boat attack ads on Senator John Kerry, they did so with exceptional zeal. The megadonors sponsoring these groups proved more polar than the traditional large contributors that the campaign finance regulators had so painstakingly targeted.

Meanwhile, aided by the Internet, the newly encouraged fundraising activity at the grass roots has excited the ideological fringes of the parties. As Thomas B. Edsall notes in his essay in the first volume of this study, the parties' web-based

43. For an excellent summary, see Malbin (2006). See also Corrado and others (2005).
44. That hyperbolic forecast came from Senator Mitch McConnell (R-Ky.). See Trevor Potter, "McCain-Feingold: A Good Start," *Washington Post,* June 23, 2006.
45. The 527s spent in excess of $500 million in the 2004 campaign. See Jacobson (2005, p. 139).

appeals and advertisements for small-scale contributions are conducted through ideological blogs. Howard Dean was the first, in 2004, to appreciate the rich lode that could be mined in that fashion. Exploiting new rules and technology, his campaign tapped into a mass donor base that proved to be well to the left of even the 2004 Democratic National Convention's delegates (who were themselves considerably more liberal than the party rank-and-file).[46]

Exactly how much these phenomena—maximalist 527s, armies of militant minidonors, and so forth—are by-products of the campaign finance regime as distinct from other factors, and also how enduring they will be, is far from certain. A prudent observer will want to watch several additional election cycles before drawing firm conclusions. Nevertheless, at least in the wake of the last presidential election, there was some reason to suspect that portions of the 2002 reform, like quite a few other good-government initiatives in this country across the years, had produced some unanticipated consequences, including more incentives to mobilize the political spectrum's extremes.

Some Preliminary Guideposts

With such cautionary tales in mind, what might be done to help repair damage wrought by the excesses of today's partisan polarization? Not much is likely to be accomplished by bewailing only the nuisances most commonly implicated (for example, the partisan redistricting of congressional seats). In addition to them, it is necessary to rethink other problematic features in every major institution of the American political system—the electoral mechanics, the congressional procedures, the president's relationship with the legislative branch, the domain of the judiciary, the role of the media, and the reach of federalism. In the remaining pages, we begin this broad reassessment at relatively high altitude and, in a subsequent section, descend where necessary into greater detail.

Electoral Revisions

The first of the institutional fundaments—the electoral component—calls for changes that would register in higher fidelity the often faint voice of the median voter. A first step in that direction would be for more states to alter the methods

46. The Pew Research Center for the People and the Press, "The Dean Activists: Their Profile and Prospects," April 6, 2005 (people-press.org/reports/display.php3?ReportID=240). Internet fundraising is still a work in progress and may be evolving into more of a mainstream sport. In 2007 Senator Barack Obama (D-Ill.) has proved to be a prodigious Internet fundraiser, even though his campaign was softer edged than Dean's.

by which candidates are slated. Dispensing with party primaries entirely would be infeasible, given how firmly institutionalized they have become in most states. Rather, here may be one instance in which the only realistic remedy for the shortcomings of the primary's "democratic impulse" may be to open a wider door for it.

Different primary systems vary widely in their aggregate effects. States with relatively open primary systems—in which Democratic, Republican, and independent voters are effectively permitted to cast ballots in either of the parties' primaries—appear to aid centrist candidacies more than states with closed primary systems do. Indeed, one study concluded, rather robustly, that representatives emerging from closed regimes tend to be significantly less aligned with the preferences of the median voter in their districts.[47]

Electoral reforms would do well to begin by improving the direct primary but ought not to stop there. A variety of measures aimed at animating potential voters are worth contemplating, for higher participation in U.S. elections, beyond the marginal improvements in recent years, might reduce the disproportionate weight of the electorate's uninhibited archpartisans. Apart from the usual efforts to ease voter registration and voting procedures, increasing the competitiveness of elections could boost turnouts. One of the troubles with the biennial contests for House seats, many of which are uncompetititive, is that they are uninspiring to millions of average citizens. More closely contested elections, being more interesting, may prompt such voters to go to the polls.

It may be, moreover, that the electoral ritual in the United States is simply too fatiguing. What Oscar Wilde said about socialism ("it takes too many evenings") is in some ways true of the American political cycle: to have any influence on it demands inordinate time, energy, and civic virtue. Arguably, a good many Americans slack off because they are called upon to vote too often. In no other major democracy does the national legislature face reelection so frequently. Maybe if federal, state, and local balloting coincided more regularly and at somewhat longer intervals (a so-called combining up of elections), more of the public might regard the overall stakes in each cycle as significant—and might tire of the whole process a bit less.[48]

Finally, though partisan gerrymanders are not the principal source of polarized politics in Congress, there is no question that the American approach to legislative redistricting is eccentric in comparison with most other democracies, and

47. Gerber and Morton (1998, p. 307).
48. For similar line of argument, see Macedo and others (2005, p. 30).

aspects of it unquestionably have some bearing at the margin.[49] Later in this chapter, we take up possible ways of countervailing their effects.

Cooling Off Congress

We have argued repeatedly in this study that much of the lament about "dysfunctional" partisanship in Congress really amounts to little more than a new-found distaste for something political scientists in an earlier day used to advocate: the advent of two parliamentary parties that are comparatively cohesive, intensely competitive, and relatively distinct programmatically. Deborah Jordan Brooks and John G. Geer, writing in another part of this book, notice much the same irony: the political parties that today are pejoratively called "polarized" have attributes of a "responsible" party system that much of the political science profession extolled in the 1950s.[50]

Partisan purposefulness, moreover, stiffens the longer a party remains in the wilderness: when the out-party finally becomes the in-party, it naturally yearns for payback or, more to the point, simply to catch up (an insight nicely expatiated upon by Christopher H. Foreman Jr. in another of this book's essays).[51] We also suspect that baked into the "broken Congress" thesis (in vogue before the Democratic takeover in 2007) were some of the bittersweet fruits of unified party control of the legislative and executive branches.

Having said that, there is no question that the frequency of debate-stifling rules has increased in the polarized House of Representatives (as David W. Brady, John Ferejohn, and Laurel Harbridge make plain in chapter 5 of this volume). And as Barbara Sinclair argues in this volume, these restrictive rules, as well as other parliamentary ploys and contrivances in recent years, have increasingly crossed a line.[52] They have been among the factors that have turned the institution into a "hothouse of partisan enmity," to borrow the apt description by Thomas E. Mann and Norman J. Ornstein.[53] The heat, moreover, shows few signs of subsiding under the control of the new Democratic Party majorities.[54] Their methods, too,

49. See Butler and Cain (1992).
50. See comments to chapter 1.
51. See comments to chapter 2.
52. See chapter 2.
53. See Mann and Ornstein (2006).
54. So far, the congressional Democrats have mostly sought to emulate, not temper, the disciplined majoritarianism formerly practiced by the GOP—prompting Ornstein to warn that the Democratic leadership was "on thin ice now," given its earlier vows to restore respect for prerogatives of the minority. Lyndsey Layton, "In Majority, Democrats Run Hill Much as GOP Did," *Washington Post*, February 18, 2007.

could continue to foment more polarization than pleases perhaps all but the most partisan American voters and will keep more ill-will simmering than the legislative process can tolerate if it is to address seriously the country's most critical policy dilemmas.

The search for solutions to this situation comes down to how a better balance might be restored between the competing values of majority rule and minority rights. In the Senate, where the minority has traditionally enjoyed parliamentary prerogatives that are extraordinary by the standards of any other democracy, obstructionism by the few against the many has become so indiscriminate as to border on abuse of the spirit, if not the letter, of the Constitution. For example, the most peculiar of the Senate's customs, the filibuster, had been used sparingly throughout most of American history.[55] In recent decades, by contrast, it has turned into a routine activity—deployed in attempts to derail as many as *half* of all major bills, by one estimate.[56] This trend, which in effect now regularly requires supermajorities for Congress to do business, is unhealthy.

No less lamentable were the days when popular majorities found themselves continually at the mercy of a different, but firmly ensconced, minority in the House as well. Contemplate the year 1958. By then, the seniority system had cemented Southern Democrats into more than 70 percent of Congress's committee chairs.[57] The House Rules Committee, an oligarchy effectively unaccountable to the majority party caucus and the Speaker, often thwarted the rest of the chamber's agenda at will. Institutional reforms under way in the House since the 1970s, culminating with the Gingrich revolution in 1995, have hosed out these stalls. By term limiting committee chairmanships, expanding the Speaker's control over assignments, abolishing proxy voting in committees, and so on, the new regime brought a welcome restoration of power to the ruling majority and its leadership.[58]

The last thing one would wish for Capitol Hill today is a reversion to the status quo ante. However, majoritarianism taken to the point of suffocating legitimate parliamentary dissent is a backward step as well; it does a disservice not only

55. Binder and Smith (1997) count only 23 manifest filibusters during the entire nineteenth century. In the 1940s through the 1960s there had been a total of 38. Then, from 1970 through 1994, the number rose to 191, with a record 35 in the two years 1991 and 1992.

56. Sinclair (2002).

57. Mackenzie (1996, p. 69).

58. See Evans (2005, p. 509). The practice of proxy voting had enabled a handful of barons chairing committees to cast votes on behalf of absent colleagues during markups.

to the loyal opposition but to Congress's deliberative capacity in general.[59] The first obligation of the legislative branch is to *debate* questions of public policy in a reasonably receptive mode. A congressional majority whose leaders legislate by turning a tin ear to their critics (for example, systematically screening out representatives of the minority party from conference committees) is a body more prone to amplify its biases and immoderation.[60]

We will have more to say about such shortcomings toward the end of this essay, and will recommend some specific procedural adjustments that could help Congress recover a greater measure of comity.

Presidential Participation

In the election of 2000, for the fourth time in U.S. history, a presidential candidate who did not gain a plurality of the popular vote was declared to have won. The contested vote count in the pivotal state of Florida was ultimately resolved only when the Supreme Court intervened. Doubts as to the legitimacy of this outcome would bedevil George W. Bush for years. Naturally, a president chosen in this inauspicious fashion could claim no explicit mandate for bold leadership. Bush became perceived as a divisive figure when, in several important respects, he opted to govern decisively. With a narrow but disciplined congressional majority, he pushed serial tax reductions and later a prolonged military entanglement— both anathema to the opposing political party.

A consequential president is bound to be more provocative than a diffident caretaker. Still, it is worth musing about how some of the rough edges of a polarizing presidency might be smoothed. In Bush's case, his modus operandi might have been regarded as less imperious and discordant if a clear majority of voters, not merely the idiosyncratic Electoral College (and Supreme Court), had put him in office. But more generally, we wonder whether the American presidency now needs essential refinement, most notably in regard to how it communicates with critics and across the aisles of the legislative branch.

The essence of presidential authority, in the late Richard Neustadt's famous phrase, is the power to persuade.[61] Although that naturally means much more than just chatting up both friends and foes, the importance of a disposition to engage

59. For a fascinating empirical examination of much the same preaching-to-the-choir bias in another kind of decisionmaking body—politically homogeneous appeals courts—see Sunstein and others (2006).
60. On the manipulation of conference committees, see Rohde (2005).
61. Neustadt (1990).

cogently in public discourse should not be underestimated. A chief executive pursuing a controversial course of action should have to account for his decisions and do so on a regular basis—not in scripted public orations and encounters with canned audiences but more often before less congenial gatherings, whence criticism is to be expected.

In this respect, we suspect that British parliamentary practice may be superior to the increasingly stilted separation—indeed the cloistering—of the executive in the American system. The regular appearance of the British prime minister and cabinet before the House of Commons, where "the government" is expected to explain and defend its policies in the face of critical questioning, strikes us as an especially admirable tradition—one that invites those in power to make their case but also gives the opposition a frequent, direct, and highly visible opportunity to speak its mind. The give-and-take is often contentious, even unruly, and does not necessarily draw the adversaries closer, but at least it routinely brings them face to face, ventilates their differences forthrightly, helps expose the public to both sides of the story, and sometimes even humbles the mighty.

Britain's parliamentary institutions, needless to say, are so utterly at odds with America's constitutional design that thoughts of transplanting almost any of them would be impracticable. In Washington the nearest approximation to a "question period" is the presidential press conference. It has never amounted to an adequate substitute, but surely it could be reconditioned to be better than it has been in recent years. In the nine months between June 2001 and February 2002, the White House held no presidential press conferences at all. Then between March 2002 and February 2003, the president made two appearances. From March 2003 through February 2004, three took place. The overall rate has since improved. (To his credit, President Bush began meeting the press once every month in the period November 2004 through May 2005, and then again monthly between March 2006 and the end of that year.) Yet long lapses also occurred; for example, over a critical six-month period from June to November in 2005, only one press conference was scheduled.

Sequestering a president from a steady interaction with skeptics does not seem like a constructive convention in a body politic where increasingly bitter partisans are quicker to talk past one another than to respect a frank exchange of views. We recommend that, at a minimum, regular press conferences for the U.S. presidency be recognized as an obligation rather than as an inconvenience to be avoided or as a favor to be granted intermittently. Ideally, we would also go a step further: regularizing an appropriate ("American") form of interbranch dialogue that would put presidents in the company of congressional leaders of both parties on a reasonably routine basis.

A Truce in the Judicial Confirmation Wars

Only a naïf would suppose that, somehow, Congress's treatment of judicial appointments can be depoliticized. Regardless of whether the federal judiciary tilts left or right, judicial activism in one form or another is here to stay. Martin Shapiro touches on the reasons in his discussion of Sarah Binder's chapter in this volume.[62] For one thing, novel rights continue to multiply in modern America, and their claimants can be counted upon to anchor them through legal recourse. The nearly boundless standing to sue in federal courts pretty much guarantees that their policymaking status will not be subordinated. Because of that immutable reality, judicial nominees will continue to be fair game for sharply partisan squabbling in the Senate. With nothing in the Constitution to prevent them, dissident senators are not going to roll over and give a president carte blanche today any more than they ever have.

Indeed, pause a moment to recollect how aggressive the Senate's oppositional ways have been in other times. In 1795 a coalition of cranky senators got George Washington off to a rough start by rejecting his nominee for chief justice, John Rutledge. Their grounds? Rutledge had criticized the Jay Treaty. In 1844 and 1845, no fewer than four different individuals nominated for the Supreme Court by President John Tyler were rejected—three of them twice. In 1869 Ulysses S. Grant nominated a particularly worthy candidate, Ebenezer Hoar, who was summarily turned back for having advocated civil service reform. From the beginning, as Benjamin Wittes has shown, the Senate has examined judicial nominations through ideological lenses and periodically "just said no" to nominees that did not suit its taste.[63]

We are not yet convinced that the current travails of judicial appointments warrant wholesale reconsideration of the Senate's historical role, even if that were constitutionally possible (which it almost certainly is not). We posit, however, that the confirmation process could benefit from three modifications: use of bipartisan nominating commissions to put forth candidates for district and appellate judgeships; a clearer demarcation between permissible parliamentary behavior regarding nominations to these lower and appellate courts, in contrast to those for the

62. See comments to chapter 3.
63. Wittes (2006, p. 129).

highest tribunal; and a simplification of the proceedings, including an end to the divisive public spectacle of congressional hearings.

Regarding the concept of commissions, one way to render their services attractive to an unreceptive White House would be to hitch them inextricably to a fast-track procedure: judicial nominees selected on a bipartisan basis would have Senate Judiciary Committee hearings expedited and would be assured a prompt up-or-down vote on the floor. The use of Senate "holds" and filibusters would be ruled inadmissible.

While judges at all levels make policy (some believe too much policy) in the American system, it is at the Supreme Court that the stakes are colossal. To hand a president with a bare majority of the Senate the unchecked power to compose a body so formidable strikes us as an unacceptable imbalance. There are two possible ways of righting the scales: lighten the significance of each Supreme Court confirmation, or ensure that justices are selected by more than a narrow majority of the Senate.

Take the first of these options. During the past decade, a number of legal scholars across the political spectrum have questioned the wisdom of maintaining life tenure for Supreme Court justices. These writers point out that no other major democratic nation employs such a system and that all but one of the U.S. states have rejected it for their own high courts. Life tenure these days can seem like an eternity, thanks to increased longevity and an incentive for presidents to lock in youthful nominees. Average tenure on the court has more than tripled, from 7.5 years in the founding era to 25.6 in recent decades. Average age at death or resignation has increased by more than ten years since the middle of the past century, from nearly sixty-eight years (1941–70) to almost seventy-nine (1971–2005).[64]

These developments have worrisome consequences. With justices sitting on the court so much longer, the frequency of new appointments declines, and the age-old question of the high court's democratic accountability, an inherently problematic matter, becomes more glaring. The fact that a justice confirmed in 2007 may well be serving through 2040 has inflated the political salience of each confirmation struggle.[65]

Pious pleas for more civility in the confirmation process are not apt to make much difference under these conditions. What could? The most direct course would be the boldest: shift from life tenure for Supreme Court justices to single

64. Calabresi and Lindgren (2006).
65. For a lucid and comprehensive compilation of evidence and argument on these and related points, see Calabresi and Lindgren (2006).

nonrenewable terms of, say, eighteen years. Such a reform could be phased in so that over time, every president would get to make two appointments in each four-year term.

While some scholars believe such a change could be instituted by mere statute, we doubt it. A constitutional amendment is likely to be necessary, and its prospects would seem remote. For the foreseeable future, therefore, de facto governance by supermajorities in the Senate will, and arguably should, continue. We simply see no other means of restraining the possibility that now, by the slimmest of margins, presidents may embed fellow partisans on the Supreme Court for spans of a quarter-century or more. So, like it or not, both parties ought to come to terms with the threatened or actual use of filibusters to block divisive appointments to the high court. Unless the president's party dominates the Senate overwhelmingly, the effective sixty-vote supermajority hurdle induces the White House to do what presidents typically do in circumstances of divided government—namely, vet potential nominees with the leaders of both parties.

For the rest of the judiciary, on the other hand, limits ought to be sought on the time senators can indulge in miring nominees. Not only should senatorial delaying tactics be curbed, a simple majority standard should generally apply. At a minimum, as recommended earlier, nominees enlisted through a commission process ought to have their fate decided expeditiously. Lessening the ease with which contrarian factions in the Senate can take hostages below the level of Supreme Court nominations could go a considerable way toward de-escalating, or at least containing, the current extent of partisan guerilla warfare, which now threatens to engulf the entire judicial branch.

Further, we are persuaded by Wittes and other disillusioned observers of public confirmation hearings that these choreographed shows serve no useful purpose, other than to give senators televised opportunities to posture for their interest group clients in return for mostly sphinx-like testimony from the nominees. So shrill and bellicose have been the displays of partisan grandstanding at some hearings, in fact, that they became unforgettable emblems in the train of events aggravating political polarization.

Of course, exhorting members of Congress to practice self-restraint is a little like telling an alcoholic to just stop getting drunk. Little is likely to change unless both the majority and the minority of the day buy in, not only for the sake of their institution's well-being over the long haul but for their own self-interest. What could improve that prospect is the realization (ultimately inescapable in a viable democracy) that what goes around eventually comes around: today's indignant Senate majority may well be tomorrow's defiant minority, and vice versa.

Can both ignore indefinitely the likelihood that a scorched-earth approach in judicial confirmation fights is in neither side's long-term interest, and hence that the current rules of engagement need revision?

A final point: the likelihood of self-restraint in the way the Senate treats would-be judges also turns on certain behavioral modifications by the other principals— the White House and the judiciary itself. We will discuss their responsibilities separately in a little while.

Mending the Media

No political institution in the United States appears to lie closer to the epicenter of the polarization process than the news media. In the first volume of *Red and Blue Nation?* Diana C. Mutz advances several compelling arguments to that effect. But years of additional research, well beyond the work that Mutz herself has pioneered, will be required to test empirically a blame-the-media thesis. For now, the jury is still out with regard to how deeply trends in journalism roil and polarize this country's politics, or whether matters are mostly the other way around. As Thomas Rosenstiel indicates in his comment on Mutz's paper, the available evidence suggests that the causal arrow points in both directions.

Whatever the case, aspiring reformers would do well to reread Gregg Easterbrook's insights in the first volume of *Red and Blue Nation?* Even if the media contribute significantly to the nation's partisan polemics, there are major constraints on what can be done to alter the media's conduct and mitigate the effects. Not only does the First Amendment stringently limit the possibilities for regulating news content and style; consumers, aided by technology, instinctively surf their way toward edgier ("polarizing") images and subject matter, and away from what looks or sounds balanced, bland, and boring. Asks Easterbrook, "If one news channel shows angry zealots enraged at each other's comments, while on another the anchor says, 'Now two experts from the Brookings Institution will debate infrastructure renewal,' who is going to get the audience?"[66]

To recognize these sobering realities, however, is not to conclude that any and all efforts to reaffirm some minimal civic standards for the conduct of at least portions of the news industry are baseless and quixotic. From their inception, the broadcast media have held a distinctive legal status. Because these producers occupy parts of the airwaves, the use of which is denied to others, the government, acting in the public interest, is entitled to allocate frequencies among competing

66. See the first volume of *Red and Blue Nation?* p. 259.

claimants and place conditions on them. The Supreme Court has affirmed this right of society rather unequivocally. As we shall show further on, the court's judgment is worth pondering fully, for it invites an exploration of ways that televised news, where possible, could be asked to meet certain basic public obligations.

Rediscovering Federalism

A blessing of the American framework of federated governance is that it provides (at least in theory) opportunities to denationalize issues too combustible for the petulant partisans in Washington to resolve satisfactorily.[67] Put another way, some of the nation's most turbulent controversies might have polarized the polity less if they had never become preoccupations of the central government and had been left to the state legislatures to decide in their diverse ways. The case for devolution is especially strong for disputes wherein no national consensus seems attainable, and where the sentiments of local or regional electorates vary widely.

Illustrative, many believe, is the abortion issue. It is conceivable that this source of passionate cultural conflict might have festered less if the Supreme Court had not produced *Roe* v. *Wade*. Suppose *Roe* had never happened. A liberalization of state abortion policies, argued political scientist Gerald N. Rosenberg, was under way before the 1973 decision, and the court actually may have done less to accelerate a peaceful transition than to provoke a backlash.[68] Granted, disparities in state law would have persisted, perhaps even widened in a number of places.[69] But paying that price might have been preferable to fighting a decades-long national culture war about the definition of human life.

The *Roe* conundrum is now probably too old and calcified to dispatch, whether with a single stroke—by overturning the opinion—or by a thousand cuts. In this instance, upending the established precedent and then so belatedly relegating policy back to the state level might ignite even wider conflict. Similar reasoning, though, does not hold for several newer wedge issues, ones still fresh enough to be consigned to the states but that leading "conservative" politicians (and sympathizers on the Supreme Court) now nevertheless appear determined to nationalize. Arguments over same-sex marriage, stem-cell science, doctor-assisted suicide, medicinal use of marijuana, and more fit that description.

67. This potential advantage has been noted in studies of political decentralization in regimes far and wide. See, for instance, Putnam (1993, chap. 2).

68. Rosenberg (1991, chap. 6).

69. For a related full discussion, see Jeffrey Rosen, "The Day after Roe," *Atlantic,* June 2006.

Why not let the state governments variously test alternative solutions in these unsettled, morally complex fields instead of insisting on national regimentation? Cluttering the central agenda—indeed, the Constitution—with uncompromising mandates and prohibitions for every new civil dilemma that surfaces in American society seems sure to fan the flames of political polarization.

It is always easier to invoke federalism, of course, than to make its principles stick. Both political parties pay lip service to states' rights and prerogatives, and both violate them without hesitation whenever it suits the interests of one partisan constituency or another. Nor do we harbor illusions that the presumptive final arbiters of the federal system, a dissonant assortment of Supreme Court justices, will ever set consistent standards for a sensible division of labor between the levels of government.[70] And there is evidence that the public, a majority of which yearns for more moderate approaches to divisive social issues, nonetheless rejects the proposition that the states should resolve these issues and seemingly favors national solutions instead.[71] Here, all we can do is merely remind whoever is listening that a good deal of the partisan rumpus in Washington might subside if the capital embroiled itself less in matters unbefitting, in Abraham Lincoln's phrase, "the majesty of the nation" and returned more of them to the statehouses.[72]

These, then, are our schematic guidelines for a course correction. In the remaining pages, we explore several prescriptions in somewhat greater depth.

Rethinking Congressional Elections

That the U.S. Congress has become increasingly polarized in recent decades is a fact acknowledged by nearly everyone. Exactly what explains that fact, however, is less widely agreed upon. Some analysts point to the electorate's underlying demographics and increases in ideological or partisan consistency; others have fastened onto the part played by politically motivated redistricting.[73] Both schools have a point. There is a tendency to overstate the explanatory power of redistricting. (How, for example, can it account for polarization of the Senate?) On the other hand, clearly in states such as California, politicians of both parties

70. For a more developed discussion of this and related questions, see Nivola (2005).
71. Pew Research Center for the People and the Press, "Pragmatic Americans Liberal and Conservative on Social Issues," August 3, 2006 (people-press.org/reports/display.php3?ReportID=283).
72. From "Address at Poughkeepsie, New York, February 19, 1861." See Lincoln (1920, p. 685).
73. For a full review, see Thomas E. Mann's chapter in the first volume of *Red and Blue Nation?*

have conspired to draw House districts in a fashion that can only be described as a fail-safe incumbent-protection plot.[74]

Redistricting Reform

To just shrug off chicanery like that in California is to be cynical or lazy. The most conservative estimates concede that gerrymanders have accounted for somewhere between 10 and 36 percent of the reduction in competitive congressional districts since 1982.[75] That effect is not trivial. The redistricting process, therefore, merits continued attention. Where does one begin?

Given the Supreme Court's reluctance to enter the thicket of redistricting controversies, any changes will be up to the state governments. In recent years, voter initiatives and referendums in four states—Washington, Idaho, Alaska, and Arizona—have established nonpartisan or bipartisan redistricting commissions.[76] These local efforts have struggled to solve a complicated riddle: how to enhance competitiveness while respecting other parameters, such as geographical compactness, jurisdictional boundaries, and the natural desire to represent "communities of interest."[77] Iowa's approach, where a nonpartisan legislative staff has the last word, is often cited as a model but may be hard to export to states with more demographic diversity and complex political cultures. Arizona has managed to fashion some workable, empirically based standards that are yielding more heterogeneous districts and more competitive elections.

How transferable this experience can be remains to be seen. Precious few Western democracies draw up their parliamentary districts in so patently politicized a fashion as do U.S. state legislatures. Parliamentary electoral commissions, operating quite independently and explicitly charged with making reasonably objective determinations, are the preferred model abroad. A reason why it may be difficult to emulate widely here is that the foreign commissions typically permit something that the Supreme Court's "one person, one vote" standard has effectively outlawed: districts of varying population size. If that flexibility

74. The most recent round of redistricting in California managed to reduce the number of vulnerable incumbents to precisely zero.

75. Jacobson (2006). For more generous calculations, see McDonald (2006). Because redistricting after 1990 and 2000 depressed competition more than it did in the 1970s and 1980s, the difference between Jacobson's and McDonald's estimates is smaller than it appears.

76. The number of states that have considered, in one way or another, redistricting commissions is considerably larger: twenty-four since the 1999–2000 legislative sessions. See Theriault, Karch, and McConnaughy (2006).

77. McDonald (2006).

existed, it would facilitate the weighing of additional criteria such as considerations of contiguity and conformity with existing community or jurisdictional
boundaries.[78]

Independent commissions may not always be able to deliver many more competitive districts than emerge, theoretically, under the present alternative practiced
in most states. Through the single-minded pursuit of safe seats, the process of
partisan gerrymandering can, paradoxically, put other seats up for grabs. Stated
another way, a party bent on providing maximal protection for its incumbents
may be distributing its finite quotient of loyal voters inefficiently—possibly for-
feiting opportunities to score gains in additional districts and potentially allowing
the rival party to compete more effectively in some of them.[79]

For all the intricacies and complexities of the redistricting game, the exertions
of the innovative redistricting authorities in the current handful of states bear
watching. In time, additional states are likely to take notice since, on balance, a
tilt toward less flagrantly partisan modes of boundary drawing seems likely to
restore somewhat greater electoral competition for the House of Representatives.
That, in turn, could nudge at least a few more of its members toward the center.

Rediscovering Multimember Districts

Because voters are largely self-segregating, even an all-out assault on gerrymanders
might not make a meaningful difference. What could have a bigger impact is a
more fundamental change: the reintroduction of multimember districting. Americans now take the ubiquity of single-member districts for granted, but the House
of Representatives actually employed a variety of modes of representation earlier
in its history. Up to 1842, individual states were free to choose their preferred
approaches. Some opted for single-member districts, others had multi-member
districts. Some elected their entire multimember delegations at large, while others
selected a mix of single-member and at-large systems. Even after 1842, when the
House tried to limit itself to single-member districts, numerous exceptions persisted. At-large representation did not die out until 1967, when an act of Congress formally put a stop to it. General-ticket elections continued here and there
until 1971.[80]

78. For illustrative discussions, see Johnston (1982); Lyons (1969). For a skeptical assessment of
the transferability of foreign experience to the U.S. case, see Butler and Cain (1992, chap. 6).
79. McDonald (2006, pp. 230–34).
80. For an illuminating history with copious details, see Calabrese (2000).

A compelling case can be made that Congress ought to deregulate itself and revive the pre-1967 tradition of letting the state legislatures decide how to elect their delegations—subject, of course, to norms of basic fairness. Bills along these lines have been introduced in the House since the late 1990s. They would permit states to use single-member, multimember, or mixed systems, provided that each option meets the constitutional standard of equal voting power and conforms to the Voting Rights Act.[81]

The Voting Rights Act undoubtedly adds a high hurdle; it is easier to comply with it by sticking with single-member districts, which, when suitably arranged, can virtually guarantee representation for minority groups. The states learned this lesson when the law forced them to reconfigure the composition of their legislatures. As recently as the early 1960s, more than three quarters of the states still retained various versions of multimember legislative districts in electing their legislatures. The share declined sharply after the Supreme Court began finding that multimember districts might restrict the representation of minorities, thus violating the Voting Rights Act.

The court, however, stopped well short of saying that multimember districts are inherently discriminatory and illegal, and a few state legislatures maintained them into the 1980s. In fact, in these states minority representation was scarcely threatened by the practice.[82] In Illinois, for example, multimember districting of the legislature's lower chamber had not prevented a larger share of African Americans and women from getting elected than prevailed in the state senate, where members were elected through single-member districts.[83]

The concern for minority representation is really part of a larger reservation about multimember districting: is the system more susceptible to the tyranny of the majority? The answer turns out to be no, at least according to one comprehensive study of the question. State legislatures based on multimember districts

81. For example, see H.R. 1173, The States' Choice of Voting Systems Act, introduced by Representative Melvin Watt (D-N.C.), March 17, 1999. For arguments that systems other than single-member districting can meet "one person, one vote" and Voting Rights Act requirements, see House of Representatives, Committee on the Judiciary, "Statement of Nathaniel A. Persily, Staff Attorney, Brennan Center for Justice at New York University School of Law," 106 Cong. 1 sess. (September 23, 1999).

82. A reanalysis of state-level data found no evidence that multimember districts disadvantage minority groups. See Richardson and Cooper (2003).

83. Richie and Hill (2001). As James H. Kuklinski, James D. Nowlan, and Philip D. Habel point out, however, neither system has produced state legislatures that "mirror the racial, ethnic, and gender composition of the population." See Kuklinski, Nowlan, and Habel (2001, p. 58).

have not been dominated disproportionately by the state's majority party. The minority party, in fact, remained intact: more than one quarter of multimember districts in the mid-1980s had representatives from both political parties.[84]

The state of Illinois offers particularly fertile ground for studying the effects of alternative electoral systems. For more than a century, Illinois used multimember districts to elect its state assembly but not the legislature's upper body. Conveniently, this enables comparisons of the two chambers over time. The state's switch to single-member legislative districts after 1982 provides an object lesson on the implications of current electoral institutions for partisan polarization.

Under the new rules, the entire state legislature became more polarized. During the era when the state's lower house, but not its senate, employed multimember districts, the parties in the former were more ideologically diverse. Democrats there were less consistently situated to the left and Republicans less consistently to the right than were their counterparts in the other body. This overlap between the parties disappeared as soon as single-member districting was adopted.[85] In addition, multimember districts decreased regional polarities: the system had ensured some Republican representation in overwhelmingly Democratic urban areas, and some Democratic presence in the rural, heavily Republican downstate areas.[86] By contrast, the advent of single-member districts all but eliminated moderate Republicans from Chicago and any Democrats from Republican-leaning suburbs.

The shift to single-member districts, then, seems to have spawned a legislature of antagonistic parties, resembling the present U.S. Congress.[87] By 1995 the *Chicago Tribune* concluded that the abolition of multimember districts had contributed to the partisan politics familiar today—increasingly shrill and confrontational, and bereft of true independents. It was time, the paper's editors urged, to consider bringing back the old electoral regime.[88]

Other Electoral Models

Illinois has been a laboratory with two complementary projects: not only multimember districting (three per district) but also a distinctive system of "cumulative" voting. Under such a system, each voter is allocated a number of votes

---

84. Niemi, Hill, and Grofman (1985).
85. Adams (1996).
86. Kuklinski, Nowlan, and Habel (2001).
87. Everson (1991).
88. "Better Politics from an Old Idea," *Chicago Tribune,* May 30, 1995.

commensurate with the number of representatives to be elected from a district, and more than one of these votes can be cast for a particular candidate. So in Illinois, if you were voting in a state legislative election with three-member districts, you would be allotted three votes. You could then either cast one vote for each candidate, or all three votes for a single candidate, or some combination thereof. The option of combining votes in this manner may enable a district's underrepresented groups (disaffected independents or moderates, for instance) to gain a voice in the legislature *if* they feel strongly enough to coordinate and bunch their votes in support of a single standard-bearer.

What may have contributed to the old, less dogmatically partisan style of the Illinois legislature was the *combination* of multimember districting *plus* the state's cumulative voting model. That inference is supported by a comparison with Arizona—a state with multimember districts but no cumulative voting. Arizona has thirty legislative districts, each represented by two legislators and one senator. Each voter in elections for the lower house may cast two votes, but no more than one for any candidate. One wonders whether the Arizona house, like the state's senate, might tend to be less ideologically polarized if, as in Illinois, blocs of moderate voters were able to bullet vote.[89] In short, multimember districting alone may not suffice to "depolarize" a legislative body.

Instant Runoff Voting

There have been other local electoral experiments of interest, ones that some reformers think various states could conceivably extend to their congressional elections. In 2002 the citizens of San Francisco passed a proposition establishing so-called instant runoff voting. This system, much like the one that was first tried in Australia as early as 1893, asks voters to rank order candidates for each office. After the votes in an initial round are tallied, the votes of voters whose first choice failed to finish high enough to remain in contention are automatically transferred to their second choices, and the process is repeated until the requisite number of winners emerges.

As the proponents of instant runoff voting argued in their successful campaign to try this new procedure, it encourages politicians to build bridges rather than ideological walls. In multicandidate races, even strong first-round finishers gain an incentive to seek votes from supporters of the also-rans. Mobilizing merely a fervent plurality is not a politically promising strategy if it antagonizes the rest of

89. Richardson, Russell, and Cooper (2004). See also Bertelli and Richardson (2004).

the electorate; in divided, multicandidate fields, the winning candidates tend to be ones that make themselves acceptable as second and third choices. They can do this only if they emphasize common ground and refrain from running campaigns that mostly attack and insult their competitors.

Early evidence suggests that the incentives have had the intended effect. "New runoff system in San Francisco has the rival candidates *cooperating*," a *New York Times* story concluded.[90] The system appears to ensure that final choices will not be made by strident pluralities of the electorate.[91] That result has not gone unnoticed. Instant runoff voting has caught on in some other U.S. cities. In November 2006, referendums like San Francisco's passed in Minneapolis and Oakland, as well as in Davis, California.

Can the methods adopted in this handful of municipalities be replicated in the electoral process for congressional seats? Primary contests, when they occur, would seem to be the place to start, for these are where multiple candidates are on offer. It is harder to see how instant runoffs would do much for typical *general* elections since, as Larry Diamond reminds us in his comment to this chapter, at that stage voters are less likely to face a multicandidate field.[92] Furthermore, where seats are safe—and hence races noncompetitive—it would scarcely matter whether an instant runoff mechanism exists or not. Its utility, in short, would seem limited in a strict two-party system. But were that duopoly to loosen, as it has from time to time in some states, the approach might be worth a closer look.[93]

Nowhere have forms of instant runoff voting operated longer than in Australia. Today that country's entire lower house of parliament is elected in this manner.[94] Not everyone is enthused. To some thoughtful theorists, the prime defect of the

90. Dean E. Murphy, "New Runoff System in San Francisco Has the Rival Candidates Cooperating," *New York Times,* September 30, 2004. Italics added.

91. Hill (2006, chap. 3). In a moment of uncharacteristic exuberance, the political theorist John Stuart Mill described this system as "among the very greatest improvements yet made in the theory and practice of government." See Mill (1862, chap. VII). For a sober comparison with other possibilities, see Brams and Fishburn (1991).

92. Constrained by two-candidate races, the alternative voting model effectively reduces to the status quo.

93. Technically, congressional races often wind up offering more than just a binary choice. Independent candidates, libertarians, and other third-party candidates on the ballot are hardly uncommon. Needless to say, given the two-party dominance in this country, these additional entries would rarely become viable candidates in the eyes of voters, regardless of whether an instant runoff option were available.

94. See FairVote, "The History of Instant Runoff Voting" (www.fairvote.org/irv/vt_lite/history.htm).

runoff procedure is its supposed virtue: voters are forced to make an "instant" *set* of complex choices—ranking a list of candidates rather than simply picking one. Thus, objected the late Nelson W. Polsby in his comment to this chapter, voters are pressed into expressing elaborate preferences based on scant knowledge. As a practical matter, though, the objection most commonly leveled against the Australian voting process is that it systematically favors center-leaning candidates at the expense of the centrifugal candidacies slated by minor parties. Unsurprisingly, the losers claim discrimination.

There is no easy way to settle the normative dilemmas associated with instant runoff voting. Those who believe that fringe parties and their off-center politicians ought to take a prominent place at the table will prefer Australia's senate, which obliges by electing its members through a version of proportional representation. But those who feel that the fringes are, if anything, too vocal in contemporary democratic politics—and that the center needs propping up—will prefer the Australian lower chamber, where minor-party representatives are comparatively scarce.

Primaries

Last but decidedly not least, we return to the question of how party primaries could be improved. As noted earlier, comparatively open primaries tend to improve the prospects of candidates who align themselves with the preferences of median voters. The relationship between primary openness and depolarization is not linear, however. Pure open primaries allow voters either to participate without declaring a party affiliation or to declare their affiliation when entering the voting booth. As it happens, rules so relaxed are not optimal for the purpose of bolstering the influence of the middle; that result can be advanced more consistently with somewhat less permissive systems (so-called semiclosed primaries). Most of these still allow broad participation, including by independents, provided they register to vote in advance.

Interestingly, members of the House of Representatives elected under these hybrid primary regimes appear to reflect their district's median voter preferences more faithfully than do members chosen under *either* tightly closed *or* overly open arrangements.[95] Primaries that are open enough to add some weakly affiliated and independent voters to a partisan pool naturally assist the campaigns of moderate politicians more than do strictly closed systems; but "openness" taken to extremes

95. Gerber and Morton (1998, p. 307).

begets diminishing returns. In free-for-alls, where anybody can simply wander into a polling place and cast any party's ballot, the heightened level of uncertainty drives candidates back into political niche markets. One way that candidates differentiate themselves in these circumstances is by staking out more, not less, ostentatious positions on hot-button issues.[96]

Whatever the case, it appears that states instituting primary election rules somewhere in the midrange, between completely closed or maximally open, are the ones most likely to further the forces of moderation.

Expand the Electorate

Beyond these modifications is one that might be the most telling of all: enlarging the active general electorate. Primaries are the elections most egregiously characterized by low voter turnout, but the problem is larger than that. Compared to, say, the French presidential election of 2007, wherein nearly 84 percent of the registered voters cast ballots, U.S. turnout tends to be comparatively low even in closely contested national elections and particularly in off years. So even these contests may be skewed toward the preferences of people with relatively strong ("polar") views more than those of moderates and independents, for they tend to be the dropouts.

Think about what actually happened at the polls in 2006, for example. Much postelection punditry portrayed the balloting that year as dominated by independents and moderates who, finally aroused, sacked Congress's right-wingers in droves, replaced them with earnest middle-of-the-roaders, and so swung the political pendulum back to the center. The reality was a bit different: moderates and independents did *not* turn out in unusually large numbers. Many of those that voted abandoned the GOP, but by battering its *centrists*. And while most of the incoming Democrats ran as pragmatists seeking the middle ground, populist and antiwar motifs were also prominent in many of the campaigns and seemed to befit the passions of the party's liberal firebrands more than the instincts of the electorate's median.

Some observers (not least the late Professor Polsby) would not view the asymmetric power of passionate partisans in U.S. elections as any cause for concern. Why *shouldn't* political decisions be made by the citizens who care most about them? Aren't those who care also better informed? And isn't their intensive

96. Kanthak and Morton (2001, pp. 117–27).

involvement an indication that the outcome of the election affects their interests more than it does the interests of the nonvoters? The logic is beguiling but, in our view, less than conclusive. Consider this analogy: some people save for the future, others do not. But just because the savers care more about saving does not necessarily mean that nonsavers have less reason to save. Similarly, whether people know it or not, elections have consequences for voters and nonvoters alike— indeed, the consequences for many nonvoters (the poor and poorly educated, for instance) may be especially significant.

A number of major democracies have made voting mandatory. Australia has instituted its own version of mandatory voting, issuing small fines for failure to vote but escalating them for recidivism, with remarkable results. The turnout rate in Australia now tops 95 percent, and more than ever, citizens regard voting as a civic obligation.[97] Near-universal voting raises the possibility that a bulge of casual voters, with little understanding of the issues and candidates, can muddy the waters. The inevitable presence of some such "donkey voters," as they are called in Australia, however, does not appear to have badly marred the democratic process in that country.

Indeed, the civic benefits of higher turnouts seem to outweigh the "donkey" effect. Candidates for the Australian house have gained an added incentive to appeal broadly beyond their partisan bases. One wonders whether members of Congress here in the United States, if subjected to wider suffrage, might also spend less time transfixed by symbolic issues that are primarily objects of partisan fascination, and more time coming to terms with the nation's larger priorities. At least campaigns continually tossing red meat to the party faithful might become a little less pervasive.

Nevertheless, the United States is not Australia. Although both are federal systems, the U.S. Constitution confers on state governments much more extensive control over voting procedures. While it might not be flatly unconstitutional to mandate voting nationwide, it would surely chafe with American custom and provoke opposition in many states. Short of forcing citizens to vote, there are other steps that should be taken.

Rates of voter participation can be measured in at least two different ways: ballots cast as a percentage of a nation's voting-age population, and ballots cast as a percentage of registered voters. By the first test, the United States unquestionably fares poorly in comparison with other Western democracies; by the second,

97. Norman Ornstein, "Vote—or Else," *New York Times,* August 10, 2006.

it tends to fall more or less in the middle of the pack.[98] Americans who register to vote turn out at about the same rate as, say, the Dutch and the British. Registering voters is no panacea; the hopelessly unmotivated will be no-shows regardless. Still, states ought to redouble efforts to facilitate registration—no easy thing in a society where each year tens of millions change their place of residence. The evidence suggests that an ability to register on election day increases not only registration but turnout, especially among young adults.[99] And all colleges and universities should comply fully with the 1998 Higher Education Act, which requires them to make good-faith efforts to distribute registration forms to all their students.

Beyond improving registration, there are strategies for upping the turnout among previously registered voters. For example, mailing polling place information to registered voters before election day increases overall turnout appreciably, as does sending these voters sample ballots in advance.[100] While estimates vary, it appears that declaring election day a holiday or moving it to the weekend could produce even larger gains. The simple idea has been floated by Martin P. Wattenberg, another contributor to this volume.[101] In Puerto Rico, where election day has been designated a holiday, voters turn out at a high rate.[102]

It is important to remember that earlier in American history, turnout rates were considerably higher, in no small part because political parties reached out to citizens not only at election time but year-round. Whatever else might be said about the political parties of yore, they proved to be efficient machines for engaging voters. Though the parties of the twenty-first century remain a far cry from the formidable engines of political mobilization of an earlier era, the parties have begun to reinvent themselves as effective grassroots organizations. No less important, Democratic and Republican party platforms and core values now display significant contrasts on a range of critical questions, recalling the robust parties of the latter nineteenth century.

These trends carry an underappreciated implication: the renewed ideological and organizational energy of both the parties—and, yes, the pyrotechnics of their polarizing rivalry—spark voter interest. Therefore, latter-day "Progressives"

---

98. See Glass, Squire, and Wolfinger (1984); Dalton and Wattenberg (1993, p. 210).
99. Macedo and others (2005, p. 55).
100. Macedo and others (2005, p. 54).
101. Martin P. Wattenberg, "Should Election Day Be a Holiday?" *Atlantic,* October 1998.
102. Macedo and others (2005, p. 55).

urging depolarization should be careful what they wish for. It may be hard, if not impossible, to rid the Republic of the incendiary and destructive aspects of our polarized parties without perforce engineering a further decline in voter participation.

Righting the Congressional Rules

While selecting representatives less tethered to their party bases would help depolarize Congress, so would improving its rules. We have already suggested that a more selective use of supermajority requirements would be beneficial. In this section, and in the same spirit, we offer three additional proposals.

Moderating the Application of Closed Rules

With 435 full members, hundreds of legislative committees and subcommittees, and a staff of thousands, the U.S. House of Representatives is the world's heftiest representative body. Maintaining an orderly flow of business in it is no easy matter. The Rules Committee helps keep order by determining the parliamentary procedures under which specific bills are debated on the floor—the number of amendments, for example, and often their content and the order in which they will be presented. Open rules permit a wide range of amendments; closed rules do not.

During the final decade of their forty-year reign, House Democrats increasingly resorted to closed rules to hobble the Republican minority's attempts to influence legislation. When the GOP finally regained control of the House in 1994, the party's leaders vowed to treat the minority more magnanimously, and for a few years they did. In the late 1990s, however, they began to revert to the same abuses they had once denounced; by 2005, the incidence of bills coming to the floor under closed rules had matched its previous peak. On several important occasions, the minority was not even permitted to offer its own substitute bill and was given only one choice—to support or oppose the majority's bill as drafted. Not surprisingly, the Democratic opposition resented this straitjacket no less than the Republicans did when they had been in the minority. Relations between the congressional parties grew more hostile.[103]

In the Senate, where the functional equivalent of an open rule is the default position, bipartisan agreements to curb amendments are often the only way to

---

103. For an up-to-date account of this sorry history, see Mann and Ornstein (2006).

sustain fragile coalitions of the center on difficult pieces of legislation. Lacking such agreement, individual senators intent on killing a controversial compromise, such as the immigration reform bill of mid-2007, are free to lace it with "poison pills"—amendments potentially toxic to the overall measure.[104] The House is different. There, a tendency to restrict amendments frequently makes it *harder* to form centrist coalitions because it puts moderates in this bind: unable to reshape legislation written by their party's base-runners, moderates must either bolt or sign on. But bolting risks retribution from the party leadership and the partisan base; signing on risks alienating swing voters on election day. No wonder centrism is regarded as hardship duty by most contemporary members of Congress—and fewer brave souls are volunteering for it.

Now that both parties have been burned by the overuse of closed rules, it is time for a bipartisan pact to cut down on them. As we noted earlier, the parties would be foolish to forget the fact that abuse begets abuse and that no majority, however well entrenched, is permanent. We urge that an understanding be reached, securing for the out-party reasonable opportunities to offer amendments and substitutes. To be sure, this rule change might pacify the parliamentary minority only at the cost of further frustrating the majority. Such trade-offs, however, are unavoidable in any representative democracy. The challenge for sensible rule makers is to seek a suitable equilibrium, one respectful of majoritarian principles but also of parliamentary dissent. The net effect, we conjecture, might be a little less partisan enmity in Congress.

Real Conferences

Our second proposal concerns the conduct of conference committees, whose business is to reconcile differing House and Senate versions of bills and to craft compromises for final passage. For most of modern history, representatives of both the minority and majority participated in these mediating sessions and wrote the final drafts of legislation. Typically, the latter were supposed to conform to the contours of the two chambers' separate bills. In recent years, however, minority participation has been curbed, sometimes drastically, and the "conference" has occasionally been anything but an honest broker: the sidelined minority watches helplessly as legislation emerges bearing no relationship to the rendition passed by one of the houses, and sometimes to neither. Adding

104. The tribulations of a crucial compromise immigration bill in 2007 were illustrative. A key to keeping the compromise intact was to restrict the free-wheeling Senate amendment process. The bill died because its managers lacked sufficient votes in the Senate to impose the curb.

insult to injury, the minority has often been powerless to prevent a waiver of the parliamentary rule requiring that a conference report be available to members several days before it is brought to a floor vote. Hence, when the roll is called, only the insiders privy to the legislation know what is in it. A natural reaction to all this is obstruction: distrustful lawmakers try every trick in the book to block bills from reaching the conference stage in the first place.

We think that the old-fashioned conference process (however imperfect it too could be) had more to recommend it than what has developed in recent years. The former process enabled Congress to overcome wide differences that otherwise threatened to grind the legislative machinery to a halt at critical junctures. Here's a thought experiment. Immigration reform was debated in both 2006 and 2007. Would it have suffered a dismal fate the first time around if Congress's conference procedures had been more reliably evenhanded? A pragmatic compromise might have been salvaged if key senators had been confident that a conference committee would actually *mediate,* not simply let the House stiff them in a one-sided showdown.[105]

Whatever else it must do, any sound set of rules has to further two objectives: predictability and trust. The members of both chambers have to be able to proceed to conference with some advance assurance that it will duly reflect their work and not act like an autonomous rump parliament, writing its own legislation from scratch.

Showing Up for an Honest Day's Work

Our final suggestion may seem like mundane minutia, but it is actually of considerable importance. The legislative calendar has contracted to the point that floor deliberations now are basically limited to a Tuesday-Thursday schedule. Too many members spend more days back in their states and districts campaigning and fundraising than on Capitol Hill performing what should also be a congressman's job—thinking, deliberating, and legislating. Many toil at home so much of the time, they have even declined to move their families to Washington.

We are at a loss how to reverse the main magnetic force that draws members out of town—namely, the quest for money to fund perpetual campaigns.

---

105. The parliamentary tactics of the Democratic leadership in the Senate stalled an immigration bill in the spring of 2006. The minority leadership declined to allow votes on conservative amendments to the Senate's moderate bill, even though its sponsors, Senators John McCain (R-Ariz.) and Edward Kennedy (D-Mass.), probably had enough support to keep it intact. Many Democrats feared that if the Senate went to conference, the far more restrictive House version would prevail.

Repeated attempts to regulate campaign finance have been more notable for their unforeseen twists, turns, and contortions than for slowing the runaway spending in U.S. elections. Facing up to what the money chase means, however, remains imperative. A Congress composed of commuters and part-timers is a shakier institution. Its shortened calendar tempts the legislative majority to rush its agenda impatiently. The minority naturally responds with obstructionism and subterfuge. And because they spend most of their days out of town, the members have fewer opportunities to acquaint themselves with their colleagues. This "government of strangers," to borrow political scientist Hugh Heclo's phrase, is an impersonal place where working relationships are hard to build and antipathies are harder to overcome.

We wish members of both houses would take the time to create a greater sense of community. At a minimum, they ought to devote larger blocks of time to deliberating and legislating on the floor. One possibility would be to stagger the work schedule rather differently: during most months, members would be expected to show up in Washington for at least two consecutive weeks, followed by a week or two in which they could, if they wish, return home or otherwise wander off.[106]

The Presidency

In his comments on our chapter, Joel D. Aberbach shifts attention to the second branch of government where another agent of hardcore partisan politics looms large: the White House. Too often asserting executive prepotency, the tenor of the contemporary presidency, Aberbach implies, tends to grate and polarize. What might a less imperious presidential style look like, one perhaps truer to the Madisonian spirit of coequal status among the branches of government?

On April 8, 1913, just a month after he was sworn into office, President Woodrow Wilson walked up to the Capitol and proceeded to speak to members of the House and Senate about his policy agenda. Wilson began his remarks by expressing his gratitude for the opportunity to show "that the President of the United States is a person, not a mere department of the Government hailing Congress from some isolated island of jealous power, sending messages, not speaking naturally and with his own voice."[107] He was there, he stressed, to prove that a

---

106. For a version of this idea, see Mann and Ornstein (2006, pp. 232–33).

107. The full text of Wilson's "Address on Tariff Reform to a Joint Session of Congress," is contained in Wilson (1978a).

president "is a human being trying to co-operate with other human beings in a common service."

Then he got down to business. The new president's first priority was to reduce the tariff, and he asked Congress for help in tackling this Herculean political task. After presenting his case formally before both houses, he did something that no president since Lincoln had tried (and that, alas, no president after Wilson has been willing to do): in the ensuing weeks, Wilson not only conferred with delegations of skeptical lawmakers at the White House, he repeatedly spent days in a room just off the Senate chamber, actively negotiating with members until the tariff reduction materialized. He believed, in his words, in pursuing "a much more habitual and informal, and yet at the same time much more public and responsible, interchange of opinion between the Executive and Congress."[108]

It is not fashionable nowadays to invoke Woodrow Wilson, the consummate idealist, as a presidential role model. But the fact is, before the First World War consumed his presidency, what this unusual leader managed to achieve by conversing closely with Congress was nigh miraculous. Through most of the nineteenth century, and into the twentieth, few questions in U.S. politics had been more divisive than the tariff. It is not too much to say that no issue today—abortion, Iraq, you name it—has come anywhere near polarizing the country as profoundly as the tariff did then. To lower the tariff as significantly as Wilson was able to do in short order was, in the annals of American legislative history, a feat second to none.

And that was not all. Within a few months, the Wilson administration chalked up a second monumental accomplishment: the establishment of the Federal Reserve System. Here, too, Wilson's distinctive style—again going to the Hill, addressing a joint session, and then patiently following up with the legislators—went a long way. His eloquence and tenacity, but also his regard for the spectrum of views in the legislative branch ("I have come to you," he explained, "to serve the country deliberately and as we should, in a clear air of common counsel"), served the Republic well.[109] We believe modern presidents could do worse than take a page from Woodrow Wilson's approach (at least in 1913), for it has

108. Wilson (1889, p. 566).

109. This quote is from Wilson's 1913 "Address on Banking and Currency Reform to a Joint Session of Congress" (Wilson 1978b). Wilson's ability to persuade the critics of his plan for the central banking system—including such political giants as William Jennings Bryan, as well as Bryan's many followers in Congress—was nothing short of astounding at the time.

much to teach about how the chief executive can help bridge severe polarities in Congress and even win cooperation in unlikely political circles.[110]

Our Question Time

Earlier in this chapter we expressed admiration for the custom in certain parliamentary regimes of routinely exposing the executive and the legislature to a face-to-face exchange of questions and answers about government policy decisions. The concept of importing something similar to the United States is not novel. Presidents Wilson, Taft, and Hoover all saw merit in the idea, and during World War II, some members of Congress—most notably, Senator Estes Kefauver (D-Tenn.)—even introduced formal resolutions to institute a question period.[111]

These initiatives came to naught, and doubtless any new ones would, too. The most we can hope for is that a distant cousin—the periodic presidential news conference—might regain more stature. A president should hold at least two full-scale press conferences every month. Preparing to meet the press, and fielding its queries, can heighten a president's awareness of the vagaries of the executive establishment. The interface also serves the useful purpose of refining the art of presidential persuasion and, no less important, opening an ongoing dialogue with persons who often harbor doubts about a president's policies. Addressing those concerns on a consistent basis may not allay them, nor necessarily clear the air, but it probably would temper the propensity of critics to demonize a president and his or her administration gratuitously.

Executive-Legislative Contact

More fundamentally, we commend Wilsonian engagement with the legislative branch. Once a month, a president and various cabinet officers should meet with the bipartisan congressional leadership plus a limited number of senators and representatives recognized for their expertise in the major topics to be discussed.[112] The number of participants should be small enough to fit comfortably around a table in, say, the Cabinet Room of the White House. These encounters should

---

110. Apart from their annual State of the Union appearances, presidents other than Wilson have occasionally used visits to Congress to plead for support of key presidential initiatives. George W. Bush did so for his Central American Free Trade Agreement, for example. See Roman (2005, p. 45). Wilson, however, exalted the practice.

111. See Kefauver (1944).

112. We hardly pretend to be alone in floating a suggestion along these lines. See, for example, Roman (2005, p. 48).

not be mere photo-ops or invitations to grandstand; in order to allow for a serious colloquy, each session should be scheduled for at least a couple of hours, with no representatives of the media present. Afterward the congressional delegation could make itself available to the press corps, and the White House press secretary could brief reporters as well.

Institutionalizing such interbranch communication might not often change a lot of hearts and minds, but at least it would give lawmakers—including those of the minority—regular access to the president and affirm that his views and theirs are to be *discussed,* instead of bypassed contemptuously.[113]

A Further Note on Judicial Selection

Our principal recommendations regarding the selection of federal judges, which has become inordinately contentious in recent decades, have already been outlined. But to them we would add one more item to think about: when making appointments, presidents would do well to recognize that a judiciary composed of diverse jurists is more likely to be rigorous as well as measured—and hence perhaps less divisive—in its jurisprudence than is a bench made up of political doppelgangers.

This consideration has important implications for the appointments process at the federal district and appellate levels, not just the Supreme Court. The recent practice of granting writs of certiorari to fewer appeals means that lower court decisions are increasingly left to stand. In other words, the judgments of the lower courts tend to become final law in the majority of cases.

Judges at all levels are indeed "political." Openly recognizing the fact is wiser than denying it—a point implicit in Shapiro's comments to chapter 3 in this volume and backed by the research of Cass Sunstein and his colleagues. Voting patterns of Democratic and Republican appointees exhibit differences.[114] What is more, homogeneous judicial panels tend to hand down ideologically polarized

---

113. It is scarcely uncommon for presidents to meet with key legislators on a fairly frequent basis. When the 110th Congress took over, President Bush began inviting House Speaker Nancy Pelosi (D-Calif.), Senate Majority Leader Harry M. Reid (D-Nev.), and their GOP counterparts to the White House every few weeks. Although press accounts of these encounters described them as "rarely productive," it is difficult to believe they were of no value whatsoever, at least with regard to certain issues. Michael Abramowitz, "Bush's Relations with Capitol Hill Chilly," *Washington Post,* May 13, 2007. Thus we posit that formalizing presidential communication with congressional leaders is an essential confidence-building step.

114. Sunstein and others (2006, p. 129).

decisions more than do mixed panels. Why does such a pattern occur? The mixed panels deliberate differently; their members are exposed to differing arguments. Homogeneity, by contrast, creates an echo chamber in which ideological predilections get amplified.

These findings argue for diversity in the composition of courts, just as they would for other types of adjudicative bodies. In fact, presidents ought to contemplate the rules that govern those other tribunals. Statutes often require bipartisan membership (in many cases, nearly even balance) on independent regulatory commissions, for instance. Why? Because in its wisdom, Congress duly understood that these agencies make a lot of law yet are seldom really apolitical.[115] It is time to acknowledge the same truth about the judiciary: this weighty branch of government is not above politics either and also should be staffed in a fashion that helps keep its partisan biases in check.

All of which is not to absolve judges of their own duty to help lower the political decibel level. Polarization is abetted or restrained not only by the makeup of the courts but by how they choose to behave. When leading judges strive to reduce the frequency of split decisions and press for consensus, judicial outcomes carry greater authority and popular assent. As it happens, though, politically diverse courts are those that are most likely to adopt this style, seeking agreement by, for example, sticking closer to the facts and deciding cases at a lower level of generality, hence stirring less hostility. Chief Justice John Roberts could steer the Supreme Court in this direction.[116] Applying "judicial minimalism," as Sunstein calls it, may lack the grandeur of more principled adjudication, but such an approach might gradually help unify the court and ultimately offer a less controversial model of jurisprudence for the judiciary as a whole.[117]

A Modest Concession from the Media

To what extent political rifts in American society are deepened by the conduct of the news media is, as we have seen, a subject of extensive debate among experts. Such dispute may seem academic, not because many believe the media play *no* part in political polarization but because the First Amendment vigorously constrains what public policy can do to make any difference. To acknowledge that

---

115. Sunstein and others (2006, pp. 136–37).
116. Chief Justice John G. Roberts Jr., Georgetown University Law Center commencement address, May 21, 2006.
117. Sunstein (1999).

little can be changed, however, is not to concede that *nothing* ought to be tried, at least with respect to the broadcast media.

The latter, after all, are public *licensees;* they have no inherent right, as the Supreme Court opined three decades ago, to an "unconditional monopoly of a scarce resource which the Government has denied others the right to use."[118] Nor, the Court continued, does the First Amendment in any sense preclude society's goal of "producing an informed public capable of conducting its own affairs"—a public served, for example, by expecting "a broadcaster to permit answers to personal attacks occurring in the course of discussing controversial issues" or requiring that the political opponents of candidates endorsed by a station be given a chance to communicate and respond. In sum, according to the Court, there could be "no sanctuary in the First Amendment for unlimited private censorship operating in a medium not open to all."

This reasoning sustained the fairness doctrine, which, before being abandoned by the Federal Communications Commission (FCC) in 1987, required licensees to give all sides of public issues reasonably balanced coverage. Bipartisan efforts were made to reinstate the doctrine but were vetoed by President Reagan and then also opposed by President George H. W. Bush.

The fairness doctrine may be dead and buried, yet the principle underlying it should not be. Licensed broadcasting ought to be subject to some sort of public interest standard, not just a market test. The civic health of the polity is a collective good that the "invisible hand" of market forces does not infallibly attend to. Indeed, a classic and legitimate pursuit of government is to promote public goods that are undersupplied by disaggregated market decisions. That pursuit, moreover, is not always consistent with maximizing individual choices. There can come a point where ever-expanding choice may cease to net gains for society.

Short of heavy-handed regulation, what might be worth considering? We think it would not be too much to encourage broadcast networks (and ideally cable and satellite outlets as well) to meet some elementary public service obligations. The FCC, for example, could request that licensed television stations voluntarily provide live coverage for an agreed-upon number of presidential press conferences. Technically, this mild intervention in the media marketplace would impinge on consumer sovereignty to some small degree. No doubt some fickle viewers would flee to other media and forms of entertainment. But some others, who would not

118. The case was *Red Lion Broadcasting Co., Inc.* v. *Federal Communications Commission,* 395 U.S. 367 (1969).

have *chosen* to see the president answer press inquiries, now might stick around and watch.[119]

Would a modest attempt to recapture the dwindling audiences for televised presidential news conferences elevate U.S. politics in any sense? At times, more of the public might bear witness to the abrasively adversarial attitude of many a contemporary journalist and to the defensive tone of the White House. However, larger audiences might be edified by listening to their president confront skeptics squarely, defend important policy decisions, and simply answer questions that are on people's minds.[120] At least one empirical study has identified precisely that kind of civic upgrade in various other democratic societies where, for example, "question times" are fully aired. "Open and spontaneous question periods," concludes its author, are "associated with higher levels of citizen knowledge about politics," and interestingly, "higher turnout in elections."[121]

Conclusion

One can debate how strong and enduring the polarizing currents in American society are, but to contend that all are superficial and will ebb soon is at variance with reality. The story is about much more than fierce feuding between the parties provoked by the eventful presidency of George W. Bush. No doubt a number of his political and policy choices heightened partisan antipathies. But recall that Bill Clinton had managed to become an equally polarizing figure. President Reagan, too, was battered by partisan tempests. The political storm churned up by U.S. actions in Central America nearly laid waste to his administration and

119. An obvious difficulty with asking the broadcast networks, but not their cable and satellite competitors, to air any quotient of public affairs programming is that most viewers now subscribe to non-network TV. Indeed, research has shown that whereas most American households tended to watch presidential prime-time news conferences in Richard Nixon's day, a much smaller percentage did so by the 1990s, thanks largely to the diffusion of cable. See Baum and Kernell (1999). Furthermore, the FCC lacks plenary jurisdiction over cable and satellite television; local franchising authorities regulate cable. However, the authorities in many cities might be sympathetic to some sort of public affairs requirement as a franchise condition, and in any event, Congress theoretically has authority to regulate all three forms of TV. We are indebted to Professor Jerome A. Barron of the George Washington University Law School for his insights on such questions.

120. On the importance of presidents retaining their prime-time audiences, see Baum and Kernell (1999).

121. Salmond (2005). For a discussion of the question period in the Canadian system, including the implications of extensive media coverage, see Franks (1987, especially chap. 7). In the United Kingdom, live coverage of the prime minister's question time can draw seven-figure audiences. See Norton (1993, p. 183).

came closer to creating a constitutional crisis than anything that has occurred during the Bush years.

Nearly two-thirds of the electorate have sorted themselves into divergent partisan camps. For some of these voters—those with politically eclectic instincts—the sorting may be akin to herding themselves, or being herded, into awkward coalitions. But it strains credulity to suppose that *most* of the voters align that way—in essence, siding with a party either just for the heck of it or because they have been involuntarily boxed in.

Most people who choose sides do so because they discern at least some significant philosophical daylight between the parties and find one side or the other more agreeable. This fact of modern political life is of consequence. It means that a substantial share of the electorate is, quite literally, at home with today's increased partisan polarization. By implication, reform that seeks to dislodge such people from their political comfort zone may be of questionable validity. On what basis should their ("polarized") preferences be disqualified in favor of the reformer's (presumptively "centrist") ones? After all, America's discordant parties are partly here, so to speak, by popular demand.

But deference to that inconvenient truth also has limits. A plurality of Americans might well prefer a less disharmonious political environment. Whether or not they know why, they are on to something. Several of the nation's most troubling predicaments—a near collapse of consensus on foreign affairs and an inability to confront the welfare state's looming fiscal crisis, to cite but two examples—are not just products of the inevitably short time horizons of politicians but also of their inability to drive bipartisan bargains where they are most needed. It is in light of these ailments that we consider the various conceivable cures advanced in these pages.

We labor under no illusion that our suggestions are faultless or an easy sell to a variety of skeptics. Some commentators—those who believe America's political polarization is largely a fiction—might ridicule our agenda for appearing disproportionate and infeasible. Others—those who think the country is most deeply divided—might scorn it as cosmetic and ineffectual. The latter group could point to important research in recent years suggesting that a rise in income inequality has arguably fueled a politics more bitterly class based than is commonly acknowledged.[122] Furthermore, levels of immigration not seen for nearly a century are said to have contributed to social division and mistrust, a result exacerbated by the

122. McCarty, Poole, and Rosenthal (2006).

tendency of more Americans to create enclaves of persons sharing a common lifestyle and ideological orientation. At the same time, many believe, various mediating institutions that could help narrow the divides of class, education, and ethnicity have seen better days.[123] Presumably, if all this is really at the root of bipartisanship's demise, the economic and social transformation needed to set things right would have to be quite grandiose and radical.

We are not inclined to go there. Social scientists will be debating the nature and extent—never mind the supposed polarizing impact—of income inequalities, immigration patterns, geographic population patterns, and other secular trends for years to come. Even if every one of these underlying forces proved definitively complicit in intensifying polarization (a big "if"), policymakers would have precious little room to maneuver in an attempt to tame them. Aggressively redistributive economic policies would run the risk of depressing economic growth without appreciably reducing income disparities. Restricting immigration sharply could worsen these effects. And altering the geographic distribution of the population would require a level of social engineering that would make the ill-fated mandatory school busing of decades past seem like a joy ride. With these thoughts in mind, the midrange revisions of political institutions that we have proposed may look worthier.

123. See Putnam (2000); Skocpol (2003).

Comments on Chapter Six

COMMENT

Nelson W. Polsby

It may be useful as a preface to a discussion of measures encouraging depolarization to ask precisely what it is about polarization that is objectionable in a political system in which each adult is legally and morally presumed to be the rightful keeper of his or her own conscience. The mere existence of disagreement cannot in and of itself be unacceptable. People will see things differently owing, perhaps, to different core beliefs, talents, or interests. All of these wellsprings of differing opinions seem to me to be beyond the capacity of a liberal democratic society to alter in any fundamental way, at least in the short run. And even if a society did have the means to do so, it should not want to do so.

Under what conditions, then, would we wish to pursue depolarization as a matter of public policy? I can think of at least two possibilities. First, polarization may be so severe or pervasive as to threaten the existence of the state or of a significant population within its boundaries. Second, polarization may express disagreements that are not in fact entertained by the great preponderance of people on whose behalf they are put forth. I will proceed on the assumption that what we are discussing is the second condition.

The chapter I've been asked to comment on inclusively accepts the proposition that Americans are mostly moderate, although their leaders may not be. And so what is required is to design or remodel institutions so as to permit this essential moderation to be more easily expressed in public policy. This bedrock commitment, as I see it, requires the authors to tack, somewhat unpredictably, between favorable and unfavorable positions on such matters as whether decisionmaking should be in the hands of majorities or supermajorities, whether political institutions should encourage or discourage competition, and whether contentiousness and conflict are good or bad for the health of the body politic.

For instance, is the Supreme Court "a dissonant assortment" of justices as Nivola and Galston state at one point, or are the federal courts insufficiently

The late Nelson W. Polsby (1934–2007) was an engaged and inspiring participant at the authors' conference on this volume, held at Stanford in January 2007, where he delivered a version of these remarks.

diverse, as they suggest at another? Can they be both at the same time? Should congressional districts be drawn so as to maximize competitiveness between the parties? Is this compatible with requiring members to stay in Washington rather than spending time, allegedly too much time, "back in their states and districts campaigning and fundraising"?

I do not know how to resolve practical problems of this kind. These problems lie on the surface of an impressively wide-ranging essay that deserves more thorough contemplation. Instead, I will succumb to the temptation to respond to a couple of the specific measures proposed in the text (there are, I think, about two dozen) in the hope that they might be severable from the general thrust of the paper, which is to advocate institutions that are workable and that do not distort underlying sentiments in the general population, favoring something approximating good government as that condition might be envisaged by a Wilsonian progressive.

Those measures are two of my pet peeves: instant runoff elections and compulsory voting. I believe they are bad ideas and inconsistent with the spirit that animates this paper. Instant runoffs require voters to express preferences without informing their choices with the results of the election that just failed to produce a winner. This introduces an artificial restriction of information, specifically on candidate viability, that many voters might need. It stifles deliberation, a feature of the decisionmaking process praised in other contexts by these authors.

Not coincidentally, it also shares with compulsory voting the fact that it treats voters like donkeys. I believe there is such a phenomenon as rational abstention. Even if it were possible to demonstrate otherwise, the herding of citizens to the polls under threat of legal sanction seems to me repugnant on its face and incompatible with democratic values, even though we are sure that such measures contribute to high turnout—no doubt they do—in such exemplary democracies as Egypt and Singapore. More to the point, it is a dubious proposition that "donkey voters," as they are called in Australia, so reliably contribute moderation to the political system as to require their presence at the polls. This is an empirical point, but there are ample theoretical grounds for skepticism about coerced voting.

While some coerced voters may discover defensible motivations for their choices, we can also count on disproportionate randomness, spoiled ballots, excessive reliance on advertising and name recognition, susceptibility to ballot placement, and acquiescence to demagogic appeals. This does not seem to me anything like good government.

Some of the authors' other concrete suggestions for institutional change—such as open primaries and redistricting reform—strike me as hostile to political parties and might profitably be considered in that light. Some—such as multimember districts, presidential question time, and requiring television networks to broadcast presidential press conferences—do not seem to take aim particularly at polarization *or* depolarization. In general, I should say I like transparency in government and I like moderation in government, but I do not think they are the same thing—and by aiming at one, we do not necessarily hit the other.

For what it is worth, I agree with most of the authors' proposals regarding congressional procedure: longer work weeks, bipartisan conferences, and fewer closed rules. But as I suppose one would expect from a student of Congress, I did miss the underlying analysis that might help to explain why we have the conditions that at present prevail and what it would cost to move in the desired directions. For example, a longer work week implies readiness to move power back to committees and away from party leadership, but it also interacts with the recommendations for increasing the competitiveness of congressional elections.

As a final point, I agree very much with the authors' view that the judicial confirmation process is an unpleasant spectacle. (I think Anthony Lake said it best when he described the confirmation process for his failed nomination to be CIA director as "nasty and brutish without being short.")[1] Well, the confirmation process *is* an unpleasant spectacle, but so these days is the judicial selection process. And these two observations cannot be unrelated. Bill Clinton made two relatively uncontentious and high-quality appointments to the Supreme Court, in part by consulting influential members of the body entitled to advise and consent. George W. Bush has followed a different course. I myself favor messy confirmations as a necessary feature of checks and balances, especially when a president lacks the wisdom to work with the political system the framers of the Constitution provided.

I do not know how comfortable the sponsors of this project would be if the authors would have put in more politics as a way of explaining how the defects of government they identify came to be. To do so, I believe, would strengthen the case for some of the measures that the authors suggest and weaken the case for others, but it would certainly fortify their overall argument.

1. See "Anthony Lake's Letter to President Clinton," March 17, 1997 (www.fas.org/irp/news/1997/12353091-12359687.htm).

COMMENT
Joel D. Aberbach

Politics is about conflict and attempts to resolve conflict, so polarization of some sort is inevitable in any political system. How political conflict is configured, however, is not preordained. It may be rich against poor, urban against rural, one ethnic group against another, one religious group against another, liberals versus conservatives, or any other cleavage (or set of cleavages) that matters in a society. And the way those cleavages are structured matters as well. If they cumulate— that is, if the categories overlap and reinforce one another—then conflicts are likely to be harder to resolve; if they are nonoverlapping, then it may be easier to reach agreement because one's foe on one issue is likely to be one's ally on another.[2]

Whether one characterizes what has happened in the United States over the past few decades as sorting or polarization, the data seem rather conclusive that American politics is now more clearly structured than it was in the previous era. The Democratic Party was once an uncomfortable alliance of southern whites and more progressive northerners—an alliance often challenged from within by the cross-cutting "conservative coalition" of southern Democrats and conservative Republicans. The Republican triumph in the South, a process that took many years but is now nearly complete, and the increasingly Democratic colorization of the North—to use the red state–blue state imagery so popular now—have produced a much more coherent set of parties. Today, both parties are much more internally consistent and, if only because of sorting, at greater ideological distance from one another. This consistency means that the cleavages in politics are more distinct, with less overlap on issues.

Sorting and Its Consequences

Is this a problem, or is it better characterized as the flowering of what many political scientists and others have long hoped for: more coherent and consistent parties that would "provide the electorate with a proper range of choice between

2. See, for example, the discussion of conflicts and cleavages in Dahl (1982). Dahl contends that "in postindustrial countries, if intense polarization occurs at all, it is more likely to reflect cleavages resulting from conflicting ideas and ideologies that are not strongly related to such time-honored categories of explanation as occupation, social status, and income," though he cautions against "overinterpret[ing]" the evidence and argument behind this statement.

alternatives of action"?[3] That question is implicit in our debates. But we could go further and ask whether much of the complaining about polarization is simply a reaction to the fact that the sorting of the electorate has brought to the fore a political configuration that liberal intellectuals (and many others, of course) find anathema.

Indeed, there may be some of this sort of "bad sport" sentiment at work, reflecting discontent with the outcome of recent elections. But there is a deeper problem that has also manifested itself contemporaneously with the rise in party polarization: a marked increase in presidential assertiveness. One can argue about the precise starting date, but certainly most would agree that the Nixon administration abused executive power extensively. One can also make a strong argument that two of Nixon's Republican successors—Ronald Reagan and George W. Bush—have been especially assertive in their conception and use of executive power.[4] Split party control during the Nixon administration and partially split party control during the Reagan administration may have been responsible for some of this, with those presidents stymied by reluctant Congresses.[5] But President Bush had a Republican Congress for much of his first six years in office— and that Congress, as Thomas E. Mann and Norman J. Ornstein observe in *The Broken Branch,* did little or nothing to check him.[6] In brief, as political scientist John Ferejohn has stated, the institutions of American government designed as checking structures in the Madisonian system "are extremely vulnerable to polarized parties in the sense that polarized parties are a way in which abusive and tyrannical majorities can grab hold of the institutions and override constitutional and other restrictions."[7]

I will return to this theme later, but first I will look at the central elements in the chapter by Pietro Nivola and William Galston. What they hold is that, whatever one chooses to call it, there has been a demonstrable sorting out of much of the electorate into "opposing camps" where political party preferences are fused with ideology, leading to strong divisions on certain "critical issues." This has been

3. See Committee on Political Parties, American Political Science Association (1950).

4. See, for example, Aberbach (2004, 2007).

5. Democrats controlled both houses of Congress during the Nixon administration. The House of Representatives was in Democratic hands throughout Ronald Reagan's administration, and both chambers were in Democratic hands the final two years.

6. Mann and Ornstein (2006).

7. Ferejohn's remarks are taken from the transcript of the Brookings-Hoover conference, "Red and Blue Nation? Consequences and Correction of America's Polarized Politics," Hoover Institution, Palo Alto, Calif., January 25–26, 2007.

accompanied by "increasingly polarized comportment" in key institutions such as the news media and Congress. And it has had significant consequences. The truculent partisanship in the nation's politics, Nivola and Galston say, has increased distrust of "core governmental institutions," helped deadlock needed fiscal retrenchment, and encumbered foreign affairs, straining "the capacity to lead an enlightened approach to global trade, immigration, and, most notably, a resolute foreign policy." It also has hobbled the judiciary, causing overly politicized recruitment criteria for court appointments as well as the use of such appointments to rouse the party faithful and inspire party contributors.

The sour mood around polarization and the strong passions that accompany it have surely contributed to political distrust. And while clearly not the only source of the nation's fiscal problems, polarization has made solutions more difficult. Beyond that, the last two problems on Nivola and Galston's list have been keenly affected by (and have affected) partisan polarization. Foreign policy and policy on terrorism are now highly partisan issues. The spectacle and conflict surrounding the selection and approval of judicial appointments is now so highly linked to issues that roil the political base of each party that they are eventually likely to undermine the legitimacy of the courts and thereby cost the nation dearly when it needs an institution to make judicious determinations on contentious issues.

Solutions

True to the tradition of such enterprises, the final chapter of the Brookings-Hoover project on political polarization seeks solutions to the stipulated problems that the nature and magnitude of current political divisions present for the nation. This is obviously not an easy task. Proposing policy changes is a risky business. Leaving aside for the moment the relatively low likelihood that proposals made will be adopted (or that they may even be particularly wise), it is also difficult to predict the full consequences of any specific reform. As the authors rightly caution, the reforms the Progressives instituted to suppress partisanship "have had a long and less than illustrious history in this country," and many reforms have gone awry. Nivola and Galston therefore approach the task of curing the problems with a welcome sense of humility and caution.

Cautions aside, however, Nivola and Galston offer quite a full menu of reform proposals designed to "help repair damage wrought by the excesses of today's partisan polarization." These include electoral reforms aiming to increase participation and give independents a greater role in nominating decisions, with the intent of aiding centrist candidacies; cooling off Congress by making procedural adjustments to "help Congress recover a greater measure of comity"; depolarizing the presidency by getting the president to account for his decisions in public appearances, particularly press conferences; facilitating "a truce in the judicial confirmation wars," particularly through the use of bipartisan nominating commissions for district and appellate judgeships and limiting the time for confirming nominees below the Supreme Court level; devising ways to moderate the media by requiring some public service obligations, such as broadcasting the presidential press conferences mentioned above; and encouraging the devolution of controversial issues and policies to the state level.

Many of the reforms and improvements the authors propose—such as a truce in the judicial confirmation wars or an effective system for moderating the application of closed rules in the House—are likely to come about only *after* depolarization has been achieved. Others, such as mechanisms for exposing the president to open dialogue, would quickly be subverted by White House flacks aiming to guarantee softball questions for the incumbent. There is one set of proposals, however, that is most interesting because it goes to the heart of the situation Nivola and Galston want to change—a falloff in the representation of moderate voters.

Without going into detail, changes in the electoral system could have an impact on the outcome of elections and particularly on the behavior of those elected by changing their incentives. For example, more open primaries, such as those endorsed by Nivola and Galston, would presumably bring more centrist voters into play and thereby dilute the influence of the current set of core party voters who now dominate closed primary states. But the authors' big set of electoral reforms goes well beyond more open primaries. They endorse a combination of multimember districting and cumulative voting, and they also give very favorable mention to instant runoff voting schemes in which voters rank order the candidates for each office, with their votes transferred to their second choices if there is no winner on the first count, and so on.

I am not expert enough on electoral systems to evaluate the particular reforms suggested, but there are related literatures, such as the well-developed body of work on moderating ethnic conflict, that also suggest electoral solutions for making candidates reciprocally dependent on voters from groups other than just their own.[8] In short, electoral reforms must receive the most careful consideration if one wants a counterweight to the current partisan polarization.

---

8. See Horowitz (1991) for a particularly clear exposition of electoral techniques to control ethnic conflict.

Why Reform?

Now back to the central question: why bother to reform a system that is giving passionate voters some passionate politics and political responses? Won't the government eventually be forced by markets to some type of fiscal retrenchment, and hasn't reality begun to dominate in foreign affairs because defeat in war and loss of influence are ultimately hard to ignore? Perhaps. However, one can argue that there are signs of a more fundamental set of problems at work. Two trends, as I suggested above, are coming together that may eventually threaten a near-perfect storm for the Madisonian system that is at the heart of our political order. Those trends are the simultaneous rise of unilateral presidential power and of disciplined, polarized parties.

Federalist No. 10 and *No. 51* are perhaps the most extraordinary of *The Federalist Papers. Federalist No. 10* makes a strong argument for "curing the mischiefs of faction" not by attempting to control its causes (and thereby threatening liberty), but by controlling its effects. And *Federalist No. 51* argues strongly for an institutional structure in which "ambition must be made to counteract ambition," with the interest of the man "connected with the constitutional rights of the place." The author of *Federalist No. 51* famously went on:

> In framing a government which is to be administered by men over men, the great difficulty lies in this; you must first enable the government to control the governed; and in the next place oblige it to control itself. A dependence on the people is, no doubt, the primary control on the government; but experience has taught mankind the necessity of auxiliary precautions. This policy of supplying, by opposite and rival interests the defect of better motives, might be traced through the whole system of human affairs, private as well as public.[9]

The goal was to give "to those who administer each department the necessary constitutional means and personal motives to resist encroachments of the others." Such a system, in theory, serves as a counterweight to any factional interest. While political parties were not in the original plan, the institutional structures and incentive systems that were assumed to flow from the institutional design were certainly meant to contain dominance by any potentially ascendant alliance of

---

9. The full text of the *The Federalist Papers* is available on the Library of Congress website at thomas.loc.gov/home/histdox/fedpapers.html.

interests such as a political party. Through this design the Founders hoped to sup-ply "auxiliary precautions" that would protect the liberty of the people. Recently, however, there are clear signs that the precautions laid out in *Federalist No. 51* are breaking down.

First, there has been a surge in claims for—and exercise of—unilateral presi-dential power. President George W. Bush has been relentless in his efforts to assert breathtaking powers for the presidency, from complete control over the executive branch as part of the well-named "unitary executive," to sweeping powers as com-mander-in-chief, to the authority to determine which elements of signed laws are actually applicable and which he can safely ignore.[10] That presidents might be ambitious to control as much as possible is hardly news. What is news—beyond the extent of the Bush administration's claims—is the way Congress reacted to these claims. For most of the first six years of the Bush administration, Congress was, in Mann and Ornstein's phrase, the broken branch of government. Contrary to the expectations of the Founders, it did little or noth-ing of note to check the president. Why not? Because, as Mann and Ornstein argue, party and ideology have apparently replaced institutional identity as pri-mary orientations for members of Congress. So when the Clinton administration was replaced by a Republican one, the junkyard dog mentality of the Republican Congress during the Clinton years changed to one that could reasonably be described as that of "a deferential and supine body, one extremely reluctant to demand information, scrub presidential proposals, or oversee the executive."[11]

Data from surveys conducted in 2004–05 for the Annenberg Foundation's Institutions of Democracy Project provide additional disquieting findings about the relationship of political party affiliation and attitudes toward the exercise of executive power.[12] Simply stated, Republicans are much more likely than Democrats to endorse strong assertions of presidential power (that some would

10. See the literature summarized in Aberbach (2004, 2007). In addition, see the excellent intro-duction to a special issue of *Presidential Studies Quarterly* by Louis Fisher of the Library of Congress. Fisher's introduction argues that "at no time in American's history have inherent powers been claimed with as much frequency and breadth as the presidency of George W. Bush." He warns that "the claim and exercise of inherent powers move a nation from one of limited powers to boundless and ill-defined authority. . . . Sovereignty moves from the constitutional principles of self-government, popular control, and republican government to the White House." Fisher (2007, p. 2).

11. Mann and Ornstein (2006, p. 215).

12. For information on the Annenberg surveys, see Annenberg Democracy Project (2007, pp. 243–46.) See also Annenberg Public Policy Center, "Institutions of American Democracy Sur-vey Data Sets," April 15, 2007 (www.annenbergpublicpolicycenter.org/ResearchDataSets.aspx). For analysis of the relationship between party and views on executive power, see Aberbach (2008).

consider beyond constitutional limits), and this holds for respondents to the Annenberg elite surveys (Bush and Clinton administration appointees, Republican and Democratic congressional staffers, Senior Executive Service career civil servants) and for respondents from the general public as well. In short, the issue of executive power has become remarkably partisan, at least during the Bush administration.

There was, for example, a vast difference in how Democratic and Republican congressional staffers responded to a question about whether the president has the authority to take preemptive military action without the consent of Congress, even if an attack on the United States is not imminent. Eighty-nine percent of Democratic staffers said no, compared to only 32 percent of Republican staffers. On the executive side, 82 percent of Clinton's former appointees said no, compared to 35 percent of Bush's appointees to high office. These figures are generally mirrored, once one controls for party identification, for Senior Executive Service career civil servants and the general public. Similar relationships can be found for other indicators, although, not unexpectedly, congressional staffers of both parties are somewhat less likely than others to endorse a blanket statement that other officials should defer to the president on important national issues.[13]

Not all Republican officials and Republican identifiers among the public have bought into every aspect of the presidential supremacy agenda. However, there is a big difference by party, and the survey data clearly indicate that this perspective has made significant inroads into the Republican part of the body politic, both at the elite and general public levels. This calls into question a basic assumption that underlies the separation of powers system since there are clear signs of a culture in the Republican Party that is extraordinarily deferential to the executive branch, certainly when that party controls both of the major elected branches of the government.

Time will tell whether this culture survives the political recriminations accompanying the policies of the Bush administration, or whether Democrats will adopt similar views once they come to control the executive branch (or, for that matter, whether Republicans will shift their views radically in the face of the election of a Democratic president). Regardless of the party in ascendance, acceptance of executive supremacy should be equally disturbing for advocates of the kind of institutional system proposed in *Federalist No. 51,* one in which the incumbents of the various institutions are expected to defend those institutions strongly,

13. See Aberbach (2008, especially pp. 173–77 and note 35 on pp. 191–92).

check the encroachments of others, and thereby contribute to the protection of the underlying liberties of citizens.

The "auxiliary precaution" we may need at this point is one that helps overcome the polarized party positions that dominate politics, especially on issues of institutional power. It is primarily for this reason, in my view, that the type of voting system reforms suggested by Nivola and Galston might be well worth a try. Polarized (or sorted) party positions on the policy issues of the day are probably not much of a threat to the body politic; often, they serve to increase interest and participation. But there is much potential benefit in trying to stimulate the election of enough moderates in both parties to give advocates of institutional interests and cross-party bargaining a more solid foothold in Congress. Think of it as an insurance policy.

COMMENT

Larry Diamond

Pietro Nivola and William Galston have given us a shrewd, comprehensive, and judicious agenda for moving American politics "toward depolarization." Like the substance of their chapter, their title is carefully crafted—for it is neither possible nor desirable to completely depolarize American politics. Democracy is a system of institutionalized competition for power, and in the modern world, this requires distinct, competing political parties. Party competition can be based on ideological and programmatic differences; on ethnic, religious, or nationality differences; on the distribution of particularistic benefits from patrons to clients; or on the charisma of an individual leader. Or, if parties are merely "catchall" electoral vehicles for contending groups of aspiring candidates and power-holders, they can be based on very little that is distinctive at all.[14]

Before we condemn the ideological and normative polarization that seems increasingly to suffuse American politics, it is worth pondering the alternatives. When parties are based primarily on ethnicity, religion, or some other fundamental identity that divides society tribally, democracy is much more vulnerable to collapse. This is why so much scholarly attention has been devoted to

14. For a typology and historical overview of models of political parties, see Gunther and Diamond (2001).

trying to depolarize ethnicity in politics, by creating cross-cutting cleavages and inducing party organizations and voter alignments that transcend raw identity lines. When parties have no enduring and readily recognizable substantive distinctions but are mainly electoral alliances for capturing power, they have more difficulty capturing any lasting affection and commitment from citizens, and the public more readily grows disillusioned with party politics and with democracy itself. During the late 1960s and 1970s, that was, in fact, a common complaint about American politics from both the left and the right. A man on a white horse may rescue a country from such disaffections, but it is invariably a temporary fix.

For all their risks and problems, then, party systems based on reasonably coherent programmatic differences—another way of saying "ideology"—offer the best bet for mobilizing democratic energy and support without overheating the system. And having a lot of party identifiers also gives democracy a healthy degree of stability. In fact, it would be hard to imagine a healthier profile for a two-party democracy than one in which the electorate is roughly divided into thirds: reasonably stable partisans of one party or the other, with a group of independents floating in the middle—roughly the situation in the United States today. Programmatic and philosophical differences are a good thing in a democracy. The challenge is to contain these differences so that they do not infect, embitter, and paralyze every issue and dimension of political life.

There are reasons to worry that party politics in the United States has become too polarized. However, I am not sure the problem is entirely ideological polarization. A wide gulf separates the parties, but it is not purely ideological. Race, religion, and (connected to them) social values play important roles. And it often seems that the parties themselves represent a kind of tribal identity, in which "red and blue" displace "black, brown, and white" as the constituent elements of a national color divide.

In the first volume of *Red and Blue Nation?* political scientists Morris Fiorina and Matthew Levendusky present intriguing evidence suggesting that partisan polarization is a more serious problem at the level of America's political elite (its public officials, party activists, fundraisers, and interest group leaders, for example) than among the general voting public. They point to the structure of party primaries as a likely important cause of this "disconnect," an explanation that also figures prominently—with good reason—among Nivola and Galston's prescriptions for depolarizing America's politics. But before turning in detail to those prescriptions, it is worth underscoring why the polarizing trends in American democracy are so worrisome.

The United States is facing a series of policy challenges that are epochal in scale and will require, if they are to be effectively managed, broad national consensus and shared national sacrifice. They include:

—ending the military involvement in Iraq and redeploying hard and soft power assets for what will likely be a long-term struggle against international terrorist networks and movements;
—halting the spread of weapons of mass destruction, especially nuclear weapons;
—averting a global climate catastrophe by reducing greenhouse gas emissions and switching to alternative fuels;
—crafting (and recrafting) international alliances and institutions for the above challenges and others, such as reducing global hunger, poverty, disease, corruption, and other drivers of state failure and violence;
—modernizing the "social compact" to deal with the looming fiscal crises in Social Security and (especially) Medicare; and
—repairing badly decayed and antiquated physical infrastructure, while undertaking other investments to increase the country's ability to repel, contain, or recover from a terrorist attack or natural disaster.[15]

If there is a common thread running through each of these challenges to the national security and economic well-being of the United States (and quite possibly to its survival as a superpower), it is that none of them can be addressed effectively with the level of partisan polarization and political sniping that permeates policy-making and political debate in the country today. Individually, each challenge is so massive, its management or resolution so intricate and costly, that it will require an unusual degree of national resolve and a shared sense of sacrifice. This resolve may come from a decisive partisan realignment that gives a president the legislative and political power to craft a new policy course, as happened in 1932. Or, if we do not get ahead of the game, it may well come from a national disaster as crushing as the Great Depression or Pearl Harbor. And in the case of global warming, which threatens not only the health and quality of American life but of civilization globally to a degree unmatched in human history, the resolve to act may come too late to arrest the destructive progression of the changing climate.

This highlights a second feature common to several of these problems: the enormous intergenerational inequality of their effects. Older Americans enjoy the

---

15. The essential work on this challenge, which should be read by every presidential candidate and public-minded citizen, is Flynn (2007).

benefits of current consumption, but it is younger Americans—particularly those under the age of forty, and most especially those not yet born—who will bear the heaviest burden if we do not arrest the rise in global temperatures, reform the social contract with aging Americans, and repair and modernize the country's dilapidated physical infrastructure. These problems are therefore particularly difficult to resolve because effective policy responses require a long-term collective vision, and highly competitive democracies dominated by powerful interest groups and lobbies—like the United States—tend to be captives of shorter-term interests.

The United States, then, is entering a distinctive era of policy challenges when it can no longer afford the politics of partisan warfare, gridlock, and the obsessive pursuit of narrow advantage. If there is one criticism I have of Nivola and Galston's chapter, then, it is that they understate the urgency of what is at stake in the quest to diminish partisan polarization and to craft new mechanisms for inducing cooperation and building consensus across partisan divides.

Promising Approaches

Some of the authors' recommendations—such as expanding voter participation by allowing registration on election day and declaring that day a national holiday—are worth doing because they would improve the vigor and quality of American democracy, even if they do nothing to depolarize it. Others—such as reconsidering multimember congressional districts—strike me as unrealistic in an era in which citizens want more direct contact with their representatives, not the diminished level that would inevitably come with larger, multimember districts.[16] I am generally supportive of their recommendations, but I do not think they go far enough in some key respects.

I endorse their analytic emphasis on the role of party primaries in "purifying" parties ideologically and pressing them toward the extremes. A natural counter to this is to open up primary elections to a wider range of voters (for example, by allowing independents to vote in either party's primary election, as they are able

---

16. I do agree with the authors that the United States needs more institutional experimentation using the great laboratory of American federalism. But in terms of the size of legislative districts, I would recommend limiting this for some time to city and county councils and state legislatures. At the level of Congress, to have multimember districts of five or more representatives, or even as few as three, would significantly reduce the ties between members and geographic communities, increasing the already dispiriting distance between the people and their representatives.

to do in New Hampshire presidential primaries). Indeed, this is one of the most important reforms proposed by Nivola and Galston. Its practical effect would probably be to accelerate the growth in the number of voters registered as independents, since in states with closed primaries some voters register for a party in order not to be disenfranchised in the primary election process. But the more candidates in primary elections have to appeal to swing voters, the greater the chance that moderates will win and make it to the general election.

I am less confident that significant depolarization can be achieved by changing the electoral system, especially for the House of Representatives. The alternative vote (instant runoff) system would only induce moderation if there were more than two significant options, if the district were reasonably competitive, *and* if one of the additional options was toward the center, between the poles of conservative Republican and liberal Democrat. The presence of this moderate third candidate would force the Republican and Democratic candidates to move toward the center to capture the "second preference" votes of supporters of the moderate candidate. But my guess is that most House districts would remain uncompetitive— either solidly Republican or Democratic—and that the introduction of the instant runoff system would likely have no effect in those districts.[17]

However, there is one district that is usually competitive, and in which the instant runoff could very well induce and enable a serious centrist challenge: the United States as a whole, in a presidential election. In the United States today, a moderate Republican or Democrat hesitates to mount an independent challenge for fear of doing to his party what Teddy Roosevelt did to the incumbent Republican president, William Howard Taft, in 1912: splitting the party and enabling Woodrow Wilson, the Democrat, to win with only 42 percent of the popular vote. Any serious third-party or independent candidate for president must also worry

---

17. It is also possible that the instant runoff system might induce a more extreme candidate to run to the right of the Republican or the left of the Democrat, knowing that voters could "safely" vote for him or her while listing their traditional party as a second choice. In competitive districts, this problem of extreme flanking might become more serious. We could see, for example, Libertarian and Green Party candidates challenging the established parties from the right and the left, forcing them, on some key issues, to retreat from moderation in order to hold on to their political base. Perhaps that would only make the Democratic and Republican candidates seem more moderate. Or perhaps the established party candidates would ignore the challenge, trusting that voters on the flank would have to name them as their second preference. No doubt, the presence of new and more serious competition would have other invigorating effects on the democratic process, but it is by no means clear that the instant runoff would contribute to the depolarization of American politics. In the foregoing scenario, with more ideological candidates pressing the main party nominees from the flanks, the effect could be to stimulate ideological polarization in some districts.

whether his or her campaign can even be viable because voters, in the end, will retreat to the two major party candidates for fear of throwing the election to the main opposing party.

Some combination of these two concerns inhibits a genuine and resourceful centrist such as New York City mayor Michael Bloomberg from competing for the presidency in 2008. But in an instant runoff system, an independent like Bloomberg would probably run, and possibly even win, since moderate Democrats and moderate Republicans could safely vote for him as their first choice while listing their party's candidate as their second choice. This possibility, in turn, raises another question: whether an independent could govern effectively as president, with no reliable base of support in Congress. Nevertheless, a viable independent candidate would help to strengthen the centrist dynamic in the presidential race, since the second preferences of voters for the moderate independent would be vital to victory for either of the two major party candidates.

Depolarization through Depoliticization

The two parties have a duopoly on American electoral politics that they will not willingly surrender any time soon. This makes electoral reforms such as the instant runoff little more than interesting academic speculation. A more politically feasible path to depolarization, then, might lie in using bipartisan or nonpartisan commissions to *depoliticize* policy choices. One laudable and long overdue innovation mentioned by Nivola and Galston would have bipartisan commissions nominate federal judges below the level of the Supreme Court, with an expedited process for Senate confirmation. This innovation, and the designation of a single long (but not lifelong) term for Supreme Court justices, would offer a good prospect of reducing the stakes in judicial politics and thus the polarization. But since restricting the terms of Supreme Court justices would require an amendment to the Constitution, the most realistic course (as the authors recommend) is to recognize—and even affirm—the filibuster as a legitimate method for blocking objectionable nominations, thus mandating a sixty-vote supermajority and hence bipartisan support for a nominee.

I also strongly endorse their recommendation for "less flagrantly partisan modes" of congressional redistricting. Here again my preference is to remove the process from partisan politics altogether and hand it over to a nonpartisan commission. But why not go further? Among established and emerging democracies, the United States is an outlier in not having an independent, professional national electoral commission. American federalism will probably not allow a

national electoral commission to do anything more than set standards and identify best practices, but surely the country can do better than the sorry spectacle of
having a partisan elected official be the chief election official of a state (as in Florida
and California, for instance). Such a practice can only diminish confidence in the
process when the chads hang or the voting machines malfunction. Some things in
a democracy—such as administering elections, or for that matter justice—are
better left to nonelected professionals. Each state in the United States should have
a career, nonpartisan official administering elections.

If we can depoliticize federal judicial nominees (and maybe even elections)
through nonpartisan commissions, can we do so for other issues? One possible
model would be the Base Realignment and Closure process used by the Department of Defense since 1988. Under this process, an independent commission,
consisting of nine distinguished experts, assesses the Pentagon's proposed changes
to military bases (closures, reductions, and enlargements) by conducting site visits and hearings. The president must either accept or reject the commission's entire
list of recommendations, and if he accepts it, Congress has forty-five days to enact
a joint resolution to disapprove the entire list. If it fails to do so, the list is imple-
mented. Stephen Flynn of the Council on Foreign Relations recommends this
model to set priorities for repairing and modernizing the country's disintegrating
physical infrastructure. An "infrastructure resiliency commission" of fifteen members appointed and approved through bipartisan congressional committees would
"identify the investments that need to be made most urgently, regardless of which
congressional district a project will reside in."[18]

I would go much further toward depoliticization. At work in the Base Realignment and Closure Commission and in the bipartisan commissions convened to
investigate the September 11 attacks and to propose a new U.S. strategy in Iraq
are three basic operational principles.[19] First, the commissions are evenly balanced
in their representation of the two parties, drawing in former members of Congress, governors, cabinet secretaries, and other respected individuals. The Iraq
Study Group, for example, was cochaired by former secretary of state James Baker
(a prominent Republican who had served in the Reagan White House and served
or aided both Bush administrations) and Lee Hamilton (the former chairman
of the House Foreign Affairs Committee and vice chairman of the 9-11 Commission), and included prominent and esteemed luminaries of each party such

18. See Flynn (2007, p. 112).
19. See National Commission on Terrorist Attacks upon the United States (2004); Iraq Study
Group (2006).

as former defense secretary William Perry, former attorney general Edwin Meese, and retired Supreme Court justice Sandra Day O'Connor.

The second operational principle is that most commission members are retired from active political life, which leaves them more room to consider the substantive issues, free of short-term political imperatives and constraints. Finally, the third principle is that commissions search for consensus. If, as in the case of Iraq, their recommendations are controversial, then at least the representatives of the two parties are committed to jumping off the cliff hand-in-hand.

There is something undemocratic about entrusting the formation of big policy decisions to expert commissions. But the process is not less democratic than having nine unelected justices with lifetime tenure and no political accountability to anyone but themselves decide such basic questions as when a woman can have an abortion and where a child can go to school. Moreover, the commissions would not legally decide such fundamental issues as how to restructure Medicare or reduce carbon-based emissions. But they would (and could) take some of the partisan sting and shameless maneuvering out of the debate by establishing a common, agreed-upon basis of facts and analysis, and then providing partisan cover for members of Congress to take painful policy steps that may offend key constituencies.

With something as complicated and consequential as entitlement reform or fighting global warming, it is unreasonable to expect Congress simply to vote a set of recommendations up or down, with no right of amendment. But a bipartisan commission consensus on basic principles could give key members of Congress the courage and the political insulation to do what is right by claiming—honestly—to their offended constituencies that it was "the best reform we could get." Something of this kind of political insulation will be needed if we are to tackle issues of intergenerational justice. Someone has to stand up for the rights of the unborn to live in a country that is not saddling them with oppressive debt or drowning their habitats with melting polar ice caps. Even the most adamant pro-life political constituencies have shown little or no interest in *these* rights of the unborn.

Presidential Leadership

America is a presidential democracy. Its politics will not be significantly depolarized unless it has a president that is less polarizing than recent presidents have been. It is fair to ask whether this can happen given the current media climate and with current institutional structures. But presidents have enormous power to shape the political agenda and the larger political climate. The key to this vital aspect of depolarization is not for the president to hold, as Nivola and Galston suggest, "at least two full-scale press conferences every month," desirable though that may be. Rather, by the appointments the president makes and the issues he or she focuses on, the president must reach across the partisan divide more effectively and consistently, not necessarily always toward the policy center (because sometimes the solutions needed do not lie in the center), but in a spirit of partisan dialogue and accommodation. It would help to have a prominent member or two (or three) of the opposing party in the cabinet. But most of all, it would help to have the president work with the Congress to appoint—and then take very seriously the recommendations of—bipartisan commissions to analyze and frame the debate on some of the most difficult foreign and domestic policy issues.

This model has potential to defuse many of the partisan landmines along the path of serious policy response, and I think it has more promise than most of the institutional recommendations offered by Nivola and Galston. But it will only work if there is a president who will listen to what the commissions recommend and use the cover they provide to build a coalition from the center out.

So how do we get a president so inclined toward bipartisanship? This brings us back to how our presidents are elected (and the potential value of partially open primaries), the role of the mass media, and the value of having more (and more focused) presidential debates in the general election. One thing that can help pave the way is a climate of broader policy dialogue and debate that reaches across established philosophical and political divides. Polarization has not only afflicted our political institutions and mass media, it has also been increasingly evident in the burgeoning world of policy think tanks. That two of the most prominent and philosophically distinct policy institutes have collaborated so fruitfully in this project is one small sign that the polarization of American politics and public policy can gradually and thoughtfully be reversed.

References

Aberbach, Joel D. 2004. "The State of the Contemporary American Presidency: Or, Is Bush II Actually Ronald Regan's Heir?" In *The George W. Bush Presidency: First Appraisals,* edited by Colin Campbell and Bert A. Rockman, pp. 46–72. Washington: CQ Press.

————. 2007. "The Executive Branch in Red and Blue." In *Institutions of American Democracy: A Republic Divided,* pp. 157–93. Oxford University Press.

————. 2008. "Supplying the Defect of Better Motives? The Bush II Administration and the Constitutional System." In *The George W. Bush Legacy,* edited by Colin Campbell, Bert A. Rockman, and Andrew Rudalevige, pp. 112–34. Washington: CQ Press.

Adams, Greg D. 1996. "Legislative Effects of Single-Member vs. Multi-Member Districts." *American Journal of Political Science* 40 (1): 129–44.

Annenberg Democracy Project. 2007. *A Republic Divided.* Oxford University Press.

Banfield, Edward C., and James Q. Wilson. 1965. *City Politics.* Harvard University Press.

Baum, Matthew A., and Samuel Kernell. 1999. "Has Cable Ended the Golden Age of Presidential Television?" *American Political Science Review* 93 (1): 99–114.

Beinart, Peter. 2006. *The Good Fight: Why Liberals—and Only Liberals—Can Win the War on Terror and Make America Great Again.* New York: HarperCollins.

Bertelli, Anthony, and Lilliard E. Richardson Jr. 2004. "Multi-Dimensional Ideology in the Multi-Member District: An Analysis of the Arizona Legislature." Report 45-2004. University of Missouri-Columbia, Institute of Public Policy, Harry S. Truman School of Public Affairs.

Binder, Sarah A., and Steven S. Smith. 1997. *Politics or Principle? Filibustering in the United States Senate.* Brookings.

Brams, Steven J., and Peter C. Fishburn. 1991. "Alternative Voting Systems." In *Political Parties and Elections in the United States: An Encyclopedia,* vol. 1, edited by L. Sandy Maisel, pp. 23–31. New York: Garland.

Burden, Barry C. 2001. "The Polarizing Effects of Congressional Primaries." In *Congressional Primaries and the Politics of Representation,* edited by Peter F. Galderisi, Marni Ezra, and Michael Lyons, pp. 95–115. Lanham, Md.: Rowman & Littlefield.

Butler, David, and Bruce E. Cain. 1992. *Congressional Redistricting: Comparative and Theoretical Perspectives.* New York: Macmillan.

Calabrese, Stephen. 2000. "Multimember District Congressional Elections." *Legislative Studies Quarterly* 25 (4): 611–643.

Calabresi, Steven G., and James Lindgren. 2006. "Term Limits for the Supreme Court: Life Tenure Reconsidered." *Harvard Journal of Law and Public Policy* 29 (3): 769–877.

Committee on Political Parties, American Political Science Association. 1950. "Toward a More Responsible Two-Party System." *American Political Science Review* 44 (Supplement).

Corrado, Anthony, and others. 2005. *The New Campaign Finance Sourcebook.* Brookings.

Cox, Archibald. 1976. *The Role of the Supreme Court in American Government.* Oxford University Press.

Dahl, Robert A. 1982. *Dilemmas of Pluralist Democracy: Autonomy vs. Control.* Yale University Press.

Dalton, Russell J., and Martin P. Wattenberg. 1993. "The Not So Simple Act of Voting." In *Political Science: The State of the Discipline,* 2nd ed., edited by Ada W. Finifter, pp. 193–218. Washington: American Political Science Association.

Davidson, Roger H., David M. Kovenock, and Michael K. O'Leary. 1968. *Congress in Crisis: Politics and Congressional Reform.* Belmont, Calif.: Wadsworth.

Drew, Elizabeth. 1999. *The Corruption of American Politics: What Went Wrong and Why.* Secaucus, N.J.: Birch Lane Press.

Evans, C. Lawrence. 2005. "Politics of Congressional Reform." In *The Legislative Branch*, edited by Paul J. Quirk and Sarah A. Binder, pp. 490–524. Oxford University Press.

Everson, David H. 1991. "The Cutback at 10: Illinois House without Cumulative Voting and 59 Members." *Illinois Issues* 17 (7): 13–15.

Fisher, Louis. 2007. "Invoking Inherent Powers: A Primer." *Presidential Studies Quarterly* 37 (1): 1–22.

Flynn, Stephen. 2007. *The Edge of Disaster: Rebuilding a Resilient Nation*. New York: Random House.

Franks, C. E. S. 1987. *The Parliament of Canada*. University of Toronto Press.

Gerber, Elisabeth R., and Rebecca B. Morton. 1998. "Primary Election Systems and Representation." *Journal of Law, Economics, and Organization* 14 (2): 304–24.

Glass, David, Peverill Squire, and Raymond Wolfinger. 1984. "Voter Turnout: An International Comparison." *Public Opinion* 6 (December-January): 49–55.

Gunther, Richard, and Larry Diamond. 2001. "Types and Functions of Parties." In *Political Parties and Democracy*, edited by Larry Diamond and Richard Gunther, pp. 3–39. Johns Hopkins University Press.

Hetherington, Marc J. 2005. *Why Trust Matters: Declining Political Trust and the Demise of American Liberalism*. Princeton University Press.

Hetherington, Marc J., and Jonathan Weiler. 2005. "Rigidity and Political Disposition." Paper prepared for the annual meeting of the American Political Science Association, Washington, September 1–4.

Hill, Steven. 2006. *10 Steps to Repair American Democracy*. Sausalito, Calif.: PoliPointPress.

Horowitz, Donald L. 1991. "Ethnic Conflict Management for Policymakers." In *Conflict and Peacemaking in Multiethnic Societies*, edited by Joseph V. Montville, pp. 115–30. Lexington, Mass: Lexington Books.

Iraq Study Group. 2006. *The Iraq Study Group Report: The Way Forward—A New Approach*. New York: Vintage Books.

Jacobs, Lawrence R., and Robert Y. Shapiro. 2000. *Politicians Don't Pander: Political Manipulation and the Loss of Democratic Responsiveness*. University of Chicago Press.

Jacobson, Gary C. 2005. "Modern Campaigns and Representation." In *The Legislative Branch*, edited by Paul J. Quirk and Sarah A. Binder, pp. 109–47. Oxford University Press.

———. 2006. "Competition in U.S. Congressional Elections." In *The Marketplace of Democracy: Electoral Competition and American Politics*, edited by Michael P. McDonald and John Samples, pp. 27–52. Brookings.

Johnston, R. J. 1982. "Redistricting by Independent Commissions: A Perspective from Britain." *Annals of the Association of American Geographers* 72 (4): 457–70.

Kanthak, Kristin, and Rebecca Morton. 2001. "The Effects of Electoral Rules on Congressional Primaries." In *Congressional Primaries and the Politics of Representation*, edited by Peter F. Galderisi, Marni Ezra, and Michael Lyons, pp. 116–31. Lanham, Md.: Rowman & Littlefield.

Kefauver, Estes. 1944. "The Need for Better Executive-Legislative Teamwork in the National Government." *American Political Science Review* 38 (2): 317–25.

King, David C. 1997. "The Polarization of American Parties and Mistrust of Government." In *Why People Don't Trust Government*, edited by Joseph S. Nye Jr., Philip D. Zelikow, and David C. King, pp. 155–78. Harvard University Press.

Kuklinski, James E., James D. Nowlan, and Philip D. Habel. 2001. "Voting for the Illinois House: Experience and Lessons from the Illinois Laboratory." In *Illinois Assembly on Political Representation and Alternative Electoral Systems: Final Report and Background Papers*, pp. 49–63. University of Illinois, Institute of Government and Public Affairs.

Lanoue, David J., and Craig F. Emmert. 1999. "Voting in the Glare of the Spotlight: Representatives' Votes on the Impeachment of President Clinton." *Polity* 32 (2): 253–69.

Lincoln, Abraham. 1894. "Address at Poughkeepsie, New York, February 19, 1861." In *Complete Works of Abraham Lincoln,* vol. 6, edited by John G. Nicolay and John Hay, pp. 142–44. Lincoln Memorial University.

Lyons, W. E. 1969. "Legislative Redistricting by Independent Commissions: Operationalizing the One Man–One Vote Doctrine in Canada." *Polity* 1 (4): 428–59.

Macedo, Stephen, and others. 2005. *Democracy at Risk: How Political Choices Undermine Citizen Participation, and What We Can Do about It.* Brookings.

Mackenzie, G. Calvin. 1996. *The Irony of Reform: Roots of American Political Disenchantment.* Boulder, Colo.: Westview Press.

Malbin, Michael J. 2006. "Assessing the Bipartisan Campaign Reform Act." In *The Election after Reform: Money, Politics and the Bipartisan Campaign Reform Act,* edited by Michael J. Malbin, pp. 1–16. Lanham, Md.: Rowman & Littlefield.

Maltzman, Forrest. 2005. "Advice and Consent: Cooperation and Conflict in the Appointment of Federal Judges." In *The Legislative Branch,* edited by Paul J. Quirk and Sarah A. Binder, pp. 407–31. Oxford University Press.

Mann, Thomas E., and Norman Ornstein. 2006. *The Broken Branch: How Congress Is Failing America and How to Get It Back on Track.* Oxford University Press

McCarty, Nolan, Keith T. Poole, and Howard Rosenthal. 2006. *Polarized America: The Dance of Ideology and Unequal Riches.* MIT Press.

McDonald, Michael P. 2006. "Redistricting and Competitive Districts." In *The Marketplace of Democracy: Electoral Competition and American Politics,* edited by Michael P. McDonald and John Samples, pp. 222–44. Brookings.

Mill, John Stuart. 1862. *Considerations on Representative Government.* New York: Harper & Brothers.

National Commission on Terrorist Attacks upon the United States. 2004. *The 9/11 Commission Report: Final Report of the National Commission on Terrorist Attacks upon the United States.* New York: W. W. Norton.

Neustadt, Richard E. 1990. *Presidential Power and the Modern Presidents: The Politics of Leadership from Roosevelt to Reagan.* New York: Free Press.

Niemi, Richard G., Jeffrey S. Hill, and Bernard Grofman. 1985. "The Impact of Multimember Districts on Party Representation in U.S. State Legislatures." *Legislative Studies Quarterly* 10 (4): 441–55.

Nivola, Pietro S. 2005. "Making Sense of Subsidiarity: Why Federalism Matters." Paper prepared for the annual meeting of the American Political Science Association, Washington, September 1–4.

Norton, Philip. 1993. "Questions outside Parliament." In *Parliamentary Questions,* edited by Mark N. Franklin and Philip Norton, pp. 176–93. Oxford: Clarendon Press.

Putnam, Robert D. 1993. *Making Democracy Work: Civic Traditions in Modern Italy.* Princeton University Press.

———. 2000. *Bowling Alone: The Collapse and Revival of American Community.* New York: Simon & Schuster.

Richardson, Lilliard E., Jr., and Christopher A. Cooper. 2003. "The Mismeasure of MMD: Reassessing the Impact of Multi-Member Districts on Descriptive Representation in U.S. State Legislatures." Paper prepared for the Third Annual Conference on State Politics and Policy, Tucson, March 14–15.

Richardson, Lilliard E., Jr., Brian E. Russell, and Christopher A. Cooper. 2004. "Legislative Representation in a Single-Member versus Multiple-Member District System: The Arizona State Legislature." *Political Research Quarterly* 57 (2): 337–44.

Richie, Rob, and Steven Hill. 2001. "Instant Runoffs, Proportional Representation, and Cumulative Voting—Reclaiming Democracy in the 21st Century." *Synthesis/Regeneration* 25 (Summer).

Rohde, David W. 2005. "Committees and Policy Formulation." In *The Legislative Branch,* edited by Paul J. Quirk and Sarah A. Binder, pp. 201–23. Oxford University Press.

Roman, Nancy E. 2005. *Both Sides of the Aisle: A Call for Bipartisan Foreign Policy.* New York: Council on Foreign Relations.

Rosenberg, Gerald N. 1991. *The Hollow Hope: Can Courts Bring About Social Change?* University of Chicago Press.

Salmond, Rob. 2005. "Parliamentary Question Times: How Legislative Accountability Mechanisms Affect Mass Political Engagement." Paper prepared for the annual meeting of the American Political Science Association, Washington, September 1–4.

Schickler, Eric. 2005. "Institutional Development of Congress." In *The Legislative Branch,* edited by Paul J. Quirk and Sarah A. Binder, pp. 35–62. Oxford University Press.

Sinclair, Barbara. 2002. "The '60-Vote Senate': Strategies, Process, and Outcomes." In *U.S. Senate Exceptionalism,* edited by Bruce I. Oppenheimer, pp. 241–61. Ohio State University Press.

Skocpol, Theda. 2003. *Diminished Democracy: From Membership to Management in American Civic Life.* University of Oklahoma Press.

Sunstein, Cass R. 1999. *One Case at a Time: Judicial Minimalism on the Supreme Court.* Harvard University Press.

Sunstein, Cass R., and others. 2006. *Are Judges Political? An Empirical Analysis of the Federal Judiciary.* Brookings.

Theriault, Sean, Andrew Karch, and Corrine McConnaughy. 2006. "The Politics of Redistricting Commissions." Paper prepared for the annual meeting of the American Political Science Association, Philadelphia, August 30–September 3.

U.S. House of Representatives. 2007. *Declaring That the United States Will Prevail in the Global War on Terror, the Struggle to Protect Freedom from the Terrorist Adversary.* H. Res. 861. 109 Cong. 2 sess. Government Printing Office.

Wilson, Woodrow. 1889. *The State: Elements of Historical and Practical Politics.* Boston: D.C. Heath.

———. 1978a. "An Address on Tariff Reform to a Joint Session of Congress." In *The Papers of Woodrow Wilson,* vol. 27, edited by Arthur S. Link, pp. 269–72. Princeton University Press.

———. 1978b. "An Address on Banking and Currency Reform to a Joint Session of Congress." In *The Papers of Woodrow Wilson,* vol. 27, edited by Arthur S. Link, pp. 570–73. Princeton University Press.

Wittes, Benjamin. 2006. *Confirmation Wars: Preserving Independent Courts in Angry Times.* Lanham, Md.: Rowman & Littlefield.

Contributors

Joel D. Aberbach
Distinguished Professor of Political Science and Public Policy and director, Center for American Politics and Public Policy, University of California– Los Angeles

Peter Beinart
Senior fellow for U.S. Foreign Policy, Council on Foreign Relations

Sarah A. Binder
Senior fellow, Governance Studies, Brookings Institution, and professor of political science, George Washington University

David W. Brady
Deputy director and senior fellow, Hoover Institution, Bowen H. and Janice Arthur McCoy Professor of Political Science and Leadership Values, Stanford Graduate School of Business

Deborah Jordan Brooks
Assistant professor of government, Dartmouth College

Andrea L. Campbell
Associate professor of political science, Massachusetts Institute of Technology

LARRY DIAMOND
Senior fellow, Hoover Institution, Stanford University

JOHN FEREJOHN
*Senior fellow, Hoover Institution, and Carolyn S. G. Munro Professor of
Political Science, Stanford University*

CHRISTOPHER H. FOREMAN JR.
*Professor, School of Public Policy, University of Maryland, College Park, and
nonresident fellow, Governance Studies, Brookings Institution*

WILLIAM A. GALSTON
Senior fellow, Governance Studies, Brookings Institution

JOHN G. GEER
*Professor of political science and Professor of Leadership, Policy, and Organizations,
Peabody College of Education, Vanderbilt University*

LAUREL HARBRIDGE
Ph.D. candidate, Department of Political Science, Stanford University

MARC J. HETHERINGTON
Associate professor of political science, Vanderbilt University

KEITH KREHBIEL
Edward B. Rust Professor of Political Science, Stanford Graduate School of Business

PIETRO S. NIVOLA
*Douglas Dillon Chair, vice president, and director, Governance Studies,
Brookings Institution*

ERIC M. PATASHNIK
*Associate professor of politics and associate director, Public Policy Program,
University of Virginia*

NELSON W. POLSBY
Heller Professor of Political Science, University of California–Berkeley

JONATHAN RAUCH
*Guest scholar, Governance Studies, Brookings Institution, and senior writer,
National Journal*

MARTIN SHAPIRO
*James W. and Isabel Coffroth Professor of Law, School of Law, University of
California–Berkeley*

BARBARA SINCLAIR
Marvin Hoffenberg Professor of American Politics, University of California–Los Angeles

MARTIN P. WATTENBERG
Professor of political science, University of California–Irvine

JAMES Q. WILSON
Ronald Reagan Professor of Public Policy, Pepperdine University

BENJAMIN WITTES
Fellow and research director in public law, Governance Studies, Brookings Institution

Index

320

INDEX

Shays, Christopher, 68, 236
Sinclair, Barbara: anecdotes of incivility, 90;
Binder, Sarah, comments, 110; on closed
rule use, 253; as contributor, 55–87;
Foreman, Christopher H., Jr., comments, 88–93; Krehbiel, Keith, comments, 93–103, 223; on procedural consequences of polarization, 110
Smart, Elizabeth, 130
Smith, Chris, 69
Snowe, Olympia, 96, 193, 195
Social Security Amendments (1983), 203,
222, 230
Social Security reform, 83, 222–23, 242
Stimson, Henry, 165
Supreme Court: confidence-polarization
relation, 190–91; democratic accountability, 258; depolarization strategies,
280, 300; judicial policymaking,
134–35, 139–40, 246; life tenure,
258–59, 300; New Deal in obscuring
political role, 135–37; salary erosion,
130–31. See also Judicial branch, polarization and

Taft, Robert, 152
Taft, William Howard, 278, 299
Talent, Jim, 25
Tax Reform Act (1986), 203, 222
Terrorism, role in shaping voter attitudes,
12–13
Tester, Jon, 25
Theiss-Morse, Elizabeth, 39
Thomas, Bill, 81
Thomas, Clarence, 113
Tito, 154
True, James, 195
Truman, Harry, 148, 152–53, 169, 245
Trust, political: 1964–2000, presidential
election years, 19–22; defined, 19;
increasing, consequences of, 23–24, 39;
party identification and, 48–49; polar-
ization effect on, 39, 187–91, 219–20,
240–42; public policy and, 187–91,
219–20; and support for government
action, 22, 23, 29; U.S. vs. other established democracies, 49–50
Turnout: 1952–2004 presidential elections,
4–5; 1980–2004 presidential elections,

6; 2004 presidential election, 41; 2006
elections, 2; compulsory voting solution,
50–51, 286; depolarization strategies
involving, 247–48, 270–73; determinants, 3, 5–9, 13, 31–33, 38–39;
engagement and, 4–8, 50–51; gender
differences, 38–39; by moderates,
31–33; negative advertising and, 3, 38.
See also Electorate
Tyler, John, 257

United States, other democracies compared,
41–50
USA PATRIOT ACT, 59, 72, 76, 195

Vietnam war, 23, 154–57, 165–71, 173,
177, 242–45
Voinovich, George, 193
Voters. See Electorate; Turnout
Voting: compulsory, 50–51, 286; cumulative, 266–67; instant runoff, 267–69,
286; multimember districts, 264–66;
redistricting reform, 263–64
Voting Rights Act, 265

Wallace, George, 39
Wallace, Henry, 152
Warner, John, 171
War on terror, 151–52, 158–65
Warren, Earl, 118, 135, 144
Washington, George, 257
Wattenberg, Martin P., 272
Waxman, Henry, 90–91
Webb, James, 2
Welfare reform legislation, 91
Wellstone, Paul, 171
West, Darrell, 37
Wilde, Oscar, 252
Wilson, James Q., 247
Wilson, Woodrow, 276–78, 299
Wittes, Benjamin, 120–21
Wittkopf, Eugene R., 153–54, 156
Wolfensberger, Don, 64, 206
Work week, congressional, 65, 67, 83, 85,
90, 275–76
Wright, Jim, 67

Zaller, John, 172